Application Environment Specification (AES) User Environment Volume

Revision A

Open Software Foundation

Prentice Hall, Englewood Cliffs, New Jersey 07632

Cover design
and cover illustration: BETH FAGAN

This book was formatted with troff

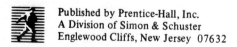

Published by Prentice-Hall, Inc.
A Division of Simon & Schuster
Englewood Cliffs, New Jersey 07632

The information contained within this document is subject to change
without notice.

Printed in the United States of America
10 9 8 7 6 5 4 3 2

ISBN   0-13-640483-9

Prentice-Hall International (UK) Limited, *London*
Prentice-Hall of Australia PTY. Limited, *Sydney*
Prentice-Hall Canada Inc., *Toronto*
Prentice-Hall Hispanoamericana, S.A., *Mexico*
Prentice-Hall of India Private Limited, *New Delhi*
Prentice-Hall of Japan, Inc., *Tokyo*
Simon & Schuster Asia Pte. Ltd., *Singapore*
Editora Prentice-Hall do Brasil, Ltda., *Rio de Janeiro*

Contents

i

List of Figures

List of Tables

Preface

Part of the charter of the Open Software Foundation [TM] (OSF[TM]) is to foster the development of portable software that will run on a variety of hardware platforms. The Application Environment Specification (AES) specifies the interfaces that support such software.

Specifically, this document (the Application Environment Specification (AES) User Environment Volume, Revision 1.0) specifies interfaces for the user environment portion of OSF's Applications Environment.

Chapter 1 describes the purpose of the Application Environment Specification, incorporating a document originally published by itself as "The AES Definition." It provides a detailed description of the relationship of the AES to:

- Formal (de jure) standards and specifications.

- Implementations; for example, operating systems like OSF's operating system component (OSC).

- Portable applications software.

Audience

This document is written for:

- Software engineers developing AES-compliant applications to run on AES-compliant implementations.

- Software engineers developing AES-compliant implementations on which AES-compliant applications can run.

- Organizations (for example, standards-setting bodies) for whom the AES (or some part of it) is an appropriate part of the formal, de jure process.

Contents

This document is organized into two chapters and three appendices.

- *Chapter 1* introduces the AES, providing the general AES definition, and the general rationale for inclusion and specification of interfaces in the AES.

- *Chapter 2* contains manual pages for all of the AES/UE interfaces. They are ordered alphabetically within commands and functions.

- *Appendix A* provides the System Service Table.

- *Appendix B* provides the System Service Table ordered by functional area.

- *Appendix C* describes the rationale for excluding interfaces considered for inclusion in the AES/UE.

Typographical Conventions

This volume uses the following typographical conventions:

- **Boldfaced** strings represent literals; type them exactly as they appear.

- *Italicized* strings represent variables (for example, function or macro arguments).

- Ellipses (...) indicate that additional arguments are optional.

Interface Definition Manual Page Format

The manual pages for interface definitions in this volume use the following format:

Purpose

This section gives a short description of the interface.

AES Support Level

This section indicates whether the interfaces's AES support status is full-, trial-, or temporary-use.

Compatibility

This section lists the standards and industry specifications in which the interface exists.

Synopsis

This section describes the appropriate syntax for using the interface.

Description

This section describes the behavior of the interface. On widget man pages there are tables of resource values in the descriptions. Those tables have the following headers:

Name   Contains the name of the resource. Each new resource is described following the new resources table.

Class   Contains the class of the resource.

Type   Contains the type of the resource.

Default   Contains the default value of the resource.

Access   Contains the access permissions for the resource. A C in this column means the resource can be set at widget creation time. A S means the resource can be set anytime. A G means the resource's value can retrieved.

Return Value

This lists the values returned by function interfaces.

Errors

This section describes the error conditions associated with using this interface.

Related Information

This section provides cross references to related interfaces and header files described within this document.

Chapter 1

Introduction

This chapter introduces the user enviromnent volume of the AES. Section 1.1 defines the AES. Section 1.2 decribes the rational for exclusion of services from this AES. Section 1.3 is the AES/UE system service outline. Section 1.4 is a table of AES support level ordered by functional area.

1.1 The Application Environment Specification Definition

This section provides a detailed description of the AES.

1.1.1 Introduction to the AES Definition

Part of the charter of OSF is to foster the development of portable software applications that will run on a wide variety of hardware platforms. The software required to support such applications is an "application environment" provided by systems or software vendors. An application environment is a set of programming and user interfaces and their associated semantics, available to applications and users.

An operating system may be a key part of an application environment, as are other base software technologies that run on operating systems and support applications. The AES is a specification for a consistent application environment across different hardware platforms. This definition uses the term implementation to describe the application environment that vendors supply to application developers, because such software is an implementation of the AES.

The AES specifies the following:

- Application-level interfaces that an implementation must provide in order to support portable applications

- Semantics or "protocols" associated with each of these interfaces

This definition describes the purpose, contents, and organization of the AES. It also discusses the meaning of AES compliance for applications and implementations, the relationship of the AES to other industry documents (standards and specifications) and to implementations. Finally, the document describes the AES development process and the support levels used to characterize interfaces within the AES.

1.1.2 Purpose of the AES

The primary purpose of the AES is to provide a common definition of application interfaces that both systems providers and systems users can rely on in the development of portable applications. The composite AES defines the stable, reliable, application-level interfaces in several functional areas. Systems sellers who comply with the AES know exactly what interfaces they must provide, and how each element of those interfaces must behave. Systems buyers who look for AES compliance know unequivocally the interfaces they can rely on.

A secondary purpose of the AES is to take advantage of OSF's organizational charter to expedite the specification of application environments. Unlike specifications and standards bodies, OSF also provides vendor-neutral, hardware-independent implementations. The task of providing these implementations gives practical experience and feedback that enables the AES to expand faster than standards documents can. Also, OSF's technical staff is chartered to provide an expeditious resolution of the conflicts that can delay the decision process in other types of organizations.

By integrating functionality that is already standardized with newer functionality that is suitable for eventual standardization, the AES provides material that contributes to future standards. Because of OSF's timely, vendor-neutral decision process, this newer functionality can be added relatively quickly.

1.1.3 Content of the AES

As previously stated, the AES is a set of specifications for programming and user interfaces and their associated semantics. This definition refers to units within these interfaces as "elements." For example, a particular library routine, user command, or object is an element. The elements specified in the AES have the following characteristics:

- They can be implemented on a wide variety of hardware platforms.

- They support hardware-independent applications.

- They are stable (they are not likely to need to change).

- They are reliable (because they are tightly specified, applications writers can rely on consistent behavior across applications platforms).

- They do not duplicate other elements specified in the AES.

We call AES-specified program and user interfaces "portability interfaces", because they provide support for portable (hardware-independent) applications.

The criteria listed above for inclusion of interfaces in the AES dictate a conservative approach to its development. In order to be useful for applications development within these criteria, the AES must provide the richest possible function set. Development of the AES requires a balance between expansion to provide richer functionality, and conservatism to guarantee the stability of included interfaces.

Internal interfaces are interfaces that are not visible to applications. Internal interfaces are not part of the AES. The AES specifies only application-level portability interfaces (as previously defined).

1.1.4 Organization of the AES

The AES is an evolving set of *area specifications*. Each area specification describes portability interfaces for one *functional area* of the application environment. OSF has identified the following functional areas:

- Operating System

- Network Services

- User Environment Services

- Graphics Services

- Database Management Services

- Programming Languages (BASIC, FORTRAN, Pascal, C, COBOL, Ada, and LISP)

In certain functional areas, OSF publishes its own area specifications, which add to or extend existing standards and specifications. This definition focuses on the development process for the specifications that OSF publishes. In other areas, the AES just points to widely-known existing standards and specifications.

The initial AES area specifications for OSF publication are in three functional areas. The *AES/Operating System* area specification describes the portability interfaces that an AES-compliant operating system must provide, and consists of two volumes (describing programming interfaces and commands and utilities, respectively). This area specification also includes protocol-independent interfaces to communications services. The *AES/Network Services* area specification describes protocol-specific interfaces to network services. The *AES/User Environment* area specification describes the portability interfaces that an AES-compliant user interface must provide, and consists of one volume (describing user interface and window management services).

As the descriptions above show, an area specification can consist of one or more volumes, and the term "AES Volume" describes the document that contains all or part of an area specification. Figure 1 shows the organization of the initial AES volumes, including the *AES/Operating System, AES/Network Services* and *AES/User Environment* volumes.

Figure 1. The Current Organization of AES Documents

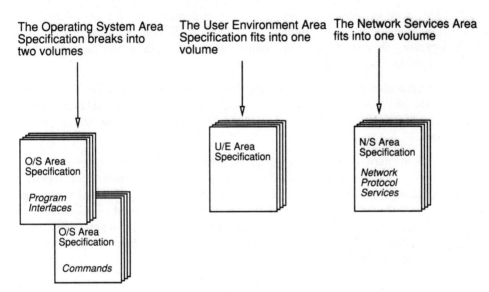

The Operating System Area Specification breaks into two volumes

The User Environment Area Specification fits into one volume

The Network Services Area fits into one volume

O/S Area Specification

Program Interfaces

O/S Area Specification

Commands

U/E Area Specification

N/S Area Specification

Network Protocol Services

OSF's goal is to promote usability and coherence of the AES documents themselves; therefore, document titles are as descriptive as possible. Also, OSF uses revisions, rather than supplements, to add functions to existing AES volumes.

Each revision of an AES Volume includes, for reference, the complete list of standards and specifications that comprise the Application Environment. (This list first appeared as "AES Level 0" in May, 1988.) Because unless otherwise stated, the standards and specifications that comprise the Application Environment are independent of one another, this list is provided only for user reference. Any direct dependencies that an area AES has on specifications in another area are listed within the AES Volume for the first area.

1.1.5 The Meaning of AES Compliance

This section provides a brief, general discussion of AES compliance for implementations and applications. Other OSF publications discuss the specific means of proving compliance, and such issues as validation, branding, and waivers.

Implementations and applications that comply with the AES do so on the basis of *area functionality*. An implementation or application that is compliant with one AES area is considered to be AES-compliant for that area.

Implementations and applications comply with the AES differently, since implementations *provide* services and applications *use* interfaces specified in the AES to access these services. A compliant implementation provides *at least* the interfaces defined in the AES. A compliant application uses *only* the interfaces defined in the AES, and those defined in any standards or specifications that the AES depends on. Such dependencies are called out explicitly in AES area specifications.

1.1.5.1 AES Compliance for Implementations

If an implementation claims AES compliance in a functional area, it must, at a minimum:

- Provide every interface specified by the AES volume for that functional area

- Implement each interface element as specified by the AES volume for that functional area

AES area-compliant implementations may offer additional interfaces not specified in the AES, or extensions to AES interfaces, provided they do not affect the compliance of any element of the AES-specified interfaces.

Unless specifically called out within the area specification, an implementation that complies with one functional area need not provide services from other functional areas, or be compliant with other functional areas.

Vendors of AES-compliant implementations must provide to their customers a compliance document that describes:

- The AES area and version the implementation complies with.

- The values of all implementation-defined variables. For those variables whose values can be changed, the document must describe the means of changing the values.

- For any implementation-defined behaviors, the behavior that applications can expect.

If this information exists in other documents provided with the implementation, the AES compliance document can point to the information rather than repeat it.

1.1.5.2 AES Compliance for Applications

If an application claims AES compliance in a functional area, it uses only the interfaces in the relevant AES area specification or those in other standards and specifications the area specification depends on. Standards or specifications included by reference are considered to be part of the AES for compliant applications.

The application must depend only on AES-specified behavior for AES interfaces. An application should not depend on any behavior that the AES describes as unspecified, undefined, or implementation-dependent.

1.1.5.3 AES Support Levels and Compliance

Each AES interface element has a support level, which specifies the commitment OSF makes to its definition. The higher the support level, the longer the warning period required before OSF can delete the element, or make an incompatible change in the element's definition. (An incompatible change is one that requires compliant applications to be rewritten.)

Compliant implementations provide all AES interfaces for the relevant area, at all support levels. Developers of compliant applications can choose to use or not use elements at any support level. Support levels serve as advisories for application developers, because they indicate how difficult it is for an element's definition to change.

During the AES development process, OSF staff members propose support levels for interface elements, based on criteria defined later in this document. OSF members review and comment on these support levels along with the rest of the document.

Section 1.1.9 provides detailed information about AES support levels.

1.1.6 Relationship of the AES to Standards and Other Specifications

The AES incorporates relevant industry standards and selected industry specifications. When an AES area specification incorporates an industry standard or specification, the area specification either points to that standard or specification, or includes the text. (Document revision schedules, source availability, and document usability dictate the use of pointers or text.)

The AES may extend or further specify interface elements derived from an included standard or specification, and when these occur, they are clearly marked as such within the appropriate AES Volume.

An AES-compliant implementation of an interface should also comply with all included standards and specifications that contain the interface. If this is not possible because of conflicts between definitions in included standards, the AES resolves conflicts based on a defined precedence order of standards. AES Volumes define, in an introductory chapter, the order of precedence of any included standards and specifications.

Inclusion of whole standards and specifications in the AES sometimes results in inclusion of interfaces, or interface elements, that might not have been selected for inclusion on their own merit. In such cases, OSF still includes the element, because it is in the standard and the standard takes precedence. However, the AES interface definition notes any problems and discourages applications' use of the problematic interface. OSF also works within the standards or specification bodies to remove or modify such interfaces.

1.1.7 Relationship of the AES to Implementations

The AES is a specification to which vendors can build implementations. OSF itself provides implementations for some of the AES functional areas. These OSF implementations include the portability interfaces defined in the AES, and may also include interfaces not specified in the AES, or extensions to AES-specified interfaces. Some of the interfaces that are not in the AES may be candidates for inclusion in a subsequent AES revision. Figure 2 shows how AES-specified interfaces are a subset of the interfaces provided in an implementation.

Figure 2. Services within OSF's Implementation (OSF-1)

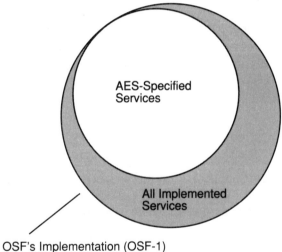

OSF's Implementation (OSF-1)

1.1.8 The AES Development Process

This section describes the processes for development of the AES, for document revision control, and for membership review cycles.

For each functional area, OSF produces one or more AES area specification drafts for its membership to review (see "Membership Review"). After incorporating review comments, OSF produces a final AES area specification. A final AES area specification for a particular revision includes the interface definitions for a stable set of portability interfaces in one functional area of the OSF-supported Application Environment.

1.1.8.1 Document Control and the AES

OSF labels the AES for each functional area with a *Revision Letter*. As the collection of revisions grows, OSF may group the existing revisions into an *AES Level*. For example, an AES Level might include AES/UE Revision B, AES/OS Revision A, and so on.

1.1.8.2 The Service Outline

A Service Outline is a document that lists all the elements in each AES interface for a functional area and describes the support level OSF plans to give the element. OSF makes two uses of Service Outlines.

- In some functional areas, a Service Outline may be a draft document that precedes a Full AES volume. (A full AES volume provides complete interface definitions or pointers to other information or conceptual descriptions.) A draft Service Outline proposes the interfaces to be included in a full AES volume. In this case, the full AES volume draft, when complete, supersedes the Service Outline draft.

- In other functional areas, a Service Outline may become a permanent document. If all the interfaces for a functional area are completely specified, with no conflicts, in industry standards or other specification documents, the AES area specification for that functional area may remain as a Service Outline and never evolve into a full AES volume.

When appropriate, a Service Outline also contains a table that shows each element, and lists relevant industry standards, specifications, and implementations that include the element.

Complete AES documents (not Service Outlines) provide complete interface definitions, and pointers to other information or conceptual descriptions.

1.1.8.3 The Membership Review

In general, membership review proceeds as follows:

1. OSF prepares a draft Service Outline and/or AES Volume for a functional area, and circulates it to OSF members. This review period may last from one to several months.

2. Members comment using a prescribed "comment template".

3. OSF responds to members' comments in the next version of the document, or in a discussion that takes place in an electronic newsgroup or at a meeting.

OSF considers all review comments during the development of AES documents, and brings important or controversial issues up for further discussion. However, the review process is not a voting process, and OSF does not wait for consensus among the membership before adding new interfaces to the AES.

1.1.9 AES Support Levels

This section defines the support levels assigned to each AES interface element. As previously mentioned, support levels define OSF's commitment to interface definitions by indicating the warning period required to make an incompatible modification or deletion of the definition.

The support levels are:

- Full-use

- Trial-use

- Temporary-use

Typically, elements in the AES have full-use or trial-use support levels. Compliant implementations must provide them, and application developers can use them freely (with the knowledge that trial-use elements are subject to more rapid change than full-use elements). The temporary-use support level appears only rarely in area specifications; it is for special cases, as described below. Implementations must provide temporary-use elements too, when they appear.

The paragraphs that follow explain each support level. The last part of the section describes how elements move from proposed status (in draft specifications) to final status (in published specifications).

1.1.9.1 Full-Use

A full-use element has the highest support level, so it is the most protected from incompatible modification or deletion from the AES.

OSF assigns a support level of full-use to elements for reasons such as the following:

- The element already exists in an approved de-jure standard. (A de-jure standard is one that is set by an official standards body.)

- The element as specified in the AES is considered stable and already in use in applications.

- The element has been upgraded to full-use status after a period of trial-use status in an earlier AES revision.

There should rarely be a need to remove a full-use element, or make incompatible modifications to it. However, if this ever becomes necessary, a full-use element keeps its full-use status, with warnings about its removal or incompatible change, for at least two full revisions of the AES. This provides time for applications to be altered to deal with a different behavior, and for implementations to prepare for the change.

For example, suppose it becomes necessary to modify a full-use element that appeared in Revision A of an AES Volume. The draft for Revision B shows the element as "proposed-for-modification/removal." Assuming the review concludes that this change is appropriate, the element in Revision B still has full-use status, but is accompanied by a warning. The warning states that the element is slated for modification after Revision C, and describes the modified behavior. Application developers can now allow for either the original or the modified behavior. Revision C contains the same warning. Revision D provides the modified definition only. The History section of the interface element definition documents the history of such changes.

1.1.9.2 Trial-Use

A trial-use element is easier to modify or delete than a full-use element. There are several reasons that OSF classifies elements as trial-use instead of full-use. An element may be under consideration for inclusion in a de-jure standard, and likely to change as a result of the standards process. Or, OSF may perceive that the element is new compared to other included elements, and therefore more likely to require changes in definition.

If it becomes necessary to modify or delete a trial-use element, it keeps its trial-use status, with warnings about its removal or incompatible change, for one full revision of the AES. So, in the example above, if the element to be modified were a trial-use element, Revision B would include the unmodified definition with a warning and description of the change, and Revision C would include the modified definition only.

1.1.9.3 Temporary-Use

A temporary-use element is a special case. Because it is limited in use, not sufficiently general, or faulty in some other way, it is likely to be changed. As such, it does not meet the criteria for inclusion in the AES with a full-use or trial-use support level, but it provides necessary functionality not available through other full-use or trial-use interface elements. Compliant applications may use these elements as necessary; an application containing a temporary-use element should be labelled as such. The AES replaces temporary-use interface elements when appropriate full- or trial-use elements become available.

Giving an element temporary-use status makes it clear from the outset that OSF intends to replace it. In the meantime, the element provides necessary and clearly specified functionality. Compliant implementations must provide services classified as temporary-use, and applications can use them, although it is clear that the element will eventually be replaced. Once a replacement exists, the AES includes a warning in the temporary-use element's definition and lists the removal date. As in the case of a trial-use element, the warning exists for one revision only.

For example, certain network interfaces provide a general service using a protocol-specific algorithm. These might be candidates for temporary-use status, because as time passes, interfaces based on protocol-independent algorithms will become available to replace them.

1.1.9.4 Proposed Usage Levels

Draft versions of specifications give newly added or changed elements a "proposed-for-*level*" status, where *level* is one of those defined above. In final versions, these elements move from "proposed-for-*level*" status to *level* status.

In the review draft of the first version of an AES area specification, all elements are at "proposed-for *level*" status. In review drafts of subsequent versions, the elements may have one of several statuses. Most existing elements retain their support level from the existing revision. A few may carry a proposed- for-*change* status (described below). New elements carry a proposed-for *level*.

The following define more exactly the AES proposed-for-inclusion and proposed for-change levels.

Proposed-for-*level*-use

> A review level leading to *level*-use inclusion on acceptance, and no change in status otherwise. This status may be used to propose a new element for *level*-use, or to move an existing element to a higher status.

Proposed-for-modification/removal

> A review level for existing elements that OSF proposes to make an incompatible modification in or remove from the AES. If this proposal is accepted during the review process, a full-use element remains as is, with a warning, for two revisions; a trial-use element remains as is with a warning, for one revision. If the proposal is rejected, the element just remains as is.

Proposed-for-correction

> A review level for elements, of any support level, in which OSF wishes to correct a specification error. OSF will propose correcting an element if a definition was obviously wrong (and implementations and applications could never follow the specification as it is written), if clarification of an unclear section is required, or if an error makes a definition clearly internally inconsistent or inappropriate. Elements proposed for correction return to their original status, in corrected form, on acceptance of the correction. They return to their original status in uncorrected form on rejection of the correction. (Proposal for correction is not required for OSF to fix a typographical error.)

Proposed-for-enhancement

> A review level for elements in which OSF wants to make an upwardly compatible change in definition. If accepted, the definition change is effective in the published version after the draft in which the proposal for enhancement occurred.

1.2 Rationale for Exclusion of Services

This section provides a rationale for the exclusion of services considered for the AES/UE.

uil and Mrm Functions

Preliminary feedback from builders of interactive design tools and user interface management systems indicates that as is, uil does not completely support their needs. While we hope and expect that future changes will be upward compatible, this cannot be guaranteed at this time. We are still evaluating whether some uil interfaces are stable enough for inclusion in the AES.

Functions Supporting WM_PROTOCOLS: XmActiveWMProtocol, XmAddWMProtocolCallbacks, XmWMAddProtocols, XmDeactivateWMProtocol, XmRemoveWMProtocolCallbacks, XmRemoveWMProtocols, XmSetWMProtocolHooks

Support for WM_PROTOCOLS is not being considered for the X Consortium's R4 Intrinsics, but may be considered in R5. When it is, Intrinsics support could make these routines obsolete.

Functions Supporting Other Protocols: XmActiveProtocol, XmAddProtocolCallbacks, XmAddProtocols, XmDeactivateProtocol, XmRemoveProtocolCallbacks, XmRemoveProtocols, XmSetProtocolHooks

These functions are used to support application writers who add entries to the system menu. The functions as provided are meant to support the WM_PROTOCOL functions as well. Decisions about AES inclusion will depend upon the resolution of WM_PROTOCOL functions.

String and FontList Functions and the Resource XmNstringDirection

XmString and its associated functions support mixed-character-set strings. At present, they are used for static strings only and do not incorporate information about the language that character segments represent. It is hoped that the interfaces will prove adequate for support of editable mixed-text strings with language identification, but until that is demonstrated, these functions are not part of the AES. Functions that require string and fontlist functions, resources and types are still available. The functions of those elements are just not defined in this AES.

Convert Functions: XmConvertUnits, XmCvtStringToUnitType

These support the Motif resolution independence model. This model has not been field tested enough for inclusion in the AES at this time.

The XmNdoubleClickInterval Resource

This resource is used in XmList and will be replaced by an application resource in the R4 intrinsics.

1.3 System Service Outline

This system service outline lists all the services considered for inclusion in the AES/UE. The first column is the name of the service. The table is organized alphabetically by this column. The second column is the type of the service. The type is widget, function, command, or file format. The third column is the proposed AES support level. All the services in this table are proposed as either full-use or excluded.

Table 1. System Service Outline

Service Name	Service Type	AES Level
ApplicationShell	widget	full-use
Composite	widget	full-use
Constraint	widget	full-use
Core	widget	full-use
MrmCloseHierarchy	function	excluded
MrmFetchColorLiteral	function	excluded
MrmFetchIconLiteral	function	excluded
MrmFetchInterfaceModule	function	excluded
MrmFetchLiteral	function	excluded
MrmFetchSetValues	function	excluded
MrmFetchWidget	function	excluded
MrmFetchWidgetOverride	function	excluded
MrmInitialize	function	excluded
MrmOpenHierarchy	function	excluded
MrmRegisterClass	function	excluded
MrmRegisterNames	function	excluded
Object	widget	full-use
OverrideShell	widget	full-use
RectObj	widget	full-use

Service Name	Service Type	AES Level
Shell	widget	full-use
TopLevelShell	widget	full-use
TransientShell	widget	full-use
Uil	function	excluded
UilDumpSymbolTree	function	excluded
VendorShell	widget	full-use
WMShell	widget	full-use
WindowObject	widget	full-use
XmActivateProtocol	function	excluded
XmActivateWMProtocol	function	excluded
XmAddProtocolCallbacks	function	excluded
XmAddProtocols	function	excluded
XmAddTabGroup	function	full-use
XmAddWMProtocolCallbacks	function	excluded
XmAddWMProtocols	function	excluded
XmArrowButton	widget	full-use
XmArrowButtonGadget	widget	full-use
XmBulletinBoard	widget	full-use
XmCascadeButton	widget	full-use
XmCascadeButtonGadget	widget	full-use
XmCascadeButtonHighlight	function	full-use
XmClipboardCancelCopy	function	full-use
XmClipboardCopy	function	full-use
XmClipboardCopyByName	function	full-use
XmClipboardEndCopy	function	full-use
XmClipboardEndRetrieve	function	full-use
XmClipboardInquireCount	function	full-use
XmClipboardInquireFormat	function	full-use
XmClipboardInquireLength	function	full-use
XmClipboardInquirePendingItems	function	full-use

Service Name	Service Type	AES Level
XmClipboardLock	function	full-use
XmClipboardRegisterFormat	function	full-use
XmClipboardRetrieve	function	full-use
XmClipboardStartCopy	function	full-use
XmClipboardStartRetrieve	function	full-use
XmClipboardUndoCopy	function	full-use
XmClipboardUnlock	function	full-use
XmClipboardWithdrawFormat	function	full-use
XmCommand	widget	full-use
XmCommandAppendValue	function	full-use
XmCommandError	function	full-use
XmCommandGetChild	function	full-use
XmCommandSetValue	function	full-use
XmConvertUnits	function	excluded
XmCreateArrowButton	function	full-use
XmCreateArrowButtonGadget	function	full-use
XmCreateBulletinBoard	function	full-use
XmCreateBulletinBoardDialog	function	full-use
XmCreateCascadeButton	function	full-use
XmCreateCascadeButtonGadget	function	full-use
XmCreateCommand	function	full-use
XmCreateDialogShell	function	full-use
XmCreateDrawingArea	function	full-use
XmCreateDrawnButton	function	full-use
XmCreateErrorDialog	function	full-use
XmCreateFileSelectionBox	function	full-use
XmCreateFileSelectionDialog	function	full-use
XmCreateForm	function	full-use
XmCreateFormDialog	function	full-use
XmCreateFrame	function	full-use

Service Name	Service Type	AES Level
XmCreateInformationDialog	function	full-use
XmCreateLabel	function	full-use
XmCreateLabelGadget	function	full-use
XmCreateList	function	full-use
XmCreateMainWindow	function	full-use
XmCreateMenuBar	function	full-use
XmCreateMenuShell	function	full-use
XmCreateMessageBox	function	full-use
XmCreateMessageDialog	function	full-use
XmCreateOptionMenu	function	full-use
XmCreatePanedWindow	function	full-use
XmCreatePopupMenu	function	full-use
XmCreatePromptDialog	function	full-use
XmCreatePulldownMenu	function	full-use
XmCreatePushButton	function	full-use
XmCreatePushButtonGadget	function	full-use
XmCreateQuestionDialog	function	full-use
XmCreateRadioBox	function	full-use
XmCreateRowColumn	function	full-use
XmCreateScale	function	full-use
XmCreateScrollBar	function	full-use
XmCreateScrolledList	function	full-use
XmCreateScrolledText	function	full-use
XmCreateScrolledWindow	function	full-use
XmCreateSelectionBox	function	full-use
XmCreateSelectionDialog	function	full-use
XmCreateSeparator	function	full-use
XmCreateSeparatorGadget	function	full-use
XmCreateText	function	full-use
XmCreateToggleButton	function	full-use

Service Name	Service Type	AES Level
XmCreateToggleButtonGadget	function	full-use
XmCreateWarningDialog	function	full-use
XmCreateWorkingDialog	function	full-use
XmCvtStringToUnitType	function	excluded
XmDeactivateProtocol	function	excluded
XmDeactivateWMProtocol	function	excluded
XmDestroyPixmap	function	full-use
XmDialogShell	widget	full-use
XmDrawingArea	widget	full-use
XmDrawnButton	widget	full-use
XmFileSelectionBox	widget	full-use
XmFileSelectionBoxGetChild	function	full-use
XmFileSelectionDoSearch	function	full-use
XmFontListAdd	function	excluded
XmFontListCreate	function	excluded
XmFontListFree	function	excluded
XmForm	widget	full-use
XmFrame	widget	full-use
XmGadget	widget	full-use
XmGetAtomName	function	full-use
XmGetMenuCursor	function	full-use
XmGetPixmap	function	full-use
XmInstallImage	function	full-use
XmInternAtom	function	full-use
XmIsMotifWMRunning	function	full-use
XmLabel	widget	full-use
XmLabelGadget	widget	full-use
XmList	widget	full-use
XmListAddItem	function	full-use
XmListAddItemUnselected	function	full-use

Service Name	Service Type	AES Level
XmListDeleteItem	function	full-use
XmListDeletePos	function	full-use
XmListDeselectAllItems	function	full-use
XmListDeselectItem	function	full-use
XmListDeselectPos	function	full-use
XmListItemExists	function	full-use
XmListSelectItem	function	full-use
XmListSelectPos	function	full-use
XmListSetBottomItem	function	full-use
XmListSetBottomPos	function	full-use
XmListSetHorizPos	function	full-use
XmListSetItem	function	full-use
XmListSetPos	function	full-use
XmMainWindow	widget	full-use
XmMainWindowSep1	function	full-use
XmMainWindowSep2	function	full-use
XmMainWindowSetAreas	function	full-use
XmManager	widget	full-use
XmMenuPosition	function	full-use
XmMenuShell	widget	full-use
XmMessageBox	widget	full-use
XmMessageBoxGetChild	function	full-use
XmOptionButtonWidget	function	full-use
XmOptionLabelWidget	function	full-use
XmPanedWindow	widget	full-use
XmPrimitive	widget	full-use
XmPushButton	widget	full-use
XmPushButtonGadget	widget	full-use
XmRemoveProtocolCallbacks	function	excluded
XmRemoveProtocols	function	excluded

Service Name	Service Type	AES Level
XmRemoveTabGroup	function	full-use
XmRemoveWMProtocolCallbacks	function	excluded
XmRemoveWMProtocols	function	excluded
XmResolvePartOffsets	function	full-use
XmRowColumn	widget	full-use
XmScale	widget	full-use
XmScaleGetValue	function	full-use
XmScaleSetValue	function	full-use
XmScrollBar	widget	full-use
XmScrollBarGetValues	function	full-use
XmScrollBarSetValues	function	full-use
XmScrolledWindow	widget	full-use
XmScrolledWindowSetAreas	function	full-use
XmSelectionBox	widget	full-use
XmSelectionBoxGetChild	function	full-use
XmSeparator	widget	full-use
XmSeparatorGadget	widget	full-use
XmSetFontUnits	function	excluded
XmSetMenuCursor	function	full-use
XmSetProtocolHooks	function	excluded
XmSetWMProtocolHooks	function	excluded
XmStringBaseline	function	excluded
XmStringByteCompare	function	excluded
XmStringCompare	function	excluded
XmStringConcat	function	excluded
XmStringCopy	function	excluded
XmStringCreate	function	excluded
XmStringCreateLtoR	function	excluded
XmStringDirectionCreate	function	excluded
XmStringDraw	function	excluded

Service Name	Service Type	AES Level
XmStringDrawImage	function	excluded
XmStringDrawUnderline	function	excluded
XmStringEmpty	function	excluded
XmStringExtent	function	excluded
XmStringFree	function	excluded
XmStringFreeContext	function	excluded
XmStringGetLtoR	function	excluded
XmStringGetNextComponent	function	excluded
XmStringGetNextSegment	function	excluded
XmStringHeight	function	excluded
XmStringInitContext	function	excluded
XmStringLength	function	excluded
XmStringLineCount	function	excluded
XmStringNConcat	function	excluded
XmStringNCopy	function	excluded
XmStringPeekNextComponent	function	excluded
XmStringSegmentCreate	function	excluded
XmStringSeparatorCreate	function	excluded
XmStringWidth	function	excluded
XmText	widget	full-use
XmTextClearSelection	function	full-use
XmTextGetEditable	function	full-use
XmTextGetMaxLength	function	full-use
XmTextGetSelection	function	full-use
XmTextGetString	function	full-use
XmTextReplace	function	full-use
XmTextSetEditable	function	full-use
XmTextSetMaxLength	function	full-use
XmTextSetSelection	function	full-use
XmTextSetString	function	full-use

Service Name	Service Type	AES Level
XmToggleButton	widget	full-use
XmToggleButtonGadget	widget	full-use
XmToggleButtonGadgetGetState	function	full-use
XmToggleButtonGadgetSetState	function	full-use
XmToggleButtonGetState	function	full-use
XmToggleButtonSetState	function	full-use
XmUninstallImage	function	full-use
XmUpdateDisplay	function	full-use
mwm	command	full-use
uil	command	excluded

1.4 Overview of the Services Type and Function

All the services are broken into four types in the tables below.

- Window manager
- Widgets and widget functions
- Toolkit functions
- User interface language

Within each table components are organized by function.

1.4.1 Window manager

Table 2. Window Manager Services

Service Name	Service Type	AES Level
mwm	command	full-use

1.4.2 Widgets and Widget Functions

This table organizes widgets by hierarchy. Position in the hierarchy is shown by the indentation of the service name. The functions for each widget immediately follow the widget.

Table 3. Widget Services

Service Name	Service Type	AES Level
Core	widget	full-use
Object	widget	full-use
RectObj	widget	full-use
WindowObj	widget	full-use
XmPrimitive	widget	full-use
XmArrowButton	widget	full-use
XmCreateArrowButton	function	full-use
XmLabel	widget	full-use
XmCreateLabel	function	full-use
XmCascadeButton	widget	full-use
XmCreateCascadeButton	function	full-use
XmCascadeButtonHighlight	function	full-use
XmDrawnButton	widget	full-use
XmCreateDrawnButton	function	full-use
XmPushButton	widget	full-use
XmCreatePushButton	function	full-use
XmToggleButton	widget	full-use
XmCreateToggleButton	function	full-use
XmToggleButtonGetState	function	full-use
XmToggleButtonSetState	function	full-use
XmList	widget	full-use
XmCreateList	function	full-use

Service Name	Service Type	AES Level
XmListAddItem	function	full-use
XmListAddItemUnselected	function	full-use
XmListDeleteItem	function	full-use
XmListDeletePos	function	full-use
XmListDeselectAllItems	function	full-use
XmListDeselectItem	function	full-use
XmListDeselectPos	function	full-use
XmListItemExists	function	full-use
XmListSelectItem	function	full-use
XmListSelectPos	function	full-use
XmListSetBottomItem	function	full-use
XmListSetBottomPos	function	full-use
XmListSetHorizPos	function	full-use
XmListSetItem	function	full-use
XmListSetPos	function	full-use
XmScrollBar	widget	full-use
XmCreateScrollBar	function	full-use
XmScrollBarGetValues	function	full-use
XmScrollBarSetValues	function	full-use
XmSeparator	widget	full-use
XmCreateSeparator	function	full-use
XmText	widget	full-use
XmCreateText	function	full-use
XmTextClearSelection	function	full-use
XmTextGetEditable	function	full-use
XmTextGetMaxLength	function	full-use
XmTextGetSelection	function	full-use
XmTextGetString	function	full-use
XmTextReplace	function	full-use
XmTextSetEditable	function	full-use

Service Name	Service Type	AES Level
XmTextSetMaxLength	function	full-use
XmTextSetSelection	function	full-use
XmTextSetString	function	full-use
Composite	widget	full-use
Shell	widget	full-use
OverrideShell	widget	full-use
XmMenuShell	widget	full-use
XmCreateMenuShell	function	full-use
WMShell	widget	full-use
VendorShell	widget	full-use
XmGetAtomName	function	full-use
XmInternAtom	function	full-use
TopLevelShell	widget	full-use
ApplicationShell	widget	full-use
TransientShell	widget	full-use
XmDialogShell	widget	full-use
XmCreateDialogShell	function	full-use
Constraint	widget	full-use
XmManager	widget	full-use
XmBulletinBoard	widget	full-use
XmCreateBulletinBoard	function	full-use
XmCreateBulletinBoardDialog	function	full-use
XmForm	widget	full-use
XmCreateForm	function	full-use
XmCreateFormDialog	function	full-use
XmMessageBox	widget	full-use
XmCreateMessageBox	function	full-use
XmCreateErrorDialog	function	full-use
XmCreateInformationDialog	function	full-use
XmCreateMessageDialog	function	full-use

Service Name	Service Type	AES Level
XmCreateQuestionDialog	function	full-use
XmCreateWarningDialog	function	full-use
XmCreateWorkingDialog	function	full-use
XmMessageBoxGetChild	function	full-use
XmSelectionBox	widget	full-use
XmCreateSelectionBox	function	full-use
XmCreatePromptDialog	function	full-use
XmCreateSelectionDialog	function	full-use
XmSelectionBoxGetChild	function	full-use
XmCommand	widget	full-use
XmCreateCommand	function	full-use
XmCommandAppendValue	function	full-use
XmCommandError	function	full-use
XmCommandGetChild	function	full-use
XmCommandSetValue	function	full-use
XmFileSelectionBox	widget	full-use
XmCreateFileSelectionBox	function	full-use
XmCreateFileSelectionDialog	function	full-use
XmFileSelectionBoxGetChild	function	full-use
XmFileSelectionDoSearch	function	full-use
XmDrawingArea	widget	full-use
XmCreateDrawingArea	function	full-use
XmFrame	widget	full-use
XmCreateFrame	function	full-use
XmPanedWindow	widget	full-use
XmCreatePanedWindow	function	full-use
XmRowColumn	widget	full-use
XmCreateRowColumn	function	full-use
XmCreateMenuBar	function	full-use
XmCreateOptionMenu	function	full-use

Service Name	Service Type	AES Level
XmCreatePopupMenu	function	full-use
XmCreatePulldownMenu	function	full-use
XmCreateRadioBox	function	full-use
XmGetMenuCursor	function	full-use
XmMenuPosition	function	full-use
XmOptionButtonWidget	function	full-use
XmOptionLabelWidget	function	full-use
XmSetMenuCursor	function	full-use
XmScale	widget	full-use
XmCreateScale	function	full-use
XmScaleGetValue	function	full-use
XmScaleSetValue	function	full-use
XmScrolledWindow	widget	full-use
XmCreateScrolledWindow	function	full-use
XmCreateScrolledList	function	full-use
XmCreateScrolledText	function	full-use
XmScrolledWindowSetAreas	function	full-use
XmMainWindow	widget	full-use
XmCreateMainWindow	function	full-use
XmMainWindowSep1	function	full-use
XmMainWindowSep2	function	full-use
XmMainWindowSetAreas	function	full-use
XmGadget	widget	full-use
XmArrowButtonGadget	widget	full-use
XmCreateArrowButtonGadget	function	full-use
XmLabelGadget	widget	full-use
XmCreateLabelGadget	function	full-use
XmCascadeButtonGadget	widget	full-use
XmCreateCascadeButtonGadget	function	full-use
XmPushButtonGadget	widget	full-use

Service Name	Service Type	AES Level
XmCreatePushButtonGadget	function	full-use
XmToggleButtonGadget	widget	full-use
XmCreateToggleButtonGadget	function	full-use
XmToggleButtonGadgetGetState	function	full-use
XmToggleButtonGadgetSetState	function	full-use
XmSeparatorGadget	widget	full-use
XmCreateSeparatorGadget	function	full-use

1.4.3 Toolkit Functions

Table 4. Toolkit Services

Service Name	Service Type	AES Level
XmActivateProtocol	function	excluded
XmActivateWMProtocol	function	excluded
XmAddProtocolCallbacks	function	excluded
XmAddProtocols	function	excluded
XmAddTabGroup	function	full-use
XmAddWMProtocolCallbacks	function	excluded
XmAddWMProtocols	function	excluded
XmClipboardCancelCopy	function	full-use
XmClipboardCopy	function	full-use
XmClipboardCopyByName	function	full-use
XmClipboardEndCopy	function	full-use
XmClipboardEndRetrieve	function	full-use
XmClipboardInquireCount	function	full-use
XmClipboardInquireFormat	function	full-use
XmClipboardInquireLength	function	full-use
XmClipboardInquirePendingItems	function	full-use
XmClipboardLock	function	full-use
XmClipboardRegisterFormat	function	full-use
XmClipboardRetrieve	function	full-use
XmClipboardStartCopy	function	full-use
XmClipboardStartRetrieve	function	full-use
XmClipboardUndoCopy	function	full-use
XmClipboardUnlock	function	full-use
XmClipboardWithdrawFormat	function	full-use
XmConvertUnits	function	excluded

Service Name	Service Type	AES Level
XmCvtStringToUnitType	function	excluded
XmDeactivateProtocol	function	excluded
XmDeactivateWMProtocol	function	excluded
XmDestroyPixmap	function	full-use
XmFontListAdd	function	excluded
XmFontListCreate	function	excluded
XmFontListFree	function	excluded
XmGetPixmap	function	full-use
XmInstallImage	function	full-use
XmIsMotifWMRunning	function	full-use
XmRemoveProtocolCallbacks	function	excluded
XmRemoveProtocols	function	excluded
XmRemoveTabGroup	function	full-use
XmRemoveWMProtocolCallbacks	function	excluded
XmRemoveWMProtocols	function	excluded
XmResolvePartOffsets	function	full-use
XmSetFontUnits	function	excluded
XmSetProtocolHooks	function	excluded
XmSetWMProtocolHooks	function	excluded
XmStringBaseline	function	excluded
XmStringByteCompare	function	excluded
XmStringCompare	function	excluded
XmStringConcat	function	excluded
XmStringCopy	function	excluded
XmStringCreate	function	excluded
XmStringCreateLtoR	function	excluded
XmStringDirectionCreate	function	excluded
XmStringDraw	function	excluded
XmStringDrawImage	function	excluded
XmStringDrawUnderline	function	excluded

Service Name	Service Type	AES Level
XmStringEmpty	function	excluded
XmStringExtent	function	excluded
XmStringFree	function	excluded
XmStringFreeContext	function	excluded
XmStringGetLtoR	function	excluded
XmStringGetNextComponent	function	excluded
XmStringGetNextSegment	function	excluded
XmStringHeight	function	excluded
XmStringInitContext	function	excluded
XmStringLength	function	excluded
XmStringLineCount	function	excluded
XmStringNConcat	function	excluded
XmStringNCopy	function	excluded
XmStringPeekNextComponent	function	excluded
XmStringSegmentCreate	function	excluded
XmStringSeparatorCreate	function	excluded
XmStringWidth	function	excluded
XmUninstallImage	function	full-use
XmUpdateDisplay	function	full-use

1.4.4 User Interface Language

Table 5. User Interface Language Services

Service Name	Service Type	AES Level
MrmCloseHierarchy	function	excluded
MrmFetchColorLiteral	function	excluded
MrmFetchIconLiteral	function	excluded
MrmFetchInterfaceModule	function	excluded
MrmFetchLiteral	function	excluded
MrmFetchSetValues	function	excluded
MrmFetchWidget	function	excluded
MrmFetchWidgetOverride	function	excluded
MrmInitialize	function	excluded
MrmOpenHierarchy	function	excluded
MrmRegisterClass	function	excluded
MrmRegisterNames	function	excluded
Uil	function	excluded
UilDumpSymbolTable	function	excluded
uil	command	excluded

mwm

Purpose

A Window Manager

AES Support Level

Full-use

Synopsis

mwm [*options*]

Description

mwm is an X11 client that provides window management functionality and some session management functionality. It provides functions that facilitate control (by the user and the programmer) of elements of window states such as placement, size, icon/normal display, input focus ownership, etc. It also provides session management functions such as stopping a client.

Options

-display *display*
> This option specifies the display to use; see *X(1)*.

-xrm *resourcestring*
> This option specifies a resource string to use.

Appearance

The following sections describe the basic default behaviors of windows, icons, the icon box, input focus, and window stacking. The appearance and behavior of the window manager can be altered by changing the configuration of specific resources. Resources are defined under the heading "X DEFAULTS."

Windows

Default **mwm** window frames have distinct components with associated functions:

Title Area	In addition to displaying the client's title, the title area is used to move the window. To move the window, place the pointer over the title area, press button 1 and drag the window to a new location. A wire frame is moved during the drag to indicate the new location. When the button is released, the window is moved to the new location.
Title Bar	The title bar includes the title area, the minimize button, the maximize button and the window menu button.
Minimize Button	To turn the window back into its icon, click button 1 on the minimize button (the frame box with a *small* square in it).

Maximize Button | To make the window fill the screen (or enlarge to the largest size allowed by the configuration files), do a button 1 click on the maximize button (the frame box with a *large* square in it).

Window Menu Button | The window menu button is the frame box with a horizontal bar in it. To pop up the window menu, press button 1. While pressing, drag the pointer on the menu to your selection, then release the button when your selection is highlighted. Alternately, you can click button 1 to pop up the menu and keep it posted; then position the pointer and select.

Default Window Menu		
Selection	**Accelerator**	**Description**
Restore	Alt+F5	Inactive (not an option for windows)
Move	Alt+F7	Allows the window to be moved with keys or mouse
Size	Alt+F8	Allows the window to be resized
Minimize	Alt+F9	Turns the window into an icon
Maximize	Alt+F10	Makes the window fill the screen
Lower	Alt+F11	Moves window to bottom of window stack
Close	Alt+F4	Removes client from **mwm** management

Resize Border Handles | To change the size of a window, move the pointer over a resize border handle (the cursor will change), press button 1, and drag the window to a new size. When the button is released, the window is resized. While dragging is being done, a rubber-band outline is displayed to indicate the new window size.

Matte | An optional matte decoration can be added between the client area and the window frame. A matte is not actually part of the window frame. There is no functionality associated with a matte.

Icons

Icons are small graphic representations of windows. A window can be minimized (iconified) using the minimize button on the window frame. Icons provide a way to reduce clutter on the screen.

Pressing mouse button 1 when the pointer is over an icon will cause the icon's window menu to pop up. Releasing the button (press + release without moving mouse = click) will cause the menu to stay posted. The menu contains the following selections:

Icon Window Menu		
Selection	**Accelerator**	**Description**
Restore	Alt+F5	Opens the associated window
Move	Alt+F7	Allows the icon to be moved with keys
Size	Alt+F8	Inactive (not an option for icons)
Minimize	Alt+F9	Inactive (not an option for icons)
Maximize	Alt+F10	Opens the associated window and makes it fill the screen
Lower	Alt+F11	Moves icon to bottom of icon stack
Close	Alt+F4	Removes client from **mwm** management

Double-clicking button 1 on an icon normalizes the icon into its associated window. Double-clicking button 1 on the icon box's icon opens the icon box and allow access to the contained icons. (In general, double-clicking a mouse button is a quick way to perform a function. Double-clicking button 1 with the pointer on the window menu button. This closes the window.)

Icon Box

When icons begin to clutter the screen, they can be packed into an icon box. (To use an icon box, **mwm** must be started with the icon box configuration already set.) The icon box is a **mwm** window that holds client icons. Icons in the icon box can be manipulated with the mouse. The following table summarizes the behavior of this interface. Button actions apply whenever the pointer is on any part of the icon.

Button Action	Description
Button 1 click	Selects the icon
Button 1 drag	Moves the icon
Button 1 double click	Normalizes (opens) the associated window
Button 1 double click	Raises an already *open* window to the top of the stack

The window menu of the icon box differs from the window menu of a client window: the Close selection is replaced with the PackIcons Alt+F12 selection. When selected, PackIcons packs the icons in the box to achieve neat rows with no empty slots.

Input Focus

mwm supports (by default) a keyboard input focus policy of explicit selection. This means when a window is selected to get keyboard input, it continues to get keyboard input until the window is withdrawn from window management, another window is explicitly selected to get keyboard input, or the window is iconified. Several resources that control the input focus. The client window with the keyboard input focus has the active window appearance with a visually distinct window frame.

The following tables summarize the keyboard input focus selection behavior:

Button Action	Object	Function Description
Button 1 press	Window / window frame	Keyboard focus selection
Button 1 press	Icon	Keyboard focus selection

Key Action	Function Description
[Alt][Tab]	Move input focus to next window in window stack
[Alt][Shift][Tab]	Move input focus to previous window in window stack

Window stacking

The stacking order of windows may be changed as a result of setting the keyboard input focus, iconifying a window, or by doing a window manager window stacking function.

When a window is iconified, the window's icon is placed on the bottom of the stack.

The following table summarizes the default window stacking behavior of **mwm**:

Key Action	Function Description
[Alt][ESC]	Put bottom window on top of stack
[Alt][Shift][ESC]	Put top window on bottom of stack

A window can also be raised to the top when it gets the keyboard input focus (for example, by pressing button 1 on the window or by using [Alt][Tab]) if this auto-raise feature is enabled with the **focusAutoRaise** resource.

X Defaults

mwm is configured from its resource database. This database is built from the following sources. They are listed in order of precedence, low to high:

app-defaults/Mwm
RESOURCE_MANAGER root window property or $HOME/.Xdefaults
XENVIRONMENT variable or $HOME/.Xdefaults-host
mwm command line options

Entries in the resource database may refer to other resource files for specific types of resources. These include files that contain bitmaps, fonts, and **mwm** specific resources such as menus and behavior specifications (for example, button and key bindings).

Mwm is the resource class name of **mwm** and **mwm** is the resource name used by **mwm** to look up resources. In the following discussion of resource specification "Mwm" and "mwm" can be used interchangeably.

mwm uses the following types of resources:

Component Appearance Resources:

These resources specify appearance attributes of window manager user interface components. They can be applied to the appearance of window manager menus, feedback windows (for example, the window reconfiguration feedback window), client window frames, and icons.

Specific Appearance and Behavior Resources:

These resources specify **mwm** appearance and behavior (for example, window management policies). They are not set separately for different **mwm** user interface components.

Client Specific Resources:

These **mwm** resources can be set for a particular client window or class of client windows. They specify client-specific icon and client window frame appearance and behavior.

Resource identifiers can be either a resource name (for example, foreground) or a resource class (for example, Foreground). If the value of a resource is a filename and if the filename is prefixed by "~/", then it is relative to the path contained in the *$HOME* environment variable (generally the user's home directory). This is the only environment variable **mwm** uses directly ($XENVIRONMENT is used by the resource manager).

Component Appearance Resources

The syntax for specifying component appearance resources that apply to window manager icons, menus, and client window frames is

Mwm*resource_id

For example, **Mwm*foreground** is used to specify the foreground color for **mwm** menus, icons, and client window frames.

The syntax for specifying component appearance resources that apply to a particular **mwm** component is

Mwm*[menu|icon|client|feedback]*resource_id

If *menu* is specified, the resource is applied only to **mwm** menus; if *icon* is specified, the resource is applied to icons; and if *client* is specified, the resource is applied to client window frames. For example, **Mwm*icon*foreground** is used to specify the foreground color for **mwm** icons, **Mwm*menu*foreground** specifies the foreground color for **mwm** menus, and **Mwm*client*foreground** is used to specify the foreground color for **mwm** client window frames.

The appearance of the title area of a client window frame (including window management buttons) can be separately configured. The syntax for configuring the title area of a client window frame is:

Mwm*client*title*resource_id

For example, **Mwm*client*title*foreground** specifies the foreground color for the title area. Defaults for title area resources are based on the values of the corresponding client window frame resources.

The appearance of menus can be configured based on the name of the menu. The syntax for specifying menu appearance by name is:

Mwm*menu**menu_name*******resource_id*

For example, **Mwm*menu*my_menu*foreground** specifies the foreground color for the menu named **my_menu**.

The following component appearance resources that apply to all window manager parts can be specified:

Component Appearance Resources - All Window Manager Parts			
Name	**Class**	**Value Type**	**Default**
background	Background	color	varies*
backgroundPixmap	BackgroundPixmap	string**	varies*
bottomShadowColor	Foreground	color	varies*
bottomShadowPixmap	BottomShadowPixmap	string**	varies*
fontList	FontList	string***	"fixed"
foreground	Foreground	color	varies*
saveUnder	SaveUnder	T/F	F
topShadowColor	Background	color	varies*
topShadowPixmap	TopShadowPixmap	string**	varies*

*The default is chosen based on the visual type of the screen.
**Pixmap image name. See XmInstallImage(3X).
***X11 R3 Font description.

background (class **Background**)
> This resource specifies the background color. Any legal X color may be specified. The default value is chosen based on the visual type of the screen.

backgroundPixmap (class **BackgroundPixmap**)
> This resource specifies the background Pixmap of the **mwm** decoration when the window is inactive (does not have the keyboard focus). The default value is chosen based on the visual type of the screen.

bottomShadowColor (class **Foreground**)
> This resource specifies the bottom shadow color. This color is used for the lower and right bevels of the window manager decoration. Any legal X color may be specified. The default value is chosen based on the visual type of the screen.

bottomShadowPixmap (class **BottomShadowPixmap**)

This resource specifies the bottom shadow Pixmap. This Pixmap is used for the lower and right bevels of the window manager decoration. The default is chosen based on the visual type of the screen.

fontList (class **Font**)

This resource specifies the font used in the window manager decoration. The character encoding of the font should match the character encoding of the strings that are used. The default is "fixed."

foreground (class **Foreground**)

This resource specifies the foreground color. The default is chosen based on the visual type of the screen.

saveUnder (class **SaveUnder**)

This is used to indicate whether "save unders" are used for **mwm** components. For this to have any effect, save unders must be implemented by the X server. If save unders are implemented, the X server will save the contents of windows obscured by windows that have the save under attribute set. If the saveUnder resource is True, **mwm** will set the save under attribute on the window manager frame of any client that has it set. If saveUnder is False, save unders will not be used on any window manager frames. The default value is False.

topShadowColor (class **Background**)

This resource specifies the top shadow color. This color is used for the upper and left bevels of the window manager decoration. The default is chosen based on the visual type of the screen.

topShadowPixmap (class **TopShadowPixmap**)

This resource specifies the top shadow Pixmap. This Pixmap is used for the upper and left bevels of the window manager decoration. The default is chosen based on the visual type of the screen.

The following component appearance resources that apply to frame and icons can be specified:

Frame and Icon Components			
Name	**Class**	**Value Type**	**Default**
activeBackground	Background	color	varies*
activeBackgroundPixmap	BackgroundPixmap	string**	varies*
activeBottomShadowColor	Foreground	color	varies*
activeBottomShadowPixmap	BottomShadowPixmap	string**	varies*
activeForeground	Foreground	color	varies*
activeTopShadowColor	Background	color	varies*
activeTopShadowPixmap	TopShadowPixmap	string**	varies*

*The default is chosen based on the visual type of the screen.
**See XmInstallImage(3X).

activeBackground (class **Background**)
This resource specifies the background color of the **mwm** decoration when the window is active (has the keyboard focus). The default is chosen based on the visual type of the screen.

activeBackgroundPixmap (class **ActiveBackgroundPixmap**)
This resource specifies the background Pixmap of the **mwm** decoration when the window is active (has the keyboard focus). The default is chosen based on the visual type of the screen.

activeBottomShadowColor (class **Foreground**)
This resource specifies the bottom shadow color of the **mwm** decoration when the window is active (has the keyboard focus). The default is chosen based on the visual type of the screen.

activeBottomShadowPixmap (class **BottomShadowPixmap**)
This resource specifies the bottom shadow Pixmap of the mwm decoration when the window is active (has the keyboard focus). The default is chosen based on the visual type of the screen.

activeForeground (class **Foreground**)
This resource specifies the foreground color of the **mwm** decoration when the window is active (has the keyboard focus). The default is chosen based on the visual type of the screen.

activeTopShadowColor (class **Background**)
> This resource specifies the top shadow color of the **mwm** decoration when the window is active (has the keyboard focus). The default is chosen based on the visual type of the screen.

activeTopShadowPixmap (class **TopShadowPixmap**)
> This resource specifies the top shadow Pixmap of the **mwm** decoration when the window is active (has the keyboard focus). The default is chosen based on the visual type of the screen.

Specific Appearance And Behavior Resources

The syntax for specifying *specific appearance and behavior resources* is

Mwm*resource_id

For example, **Mwm*keyboardFocusPolicy** specifies the window manager policy for setting the keyboard focus to a particular client window.

The following specific appearance and behavior resources can be specified:

Specific Appearance and Behavior Resources			
Name	**Class**	**Value Type**	**Default**
autoKeyFocus	AutoKeyFocus	T/F	T
autoRaiseDelay	AutoRaiseDelay	millisec	500
bitmapDirectory	BitmapDirectory	directory	/usr/include/\ X11/bitmaps
buttonBindings	ButtonBindings	string	NULL
cleanText	CleanText	T/F	T
clientAutoPlace	ClientAutoPlace	T/F	T
colormapFocusPolicy	ColormapFocusPolicy	string	keyboard
configFile	ConfigFile	file	.mwmrc

Name	Class	Value Type	Default
deiconifyKeyFocus	DeiconifyKeyFocus	T/F	T
doubleClickTime	DoubleClickTime	millisec.	500
enforceKeyFocus	EnforceKeyFocus	T/F	T
fadeNormalIcon	FadeNormalIcon	T/F	F
frameBorderWidth	FrameBorderWidth	pixels	5
iconAutoPlace	IconAutoPlace	T/F	T
iconBoxGeometry	IconBoxGeometry	string	6x1+0-0
iconBoxName	IconBoxName	string	iconbox
iconBoxTitle	IconBoxTitle	string	Icons
iconClick	IconClick	T/F	T
iconDecoration	IconDecoration	string	varies
iconImageMaximum	IconImageMaximum	wxh	50x50
iconImageMinimum	IconImageMinimum	wxh	32x32
iconPlacement	IconPlacement	string	left bottom
iconPlacementMargin	IconPlacementMargin	pixels	varies
interactivePlacement	InteractivePlacement	T/F	F
keyBindings	KeyBindings	string	system
keyboardFocusPolicy	KeyboardFocusPolicy	string	explicit
limitResize	LimitResize	T/F	T
lowerOnIconify	LowerOnIconify	T/F	T
maximumMaximumSize	MaximumMaximumSize	wxh (pixels)	2X screen w&h
moveThreshold	MoveThreshold	pixels	4
passButtons	PassButtons	T/F	F
passSelectButton	PassSelectButton	T/F	T

Name	Class	Value Type	Default
positionIsFrame	PositionIsFrame	T/F	T
positionOnScreen	PositionOnScreen	T/F	T
quitTimeout	QuitTimeout	millisec.	1000
resizeBorderWidth	ResizeBorderWidth	pixels	10
resizeCursors	ResizeCursors	T/F	T
showFeedback	ShowFeedback	string	all
startupKeyFocus	StartupKeyFocus	T/F	T
transientDecoration	TransientDecoration	string	system title
transientFunctions	TransientFunctions	string	-minimize -maximize
useIconBox	UseIconBox	T/F	F
wMenuButtonClick	WMenuButtonClick	T/F	T
wMenuButtonClick2	WMenuButtonClick2	T/F	T

autoKeyFocus (class **AutoKeyFocus**)

This resource is only available when the keyboard input focus policy is explicit. If autoKeyFocus is given a value of True, then when a window with the keyboard input focus is withdrawn from window management or is iconified, the focus is set to the previous window that had the focus. If the value given is False, there is no automatic setting of the keyboard input focus. The default value is True.

autoRaiseDelay (class **AutoRaiseDelay**)

This resource is only available when the focusAutoRaise resource is True and the keyboard focus policy is pointer. The autoRaiseDelay resource specifies the amount of time (in milliseconds) that **mwm** will wait before raising a window after it gets the keyboard focus. The default value of this resource is 500 (ms).

bitmapDirectory (class **BitmapDirectory**)

> This resource identifies a directory to be searched for bitmaps referenced by **mwm** resources. This directory is searched if a bitmap is specified without an absolute pathname. The default value for this resource is "/usr/include/X11/bitmaps".

buttonBindings (class **ButtonBindings**)

> This resource identifies the set of button bindings for window management functions. The named set of button bindings is specified in the **mwm resource description file**. These button bindings are *merged* with the built-in default bindings. The default value for this resource is NULL (i.e., no button bindings are added to the built-in button bindings).

cleanText (class**CleanText**)

> This resource controls the display of window manager text in the client title and feedback windows. If the default value of True is used, the text is drawn with a clear (no stipple) background. This makes text easier to read on monochrome systems where a backgroundPixmap is specified. Only the stippling in the area immediately around the text is cleared. If False, the text is drawn directly on top of the existing background.

clientAutoPlace (class **ClientAutoPlace**)

> This resource determines the position of a window when the window has not been given a user specified position. With a value of True, windows are positioned with the top left corners of the frames offset horizontally and vertically. A value of False causes the currently configured position of the window to be used. In either case, **mwm** will attempt to place the windows totally on-screen. The default value is True.

colormapFocusPolicy (class **ColormapFocusPolicy**)

> This resource indicates the colormap focus policy that is to be used. If the resource value is explicit then a colormap selection action is done on a client window to set the colormap focus to that window. If the value is pointer then the client window containing the pointer has the colormap focus. If the value is keyboard then the client window that has the keyboard input focus will have the colormap focus. The default value for this resource is keyboard.

configFile (class **ConfigFile**)

The resource value is the pathname for an **mwm resource description file**. The default is **.mwmrc** in the user's home directory (based on the $HOME environment variable) if this file exists, otherwise **/usr/lib/X11/system.mwmrc**.

deiconifyKeyFocus (class **DeiconifyKeyFocus**)

This resource only applies when the keyboard input focus policy is explicit. If a value of True is used, a window will receive the keyboard input focus when it is normalized (deiconified). True is the default value.

doubleClickTime (class **DoubleClickTime**)

This resource is used to set the maximum time (in ms) between the clicks (button presses) that make up a double-click. The default value of this resource is 500 (ms).

enforceKeyFocus (class **EnforceKeyFocus**)

If this resource is given a value of True, then the keyboard input focus is always explicitly set to selected windows even if there is an indication that they are "globally active" input windows. (An example of a globally active window is a scroll bar that can be operated without setting the focus to that client.) If the resource is False, the keyboard input focus is not explicitly set to globally active windows. The default value is True.

fadeNormalIcon (class **FadeNormalIcon**)

If this resource is given a value of True, an icon is grayed out whenever it has been normalized (its window has been opened). The default value is False.

frameBorderWidth (class **FrameBorderWidth**)

This resource specifies the width (in pixels) of a client window frame border without resize handles. The border width includes the 3-D shadows. The default value is 5 pixels.

iconAutoPlace (class **IconAutoPlace**)

This resource indicates whether icons are automatically placed on the screen by **mwm**, or are placed by the user. Users may specify an initial icon position and may move icons after initial placement; however, **mwm** will adjust the user-specified position to fit into an invisible grid. When icons are automatically placed, **mwm** places them into the grid using a scheme set with the iconPlacement resource. If the iconAutoPlace resource has a value of True, then **mwm** does automatic icon placement. A value of False allows user placement. The default value of this resource is True.

iconBoxGeometry (class **IconBoxGeometry**)

This resource indicates the initial position and size of the icon box. The value of the resource is a standard window geometry string with the following syntax:

$$[=][width\mathbf{x}height][\{+\text{-}\}xoffset\{+\text{-}\}yoffset]$$

If the offsets are not provided, the iconPlacement policy is used to determine the initial placement. The units for width and height are columns and rows.

The actual screen size of the icon box window will depend on the iconImageMaximum (size) and iconDecoration resources. The default value for size is (6 * iconWidth + padding) wide by (1 * iconHeight + padding) high. The default value of the location is +0 -0.

iconBoxName (class **IconBoxName**)

This resource specifies the name that is used to look up icon box resources. The default name is iconbox.

iconBoxTitle (class **IconBoxTitle**)

This resource specifies the name that is used in the title area of the icon box frame. The default value is Icons.

iconClick (class **IconClick**)

When this resource is given the value of True, the system menu is posted and left posted when an icon is clicked. The default value is True.

iconDecoration (class **IconDecoration**)

This resource specifies the general icon decoration. The resource value is label"(only the label part is displayed) or image (only the image part is displayed) or label image (both the label and image parts are displayed). A value of activelabel can also be specified to get a label (not truncated to the width of the icon) when the icon is selected. The default icon decoration for icon box icons is that each icon has a label part and an image part (label image). The default icon decoration for stand-alone icons is that each icon has an active label part, a label part and an image part (activelabel label image).

iconImageMaximum (class **IconImageMaximum**)

This resource specifies the maximum size of the icon *image*. The resource value is *width*x*height* (e.g., 64x64). The maximum supported size is 128x128. The default value of this resource is 50x50.

iconImageMinimum (class **IconImageMinimum**)

This resource specifies the minimum size of the icon *image*. The resource value is *width*x*height* (e.g., 32x50). The minimum supported size is 16x16. The default value of this resource is 32x32.

iconPlacement (class **IconPlacement**)

This resource specifies the icon placement scheme to be used. The resource value has the following syntax:

primary_layout secondary_layout

The layout values are one of the following:

top	Lay the icons out top to bottom.
bottom	Lay the icons out bottom to top.
left	Lay the icons out left to right.
right	Lay the icons out right to left.

A horizontal (vertical) layout value should not be used for both the *primary_layout* and the *secondary_layout* (e.g., don't use top for the *primary_layout* and bottom for the *secondary_layout*). The *primary_layout* indicates whether, when an icon placement is done, the icon is placed in a row or a column and the direction of placement. The *secondary_layout* indicates where to place new rows or columns. For example, top right indicates that icons should be placed top to bottom on the screen and that columns should be added from right to left on the screen. The default placement is left bottom (icons are placed left to right on the screen, with the first row on the bottom of the screen, and new rows added from the bottom of the screen to the top of the screen).

iconPlacementMargin (class **IconPlacementMargin**)

This resource sets the distance between the edge of the screen and the icons that are placed along the edge of the screen. The value should be greater than or equal to 0. A default value (see below) is used if the value specified is invalid. The default value for this resource is equal to the space between icons as they are placed on the screen (this space is based on maximizing the number of icons in each row and column).

interactivePlacement (class **InteractivePlacement**)

This resource controls the initial placement of new windows on the screen. If the value is True, then the pointer shape changes before a new window is placed on the screen to indicate to the user that a position should be selected for the upper-left hand corner of the window. If the value is False, then windows are placed according to the initial window configuration attributes. The default value of this resource is False.

keyBindings (class **KeyBindings**)

This resource identifies the set of key bindings for window management functions. If specified these key bindings *replace* the built-in default bindings. The named set of key bindings is specified in **mwm resource description file**. The default value for this resource is the set of system-compatible key bindings.

keyboardFocusPolicy (class **KeyboardFocusPolicy**)

If set to pointer, the keyboard focus policy is to have the keyboard focus set to the client window that contains the pointer (the pointer could also be in the client window decoration that **mwm** adds). If set to explicit, the policy is to have the keyboard focus set to a client window when the user presses button 1 with the pointer on the client window or any part of the associated **mwm** decoration. The default value for this resource is explicit.

limitResize (class **LimitResize**)

If this resource is True, the user is not allowed to resize a window to greater than the maximum size. The default value for this resource is True.

lowerOnIconify (class **LowerOnIconify**)

If this resource is given the default value of True, a window's icon appears on the bottom of the window stack when the window is minimized (iconified). A value of False places the icon in the stacking order at the same place as its associated window.

maximumMaximumSize (class **MaximumMaximumSize**)

This resource is used to limit the maximum size of a client window as set by the user or client. The resource value is *width***x***height* (e.g., 1024x1024) where the width and height are in pixels. The default value of this resource is twice the screen width and height.

moveThreshold (class **MoveThreshold**)

This resource is used to control the sensitivity of dragging operations that move windows and icons. The value of this resource is the number of pixels that the locator will be moved with a button down before the move operation is initiated. This is used to prevent window/icon movement when a click or double-click is done and there is unintentional pointer movement with the button down. The default value of this resource is 4 (pixels).

passButtons (class **PassButtons**)

This resource indicates whether or not button press events are passed to clients after they are used to do a window manager function in the client context. If the resource value is False, then the button press will not be passed to the client. If the value is True, the button press is passed to the client window. The window manager function is done in either case. The default value for this resource is False.

passSelectButton (class **PassSelectButton**)

This resource indicates whether or not the keyboard input focus selection button press (if keyboardFocusPolicy is explicit) is passed on to the client window or used to do a window management action associated with the window decorations. If the resource value is False then the button press will not be used for any operation other than selecting the window to be the keyboard input focus; if the value is True, the button press is passed to the client window or used to do a window management operation, if appropriate. The keyboard input focus selection is done in either case. The default value for this resource is True.

positionIsFrame (class **PositionIsFrame**)

This resource indicates how client window position information (from the WM_NORMAL_HINTS property and from configuration requests) is to be interpreted. If the resource value is True then the information is interpreted as the position of the **mwm** client window frame. If the value is False then it is interpreted as being the position of the client area of the window. The default value of this resource is True.

positionOnScreen (class **PositionOnScreen**)

This resource is used to indicate that windows should initially be placed (if possible) so that they are not clipped by the edge of the screen (if the resource value is True). If a window is larger then the size of the screen then at least the upper left corner of the window will be on-screen. If the resource value is False, then windows are placed in the requested position even if totally off-screen. The default value of this resource is True.

quitTimeout (class **QuitTimeout**)

This resource specifies the amount of time (in milliseconds) that **mwm** will wait for a client to update the WM_COMMAND property after **mwm** has sent the WM_SAVE_YOURSELF message. This protocol will only be used for those clients that have a WM_SAVE_YOURSELF atom and no WM_DELETE_WINDOW atom in the WM_PROTOCOLS client window property. The default value of this resource is 1000 (ms). (Refer to the f.kill function for additional information.)

resizeBorderWidth (class **ResizeBorderWidth**)

This resource specifies the width (in pixels) of a client window frame border with resize handles. The specified border width includes the 3-D shadows. The default is 10 (pixels).

resizeCursors (class **ResizeCursors**)

This is used to indicate whether the resize cursors are always displayed when the pointer is in the window size border. If True the cursors are shown, otherwise the window manager cursor is shown. The default value is True.

showFeedback (class **ShowFeedback**)

This resource controls when feedback information is displayed. It controls both window position and size feedback during move or resize operations and initial client placement. It also controls window manager message and dialog boxes. The value for this resource is a list of names of the feedback options to be enabled; the names must be separated by a space. The names of the feedback options are shown below:

Name	Description
all	Show all feedback. (Default value.)
behavior	Confirm behavior switch.
move	Show position during move.
none	Show no feedback.
placement	Show position and size during initial placement.
resize	Show size during resize.
restart	Confirm **mwm** restart.

The following command line illustrates the syntax for showFeedback:

Mwm*showFeedback: placement resize behavior restart

This resource specification provides feedback for initial client placement and resize, and enables the dialog boxes to confirm the restart and set behavior functions. It disables feedback for the move function.

startupKeyFocus (class **StartupKeyFocus**)

This resource is only available when the keyboard input focus policy is explicit. When given the default value of True, a window gets the keyboard input focus when the window is mapped (i.e., initially managed by the window manager).

transientDecoration (class **TransientDecoration**)

This controls the amount of decoration that Mwm puts on transient windows. The decoration specification is exactly the same as for the **clientDecoration** (client specific) resource. Transient windows are identified by the WM_TRANSIENT_FOR property which is added by the client to indicate a relatively temporary window. The default value for this resource is menu title (i.e., transient windows will have resize borders and a titlebar with a window menu button).

transientFunctions (class **TransientFunctions**)

This resource is used to indicate which window management functions are applicable (or not applicable) to transient windows. The function specification is exactly the same as for the **clientFunctions** (client specific) resource. The default value for this resource is -minimize -maximize.

useIconBox (class **UseIconBox**)

If this resource is given a value of True, icons are placed in an icon box. When an icon box is not used, the icons are placed on the root window (default value).

wMenuButtonClick (class **WMenuButtonClick**)

This resource indicates whether a click of the mouse when the pointer is over the window menu button will post and leave posted the system menu. If the value given this resource is True, then the menu will remain posted. True is the default value for this resource.

wMenuButtonClick2 (class **WMenuButtonClick2**)

When this resource is given the default value of True, a double-click action on the window menu button will do an f.kill function.

Client Specific Resources

The syntax for specifying *client specific resources* is

Mwm**client_name_or_class*****resource_id*

For example, **Mwm*mterm*windowMenu** is used to specify the window menu to be used with mterm clients.

The syntax for specifying *client specific resources* for all classes of clients is

Mwm*resource_id

Specific client specifications take precedence over the specifications for all clients. For example, **Mwm*windowMenu** is used to specify the window menu to be used for all classes of clients that don't have a window menu specified.

The syntax for specifying resource values for windows that have an unknown name and class (i.e. the window does not have a WM_CLASS property associated with it) is

Mwm*defaults*resource_id

For example, **Mwm*defaults*iconImage** is used to specify the icon image to be used for windows that have an unknown name and class.

The following client specific resources can be specified:

Client Specific Resources			
Name	**Class**	**Value Type**	**Default**
clientDecoration	ClientDecoration	string	all
clientFunctions	ClientFunctions	string	all
focusAutoRaise	FocusAutoRaise	T/F	T
iconImage	IconImage	pathname	(image)
iconImageBackground	Background	color	icon background
iconImageBottomShadowColor	Foreground	color	icon bottom shadow
iconImageBottomShadowPixmap	BottomShadow-Pixmap	color	icon bottom shadow pixmap
iconImageForeground	Foreground	color	icon foreground
iconImageTopShadowColor	Background	color	icon top shadow color
iconImageTopShadowPixmap	TopShadow-Pixmap	color	icon top shadow pixmap
matteBackground	Background	color	background
matteBottomShadowColor	Foreground	color	bottom shadow color
matteBottomShadowPixmap	BottomShadow-Pixmap	color	bottom shadow pixmap
matteForeground	Foreground	color	foreground
matteTopShadowColor	Background	color	top shadow color
matteTopShadowPixmap	TopShadow-Pixmap	color	top shadow pixmap

Client Specific Resources			
Name	**Class**	**Value Type**	**Default**
matteWidth	MatteWidth	pixels	0
maximumClientSize	MaximumClientSize	wxh	fill the screen
useClientIcon	UseClientIcon	T/F	F
windowMenu	WindowMenu	string	string

clientDecoration (class **ClientDecoration**)

This resource controls the amount of window frame decoration. The resource is specified as a list of decorations to specify their inclusion in the frame. If a decoration is preceded by a minus sign, then that decoration is excluded from the frame. The *sign* of the first item in the list determines the initial amount of decoration. If the sign of the first decoration is minus, then **mwm** assumes all decorations are present and starts subtracting from that set. If the sign of the first decoration is plus (or not specified), then **mwm** starts with no decoration and builds up a list from the resource.

Name	**Description**
all	Include all decorations (default value).
border	Window border.
maximize	Maximize button (includes title bar).
minimize	Minimize button (includes title bar).
none	No decorations.
resizeh	Border resize handles (includes border).
menu	Window menu button (includes title bar).
title	Title bar (includes border).

clientFunctions (class **ClientFunctions**)

This resource is used to indicate which **mwm** functions are applicable (or not applicable) to the client window. The value for the resource is a list of functions. If the first function in the list has a minus sign in front of it, then **mwm** starts with all functions and subtracts from that set. If the first function in the list has a plus sign in front of it, then **mwm** starts with no functions and builds up a list. Each function in the list must be preceded by the appropriate plus or minus sign and be separated from the next function by a space.

The table below lists the functions available for this resource:

Name	Description
all	Include all functions (default value)
none	No functions
resize	f.resize
move	f.move
minimize	f.minimize
maximize	f.maximize
close	f.kill

focusAutoRaise (class **FocusAutoRaise**)

When the value of this resource is True, clients are made completely unobscured when they get the keyboard input focus. If the value is False, the stacking of windows on the display is not changed when a window gets the keyboard input focus. The default value is True.

iconImage (class **IconImage**)

This resource can be used to specify an icon image for a client (e.g., "Mwm*myclock*iconImage"). The resource value is a pathname for a bitmap file. The value of the (client specific) useClientIcon resource is used to determine whether or not user supplied icon images are used instead of client supplied icon images. The default value is to display a built-in window manager icon image.

iconImageBackground (class **Background**)
> This resource specifies the background color of the icon image that is displayed in the image part of an icon. The default value of this resource is the icon background color (i.e., specified by "Mwm*background or Mwm*icon*background).

iconImageBottomShadowColor (class **Foreground**)
> This resource specifies the bottom shadow color of the icon image that is displayed in the image part of an icon. The default value of this resource is the icon bottom shadow color (i.e., specified by Mwm*icon*bottomShadowColor).

iconImageBottomShadowPixmap (class **BottomShadowPixmap**)
> This resource specifies the bottom shadow Pixmap of the icon image that is displayed in the image part of an icon. The default value of this resource is the icon bottom shadow Pixmap (i.e., specified by Mwm*icon*bottomShadowPixmap).

iconImageForeground (class **Foreground**)
> This resource specifies the foreground color of the icon image that is displayed in the image part of an icon. The default value of this resource is the icon foreground color (i.e., specified by "Mwm*foreground or Mwm*icon*foreground).

iconImageTopShadowColor (class **Background**)
> This resource specifies the top shadow color of the icon image that is displayed in the image part of an icon. The default value of this resource is the icon top shadow color (i.e., specified by Mwm*icon*topShadowColor).

iconImageTopShadowPixmap (class **TopShadowPixmap**)
> This resource specifies the top shadow Pixmap of the icon image that is displayed in the image part of an icon. The default value of this resource is the icon top shadow Pixmap (i.e., specified by Mwm*icon*topShadowPixmap).

matteBackground (class **Background**)
> This resource specifies the background color of the matte, when **matteWidth** is positive. The default value of this resource is the client background color (i.e., specified by "Mwm*background or Mwm*client*background).

matteBottomShadowColor (class **Foreground**)

This resource specifies the bottom shadow color of the matte, when **matteWidth** is positive. The default value of this resource is the client bottom shadow color (i.e., specified by "Mwm*bottomShadowColor   or Mwm*client*bottomShadowColor).

matteBottomShadowPixmap (class **BottomShadowPixmap**)

This resource specifies the bottom shadow Pixmap of the matte, when **matteWidth** is positive. The default value of this resource is the client bottom shadow Pixmap (i.e., specified by "Mwm*bottomShadowPixmap   or Mwm*client*bottomShadowPixmap).

matteForeground (class **Foreground**)

This resource specifies the foreground color of the matte, when **matteWidth** is positive. The default value of this resource is the client foreground color (i.e., specified by "Mwm*foreground or Mwm*client*foreground).

matteTopShadowColor (class **Background**)

This resource specifies the top shadow color of the matte, when **matteWidth** is positive. The default value of this resource is the client top shadow color (i.e., specified by "Mwm*topShadowColor or Mwm*client*topShadowColor).

matteTopShadowPixmap (class **TopShadowPixmap**)

This resource specifies the top shadow Pixmap of the matte, when **matteWidth** is positive. The default value of this resource is the client top shadow Pixmap (i.e., specified by "Mwm*topShadowPixmap or Mwm*client*topShadowPixmap).

matteWidth (class **MatteWidth**)

This resource specifies the width of the optional matte. The default value is 0, which effectively disables the matte.

maximumClientSize (class **MaximumClientSize**)

This is a size specification that indicates the client size to be used when an application is maximized. The resource value is specified as *width*x*height*. The width and height are interpreted in the units that the client uses (e.g., for terminal emulators this is generally characters). If this resource is not specified then the maximum size from the WM_NORMAL_HINTS property is used if set. Otherwise the default value is the size where the client window with window management borders fills the screen. When the maximum client size is not determined by the maximumClientSize resource, the maximumMaximumSize resource value is used as a constraint on the maximum size.

useClientIcon (class **UseClientIcon**)

If the value given for this resource is True, then a client supplied icon image will take precedence over a user supplied icon image. The default value is False, making the user supplied icon image have higher precedence than the client supplied icon image.

windowMenu (class **WindowMenu**)

This resource indicates the name of the menu pane that is posted when the window menu is popped up (usually by pressing button 1 on the window menu button on the client window frame). Menu panes are specified in the **mwm resource description file** file. Window menus can be customized on a client class basis by specifying resources of the form **Mwm***client_name_or_class***windowMenu** (See "Mwm Resource Description File Syntax"). The default value of this resource is the name of the built-in window menu specification.

Resource Description File

The **mwm resource description file** is a supplementary resource file that contains resource descriptions that are referred to by entries in the defaults files (.Xdefaults, app-defaults/Mwm). It contains descriptions of resources that are to be used by **mwm**, and that cannot be easily encoded in the defaults files (a bitmap file is an analogous type of resource description file). A particular **mwm resource description file** can be selected using the **configFile** resource.

The following types of resources can be described in the **mwm resource description file**:

Buttons   Window manager functions can be bound (associated) with button events.

Keys   Window manager functions can be bound (associated) with key press events.

Menus   Menu panes can be used for the window menu and other menus posted with key bindings and button bindings.

mwm Resource Description File Syntax

The **mwm resource description file** is a standard text file that contains items of information separated by blanks, tabs, and new lines characters. Blank lines are ignored. Items or characters can be quoted to avoid special interpretation (e.g., the comment character can be quoted to prevent it from being interpreted as the comment character). A quoted item can be contained in double quotes ("). Single characters can be quoted by preceding them by the back-slash character (\). All text from an unquoted # to the end of the line is regarded as a comment and is not interpreted as part of a resource description. If ! is the first character in a line, the line is regarded as a comment. Window manager functions can be accessed with button and key bindings, and with window manager menus. Functions are indicated as part of the specifications for button and key binding sets, and menu panes. The function specification has the following syntax:

$$
\begin{aligned}
&\textit{function} = &&\textit{function\_name [function\_args]} \\
&\textit{function\_name} = &&\textit{window manager function} \\
&\textit{function\_args} = &&\{\textit{quoted\_item} \mid \textit{unquoted\_item}\}
\end{aligned}
$$

The following functions are supported. If a function is specified that isn't one of the supported functions then it is interpreted by **mwm** as *f.nop*.

f.beep   This function causes a beep.

f.circle_down [**icon** | **window**]

This function causes the window or icon that is on the top of the window stack to be put on the bottom of the window stack (so that it is no longer obscuring any other window or icon). This function affects only those windows and icons that are obscuring other windows and icons, or that are obscured by other windows and icons. Secondary windows (i.e. transient windows) are restacked with their associated primary window. Secondary windows always stay on top of the associated primary window and there can be no other primary windows between the secondary windows and their primary window. If an **icon** function argument is specified, then the function applies only to icons. If a **window** function argument is specified then the function applies only to windows.

f.circle_up [**icon** | **window**]

This function raises the window or icon on the bottom of the window stack (so that it is not obscured by any other windows). This function affects only those windows and icons that are obscuring other windows and icons, or that are obscured by other windows and icons. Secondary windows (i.e. transient windows) are restacked with their associated primary window. If an *icon* function argument is specified then the function applies only to icons. If an *window* function argument is specified then the function applies only to windows.

f.exec or **!**   This function causes *command* to be executed (using the value of the *$SHELL* environment variable if it is set, otherwise */bin/sh*). The **!** notation can be used in place of the **f.exec** function name.

f.focus_color

This function sets the colormap focus to a client window. If this function is done in a root context, then the default colormap (setup by the *X Window System* for the screen where **mwm** is running) is installed and there is no specific client window colormap focus. This function is treated as *f.nop* if *colormapFocusPolicy* is not explicit.

f.focus_key This function sets the keyboard input focus to a client window or icon. This function is treated as *f.nop* if *keyboardFocusPolicy* is not explicit or the function is executed in a root context.

f.kill If the WM_DELETE_WINDOW protocol is set up, the client is sent a client message event indicating that the client window should be deleted. If the WM_SAVE_YOURSELF protocol is set up and the WM_DELETE_WINDOW protocol is not set up, the client is sent a client message event indicating that the client needs to prepare to be terminated. If the client does not have the WM_DELETE_WINDOW or WM_SAVE_YOURSELF protocol set up, this function causes a client's X connection to be terminated (usually resulting in termination of the client). Refer to the description of the *quitTimeout* resource and the *WM_PROTOCOLS* property.

f.lower [*-client*]

This function lowers a client window to the bottom of the window stack (where it obscures no other window). Secondary windows (i.e. transient windows) are restacked with their associated primary window. The *client* argument indicates the name or class of a client to lower. If the *client* argument is not specified then the context that the function was invoked in indicates the window or icon to lower.

f.maximize This function causes a client window to be displayed with its maximum size.

f.menu This function associates a cascading (pull-right) menu with a menu pane entry or a menu with a button or key binding. The *menu_name* function argument identifies the menu to be used.

f.minimize   This function causes a client window to be minimized (iconified). When a window is minimized when no icon box is used, its icon is placed on the bottom of the window stack (such that it obscures no other window). If an icon box is used, then the client's icon changes to its iconified form inside the icon box. Secondary windows (i.e. transient windows) are minimized with their associated primary window. There is only one icon for a primary window and all its secondary windows.

f.move   This function allows a client window to be interactively moved.

f.next_cmap   This function installs the next colormap in the list of colormaps for the window with the colormap focus.

f.next_key [**icon** | **window** | **transient**]

This function sets the keyboard input focus to the next window/icon in the set of windows/icons managed by the window manager (the ordering of this set is based on the stacking of windows on the screen). This function is treated as *f.nop* if *keyboardFocusPolicy* is not explicit. The keyboard input focus is only moved to windows that do not have an associated secondary window that is application modal. If the **transient** argument is specified, then transient (secondary) windows are traversed (otherwise, if only **window** is specified, traversal is done only to the last focused window in a transient group). If an **icon** function argument is specified, then the function applies only to icons. If a **window** function argument is specified, then the function applies only to windows.

f.nop   This function does nothing.

f.normalize   This function causes a client window to be displayed with its normal size. Secondary windows (i.e. transient windows) are placed in their normal state along with their associated primary window.

f.pack_icons

This function is used to relayout icons (based on the layout policy being used) on the root window or in the icon box. In general this causes icons to be "packed" into the icon grid.

f.pass_keys This function is used to enable/disable (toggle) processing of key bindings for window manager functions. When it disables key binding processing all keys are passed on to the window with the keyboard input focus and no window manager functions are invoked. If the *f.pass_keys* function is invoked with a key binding to disable key binding processing the same key binding can be used to enable key binding processing.

f.post_wmenu

This function is used to post the window menu. If a key is used to post the window menu and a window menu button is present, the window menu is automatically placed with its top-left corner at the bottom-left corner of the window menu button for the client window. If no window menu button is present, the window menu is placed at the top-left corner of the client window.

f.prev_cmap

This function installs the previous colormap in the list of colormaps for the window with the colormap focus.

f.prev_key [**icon | window | transient**]

This function sets the keyboard input focus to the previous window/icon in the set of windows/icons managed by the window manager (the ordering of this set is based on the stacking of windows on the screen). This function is treated as *f.nop* if *keyboardFocusPolicy* is not explicit. The keyboard input focus is only moved to windows that do not have an associated secondary window that is application modal. If the *transient* argument is specified, then transient (secondary) windows are traversed (otherwise, if only *window* is specified, traversal is done only to the last focused window in a transient group). If an *icon* function argument is specified then the function applies only to icons. If an *window* function argument is specified then the function applies only to windows.

f.quit_mwm This function terminates **mwm** (but NOT the X window system).

f.raise [*-client*]
This function raises a client window to the top of the window stack (where it is obscured by no other window). Secondary windows (i.e. transient windows) are restacked with their associated primary window. The *client* argument indicates the name or class of a client to raise. If the *client* argument is not specified then the context that the function was invoked in indicates the window or icon to raise.

f.raise_lower
This function raises a client window to the top of the window stack if it is partially obscured by another window, otherwise it lowers the window to the bottom of the window stack. Secondary windows (i.e. transient windows) are restacked with their associated primary window.

f.refresh This function causes all windows to be redrawn.

f.refresh_win
This function causes a client window to be redrawn.

f.resize This function allows a client window to be interactively resized.

f.restart This function causes **mwm** to be restarted (effectively terminated and re-executed).

f.send_msg *message_number*

This function sends a client message of the type _MOTIF_WM_MESSAGES with the *message_type* indicated by the *message_number* function argument. The client message will only be sent if *message_number* is included in the client's _MOTIF_WM_MESSAGES property. A menu item label is grayed out if the menu item is used to do *f.send_msg* of a message that is not included in the client's _MOTIF_WM_MESSAGES property.

f.separator This function causes a menu separator to be put in the menu pane at the specified location (the label is ignored).

f.set_behavior

This function causes the window manager to restart with the default OSF behavior (if a custom behavior is configured) or a custom behavior (if an OSF default behavior is configured).

f.title This function inserts a title in the menu pane at the specified location.

Each function may be constrained as to which resource types can specify the function (e.g., menu pane) and also what context the function can be used in (e.g., the function is done to the selected client window). Function contexts are

root No client window or icon has been selected as an object for the function.

window A client window has been selected as an object for the function. This includes the window's title bar and frame. Some functions are applied only when the window is in its normalized state (e.g., f.maximize) or its maximized state (e.g., f.normalize).

icon An icon has been selected as an object for the function.

If a function is specified in a type of resource where it is not supported or is invoked in a context that does not apply then the function is treated as *f.nop*. The following table indicates the resource types and function contexts in which window manager functions apply.

Function	Contexts	Resources
f.beep	root,icon,window	button,key,menu
f.circle_down	root,icon,window	button,key,menu
f.circle_up	root,icon,window	button,key,menu
f.exec	root,icon,window	button,key,menu
f.focus_color	root,icon,window	button,key,menu
f.focus_key	root,icon,window	button,key,menu
f.kill	icon,window	button,key,menu
f.lower	root,icon,window	button,key,menu
f.maximize	icon,window(normal)	button,key,menu
f.menu	root,icon,window	button,key,menu
f.minimize	window	button,key,menu
f.move	icon,window	button,key,menu
f.next_cmap	root,icon,window	button,key,menu
f.next_key	root,icon,window	button,key,menu
f.nop	root,icon,window	button,key,menu
f.normalize	icon,window(maximized)	button,key,menu
f.pack_icons	root,icon,window	button,key,menu
f.pass_keys	root,icon,window	button,key,menu
f.post_wmenu	root,icon,window	button,key
f.prev_cmap	root,icon,window	button,key,menu
f.prev_key	root,icon,window	button,key,menu
f.quit_mwm	root	button,key,menu
f.raise	root,icon,window	button,key,menu
f.raise_lower	icon,window	button,key,menu
f.refresh	root,icon,window	button,key,menu
f.refresh_win	window	button,key,menu
f.resize	window	button,key,menu

f.restart	root	button,key,menu
f.send_msg	icon,window	button,key,menu
f.separator	root,icon,window	menu
f.set_behavior	root,icon,window	button,key,menu
f.title	root,icon,window	menu

Window Manager Event Specification

Events are indicated as part of the specifications for button and key binding sets, and menu panes.

Button events have the following syntax:

button =	*[modifier_list]<button_event_name>*
modifier_list =	*modifier_name {modifier_name}*

All modifiers specified are interpreted as being exclusive (this means that only the specified modifiers can be present when the button event occurs). The following table indicates the values that can be used for *modifier_name*. The [Alt] key is frequently labeled [Extend] or [Meta]. Alt and Meta can be used interchangeably in event specification.

Modifier	Description
Ctrl	Control Key
Shift	Shift Key
Alt	Alt/Meta Key
Meta	Meta/Alt Key
Lock	Lock Key
Mod1	Modifier1
Mod2	Modifier2
Mod3	Modifier3
Mod4	Modifier4
Mod5	Modifier5

The following table indicates the values that can be used for *button_event_name*.

Button	Description
Btn1Down	Button 1 Press
Btn1Up	Button 1 Release
Btn1Click	Button 1 Press and Release
Btn1Click2	Button 1 Double Click
Btn2Down	Button 2 Press
Btn2Up	Button 2 Release
Btn2Click	Button 2 Press and Release
Btn2Click2	Button 2 Double Click
Btn3Down	Button 3 Press
Btn3Up	Button 3 Release
Btn3Click	Button 3 Press and Release
Btn3Click2	Button 3 Double Click
Btn4Down	Button 4 Press
Btn4Up	Button 4 Release
Btn4Click	Button 4 Press and Release
Btn4Click2	Button 4 Double Click
Btn5Down	Button 5 Press
Btn5Up	Button 5 Release
Btn5Click	Button 5 Press and Release
Btn5Click2	Button 5 Double Click

Key events that are used by the window manager for menu mnemonics and for binding to window manager functions are single key presses; key releases are ignored. Key events have the following syntax:

> *key =*   [*modifier_list*]**<Key>***key_name*
> *modifier_list =*   *modifier_name* {*modifier_name*}

All modifiers specified are interpreted as being exclusive (this means that only the specified modifiers can be present when the key event occurs). Modifiers for keys are the same as those that apply to buttons. The *key_name* is an X11 keysym name. Keysym names can be found in the keysymdef.h file (remove the *XK_* prefix).

Button Bindings

The **buttonBindings** resource value is the name of a set of button bindings that are used to configure window manager behavior. A window manager function can be done when a button press occurs with the pointer over a framed client window, an icon or the root window. The context for indicating where the button press applies is also the context for invoking the window manager function when the button press is done (significant for functions that are context sensitive).

The button binding syntax is

> **Buttons** *bindings_set_name*
> {
>   *button   context   function*
>   *button   context   function*
>   .
>
>   .
>   *button   context   function*
> }

The syntax for the *context* specification is

> *context* =   *object*[|*context*]
> *object* =   **root** | **icon** | **window** | **title** | **frame** | **border** | **app**

The context specification indicates where the pointer must be for the button binding to be effective. For example, a context of **window** indicates that the pointer must be over a client window or window management frame for the button binding to be effective. The **frame** context is for the window management frame around a client window (including the border and titlebar), the **border** context is for the border part of the window management frame (not including the titlebar), the **title** context is for the title area of the window management frame, and the **app** context is for the application window (not including the window management frame).

If an *f.nop* function is specified for a button binding, the button binding will not be done.

Key Bindings

The **keyBindings** resource value is the name of a set of key bindings that are used to configure window manager behavior. A window manager function can be done when a particular key is pressed. The context in which the key binding applies is indicated in the key binding specification. The valid contexts are the same as those that apply to button bindings.

The key binding syntax is

> **Keys** *bindings_set_name*
> {
>   *key   context   function*
>   *key   context   function*
>   .
>   .
>   *key   context   function*
> }

If an *f.nop* function is specified for a key binding, the key binding will not be done. If an *f.post_wmenu* or *f.menu* function is bound to a key, **mwm** will automatically use the same key for removing the menu from the screen after it has been popped up.

The *context* specification syntax is the same as for button bindings. For key bindings, the **frame**, **title**, **border**, and **app** contexts are equivalent to the **window** context. The context for a key event is the window or icon that has the keyboard input focus (**root** if no window or icon has the keyboard input focus).

Menu Panes

Menus can be popped up using the *f.post_wmenu* and *f.menu* window manager functions. The context for window manager functions that are done from a menu is *root*, *icon* or *window* depending on how the menu was popped up. In the case of the *window* menu or menus popped up with a key binding, the location of the keyboard input focus indicates the context. For menus popped up using a button binding, the context of the button binding is the context of the menu.

The menu pane specification syntax is

> **Menu** *menu_name*
> {
>   *label* [*mnemonic*] [*accelerator*] *function*
>   *label* [*mnemonic*] [*accelerator*] *function*
>   .
>   .
>   .
>   *label* [*mnemonic*] [*accelerator*] *function*
> }

Each line in the *Menu* specification identifies the label for a menu item and the function to be done if the menu item is selected. Optionally a menu button mnemonic and a menu button keyboard accelerator may be specified. Mnemonics are functional only when the menu is posted and keyboard traversal applies.

The *label* may be a string or a bitmap file. The label specification has the following syntax:

> *label* =   *text* | *bitmap_file*
> *bitmap_file* =   *@file_name*
> *text* =   *quoted_item* | *unquoted_item*

The string encoding for labels must be compatible with the menu font that is used. Labels are greyed out for menu items that do the *f.nop* function or an invalid function or a function that doesn't apply in the current context.

A *mnemonic* specification has the following syntax

mnemonic =   *_character*

The first matching *character* in the label is underlined. If there is no matching *character* in the label, no mnemonic is registered with the window manager for that label. Although the *character* must exactly match a character in the label, the mnemonic will not execute if any modifier (such as Shift) is pressed with the character key.

The *accelerator* specification is a key event specification with the same syntax as is used for key bindings to window manager functions.

Environment

mwm uses the environment variable **$HOME** specifying the user's home directory.

Files

/usr/lib/X11/system.mwmrc
/usr/lib/X11/app-defaults/Mwm
$HOME/.Xdefaults
$HOME/.mwmrc

Related Information

X(1)
VendorShell(3X)
XmInstallImage(3X)

ApplicationShell

Purpose

The ApplicationShell widget class

AES Support Level

Full-use

Synopsis

```
#include <Xm/Xm.h>
#include <X11/Shell.h>
```

Description

ApplicationShell is used as the main top-level window for an application. An application should have more than one ApplicationShell only if it implements multiple logical applications.

Classes

ApplicationShell inherits behavior and resources from **Core**, **Composite**, **Shell**, **WMShell**, **VendorShell**, and **TopLevelShell**.

The class pointer is **applicationShellWidgetClass**.

The class name is **ApplicationShell**.

New Resources

The following table defines a set of widget resources used by the programmer to specify data. The programmer can also set the resource values for the inherited classes to set attributes for this widget. To reference a resource by name or by class in a .Xdefaults file, remove the **XmN** or **XmC** prefix and use the remaining letters. To specify one of the defined values for a resource in a .Xdefaults file, remove the **Xm** prefix and use the remaining letters (in either lowercase or uppercase, but include any underscores between words). The codes in the access column indicate if the given resource can be set at creation time (**C**), set by using **XtSetValues** (**S**), retrieved by using **XtGetValues** (**G**), or is not applicable (**N/A**).

ApplicationShell Resource Set		
Name	**Default**	**Access**
Class	**Type**	
XmNargc	NULL	CSG
XmCNargc	int	
XmNargv	NULL	CSG
XmCNargv	String *	

XmNargc   Specifies the number of arguments given in the **XmNargv** resource. The function **XtInitialize** will set this resource on the shell widget instance it creates by using its parameters as the values.

XmNargv   Specifies the argument list required by a session manager to restart the application, if it is killed. This list should be updated at appropriate points by the application if a new state has been reached which can be directly restarted. The function **XtInitialize** will set this resource on the shell widget instance it creates by using its parameters as the values.

Inherited Resources

ApplicationShell inherits behavior and resources from the following superclasses. For a complete description of these resources, refer to the man page for that superclass.

TopLevelShell Resource Set		
Name	**Default**	**Access**
Class	**Type**	
XmNiconic	False	CSG
XmCIconic	Boolean	
XmNiconName	NULL	CSG
XmCIconName	String	

VendorShell Resource Set		
Name	**Default**	**Access**
Class	**Type**	
XmNdeleteResponse	XmDESTROY	CSG
XmCDeleteResponse	unsigned char	
XmNkeyboardFocusPolicy	XmEXPLICIT	CSG
XmCKeyboardFocusPolicy	unsigned char	
XmNmwmDecorations	-1	CSG
XmCMwmDecorations	int	
XmNmwmFunctions	-1	CSG
XmCMwmFunctions	int	
XmNmwmInputMode	-1	CSG
XmCMwmInputMode	int	
XmNmwmMenu	NULL	CSG
XmCMwmMenu	String	

WMShell Resource Set		
Name **Class**	**Default** **Type**	**Access**
XmNheightInc XmCHeightInc	-1 int	CSG
XmNiconMask XmCIconMask	NULL Pixmap	CSG
XmNiconPixmap XmCIconPixmap	NULL Pixmap	CSG
XmNiconWindow XmCIconWindow	NULL Window	CSG
XmNiconX XmCIconX	-1 int	CSG
XmNiconY XmCIconY	-1 int	CSG
XmNinitialState XmCInitialState	1 int	CSG
XmNinput XmCInput	True Boolean	CSG
XmNmaxAspectX XmCMaxAspectX	-1 int	CSG
XmNmaxAspectY XmCMaxAspectY	-1 int	CSG
XmNmaxHeight XmCMaxHeight	-1 int	CSG
XmNmaxWidth XmCMaxWidth	-1 int	CSG
XmNminAspectX XmCMinAspectX	-1 int	CSG
XmNminAspectY XmCMinAspectY	-1 int	CSG

Name Class	Default Type	Access
XmNminHeight XmCMinHeight	-1 int	CSG
XmNminWidth XmCMinWidth	-1 int	CSG
XmNtitle XmCTitle	NULL char *	CSG
XmNtransient XmCTransient	False Boolean	CSG
XmNwaitForWm XmCWaitForWm	True Boolean	CSG
XmNwidthInc XmCWidthInc	-1 int	CSG
XmNwindowGroup XmCWindowGroup	None XID	CSG
XmNwmTimeout XmCWmTimeout	fivesecond int	CSG

Shell Resource Set		

Name
   Class
	Default
	   Type
		Access

XmNallowShellResize
   XmCAllowShellResize
	False
	   Boolean
		CSG

XmNcreatePopupChildProc
   XmCCreatePopupChildProc
	NULL
	   XmCreatePopupChildProc
		CSG

XmNgeometry
   XmCGeometry
	NULL
	   String
		CSG

XmNoverrideRedirect
   XmCOverrideRedirect
	False
	   Boolean
		CSG

XmNpopdownCallback
   XmCCallback
	NULL
	   XtCallbackList
		C

XmNpopupCallback
   XmCCallback
	NULL
	   XtCallbackList
		C

XmNsaveUnder
   XmCSaveUnder
	False
	   Boolean
		CSG

Composite Resource Set		

Name
   Class
	Default
	   Type
		Access

XmNinsertPosition
   XmCInsertPosition
	NULL
	   XmRFunction
		CSG

Core Resource Set		
Name	**Default**	**Access**
Class	**Type**	
XmNaccelerators	NULL	CSG
XmCAccelerators	XtTranslations	
XmNancestorSensitive	ShellAncestorSensitive	G
XmCSensitive	Boolean	
XmNbackground	White	CSG
XmCBackground	Pixel	
XmNbackgroundPixmap	XmUNSPECIFIED_PIXMAP	CSG
XmCPixmap	Pixmap	
XmNborderColor	Black	CSG
XmCBorderColor	Pixel	
XmNborderPixmap	XmUNSPECIFIED_PIXMAP	CSG
XmCPixmap	Pixmap	
XmNborderWidth	1	CSG
XmCBorderWidth	Dimension	
XmNcolormap	ShellColormap	CG
XmCColormap	Colormap	
XmNdepth	ShellDepth	CG
XmCDepth	int	
XmNdestroyCallback	NULL	C
XmCCallback	XtCallbackList	
XmNheight	0	CSG
XmCHeight	Dimension	
XmNmappedWhenManaged	True	CSG
XmCMappedWhenManaged	Boolean	
XmNscreen	XtCopyScreen	CG
XmCScreen	Pointer	
XmNsensitive	True	CSG
XmCSensitive	Boolean	

Name	Default	Access
Class	Type	
XmNtranslations	NULL	CSG
XmCTranslations	XtTranslations	
XmNwidth	0	CSG
XmCWidth	Dimension	
XmNx	0	CSG
XmCPosition	Position	
XmNy	0	CSG
XmCPosition	Position	

Related Information

Composite(3X), Core(3X), Shell(3X), WMShell(3X), VendorShell(3X), and TopLevelShell(3X).

Composite

Purpose

The Composite widget class

AES Support Level

Full-use

Synopsis

#include <Xm/Xm.h>

Description

Composite widgets are intended to be containers for other widgets and can have an arbitrary number of children. Their responsibilities (implemented either directly by the widget class or indirectly by Intrinsics functions) include.

- Overall management of children from creation to destruction.

- Destruction of descendants when the composite widget is destroyed.

- Physical arrangement (geometry management) of a displayable subset of managed children.

- Mapping and unmapping of a subset of the managed children. Instances of composite widgets need to specify the order in which their children are kept. For example, an application may want a set of command buttons in some logical order grouped by function, and it may want buttons that represent filenames to be kept in alphabetical order.

Classes

Composite inherits behavior and resources from **Core**.

The class pointer is **compositeWidgetClass**.

The class name is **Composite**.

New Resources

The following table defines a set of widget resources used by the programmer to specify data. The programmer can also set the resource values for the inherited classes to set attributes for this widget. To reference a resource by name or by class in a .Xdefaults file, remove the **XmN** or **XmC** prefix and use the remaining letters. To specify one of the defined values for a resource in a .Xdefaults file, remove the **Xm** prefix and use the remaining letters (in either lowercase or uppercase, but include any underscores between words). The codes in the access column indicate if the given resource can be set at creation time (**C**), set by using **XtSetValues** (**S**), retrieved by using **XtGetValues** (**G**), or is not applicable (**N/A**).

Composite Resource Set		
Name	**Default**	**Access**
Class	**Type**	
XmNinsertPosition	NULL	CSG
XmCInsertPosition	XmRFunction	

XmNinsertPosition

Points to the **XtOrderProc** function described below.

The following procedure pointer in a composite widget instance is of type **XtOrderProc**:

Cardinal (* XtOrderProc) (*widget*)
    Widget   *w*;

w   Specifies the widget.

Composite widgets that allow clients to order their children (usually homogeneous boxes) can call their widget instance's insert_position procedure from the class's insert_child procedure to determine where a new child should go in its children array. Thus, a client of a composite class can apply different sorting criteria to widget instances of the class, passing in a different insert_position procedure when it creates each composite widget instance.

The return value of the insert_position procedure indicates how many children should go before the widget. Returning *zero* indicates that the widget should go before all other children; returning num_children indicates that it should go after all other children. The default insert_position function returns num_children and can be overridden by a specific composite widget's resource list or by the argument list provided when the composite widget is created.

Inherited Resources

Composite inherits behavior and resources from the following superclass. For a complete description of each resource, refer to the man page for that superclass.

Core Resource Set		
Name	**Default**	**Access**
Class	**Type**	
XmNaccelerators	NULL	CSG
XmCAccelerators	XtTranslations	
XmNancestorSensitive	True	G
XmCSensitive	Boolean	
XmNbackground	White	CSG
XmCBackground	Pixel	
XmNbackgroundPixmap	XmUNSPECIFIED_PIXMAP	CSG
XmCPixmap	Pixmap	
XmNborderColor	Black	CSG
XmCBorderColor	Pixel	
XmNborderPixmap	XmUNSPECIFIED_PIXMAP	CSG
XmCPixmap	Pixmap	
XmNborderWidth	1	CSG
XmCBorderWidth	Dimension	
XmNcolormap	XtCopyFromParent	CG
XmCColormap	Colormap	
XmNdepth	XtCopyFromParent	CG
XmCDepth	int	
XmNdestroyCallback	NULL	C
XmCCallback	XtCallbackList	
XmNheight	0	CSG
XmCHeight	Dimension	
XmNmappedWhenManaged	True	CSG
XmCMappedWhenManaged	Boolean	
XmNscreen	XtCopyScreen	CG
XmCScreen	Pointer	
XmNsensitive	True	CSG
XmCSensitive	Boolean	

Name	Default	Access
Class	Type	
XmNtranslations	NULL	CSG
XmCTranslations	XtTranslations	
XmNwidth	0	CSG
XmCWidth	Dimension	
XmNx	0	CSG
XmCPosition	Position	
XmNy	0	CSG
XmCPosition	Position	

Related Information

Core(3X).

Constraint

Purpose

The Constraint widget class

AES Support Level

Full-use

Synopsis

#include <Xm/Xm.h>

Description

Constraint widgets maintain additional state data for each child. For example, client-defined constraints on the child's geometry may be specified.

When a constrained composite widget defines constraint resources, all of that widget's children inherit all of those resources as their own. These constraint resources are set and read just the same as any other resources defined for the child. This resource inheritance extends exactly one generation down, which means only the first-generation children of a constrained composite widget inherit the parent widget's constraint resources.

Because constraint resources are defined by the parent widgets and not the children, the child widgets never directly use the constraint resource data. Instead constraint resource data is used to attach child-specific data to children.

Classes

Constraint inherits behavior and resources from **Composite** and **Core**.

The class pointer is **constraintWidgetClass**.

The class name is **Constraint**.

New Resources

Constraint defines no new resources.

Inherited Resources

Constraint inherits behavior and resources from **Composite** and **Core**. The following table defines a set of widget resources used by the programmer to specify data. The programmer can also set the resource values for the inherited classes to set attributes for this widget. To reference a resource by name or by class in a .Xdefaults file, remove the **XmN** or **XmC** prefix and use the remaining letters. To specify one of the defined values for a resource in a .Xdefaults file, remove the **Xm** prefix and use the remaining letters (in either lowercase or uppercase, but include any underscores between words). The codes in the access column indicate if the given resource can be set at creation time (**C**), set by using **XtSetValues** (**S**), retrieved by using **XtGetValues** (**G**), or is not applicable (**N/A**).

Core Resource Set		
Name	**Default**	**Access**
Class	**Type**	
XmNaccelerators	NULL	CSG
XmCAccelerators	XtTranslations	
XmNancestorSensitive	True	G
XmCSensitive	Boolean	
XmNbackground	White	CSG
XmCBackground	Pixel	
XmNbackgroundPixmap	XmUNSPECIFIED_PIXMAP	CSG
XmCPixmap	Pixmap	
XmNborderColor	Black	CSG
XmCBorderColor	Pixel	
XmNborderPixmap	XmUNSPECIFIED_PIXMAP	CSG
XmCPixmap	Pixmap	
XmNborderWidth	1	CSG
XmCBorderWidth	Dimension	
XmNcolormap	XtCopyFromParent	CG
XmCColormap	Colormap	
XmNdepth	XtCopyFromParent	CG
XmCDepth	int	
XmNdestroyCallback	NULL	C
XmCCallback	XtCallbackList	
XmNheight	0	CSG
XmCHeight	Dimension	
XmNmappedWhenManaged	True	CSG
XmCMappedWhenManaged	Boolean	
XmNscreen	XtCopyScreen	CG
XmCScreen	Pointer	
XmNsensitive	True	CSG
XmCSensitive	Boolean	

Name	Default	Access
Class	Type	
XmNtranslations	NULL	CSG
XmCTranslations	XtTranslations	
XmNwidth	0	CSG
XmCWidth	Dimension	
XmNx	0	CSG
XmCPosition	Position	
XmNy	0	CSG
XmCPosition	Position	

Related Information

Composite(3X) and **Core(3X)**.

Core

Purpose

The Core widget class

AES Support Level

Full-use

Synopsis

#include <Xm/Xm.h>

Description

Core is the Xt Intrinsic base class for windowed widgets.

To add support for windowless widgets, three additional classes have been added above Core in the class hierarchy. They are **Object**, **RectObj**, and **WindowObj**. **WindowObj** is a synonym of Core that provides no added functionality but was necessary for implementation reasons.

Classes

All widgets are built from **Core**.

The class pointer is **widgetClass**.

The class name is **Core**.

New Resources

The following table defines a set of widget resources used by the programmer to specify data. The programmer can also set the resource values for the inherited classes to set attributes for this widget. To reference a resource by name or by class in a .Xdefaults file, remove the **XmN** or **XmC** prefix and use the remaining letters. To specify one of the defined values for a resource in a .Xdefaults file, remove the **Xm** prefix and use the remaining letters (in either lowercase or uppercase, but include any underscores between words). The codes in the access column indicate if the given resource can be set at creation time (**C**), set by using **XtSetValues** (**S**), retrieved by using **XtGetValues** (**G**), or is not applicable (**N/A**).

Core Resource Set		
Name Class	**Default** Type	**Access**
XmNaccelerators XmCAccelerators	NULL XtTranslations	CSG
XmNancestorSensitive XmCSensitive	True Boolean	G
XmNbackground XmCBackground	White Pixel	CSG
XmNbackgroundPixmap XmCPixmap	XmUNSPECIFIED_PIXMAP Pixmap	CSG
XmNborderColor XmCBorderColor	Black Pixel	CSG
XmNborderPixmap XmCPixmap	XmUNSPECIFIED_PIXMAP Pixmap	CSG
XmNborderWidth XmCBorderWidth	1 Dimension	CSG
XmNcolormap XmCColormap	XtCopyFromParent Colormap	CG
XmNdepth XmCDepth	XtCopyFromParent int	CG
XmNdestroyCallback XmCCallback	NULL XtCallbackList	C
XmNheight XmCHeight	0 Dimension	CSG
XmNmappedWhenManaged XmCMappedWhenManaged	True Boolean	CSG
XmNscreen XmCScreen	XtCopyScreen Pointer	CG
XmNsensitive XmCSensitive	True Boolean	CSG

Name	Default	Access
Class	Type	
XmNtranslations	NULL	CSG
XmCTranslations	XtTranslations	
XmNwidth	0	CSG
XmCWidth	Dimension	
XmNx	0	CSG
XmCPosition	Position	
XmNy	0	CSG
XmCPosition	Position	

XmNaccelerators

> Specifies a translation table that is bound with its actions in the context of a particular widget. The accelerator table can then be installed on some destination widget.

XmNancestorSensitive

> Specifies whether the immediate parent of the widget will receive input events. Use the function **XtSetSensitive** to change the argument to preserve data integrity (see **XmNsensitive** below).

XmNbackground

> Specifies the background color for the widget.

XmNbackgroundPixmap

> Specifies a pixmap for tiling the background. The first tile is placed at the upper left-hand corner of the widget's window.

XmNborderColor

> Specifies the color of the border in a pixel value.

XmNborderPixmap

> Specifies a pixmap to be used for tiling the border. The first tile is placed at the upper left-hand corner of the border.

XmNborderWidth

> Specifies the width of the border that surrounds the widget's window on all four sides. The width is specified in pixels. A width of zero means that no border will show.

XmNcolormap
Specifies the colormap that will be used for conversions to the type **Pixel** for this widget instance. When changed, previously generated pixel values will not be affected, but newly generated values will be in the new colormap.

XmNdepth Specifies the number of bits that can be used for each pixel in the widget's window. Applications should not change or set the value of this resource as it is set by the Xt Intrinsics when the widget is created.

XmNdestroyCallback
Specifies a list of callbacks that is called when the widget is destroyed.

XmNheight Specifies the height of the widget's window in pixels, not including the border area.

XmNmappedWhenManaged
If set to True it maps the widget (makes it visible) as soon as it is both realized and managed. If set to False, the client is responsible for mapping and unmapping the widget. If the value is changed from True to False after the widget has been realized and managed, the widget is unmapped.

XmNscreen Specifies the screen on which a widget instance resides. It is read only, except for shells.

XmNsensitive
Determines whether a widget will receive input events. If a widget is sensitive, the Xt Intrinsics's Event Manager will dispatch to the widget all keyboard, mouse button, motion, window enter/leave, and focus events. Insensitive widgets do not receive these events. Use the function **XtSetSensitive** to change the sensitivity argument. Using **XtSetSensitive** ensures that if a parent widget has **XmNsensitive** set to False, the ancestor-sensitive flag of all its children will be appropriately set.

XmNtranslations
> Points to a translations list. A translations list is a list of events and actions that are to be performed when the events occur.

XmNwidth Specifies the width of the widget's window in pixels, not including the border area.

XmNx
> Specifies the x-coordinate of the widget's upper left-hand corner (excluding the border) in relation to its parent widget.

XmNy
> Specifies the y-coordinate of the widget's upper left-hand corner (excluding the border) in relation to its parent widget.

Related Information

WindowObj(3X).

Object

Purpose

The Object widget class

AES Support Level

Full-use

Synopsis

#include <Xm/Xm.h>

Description

Object is never instantiated. Its sole purpose is as a supporting superclass for other widget classes.

Classes

The class pointer is **objectClass**.

The class name is **Object**.

New Resources

The following table defines a set of widget resources used by the programmer to specify data. The programmer can also set the resource values for the inherited classes to set attributes for this widget. To reference a resource by name or by class in a .Xdefaults file, remove the **XmN** or **XmC** prefix and use the remaining letters. To specify one of the defined values for a resource in a .Xdefaults file, remove the **Xm** prefix and use the remaining letters (in either lowercase or uppercase, but include any underscores between words). The codes in the access column indicate if the given resource can be set at creation time (**C**), set by using **XtSetValues** (**S**), retrieved by using **XtGetValues** (**G**), or is not applicable (**N/A**).

Object Resource Set		
Name	**Default**	**Access**
Class	**Type**	
XmNdestroyCallback	NULL	C
XmCCallback	XtCallbackList	

XmNdestroyCallback

Specifies a list of callbacks that is called when the gadget is destroyed.

OverrideShell

Purpose

The OverrideShell widget class

AES Support Level

Full-use

Synopsis

#include <Xm/Xm.h>
#include <X11/Shell.h>

Description

OverrideShell is used for shell windows that completely bypass the window manager, for example, PopupMenu shells.

Classes

OverrideShell inherits behavior and resources from **Core**, **Composite**, and **Shell**.

The class pointer is **overrideShellWidgetClass**.

The class name is **OverrideShell**.

New Resources

OverrideShell defines no new resources, but overrides the **XmNoverrideRedirect** and **XmNsaveUnder** resources in the **Shell** class.

Inherited Resources

OverrideShell inherits behavior and resources from the following superclasses. For a complete description of these resources, refer to the man page for that superclass.

The following table defines a set of widget resources used by the programmer to specify data. The programmer can also set the resource values for the inherited classes to set attributes for this widget. To reference a resource by name or by class in a .Xdefaults file, remove the **XmN** or **XmC** prefix and use the remaining letters. To specify one of the defined values for a resource in a .Xdefaults file, remove the **Xm** prefix and use the remaining letters (in either lowercase or uppercase, but include any underscores between words). The codes in the access column indicate if the given resource can be set at creation time (**C**), set by using **XtSetValues** (**S**), retrieved by using **XtGetValues** (**G**), or is not applicable (**N/A**).

Shell Resource Set		
Name	**Default**	**Access**
Class	**Type**	
XmNallowShellResize	False	CSG
XmCAllowShellResize	Boolean	
XmNancestorSensitive	ShellAncestorSensitive	CSG
XmCSensitive	Boolean	
XmNcreatePopupChildProc	NULL	CSG
XmCCreatePopupChildProc	XmCreatePopupChildProc	
XmNdepth	ShellDepth	CSG
XmCDepth	int	
XmNgeometry	NULL	CSG
XmCGeometry	String	
XmNoverrideRedirect	True	CSG
XmCOverrideRedirect	Boolean	
XmNpopdownCallback	NULL	C
XmCCallback	XtCallbackList	
XmNpopupCallback	NULL	C
XmCCallback	XtCallbackList	
XmNsaveUnder	True	CSG
XmCSaveUnder	Boolean	

Composite Resource Set		
Name	**Default**	**Access**
Class	**Type**	
XmNinsertPosition	NULL	CSG
XmCInsertPosition	XmRFunction	

Core Resource Set		
Name	**Default**	**Access**
Class	**Type**	
XmNaccelerators	NULL	CSG
XmCAccelerators	XtTranslations	
XmNancestorSensitive	ShellAncestorSensitive	G
XmCSensitive	Boolean	
XmNbackground	White	CSG
XmCBackground	Pixel	
XmNbackgroundPixmap	XmUNSPECIFIED_PIXMAP	CSG
XmCPixmap	Pixmap	
XmNborderColor	Black	CSG
XmCBorderColor	Pixel	
XmNborderPixmap	XmUNSPECIFIED_PIXMAP	CSG
XmCPixmap	Pixmap	
XmNborderWidth	1	CSG
XmCBorderWidth	Dimension	
XmNcolormap	ShellColormap	CG
XmCColormap	Colormap	
XmNdepth	ShellDepth	CG
XmCDepth	int	
XmNdestroyCallback	NULL	C
XmCCallback	XtCallbackList	
XmNheight	0	CSG
XmCHeight	Dimension	
XmNmappedWhenManaged	True	CSG
XmCMappedWhenManaged	Boolean	
XmNscreen	XtCopyScreen	CG
XmCScreen	Pointer	
XmNsensitive	True	CSG
XmCSensitive	Boolean	

Name	Default	Access
Class	Type	
XmNtranslations	NULL	CSG
XmCTranslations	XtTranslations	
XmNwidth	0	CSG
XmCWidth	Dimension	
XmNx	0	CSG
XmCPosition	Position	
XmNy	0	CSG
XmCPosition	Position	

Related Information

Composite(3X), Core(3X), and Shell(3X).

RectObj

Purpose

The RectObj widget class

AES Support Level

Full-use

Synopsis

#include <Xm/Xm.h>

Description

RectObj is never instantiated. Its sole purpose is as a supporting superclass for other widget classes.

Classes

RectObj inherits behavior and a resource from **Object**.

The class pointer is **rectObjClass**.

The class name is **RectObj**.

New Resources

The following table defines a set of widget resources used by the programmer to specify data. The programmer can also set the resource values for the inherited classes to set attributes for this widget. To reference a resource by name or by class in a .Xdefaults file, remove the **XmN** or **XmC** prefix and use the remaining letters. To specify one of the defined values for a resource in a .Xdefaults file, remove the **Xm** prefix and use the remaining letters (in either lowercase or uppercase, but include any underscores between words). The codes in the access column indicate if the given resource can be set at creation time (**C**), set by using **XtSetValues** (**S**), retrieved by using **XtGetValues** (**G**), or is not applicable (**N/A**).

RectObj Resource Set		
Name	**Default**	**Access**
Class	**Type**	
XmNancestorSensitive	XtCopyFromParent	CSG
XmCSensitive	Boolean	
XmNborderWidth	1	CSG
XmCBorderWidth	Dimension	
XmNheight	0	CSG
XmCHeight	Dimension	
XmNsensitive	True	CSG
XmCSensitive	Boolean	
XmNwidth	0	CSG
XmCWidth	Dimension	
XmNx	0	CSG
XmCPosition	Position	
XmNy	0	CSG
XmCPosition	Position	

XmNancestorSensitive

Specifies whether the immediate parent of the gadget will receive input events. Use the function **XtSetSensitive** if you are changing the argument to preserve data integrity (see **XmNsensitive** below).

XmNborderWidth

Specifies the width of the border placed around the RectObj's rectangular display area.

XmNheight Specifies the height of the RectObj's rectangular display area.

XmNsensitive

Determines whether a RectObj will receive input events. If a RectObj is sensitive, the parent will dispatch to the gadget all keyboard, mouse button, motion, window enter/leave, and focus events. Insensitive gadgets do not receive these events. Use the function **XtSetSensitive** to change the sensitivity argument. If a parent widget has **XmNsensitive** set to False, the ancestor-sensitive flag of all its children is appropriately set.

XmNwidth Contains the width of the RectObj's rectangular display area.

XmNx

Contains the x-coordinate of the gadget's upper left-hand corner in relation to its parent's window.

XmNy

Contains the y-coordinate of the gadget's upper left-hand corner in relation to its parent's window.

Inherited Resources

RectObj inherits behavior and a resource from **Object**. For a description of this resource, refer to the **Object** man page.

Object Resource Set		
Name	**Default**	**Access**
Class	**Type**	
XmNdestroyCallback	NULL	C
XmCCallback	XtCallbackList	

Related Information

Object(3X).

Shell

Purpose

The Shell widget class

AES Support Level

Full-use

Synopsis

#include <Xm/Xm.h>
#include <X11/Shell.h>

Description

Shell is a top-level widget (with only one managed child) that encapsulates
the interaction with the window manager.

Classes

Shell inherits behavior and resources from **Composite** and **Core**.

The class pointer is **shellWidgetClass**.

The class name is **Shell**.

New Resources

The following table defines a set of widget resources used by the programmer to specify data. The programmer can also set the resource values for the inherited classes to set attributes for this widget. To reference a resource by name or by class in a .Xdefaults file, remove the **XmN** or **XmC** prefix and use the remaining letters. To specify one of the defined values for a resource in a .Xdefaults file, remove the **Xm** prefix and use the remaining letters (in either lowercase or uppercase, but include any underscores between words). The codes in the access column indicate if the given resource can be set at creation time (**C**), set by using **XtSetValues** (**S**), retrieved by using **XtGetValues** (**G**), or is not applicable (**N/A**).

Shell Resource Set		
Name	**Default**	**Access**
Class	**Type**	
XmNallowShellResize	False	CSG
XmCAllowShellResize	Boolean	
XmNcreatePopupChildProc	NULL	CSG
XmCCreatePopupChildProc	XmCreatePopupChildProc	
XmNgeometry	NULL	CSG
XmCGeometry	String	
XmNoverrideRedirect	False	CSG
XmCOverrideRedirect	Boolean	
XmNpopdownCallback	NULL	C
XmCCallback	XtCallbackList	
XmNpopupCallback	NULL	C
XmCCallback	XtCallbackList	
XmNsaveUnder	False	CSG
XmCSaveUnder	Boolean	

XmNallowShellResize

Specifies that if this resource is False, then the Shell widget instance will return **XtGeometryNo** to all geometry requests from its children.

XmNcreatePopupChildProc

Specifies the pointer to a function which is called when the Shell widget instance is popped up by **XtPopup**.

XmNgeometry

Specifies the desired geometry for the widget instance. This resource is examined only when the widget instance is unrealized and the number of its managed children is changed. It will be used to change the values of the **XmNx**, **XmNy**, **XmNwidth**, and **XmNheight** resources.

XmNoverrideRedirect

Specifies this is True if the widget instance is a short-term window which should be ignored by the window manager. Applications and users should not normally alter this resource.

XmNpopdownCallback

Specifies a list of callbacks that is called when the widget instance is popped down by **XtPopdown**.

XmNpopupCallback

Specifies a list of callbacks that is called when the widget instance is popped up by **XtPopup**.

XmNsaveUnder

Specifies a True value if it is desirable to save the contents of the screen beneath this widget instance, avoiding expose events when the instance is unmapped. This is a hint, and an implementation may save contents whenever it desires, including always or never.

Inherited Resources

Shell inherits behavior and resources from the following superclass. For a complete description of these resources, refer to the man page for that superclass.

Composite Resource Set		
Name	**Default**	**Access**
Class	**Type**	
XmNinsertPosition	NULL	CSG
XmCInsertPosition	XmRFunction	

Core Resource Set		
Name	**Default**	**Access**
Class	**Type**	
XmNaccelerators	NULL	CSG
XmCAccelerators	XtTranslations	
XmNancestorSensitive	ShellAncestorSensitive	G
XmCSensitive	Boolean	
XmNbackground	White	CSG
XmCBackground	Pixel	
XmNbackgroundPixmap	XmUNSPECIFIED_PIXMAP	CSG
XmCPixmap	Pixmap	
XmNborderColor	Black	CSG
XmCBorderColor	Pixel	
XmNborderPixmap	XmUNSPECIFIED_PIXMAP	CSG
XmCPixmap	Pixmap	
XmNborderWidth	1	CSG
XmCBorderWidth	Dimension	
XmNcolormap	ShellColormap	CG
XmCColormap	Colormap	

Name	Default	Access
Class	Type	
XmNdepth	ShellDepth	CG
XmCDepth	int	
XmNdestroyCallback	NULL	C
XmCCallback	XtCallbackList	
XmNheight	0	CSG
XmCHeight	Dimension	
XmNmappedWhenManaged	True	CSG
XmCMappedWhenManaged	Boolean	
XmNscreen	XtCopyScreen	CG
XmCScreen	Pointer	
XmNsensitive	True	CSG
XmCSensitive	Boolean	
XmNtranslations	NULL	CSG
XmCTranslations	XtTranslations	
XmNwidth	0	CSG
XmCWidth	Dimension	
XmNx	0	CSG
XmCPosition	Position	
XmNy	0	CSG
XmCPosition	Position	

Related Information

Composite(3X) and Core(3X).

TopLevelShell

Purpose

The TopLevelShell widget class

AES Support Level

Full-use

Synopsis

#include <Xm/Xm.h>
#include <X11/Shell.h>

Description

TopLevelShell is used for normal top-level windows such as any additional top-level widgets an application needs.

Classes

TopLevelShell inherits behavior and resources from **Core**, **Composite**, **Shell**, **WMShell**, and **Vendorshell**.

The class pointer is **topLevelShellWidgetClass**.

The class name is **TopLevelShell**.

New Resources

The following table defines a set of widget resources used by the programmer to specify data. The programmer can also set the resource values for the inherited classes to set attributes for this widget. To reference a resource by name or by class in a .Xdefaults file, remove the **XmN** or **XmC** prefix and use the remaining letters. To specify one of the defined values for a resource in a .Xdefaults file, remove the **Xm** prefix and use the remaining letters (in either lowercase or uppercase, but include any underscores between words). The codes in the access column indicate if the given resource can be set at creation time (**C**), set by using **XtSetValues** (**S**), retrieved by using **XtGetValues** (**G**), or is not applicable (**N/A**).

TopLevelShell Resource Set		
Name	**Default**	**Access**
Class	**Type**	
XmNiconic	False	CSG
XmClconic	Boolean	
XmNiconName	NULL	CSG
XmClconName	String	

XmNiconic   Specifies that if this is True when the widget instance is realized, then the widget instance will indicate to the window manager that the application wishes to start as an icon, irrespective of the **XtNinitialState** resource. This resource is examined by the Intrinsics only during a call to **XtRealize**; it is ignored at all other times.

XmNiconName
Specifies the short form of the application name to be displayed by the window manager when the application is iconified.

Inherited Resources

TopLevelShell inherits behavior and resources from the following superclasses. For a complete description of these resources, refer to the man page for that superclass.

VendorShell Resource Set		
Name **Class**	**Default** **Type**	**Access**
XmNdeleteResponse XmCDeleteResponse	XmDESTROY unsigned char	CSG
XmNkeyboardFocusPolicy XmCKeyboardFocusPolicy	XmEXPLICIT unsigned char	CSG
XmNmwmDecorations XmCMwmDecorations	-1 int	CSG
XmNmwmFunctions XmCMwmFunctions	-1 int	CSG
XmNmwmInputMode XmCMwmInputMode	-1 int	CSG
XmNmwmMenu XmCMwmMenu	NULL String	CSG

WMShell Resource Set		
Name **Class**	**Default** **Type**	**Access**
XmNheightInc XmCHeightInc	-1 int	CSG
XmNiconMask XmCIconMask	NULL Pixmap	CSG
XmNiconPixmap XmCIconPixmap	NULL Pixmap	CSG
XmNiconWindow XmCIconWindow	NULL Window	CSG
XmNiconX XmCIconX	-1 int	CSG
XmNiconY XmCIconY	-1 int	CSG
XmNinitialState XmCInitialState	1 int	CSG
XmNinput XmCInput	True Boolean	CSG
XmNmaxAspectX XmCMaxAspectX	-1 int	CSG
XmNmaxAspectY XmCMaxAspectY	-1 int	CSG
XmNmaxHeight XmCMaxHeight	-1 int	CSG
XmNmaxWidth XmCMaxWidth	-1 int	CSG
XmNminAspectX XmCMinAspectX	-1 int	CSG
XmNminAspectY XmCMinAspectY	-1 int	CSG

Name Class	Default Type	Access
XmNminHeight XmCMinHeight	-1 int	CSG
XmNminWidth XmCMinWidth	-1 int	CSG
XmNtitle XmCTitle	NULL char *	CSG
XmNtransient XmCTransient	False Boolean	CSG
XmNwaitForWm XmCWaitForWm	True Boolean	CSG
XmNwidthInc XmCWidthInc	-1 int	CSG
XmNwindowGroup XmCWindowGroup	None XID	CSG
XmNwmTimeout XmCWmTimeout	fivesecond int	CSG

Shell Resource Set		
Name	**Default**	**Access**
Class	**Type**	
XmNallowShellResize	False	CSG
XmCAllowShellResize	Boolean	
XmNcreatePopupChildProc	NULL	CSG
XmCCreatePopupChildProc	XmCreatePopupChildProc	
XmNgeometry	NULL	CSG
XmCGeometry	String	
XmNoverrideRedirect	False	CSG
XmCOverrideRedirect	Boolean	
XmNpopdownCallback	NULL	C
XmCCallback	XtCallbackList	
XmNpopupCallback	NULL	C
XmCCallback	XtCallbackList	
XmNsaveUnder	False	CSG
XmCSaveUnder	Boolean	

Composite Resource Set		
Name	**Default**	**Access**
Class	**Type**	
XmNinsertPosition	NULL	CSG
XmCInsertPosition	XmRFunction	

Core Resource Set		
Name	**Default**	**Access**
Class	**Type**	
XmNaccelerators	NULL	CSG
XmCAccelerators	XtTranslations	
XmNancestorSensitive	ShellAncestorSensitive	G
XmCSensitive	Boolean	
XmNbackground	White	CSG
XmCBackground	Pixel	
XmNbackgroundPixmap	XmUNSPECIFIED_PIXMAP	CSG
XmCPixmap	Pixmap	
XmNborderColor	Black	CSG
XmCBorderColor	Pixel	
XmNborderPixmap	XmUNSPECIFIED_PIXMAP	CSG
XmCPixmap	Pixmap	
XmNborderWidth	1	CSG
XmCBorderWidth	Dimension	
XmNcolormap	ShellColormap	CG
XmCColormap	Colormap	
XmNdepth	ShellDepth	CG
XmCDepth	int	
XmNdestroyCallback	NULL	C
XmCCallback	XtCallbackList	
XmNheight	0	CSG
XmCHeight	Dimension	
XmNmappedWhenManaged	True	CSG
XmCMappedWhenManaged	Boolean	
XmNscreen	XtCopyScreen	CG
XmCScreen	Pointer	
XmNsensitive	True	CSG
XmCSensitive	Boolean	

Name	Default	Access
Class	Type	
XmNtranslations	NULL	CSG
XmCTranslations	XtTranslations	
XmNwidth	0	CSG
XmCWidth	Dimension	
XmNx	0	CSG
XmCPosition	Position	
XmNy	0	CSG
XmCPosition	Position	

Related Information

Composite(3X), Core(3X), Shell(3X), WMShell(3X), and
VendorShell(3X).

TransientShell

Purpose

The TransientShell widget class

AES Support Level

Full-use

Synopsis

#include <Xm/Xm.h>
#include <X11/Shell.h>

Description

TransientShell is used for shell windows that can be manipulated by the window manager but are not allowed to be iconified separately. For example, Dialog boxes make no sense without their associated application. They are iconified by the window manager only if the main application shell is iconified.

Classes

TransientShell inherits behavior and resources from **Core**, **Composite**, **Shell**, **WMShell**, and **VendorShell**.

The class pointer is **transientShellWidgetClass**.

The class name is **TransientShell**.

New Resources

TransientShell defines no new resources, but overrides the **XmNsaveUnder** resource in **Shell** and the **XmNtransient** resource in **WMShell**.

Inherited Resources

TransientShell inherits behavior and resources from the following superclasses. For a complete description of these resources, refer to the man page for that superclass.

The following table defines a set of widget resources used by the programmer to specify data. The programmer can also set the resource values for the inherited classes to set attributes for this widget. To reference a resource by name or by class in a .Xdefaults file, remove the **XmN** or **XmC** prefix and use the remaining letters. To specify one of the defined values for a resource in a .Xdefaults file, remove the **Xm** prefix and use the remaining letters (in either lowercase or uppercase, but include any underscores between words). The codes in the access column indicate if the given resource can be set at creation time (**C**), set by using **XtSetValues** (**S**), retrieved by using **XtGetValues** (**G**), or is not applicable (**N/A**).

VendorShell Resource Set		
Name Class	**Default** Type	**Access**
XmNdeleteResponse XmCDeleteResponse	XmDESTROY unsigned char	CSG
XmNkeyboardFocusPolicy XmCKeyboardFocusPolicy	XmEXPLICIT unsigned char	CSG
XmNmwmDecorations XmCMwmDecorations	-1 int	CSG
XmNmwmFunctions XmCMwmFunctions	-1 int	CSG
XmNmwmInputMode XmCMwmInputMode	-1 int	CSG
XmNmwmMenu XmCMwmMenu	NULL String	CSG

WMShell Resource Set		
Name	**Default**	**Access**
Class	**Type**	
XmNheightInc	-1	CSG
XmCHeightInc	int	
XmNiconMask	NULL	CSG
XmCIconMask	Pixmap	
XmNiconPixmap	NULL	CSG
XmCIconPixmap	Pixmap	
XmNiconWindow	NULL	CSG
XmCIconWindow	Window	
XmNiconX	-1	CSG
XmCIconX	int	
XmNiconY	-1	CSG
XmCIconY	int	
XmNinitialState	1	CSG
XmCInitialState	int	
XmNinput	True	CSG
XmCInput	Boolean	
XmNmaxAspectX	-1	CSG
XmCMaxAspectX	int	
XmNmaxAspectY	-1	CSG
XmCMaxAspectY	int	
XmNmaxHeight	-1	CSG
XmCMaxHeight	int	
XmNmaxWidth	-1	CSG
XmCMaxWidth	int	
XmNminAspectX	-1	CSG
XmCMinAspectX	int	
XmNminAspectY	-1	CSG
XmCMinAspectY	int	

Name Class	Default Type	Access
XmNminHeight XmCMinHeight	-1 int	CSG
XmNminWidth XmCMinWidth	-1 int	CSG
XmNtitle XmCTitle	NULL char *	CSG
XmNtransient XmCTransient	False Boolean	CSG
XmNwaitForWm XmCWaitForWm	True Boolean	CSG
XmNwidthInc XmCWidthInc	-1 int	CSG
XmNwindowGroup XmCWindowGroup	None XID	CSG
XmNwmTimeout XmCWmTimeout	fivesecond int	CSG

Shell Resource Set		
Name	**Default**	**Access**
Class	**Type**	
XmNallowShellResize	False	CSG
XmCAllowShellResize	Boolean	
XmNcreatePopupChildProc	NULL	CSG
XmCCreatePopupChildProc	XmCreatePopupChildProc	
XmNgeometry	NULL	CSG
XmCGeometry	String	
XmNoverrideRedirect	False	CSG
XmCOverrideRedirect	Boolean	
XmNpopdownCallback	NULL	C
XmCCallback	XtCallbackList	
XmNpopupCallback	NULL	C
XmCCallback	XtCallbackList	
XmNsaveUnder	False	CSG
XmCSaveUnder	Boolean	

Composite Resource Set		
Name	**Default**	**Access**
Class	**Type**	
XmNinsertPosition	NULL	CSG
XmCInsertPosition	XmRFunction	

Core Resource Set		
Name	**Default**	**Access**
Class	**Type**	
XmNaccelerators	NULL	CSG
XmCAccelerators	XtTranslations	
XmNancestorSensitive	ShellAncestorSensitive	G
XmCSensitive	Boolean	
XmNbackground	White	CSG
XmCBackground	Pixel	
XmNbackgroundPixmap	XmUNSPECIFIED_PIXMAP	CSG
XmCPixmap	Pixmap	
XmNborderColor	Black	CSG
XmCBorderColor	Pixel	
XmNborderPixmap	XmUNSPECIFIED_PIXMAP	CSG
XmCPixmap	Pixmap	
XmNborderWidth	1	CSG
XmCBorderWidth	Dimension	
XmNcolormap	ShellColormap	CG
XmCColormap	Colormap	
XmNdepth	ShellDepth	CG
XmCDepth	int	
XmNdestroyCallback	NULL	C
XmCCallback	XtCallbackList	
XmNheight	0	CSG
XmCHeight	Dimension	
XmNmappedWhenManaged	True	CSG
XmCMappedWhenManaged	Boolean	
XmNscreen	XtCopyScreen	CG
XmCScreen	Pointer	
XmNsensitive	True	CSG
XmCSensitive	Boolean	

Name	Default	Access
Class	Type	
XmNtranslations	NULL	CSG
XmCTranslations	XtTranslations	
XmNwidth	0	CSG
XmCWidth	Dimension	
XmNx	0	CSG
XmCPosition	Position	
XmNy	0	CSG
XmCPosition	Position	

Related Information

Composite(3X), Core(3X), Shell(3X), VendorShell(3X), and
WMShell(3X).

VendorShell

Purpose

The VendorShell widget class

AES Support Level

Full-use

Synopsis

#include <Xm/Xm.h>
#include <X11/Shell.h>

Description

VendorShell is a Motif widget class used as a supporting superclass for all
shell classes that are visible to the window manager and that are not
override redirect. It contains the resources that describe the Mwm-specific
look and feel. It also manages the Mwm-specific communication needed by
all VendorShell subclasses. See the Mwm man page for more information.

Classes

VendorShell inherits behavior and resources from **Core**, **Composite**, **Shell**, and **WMShell** classes.

The class pointer is **vendorShellWidgetClass**.

The class name is **VendorShell**.

New Resources

The following table defines a set of widget resources used by the programmer to specify data. The programmer can also set the resource values for the inherited classes to set attributes for this widget. To reference a resource by name or by class in a .Xdefaults file, remove the **XmN** or **XmC** prefix and use the remaining letters. To specify one of the defined values for a resource in a .Xdefaults file, remove the **Xm** prefix and use the remaining letters (in either lowercase or uppercase, but include any underscores between words). The codes in the access column indicate if the given resource can be set at creation time (**C**), set by using **XtSetValues** (**S**), retrieved by using **XtGetValues** (**G**), or is not applicable (**N/A**).

VendorShell Resource Set		
Name	**Default**	**Access**
Class	**Type**	
XmNdeleteResponse	XmDESTROY	CSG
XmCDeleteResponse	unsigned char	
XmNkeyboardFocusPolicy	XmEXPLICIT	CSG
XmCKeyboardFocusPolicy	unsigned char	
XmNmwmDecorations	-1	CSG
XmCMwmDecorations	int	
XmNmwmFunctions	-1	CSG
XmCMwmFunctions	int	
XmNmwmInputMode	-1	CSG
XmCMwmInputMode	int	
XmNmwmMenu	NULL	CSG
XmCMwmMenu	String	

XmNkeyboardFocusPolicy

Determines allocation of keyboard focus within the widget hierarchy rooted at this shell. The X keyboard focus must be directed to somewhere in the hierarchy for this client-side focus management to take effect.

XmNdeleteResponse

Determines what action the shell takes in response to a **WM_DELETE_WINDOW** message. The setting can be one of three values: **XmDESTROY, XmUNMAP, and XmDO_NOTHING.** The resource is scanned, and the appropriate action is taken, after the **WM_DELETE_WINDOW** callback list (if any) that is registered with the Protocol manager has been called.

XmNmwmDecorations

Includes the decoration flags (specific decorations to add or remove from the window manager frame) for **MWM_HINTS**.

XmNmwmFunctions

Includes the function flags (specific window manager functions to include or exclude from the system menu) for **MWM_HINTS**.

XmNmwmInputMode

Includes the input mode flag (application modal or system modal input focus constraints) for **MWM_HINTS**.

XmNmwmMenu

Specifies the menu items that the Motif window manager should add to the end of the system menu. The string contains a list of items separated by **\n** with the following format:

label [mnemonic] [accelerator] function

If more than one item is specified, the items should be separated by a newline character.

Inherited Resources

VendorShell inherits behavior and resources from the following superclasses. For a complete description of these resources, refer to the man page for that superclass.

WMShell Resource Set		
Name **Class**	**Default** **Type**	**Access**
XmNheightInc XmCHeightInc	-1 int	CSG
XmNiconMask XmCIconMask	NULL Pixmap	CSG
XmNiconPixmap XmCIconPixmap	NULL Pixmap	CSG
XmNiconWindow XmCIconWindow	NULL Window	CSG
XmNiconX XmCIconX	-1 int	CSG
XmNiconY XmCIconY	-1 int	CSG
XmNinitialState XmCInitialState	1 int	CSG
XmNinput XmCInput	True Boolean	CSG
XmNmaxAspectX XmCMaxAspectX	-1 int	CSG
XmNmaxAspectY XmCMaxAspectY	-1 int	CSG
XmNmaxHeight XmCMaxHeight	-1 int	CSG
XmNmaxWidth XmCMaxWidth	-1 int	CSG
XmNminAspectX XmCMinAspectX	-1 int	CSG
XmNminAspectY XmCMinAspectY	-1 int	CSG

Name	Default	Access
Class	Type	
XmNminHeight	-1	CSG
XmCMinHeight	int	
XmNminWidth	-1	CSG
XmCMinWidth	int	
XmNtitle	NULL	CSG
XmCTitle	char *	
XmNtransient	False	CSG
XmCTransient	Boolean	
XmNwaitForWm	True	CSG
XmCWaitForWm	Boolean	
XmNwidthInc	-1	CSG
XmCWidthInc	int	
XmNwindowGroup	None	CSG
XmCWindowGroup	XID	
XmNwmTimeout	fivesecond	CSG
XmCWmTimeout	int	

Shell Resource Set		
Name	**Default**	**Access**
Class	**Type**	
XmNallowShellResize	False	CSG
XmCAllowShellResize	Boolean	
XmNcreatePopupChildProc	NULL	CSG
XmCCreatePopupChildProc	XmCreatePopupChildProc	
XmNgeometry	NULL	CSG
XmCGeometry	String	
XmNoverrideRedirect	False	CSG
XmCOverrideRedirect	Boolean	
XmNpopdownCallback	NULL	C
XmCCallback	XtCallbackList	
XmNpopupCallback	NULL	C
XmCCallback	XtCallbackList	
XmNsaveUnder	False	CSG
XmCSaveUnder	Boolean	

Composite Resource Set		
Name	**Default**	**Access**
Class	**Type**	
XmNinsertPosition	NULL	CSG
XmCInsertPosition	XmRFunction	

Core Resource Set		
Name	**Default**	**Access**
Class	**Type**	
XmNaccelerators	NULL	CSG
XmCAccelerators	XtTranslations	
XmNancestorSensitive	ShellAncestorSensitive	G
XmCSensitive	Boolean	
XmNbackground	White	CSG
XmCBackground	Pixel	
XmNbackgroundPixmap	XmUNSPECIFIED_PIXMAP	CSG
XmCPixmap	Pixmap	
XmNborderColor	Black	CSG
XmCBorderColor	Pixel	
XmNborderPixmap	XmUNSPECIFIED_PIXMAP	CSG
XmCPixmap	Pixmap	
XmNborderWidth	1	CSG
XmCBorderWidth	Dimension	
XmNcolormap	ShellColormap	CG
XmCColormap	Colormap	
XmNdepth	ShellDepth	CG
XmCDepth	int	
XmNdestroyCallback	NULL	C
XmCCallback	XtCallbackList	
XmNheight	0	CSG
XmCHeight	Dimension	
XmNmappedWhenManaged	True	CSG
XmCMappedWhenManaged	Boolean	
XmNscreen	XtCopyScreen	CG
XmCScreen	Pointer	
XmNsensitive	True	CSG
XmCSensitive	Boolean	

Name	Default	Access
Class	Type	
XmNtranslations	NULL	CSG
XmCTranslations	XtTranslations	
XmNwidth	0	CSG
XmCWidth	Dimension	
XmNx	0	CSG
XmCPosition	Position	
XmNy	0	CSG
XmCPosition	Position	

Related Information

Composite(3X), Core(3X), mwm(1X), Shell(3X), WMShell(3X),
XmGetAtomName(3X), XmInternAtom(3X),
XmIsMotifWMRunning(3X),

WMShell

Purpose

The WMShell widget class

AES Support Level

Full-use

Synopsis

#include <Xm/Xm.h>
#include <X11/Shell.h>

Description

WMShell is a top-level widget that encapsulates the interaction with the window manager.

Classes

WMShell inherits behavior and resources from **Core**, **Composite**, and **Shell** classes.

The class pointer is **wmShellWidgetClass**.

The class name is **WMShell**.

New Resources

The following table defines a set of widget resources used by the programmer to specify data. The programmer can also set the resource values for the inherited classes to set attributes for this widget. To reference a resource by name or by class in a .Xdefaults file, remove the **XmN** or **XmC** prefix and use the remaining letters. To specify one of the defined values for a resource in a .Xdefaults file, remove the **Xm** prefix and use the remaining letters (in either lowercase or uppercase, but include any underscores between words). The codes in the access column indicate if the given resource can be set at creation time (**C**), set by using **XtSetValues** (**S**), retrieved by using **XtGetValues** (**G**), or is not applicable (**N/A**).

WMShell Resource Set		
Name **Class**	**Default** **Type**	**Access**
XmNheightInc XmCHeightInc	-1 int	CSG
XmNiconMask XmCIconMask	NULL Pixmap	CSG
XmNiconPixmap XmCIconPixmap	NULL Pixmap	CSG
XmNiconWindow XmCIconWindow	NULL Window	CSG
XmNiconX XmCIconX	-1 int	CSG
XmNiconY XmCIconY	-1 int	CSG
XmNinitialState XmCInitialState	1 int	CSG
XmNinput XmCInput	True Boolean	CSG
XmNmaxAspectX XmCMaxAspectX	-1 int	CSG
XmNmaxAspectY XmCMaxAspectY	-1 int	CSG
XmNmaxHeight XmCMaxHeight	-1 int	CSG
XmNmaxWidth XmCMaxWidth	-1 int	CSG
XmNminAspectX XmCMinAspectX	-1 int	CSG
XmNminAspectY XmCMinAspectY	-1 int	CSG

Name	Default	Access
Class	Type	
XmNminHeight	-1	CSG
XmCMinHeight	int	
XmNminWidth	-1	CSG
XmCMinWidth	int	
XmNtitle	NULL	CSG
XmCTitle	char *	
XmNtransient	False	CSG
XmCTransient	Boolean	
XmNwaitForWm	True	CSG
XmCWaitForWm	Boolean	
XmNwidthInc	-1	CSG
XmCWidthInc	int	
XmNwindowGroup	None	CSG
XmCWindowGroup	XID	
XmNwmTimeout	fivesecond	CSG
XmCWmTimeout	int	

XmNheightInc

Specifies allowable height for the widget instance by the window manager if this resource is defined. The sizes are **XmNminimumHeight** plus an integral multiple of **XmNheightInc**, subject to the **XmNmaximumHeight** resource.

XmNiconMask

Specifies a bitmap which could be used by the window manager to clip the **XmNiconPixmap** bitmap to make the icon nonrectangular.

XmNiconPixmap

Specifies a bitmap which could be used by the window manager as the application's icon.

XmNiconWindow

Specifies the ID of a window which could be used by the window manager as the application's icon.

XmNiconX Specifies a suitable place to put the application's icon; this is a hint to the window manager in root window coordinates. Since the window manager controls icon placement policy, this may be ignored.

XmNiconY Specifies a suitable place to put the application's icon; this is a hint to the window manager in root window coordinates. Since the window manager controls icon placement policy, this may be ignored.

XmNinitialState

Specifies the state in which the application wishes the widget instance to start. It must be one of the constants **NormalState** or **IconicState**.

XmNinput Gives the application's input model for this widget and its descendants.

XmNmaxAspectX

Gives the maximum aspect ratio (X/Y) that the application wishes the widget instance to have.

XmNmaxAspectY

Gives the maximum aspect ratio (X/Y) that the application wishes the widget instance to have.

XmNmaxHeight

Gives the maximum height that the application wishes the widget instance to have.

XmNmaxWidth

Gives the maximum width that the application wishes the widget instance to have.

XmNminAspectX

Gives the minimum aspect ratio (X/Y) that the application wishes the widget instance to have.

XmNminAspectY

Gives the minimum aspect ratio (X/Y) that the application wishes the widget instance to have.

XmNminHeight

Specifies the minimum height that the application wishes the widget instance to have.

XmNminWidth

Specifies the minimum width that the application wishes the widget instance to have.

XmNtitle   Specifies the application name to be displayed by the window manager.

XmNtransient

Specifies a Boolean value that is True if the widget instance is a transient window that should be treated more lightly by the window manager. Applications and users should not normally alter this resource.

XmNwaitForWm

Specifies that the Intrinsics will wait the length of time given by the **XmNwmTimeout** resource for the window manager to respond to certain actions when True, before assuming that there is no window manager present. This resource will be altered by the Intrinsics as it receives, or fails to receive, responses from the window manager.

XmNwidthInc

Specifies allowable width for the widget instance by the window manager if this resource is defined. The sizes are **XmNminimumWidth** plus an integral multiple of **XmNwidthInc**, subject to the **XmNmaximumWidth** resource.

XmNwindowGroup

Specifies the ID of a window for which this widget instance is associated; a window manager may treat all windows in a group in some way, for example, by always moving or iconifying them together. If this is set on a Shell widget instance that has no parent but has pop-up children, this resource is set to the same value on all pop-up children of the widget instance, all pop-up children of these children, and so on. See also the **XmNtransient** resource.

XmNwmTimeout

Specifies the length of time that the Intrinsics will wait for the window manager to respond to certain actions before assuming that there is no window manager present.

Inherited Resources

WMShell inherits behavior and resources from the following superclasses. For a complete description of these resources, refer to the man page for that superclass.

Shell Resource Set		
Name **Class**	**Default** **Type**	**Access**
XmNallowShellResize XmCAllowShellResize	False Boolean	CSG
XmNcreatePopupChildProc XmCCreatePopupChildProc	NULL XmCreatePopupChildProc	CSG
XmNgeometry XmCGeometry	NULL String	CSG
XmNoverrideRedirect XmCOverrideRedirect	False Boolean	CSG
XmNpopdownCallback XmCCallback	NULL XtCallbackList	C
XmNpopupCallback XmCCallback	NULL XtCallbackList	C
XmNsaveUnder XmCSaveUnder	False Boolean	CSG

Composite Resource Set		
Name	**Default**	**Access**
Class	**Type**	
XmNinsertPosition	NULL	CSG
XmCInsertPosition	XmRFunction	

Core Resource Set		
Name	**Default**	**Access**
Class	**Type**	
XmNaccelerators	NULL	CSG
XmCAccelerators	XtTranslations	
XmNancestorSensitive	ShellAncestorSensitive	G
XmCSensitive	Boolean	
XmNbackground	White	CSG
XmCBackground	Pixel	
XmNbackgroundPixmap	XmUNSPECIFIED_PIXMAP	CSG
XmCPixmap	Pixmap	
XmNborderColor	Black	CSG
XmCBorderColor	Pixel	
XmNborderPixmap	XmUNSPECIFIED_PIXMAP	CSG
XmCPixmap	Pixmap	
XmNborderWidth	1	CSG
XmCBorderWidth	Dimension	
XmNcolormap	ShellColormap	CG
XmCColormap	Colormap	
XmNdepth	ShellDepth	CG
XmCDepth	int	
XmNdestroyCallback	NULL	C
XmCCallback	XtCallbackList	

Name	Default	Access
Class	Type	
XmNheight	0	CSG
XmCHeight	Dimension	
XmNmappedWhenManaged	True	CSG
XmCMappedWhenManaged	Boolean	
XmNscreen	XtCopyScreen	CG
XmCScreen	Pointer	
XmNsensitive	True	CSG
XmCSensitive	Boolean	
XmNtranslations	NULL	CSG
XmCTranslations	XtTranslations	
XmNwidth	0	CSG
XmCWidth	Dimension	
XmNx	0	CSG
XmCPosition	Position	
XmNy	0	CSG
XmCPosition	Position	

Related Information

Composite(3X), Core(3X), and Shell(3X).

WindowObj

Purpose

The WindowObj widget class

AES Support Level

Full-use

Synopsis

#include <Xm/Xm.h>

Description

WindowObj is an internal Xt Intrinsic widget class. It is a synonym of Core class that provides no added functionality but was necessary for implementation reasons.

Classes

WindowObj inherits behavior and resources from **Object** and **RectObj** classes.

The class pointer is **windowObjClass**.

The class name is **WindowObj**.

Related Information

Core(3X), **Object(3X)**, **RectObj(3X)**.

XmAddTabGroup

Purpose

A function that adds a manager or a primitive widget to the list of tab groups.

AES Support Level

Full-use

Synopsis

#include <Xm/Xm.h>

void XmAddTabGroup (*tab_group*)
    Widget   *tab_group*;

Description

AddTabGroup adds a manager or primitive widget to the list of tab groups associated with a particular widget hierarchy. Each instance of the List widget, each multiline Text edit widget, each OptionMenu widget, and each ScrollBar widget must be placed within its own tab group; do not place other widgets in these groups. This allows the arrow keys to function in their normal fashion within these widgets.

When using the keyboard to traverse through a widget hierarchy, primitive or manager widgets are grouped together into what are known as **tab groups**. Any manager or primitive widget can be a tab group. Within a tab group, move the focus to the next widget within the tab group by using the arrow keys. To move to another tab group, enter the Tab, or <Shift>Tab.

tab_group
Specifies the manager or primitive widget ID.

Related Information

XmManager(3X), **XmPrimitive(3X)** and **XmRemoveTabGroup(3X)**.

XmArrowButton

Purpose

The ArrowButton widget class

AES Support Level

Full-use

Synopsis

#include <Xm/ArrowB.h>

Description

ArrowButton consists of a directional arrow surrounded by a border shadow. When it is selected, the shadow moves to give the appearance that the ArrowButton has been pressed in. When the ArrowButton is unselected, the shadow moves to give the appearance that the ArrowButton is released, or out.

Classes

ArrowButton inherits behavior and resources from **Core** and **XmPrimitive** classes.

The class pointer is **xmArrowButtonWidgetClass**.

The class name is **XmArrowButton**.

New Resources

The following table defines a set of widget resources used by the programmer to specify data. The programmer can also set the resource values for the inherited classes to set attributes for this widget. To reference a resource by name or by class in a .Xdefaults file, remove the **XmN** or **XmC** prefix and use the remaining letters. To specify one of the defined values for a resource in a .Xdefaults file, remove the **Xm** prefix and use the remaining letters (in either lowercase or uppercase, but include any underscores between words). The codes in the access column indicate if the given resource can be set at creation time (**C**), set by using **XtSetValues** (**S**), retrieved by using **XtGetValues** (**G**), or is not applicable (**N/A**).

XmArrowButton Resource Set		
Name	**Default**	**Access**
Class	**Type**	
XmNactivateCallback	NULL	C
XmCCallback	XtCallbackList	
XmNarmCallback	NULL	C
XmCCallback	XtCallbackList	
XmNarrowDirection	XmARROW_UP	CSG
XmCArrowDirection	unsigned char	
XmNdisarmCallback	NULL	C
XmCCallback	XtCallbackList	

XmNactivateCallback

Specifies a list of callbacks that is called when the ArrowButton is activated. To activate the button, press and release mouse button 1 while the pointer is inside the ArrowButton widget. Activating the ArrowButton also disarms it. The reason sent by this callback is **XmCR_ACTIVATE**.

XmNarmCallback

Specifies a list of callbacks that is called when the ArrowButton is armed. To arm this widget, press mouse button 1 while the pointer is inside the ArrowButton. The reason this callback is sent by **XmCR_ARM**.

XmNarrowDirection

Sets the arrow direction. The following are values for this resource:

- **XmARROW_UP**.

- **XmARROW_DOWN**.

- **XmARROW_LEFT**.

- **XmARROW_RIGHT**.

XmNdisarmCallback
> Specifies a list of callbacks that is called when the ArrowButton is disarmed. To disarm this widget, press and release mouse button 1 while the pointer is inside the ArrowButton. The reason for this callback is **XmCR_DISARM**.

Inherited Resources

ArrowButton inherits behavior and resources from the following superclasses. For a complete description of each resource, refer to the man page for that superclass.

XmPrimitive Resource Set		
Name	**Default**	**Access**
Class	**Type**	
XmNbottomShadowColor	dynamic	CSG
XmCForeground	Pixel	
XmNbottomShadowPixmap	XmUNSPECIFIED_PIXMAP	CSG
XmCBottomShadowPixmap	Pixmap	
XmNforeground	dynamic	CSG
XmCForeground	Pixel	
XmNhelpCallback	NULL	C
XmCCallback	XtCallbackList	
XmNhighlightColor	Black	CSG
XmCForeground	Pixel	
XmNhighlightOnEnter	False	CSG
XmCHighlightOnEnter	Boolean	
XmNhighlightPixmap	dynamic	CSG
XmCHighlightPixmap	Pixmap	
XmNhighlightThickness	0	CSG
XmCHighlightThickness	short	
XmNshadowThickness	2	CSG
XmCShadowThickness	short	
XmNtopShadowColor	dynamic	CSG
XmCBackground	Pixel	
XmNtopShadowPixmap	XmUNSPECIFIED_PIXMAP	CSG
XmCTopShadowPixmap	Pixmap	
XmNtraversalOn	False	CSG
XmCTraversalOn	Boolean	
XmNuserData	NULL	CSG
XmCUserData	caddr_t	

Core Resource Set		
Name	**Default**	**Access**
Class	**Type**	
XmNaccelerators	NULL	CSG
XmCAccelerators	XtTranslations	
XmNancestorSensitive	True	G
XmCSensitive	Boolean	
XmNbackground	dynamic	CSG
XmCBackground	Pixel	
XmNbackgroundPixmap	XmUNSPECIFIED_PIXMAP	CSG
XmCPixmap	Pixmap	
XmNborderColor	Black	CSG
XmCBorderColor	Pixel	
XmNborderPixmap	XmUNSPECIFIED_PIXMAP	CSG
XmCPixmap	Pixmap	
XmNborderWidth	0	CSG
XmCBorderWidth	Dimension	
XmNcolormap	XtCopyFromParent	CG
XmCColormap	Colormap	
XmNdepth	XtCopyFromParent	CG
XmCDepth	int	
XmNdestroyCallback	NULL	C
XmCCallback	XtCallbackList	
XmNheight	0	CSG
XmCHeight	Dimension	
XmNmappedWhenManaged	True	CSG
XmCMappedWhenManaged	Boolean	
XmNscreen	XtCopyScreen	CG
XmCScreen	Pointer	
XmNsensitive	True	CSG
XmCSensitive	Boolean	

Name	Default	Access
Class	Type	
XmNtranslations	NULL	CSG
XmCTranslations	XtTranslations	
XmNwidth	0	CSG
XmCWidth	Dimension	
XmNx	0	CSG
XmCPosition	Position	
XmNy	0	CSG
XmCPosition	Position	

Callback Information

The following structure is returned with each callback:

typedef struct
{
    int   *reason*;
    XEvent   * *event*;
} XmAnyCallbackStruct;

reason   Indicates why the callback was invoked.

event   Points to the **XEvent** that triggered the callback. This event is NULL for the **XmNactivateCallback** if the callback was triggered when Primitive's resource **XmNtraversalOn** was True or if the callback was accessed through the **ArmAndActivate** action routine.

Behavior

<Btn1Down>:

This action causes the arrow to be armed, and the shadow to be drawn in the selected state. The callbacks for **XmNarmCallback** are called.

<Btn1Up>: If the mouse button release occurs when the pointer is within the ArrowButton, then the arrow shadows are redrawn in the unselected state. The callbacks for **XmNactivateCallback** are called, followed by callbacks for **XmNdisarmCallback**.

If the mouse button release occurs when the pointer is outside the ArrowButton, the callbacks for **XmNdisarmCallback** are called.

<Leave Window>:

If the mouse button is pressed and the cursor leaves the widget's window, the arrow shadow is redrawn in its unselected state.

<Enter Window>:

If the mouse button is pressed and the cursor leaves and re-enters the widget's window, the arrow shadow is drawn in the same manner as when the button was first armed.

Default Translations

<Btn1Down>:	**Arm()**
<Btn1Up>:	**Activate()**
	Disarm()
<Key>Return:	**ArmAndActivate()**
<Key>Space:	**ArmAndActivate()**
<EnterWindow>:	**Enter()**
<LeaveWindow>:	**Leave()**

Keyboard Traversal

For information on keyboard traversal, see the man page for **XmPrimitive(3X)** and its sections on behavior and default translations.

Related Information

Core(3X), **XmCreateArrowButton(3X)**, and **XmPrimitive(3X)**.

XmArrowButtonGadget

Purpose

The ArrowButtonGadget widget class

AES Support Level

Full-use

Synopsis

#include <Xm/ArrowBG.h>

Description

ArrowButtonGadget consists of a directional arrow surrounded by a border shadow. When it is selected, the shadow moves to give the appearance that the ArrowButtonGadget has been pressed in. When it is unselected, the shadow moves to give the appearance that the button is released, or out.

Classes

ArrowButtonGadget inherits behavior and resources from **Object**, **RectObj**, and **XmGadget** classes.

The class pointer is **xmArrowButtonGadgetClass**.

The class name is **XmArrowButtonGadget**.

New Resources

The following table defines a set of widget resources used by the programmer to specify data. The programmer can also set the resource values for the inherited classes to set attributes for this widget. To reference a resource by name or by class in a .Xdefaults file, remove the **XmN** or **XmC** prefix and use the remaining letters. To specify one of the defined values for a resource in a .Xdefaults file, remove the **Xm** prefix and use the remaining letters (in either lowercase or uppercase, but include any underscores between words). The codes in the access column indicate if the given resource can be set at creation time (**C**), set by using **XtSetValues** (**S**), retrieved by using **XtGetValues** (**G**), or is not applicable (**N/A**).

ArrowButtonGadget Resource Set		
Name	**Default**	**Access**
Class	**Type**	
XmNactivateCallback	NULL	C
XmCCallback	XtCallbackList	
XmNarmCallback	NULL	C
XmCCallback	XtCallbackList	
XmNarrowDirection	XmARROW_UP	CSG
XmCArrowDirection	int	
XmNdisarmCallback	NULL	C
XmCCallback	XtCallbackList	

XmNactivateCallback

Specifies a list of callbacks that is called when the ArrowButtonGadget is activated. To activate the button, press and release mouse button 1 while the pointer is inside the ArrowButtonGadget. Activating the ArrowButtonGadget also disarms it. The reason sent by this callback is **XmCR_ACTIVATE**.

XmNarmCallback

Specifies a list of callbacks that is called when the ArrowButtonGadget is armed. To arm this widget, press mouse button 1 while the pointer is inside the ArrowButtonGadget. For this callback the reason is **XmCR_ARM**.

XmNarrowDirection

Sets the arrow direction. The values for this resource are:

• **XmARROW_UP.**

• **XmARROW_DOWN.**

• **XmARROW_LEFT.**

• **XmARROW_RIGHT.**

XmNdisarmCallback

Specifies a list of callbacks that is called when the ArrowButtonGadget is disarmed. To disarm this widget, press and release mouse button one while the pointer is inside the ArrowButtonGadget. For this callback the reason is **XmCR_DISARM**.

Inherited Resources

ArrowButtonGadget inherits behavior and resources from the following superclasses. For a complete description of each resource, refer to the man page for that superclass.

XmGadget Resource Set		
Name	**Default**	**Access**
Class	**Type**	
XmNhelpCallback	NULL	C
XmCCallback	XtCallbackList	
XmNhighlightOnEnter	False	CSG
XmCHighlightOnEnter	Boolean	
XmNhighlightThickness	0	CSG
XmCHighlightThickness	short	
XmNshadowThickness	2	CSG
XmCShadowThickness	short	
XmNtraversalOn	False	CSG
XmCTraversalOn	Boolean	
XmNuserData	NULL	CSG
XmCUserData	caddr_t	

RectObj Resource Set		
Name **Class**	**Default** **Type**	**Access**
XmNancestorSensitive XmCSensitive	XtCopyFromParent Boolean	CSG
XmNborderWidth XmCBorderWidth	0 Dimension	CSG
XmNheight XmCHeight	0 Dimension	CSG
XmNsensitive XmCSensitive	True Boolean	CSG
XmNwidth XmCWidth	0 Dimension	CSG
XmNx XmCPosition	0 Position	CSG
XmNy XmCPosition	0 Position	CSG

Object Resource Set		
Name **Class**	**Default** **Type**	**Access**
XmNdestroyCallback XmCCallback	NULL XtCallbackList	C

Callback Information

The following structure is returned with each callback:

```
typedef struct
{
    int       reason;
    XEvent    * event;
} XmAnyCallbackStruct;
```

    reason   Indicates why the callback was invoked.

    event   Points to the **XEvent** that triggered the callback. This event is NULL for the **XmNactivateCallback** if the callback was triggered when Primitive's resource **XmNtraversalOn** was True or if the callback was accessed through the **ArmAndActivate** action routine.

Behavior

<Btn1Down>:

    This action causes the arrow to be armed, and the shadow to be drawn in the selected state. The callbacks for **XmNarmCallback** are called.

<Btn1Up>: If the mouse-button release occurs when the pointer is within the ArrowButtonGadget, then the arrow shadows are redrawn in the unselected state. The callbacks for **XmNactivateCallback** are called, followed by callbacks for **XmNdisarmCallback**.

    If the mouse-button release occurs when the pointer is outside the ArrowButtonGadget, the callbacks for **XmNdisarmCallback** are called.

<Leave Window>:

    If the mouse button is pressed and the cursor leaves the widget's window, the arrow shadow is redrawn in its unselected state.

<Enter Window>:

    If the mouse button is pressed and the cursor leaves and re-enters the widget's window, the arrow shadow is drawn in the same manner as when the button was first armed.

Keyboard Traversal

For information on keyboard traversal, see the man page for **XmGadget(3X)** and its sections on behavior and default translations.

Related Information

Object(3X), **RectObj(3X)**, **XmCreateArrowButtonGadget(3X)**, and **XmGadget(3X)**.

XmBulletinBoard

Purpose

The BulletinBoard widget class

AES Support Level

Full-use

Synopsis

#include <Xm/BulletinB.h>

Description

BulletinBoard is a composite widget that provides simple geometry management for children widgets. It does not force positioning on its children, but can be set to reject geometry requests that would result in overlapping children. BulletinBoard is the base widget for most dialog widgets and is also used as a general container widget.

Modal and modeless dialogs are implemented as collections of widgets that include a DialogShell, a BulletinBoard (or subclass) child of the shell, and various dialog components (buttons, labels, and so forth) that are children of BulletinBoard. BulletinBoard defines callbacks useful for dialogs (focus, map, unmap), which are available for application use. If its parent is a

DialogShell, BulletinBoard passes title and input mode (based on dialog style) information to the parent, which is responsible for appropriate communication with the window manager.

Classes

BulletinBoard inherits behavior and resources from **Core**, **Composite**, **Constraint**, and **XmManager** classes.

The class pointer is **xmBulletinBoardWidgetClass**.

The class name is **XmBulletinBoard**.

New Resources

The following table defines a set of widget resources used by the programmer to specify data. The programmer can also set the resource values for the inherited classes to set attributes for this widget. To reference a resource by name or by class in a .Xdefaults file, remove the **XmN** or **XmC** prefix and use the remaining letters. To specify one of the defined values for a resource in a .Xdefaults file, remove the **Xm** prefix and use the remaining letters (in either lowercase or uppercase, but include any underscores between words). The codes in the access column indicate if the given resource can be set at creation time (**C**), set by using **XtSetValues** (**S**), retrieved by using **XtGetValues** (**G**), or is not applicable (**N/A**).

XmBulletinBoard Resource Set		

Name
    Class
	Default
	    Type
		Access

XmNallowOverlap
    XmCAllowOverlap
	True
	    Boolean
		CSG

XmNautoUnmanage
    XmCAutoUnmanage
	True
	    Boolean
		CSG

XmNbuttonFontList
    XmCButtonFontList
	NULL
	    XmFontList
		CSG

XmNcancelButton
    XmCWidget
	NULL
	    Widget
		SG

XmNdefaultButton
    XmCWidget
	NULL
	    Widget
		SG

XmNdefaultPosition
    XmCDefaultPosition
	True
	    Boolean
		CSG

XmNdialogStyle
    XmCDialogStyle
	dynamic
	    unsigned char
		CSG

XmNdialogTitle
    XmCXmString
	NULL
	    XmString
		CSG

XmNfocusCallback
    XmCCallback
	NULL
	    XtCallbackList
		C

XmNlabelFontList
    XmCLabelFontList
	NULL
	    XmFontList
		CSG

XmNmapCallback
    XmCCallback
	NULL
	    XtCallbackList
		C

XmNmarginHeight
    XmCMarginHeight
	10
	    short
		CSG

XmNmarginWidth
    XmCMarginWidth
	10
	    short
		CSG

XmNnoResize
    XmCNoResize
	False
	    Boolean
		CSG

Name	Default	Access
Class	Type	
XmNresizePolicy	XmRESIZE_ANY	CSG
XmCResizePolicy	unsigned char	
XmNshadowType	XmSHADOW_OUT	CSG
XmCShadowType	unsigned char	
XmNtextFontList	NULL	CSG
XmCTextFontList	XmFontList	
XmNtextTranslations	NULL	C
XmCTranslations	XtTranslations	
XmNunmapCallback	NULL	C
XmCCallback	XtCallbackList	

XmNallowOverlap

Controls the policy for overlapping children widgets. If True, BulletinBoard allows geometry requests that result in overlapping children.

XmNautoUnmanage

Controls whether or not BulletinBoard is automatically unmanaged after a button is activated. If True, BulletinBoard adds a callback to button children (PushButtons, PushButtonGadgets, and DrawnButtons) that unmanages the BulletinBoard when a button is activated; and, the unmap callbacks are called if the parent of the BulletinBoard is a DialogShell. If False, the BulletinBoard is not automatically unmanaged.

XmNbuttonFontList

Specifies the font list used for BulletinBoard's button children (PushButtons, PushButtonGadgets, ToggleButtons, and ToggleButtonGadgets). If NULL, the **XmNtextFontList** is used for buttons.

XmNcancelButton

Specifies the widget ID of the **Cancel** button. BulletinBoard's subclasses, which define a **Cancel** button, set this resource. BulletinBoard does not directly provide any behavior for that button.

XmNdefaultButton

Specifies the widget ID of the default button. BulletinBoard's subclasses, which define a default button, set this resource. BulletinBoard defines translations and installs accelerators that activate that button when the return key is pressed.

XmNdefaultPosition

Controls whether or not the BulletinBoard is automatically positioned by its parent. If True, and the parent of the BulletinBoard is a DialogShell, then the BulletinBoard is centered within or around the parent of the DialogShell when the BulletinBoard is mapped and managed. If False, the BulletinBoard is not automatically positioned.

XmNdialogStyle

Indicates the dialog style associated with BulletinBoard. If the parent of BulletinBoard is a DialogShell, then the parent is configured according to this resource and DialogShell sets the **XmNinputMode** of VendorShell accordingly. Possible values for this resource include the following:

- **XmDIALOG_SYSTEM_MODAL** — used for dialogs that must be responded to before any other interaction in any application

- **XmDIALOG_APPLICATION_MODAL** — used for dialogs that must be responded to before some other interactions in the same application

- **XmDIALOG_MODELESS** — used for dialogs that do not interrupt interaction of any application

- **XmDIALOG_WORK_AREA** — used for non-dialog BulletinBoard widgets (parent is not a subclass of DialogShell)

XmNdialogTitle

Specifies the dialog title. If this resource is not NULL, and the parent of the BulletinBoard is a subclass of WMShell, BulletinBoard sets the **XmNtitle** of its parent to the value of this resource.

XmNfocusCallback

Specifies the list of callbacks that is called when the BulletinBoard widget or one of its descendants accepts the input focus. The callback reason is **XmCR_FOCUS**.

XmNlabelFontList

Specifies the font list used for BulletinBoard's Label children (Labels and LabelGadgets). If NULL, **XmNtextFontList** is used for labels also.

XmNmapCallback

Specifies the list of callbacks that is called only when the parent of the BulletinBoard is a DialogShell; in which case, this callback list is invoked when the BulletinBoard widget is mapped. The callback reason is **XmCR_MAP**.

XmNmarginHeight

Specifies the minimum spacing in pixels between the top or bottom edge of BulletinBoard and any child widget.

XmNmarginWidth

Specifies the minimum spacing in pixels between the left or right edge of BulletinBoard and any child widget.

XmNnoResize

Controls whether or not resize controls are included in the window manager frame around the dialog. If set to True, the **mwm** does not include resize controls in the window manager frame containing the DialogShell or TopLevelShell parent of the BulletinBoard. If set to False, the window manager frame does include resize controls. The preferred way to manipulate the set of controls provided by the **mwm** is to specify values for the mwm resources provided by VendorShell.

XmNresizePolicy

Controls the policy for resizing BulletinBoard widgets. Possible values include the following:

- **XmRESIZE_NONE** — fixed size

- **XmRESIZE_ANY** — shrink or grow as needed

- **XmRESIZE_GROW** — grow only

XmNshadowType

Describes the shadow drawing style for BulletinBoard. This resource can have the following values:

- **XmSHADOW_IN** — draws the BulletinBoard shadow so that it appears inset. This means that the bottom shadow visuals and top shadow visuals are reversed.

- **XmSHADOW_OUT** — draws the BulletinBoard shadow so that it appears outset

- **XmSHADOW_ETCHED_IN** — draws the BulletinBoard shadow using a double line giving the effect of a line etched into the window, similar to the Separator widget

- **XmSHADOW_ETCHED_OUT** — draws the BulletinBoard shadow using a double line giving the effect of a line coming out of the window, similar to the Separator widget

BulletinBoard widgets draw shadows just within their borders if **XmNshadowThickness** is greater than zero. If the parent of a BulletinBoard widget is a DialogShell, BulletinBoard dynamically changes the default for **XmNshadowThickness** from 0 to 1.

XmNtextFontList

Specifies the font list used for BulletinBoard's Text children. If there is no **XmNbuttonFontList**, then this resource is used for buttons; and, if there is no **XmNlabelFontList**, then this resource is used for labels also.

XmNtextTranslations

Adds translations to any Text widget or Text widget subclass that is added as a child of BulletinBoard.

XmNunmapCallback

Specifies the list of callbacks that is called only when the parent of the BulletinBoard is a DialogShell; in which case, this callback list is invoked when the BulletinBoard widget is unmapped. The callback reason is **XmCR_UNMAP**.

Inherited Resources

BulletinBoard inherits behavior and resources from the following superclasses. For a complete description of each resource, refer to the man page for that superclass.

XmManager Resource Set		
Name	**Default**	**Access**
Class	**Type**	
XmNbottomShadowColor	dynamic	CSG
XmCForeground	Pixel	
XmNbottomShadowPixmap	XmUNSPECIFIED_PIXMAP	CSG
XmCBottomShadowPixmap	Pixmap	
XmNforeground	dynamic	CSG
XmCForeground	Pixel	
XmNhelpCallback	NULL	C
XmCCallback	XtCallbackList	
XmNhighlightColor	Black	CSG
XmCForeground	Pixel	
XmNhighlightPixmap	dynamic	CSG
XmCHighlightPixmap	Pixmap	
XmNshadowThickness	dynamic	CSG
XmCShadowThickness	short	
XmNtopShadowColor	dynamic	CSG
XmCBackground	Pixel	
XmNtopShadowPixmap	XmUNSPECIFIED_PIXMAP	CSG
XmCTopShadowPixmap	Pixmap	
XmNuserData	NULL	CSG
XmCUserData	caddr_t	

Composite Resource Set		
Name	**Default**	**Access**
Class	**Type**	
XmNinsertPosition	NULL	CSG
XmCInsertPosition	XmRFunction	

Core Resource Set		
Name **Class**	**Default** **Type**	**Access**
XmNaccelerators XmCAccelerators	NULL XtTranslations	CSG
XmNancestorSensitive XmCSensitive	True Boolean	G
XmNbackground XmCBackground	dynamic Pixel	CSG
XmNbackgroundPixmap XmCPixmap	XmUNSPECIFIED_PIXMAP Pixmap	CSG
XmNborderColor XmCBorderColor	Black Pixel	CSG
XmNborderPixmap XmCPixmap	XmUNSPECIFIED_PIXMAP Pixmap	CSG
XmNborderWidth XmCBorderWidth	0 Dimension	CSG
XmNcolormap XmCColormap	XtCopyFromParent Colormap	CG
XmNdepth XmCDepth	XtCopyFromParent int	CG
XmNdestroyCallback XmCCallback	NULL XtCallbackList	C
XmNheight XmCHeight	0 Dimension	CSG
XmNmappedWhenManaged XmCMappedWhenManaged	True Boolean	CSG
XmNscreen XmCScreen	XtCopyScreen Pointer	CG
XmNsensitive XmCSensitive	True Boolean	CSG

Name	Default	Access
Class	Type	
XmNtranslations	NULL	CSG
XmCTranslations	XtTranslations	
XmNwidth	0	CSG
XmCWidth	Dimension	
XmNx	0	CSG
XmCPosition	Position	
XmNy	0	CSG
XmCPosition	Position	

Callback Information

The following structure is returned with each callback.

typedef struct
{
    int   *reason*;
    XEvent * *event*;
} XmAnyCallbackStruct;

reason   Indicates why the callback was invoked.

event   Points to the **XEvent** that triggered the callback.

Behavior

BulletinBoard behavior is summarized below.

<Cancel Button Activated>:
        When the **Cancel** button is pressed, the activate callbacks of the **Cancel** button are called.

\<Default Button Activated\> or **\<Key\>Return**:
> When the default button or Return key is pressed, the activate callbacks of the default button are called.

\<Help Button Activated\> or **\<Key\>F1**:
> When the **Help** button or **Function key 1** is pressed, the callbacks for **XmNhelpCallback** are called.

\<FocusIn\>: When a **FocusIn** *event* is generated on the widget window, the callbacks for **XmNfocusCallback** are called.

\<MapWindow\>:
> When a BulletinBoard, which is the child of a DialogShell, is mapped, the callbacks for **XmNmapCallback** are invoked. When a BulletinBoard that is not the child of a DialogShell is mapped, the callbacks are not invoked.

\<UnmapWindow\>:
> When a BulletinBoard that is the child of a DialogShell is unmapped, the callbacks for **XmNunmapCallback** are invoked. When a BulletinBoard that is not the child of a DialogShell is unmapped, the callbacks are not invoked.

Default Translations

The following are the default translations defined for BulletinBoard widgets:

\<EnterWindow\>:	**Enter()**
\<FocusIn\>:	**FocusIn()**
\<Btn1Down\>:	**Arm()**
\<Btn1Up\>:	**Activate()**
\<Key\>F1:	**Help()**
\<Key\>Return:	**Return()**
\<Key\>KP_Enter:	**Return()**

Default Accelerators

The following are the default accelerator translations that are added to descendants of a BulletinBoard if the parent of the BulletinBoard is a DialogShell:

#override
<Key>F1:   **Help()**
<Key>Return: **Return()**
<Key>KP_Enter: **Return()**

Keyboard Traversal

By default, if the parent of a BulletinBoard widget is a DialogShell, BulletinBoard uses the Return key for activating the default button and installs accelerators on all descendant widgets to make this possible. These accelerators disable the normal keyboard traversal behavior of the Return key. This traversal behavior may be restored (and the default button behavior disabled) by replacing BulletinBoard's default accelerators with an alternative set of translations that do not specify the Return action. For more information on keyboard traversal, see the man page for **XmManager(3X)** and its sections on behavior and default translations.

Related Information

Composite(3X), Constraint(3X), Core(3X),
XmCreateBulletinBoard(3X), XmCreateBulletinBoardDialog(3X),
XmDialogShell(3X), and XmManager(3X).

XmCascadeButton

Purpose

The CascadeButton widget class

AES Support Level

Full-use

Synopsis

#include <Xm/CascadeB.h>

Description

CascadeButton links two MenuPanes or a MenuBar to a MenuPane.

It is used in menu systems and must have a RowColumn parent with its **XmNrowColumnType** resource set to **XmMENU_PULLDOWN**, **XmMENU_POPUP** or **XmMENU_BAR**.

It is the only widget that can have a Pulldown MenuPane attached to it as a submenu. The submenu is displayed when this widget is activated within a MenuBar, a PopupMenu, or a PulldownMenu. Its visuals can include a label or pixmap and a cascading indicator when it is in a Popup or Pulldown MenuPane; or, it can include only a label or a pixmap when it is in a MenuBar.

The default behavior associated with a CascadeButton depends on the type of menu system in which it resides. By default, mouse button 1 controls the behavior of the CascadeButton if it resides in a PulldownMenu or a MenuBar; and, mouse button 3 controls the behavior of the CascadeButton if it resides in a PopupMenu. The actual mouse button used is determined by its RowColumn parent.

A CascadeButton's visuals differ from most other button gadgets. When the button becomes armed, its visuals change from a 2-D to a 3-D look, and it displays the submenu that has been attached to it. If no submenu is attached, then it simply changes its visuals.

When a CascadeButton within a Pulldown or Popup MenuPane is armed as the result of the user moving the mouse pointer into the widget, it does not immediately display its submenu. Instead, it waits a short amount of time to see if the arming was temporary (that is, the user was simply passing through the widget), or whether the user really wanted the submenu posted. This time delay is configurable via **XmNmappingDelay**.

CascadeButton provides a single mechanism for activating the widget from the keyboard. This mechanism is referred to as a keyboard mnemonic. If a mnemonic has been specified for the widget, the user may activate the CascadeButton by simply typing the mnemonic while the CascadeButton is visible. If the CascadeButton is in a MenuBar, the **meta** key must be pressed with the mnemonic. Mnemonics are typically used to interact with a menu via the keyboard interface.

If in a Pulldown or Popup MenuPane and there is a submenu attached, the **XmNmarginBottom**, **XmNmarginRight**, and **XmNmarginTop** resources enlarge to accommodate **XmNcascaadePixmap**. **XmNmarginWidth** defaults to 6 if this resource is in a MenuBar; otherwise, it takes Label's default, which is 2.

Classes

CascadeButton inherits behavior and resources from **Core**, **XmPrimitive**, and **XmLabel** classes.

The class pointer is **xmCascadeButtonWidgetClass**.

The class name is **XmCascadeButton**.

New Resources

The following table defines a set of widget resources used by the programmer to specify data. The programmer can also set the resource values for the inherited classes to set attributes for this widget. To reference a resource by name or by class in a .Xdefaults file, remove the **XmN** or **XmC** prefix and use the remaining letters. To specify one of the defined values for a resource in a .Xdefaults file, remove the **Xm** prefix and use the remaining letters (in either lowercase or uppercase, but include any underscores between words). The codes in the access column indicate if the given resource can be set at creation time (**C**), set by using **XtSetValues** (**S**), retrieved by using **XtGetValues** (**G**), or is not applicable (**N/A**).

XmCascadeButton Resource Set		
Name **Class**	**Default** **Type**	**Access**
XmNactivateCallback XmCCallback	NULL XtCallbackList	C
XmNcascadePixmap XmCPixmap	"menu-cascade" Pixmap	CSG
XmNcascadingCallback XmCCallback	NULL XtCallbackList	C
XmNmappingDelay XmCMappingDelay	100 int	CSG
XmNsubMenuId XmCMenuWidget	0 Widget	CSG

XmNactivateCallback

Specifies the list of callbacks that is called when the user activates the CascadeButton widget, and there is no submenu attached to pop up. The activation occurs by releasing a mouse button or by typing the mnemonic associated with the widget. The specific mouse button depends on information in the RowColumn parent. The reason sent by the callback is **XmCR_ACTIVATE**.

XmNcascadePixmap

Specifies the cascade pixmap displayed on the right end of the widget when a CascadeButton is used within a Popup or Pulldown MenuPane and a submenu is attached. The Label class resources **XmNmarginRight**, **XmNmarginTop**, and **XmNmarginBottom** may be modified to ensure that room is left for the cascade pixmap. The default cascade pixmap is an arrow pointing to the right.

XmNcascadingCallback

Specifies the list of callbacks that is called just prior to the mapping of the submenu associated with CascadeButton. The reason sent by the callback is **XmCR_CASCADING**.

XmNmappingDelay

Specifies the amount of time, in milliseconds, between when a CascadeButton becomes armed and when it maps its submenu. This delay is used only when the widget is within a Popup or Pulldown MenuPane.

XmNsubMenuId

Specifies the widget ID for the Pulldown MenuPane to be associated with this CascadeButton. The specified MenuPane is displayed when the CascadeButton becomes armed. The MenuPane must have been created with the appropriate parentage depending on the type of menu used. See **XmCreateMenuBar(3X)**, **XmCreatePulldownMenu(3X)**, and **XmCreatePopupMenu(3X)** for more information on the menu systems.

Inherited Resources

CascadeButton inherits behavior and resources from the following superclasses. For a complete description of each resource, refer to the man page for that superclass.

XmLabel Resource Set		
Name	**Default**	**Access**
Class	**Type**	
XmNaccelerator	NULL	CSG
XmCaccelerator	String	
XmNacceleratorText	NULL	CSG
XmCacceleratorText	XmString	
XmNalignment	XmALIGNMENT_CENTER	CSG
XmCAlignment	unsigned char	
XmNfontList	"Fixed"	CSG
XmCFontList	XmFontList	
XmNlabelInsensitivePixmap	XmUNSPECIFIED_PIXMAP	CSG
XmCLabelInsensitivePixmap	Pixmap	
XmNlabelPixmap	XmUNSPECIFIED_PIXMAP	CSG
XmCPixmap	Pixmap	
XmNlabelString	NULL	CSG
XmCXmString	XmString	
XmNlabelType	XmSTRING	CSG
XmCLabelType	unsigned char	
XmNmarginBottom	dynamic	CSG
XmCMarginBottom	short	
XmNmarginHeight	2	CSG
XmCMarginHeight	short	
XmNmarginLeft	0	CSG
XmCMarginLeft	short	
XmNmarginRight	dynamic	CSG
XmCMarginRight	short	

Name
    Class
	Default
	    Type
		Access

XmNmarginTop
    XmCMarginTop
	dynamic
	    short
		CSG

XmNmarginWidth
    XmCMarginWidth
	dynamic
	    short
		CSG

XmNmnemonic
    XmCMnemonic
	'\0'
	    char
		CSG

XmNrecomputeSize
    XmCRecomputeSize
	True
	    Boolean
		CSG

XmPrimitive Resource Set		
Name Class	**Default** Type	**Access**
XmNbottomShadowColor XmCForeground	dynamic Pixel	CSG
XmNbottomShadowPixmap XmCBottomShadowPixmap	XmUNSPECIFIED_PIXMAP Pixmap	CSG
XmNforeground XmCForeground	dynamic Pixel	CSG
XmNhelpCallback XmCCallback	NULL XtCallbackList	C
XmNhighlightColor XmCForeground	Black Pixel	CSG
XmNhighlightOnEnter XmCHighlightOnEnter	False Boolean	CSG
XmNhighlightPixmap XmCHighlightPixmap	dynamic Pixmap	CSG
XmNhighlightThickness XmCHighlightThickness	0 short	CSG
XmNshadowThickness XmCShadowThickness	2 short	CSG
XmNtopShadowColor XmCBackground	dynamic Pixel	CSG
XmNtopShadowPixmap XmCTopShadowPixmap	XmUNSPECIFIED_PIXMAP Pixmap	CSG
XmNtraversalOn XmCTraversalOn	False Boolean	CSG
XmNuserData XmCUserData	NULL caddr_t	CSG

Core Resource Set		
Name **Class**	**Default** **Type**	**Access**
XmNaccelerators XmCAccelerators	NULL XtTranslations	CSG
XmNancestorSensitive XmCSensitive	True Boolean	G
XmNbackground XmCBackground	dynamic Pixel	CSG
XmNbackgroundPixmap XmCPixmap	XmUNSPECIFIED_PIXMAP Pixmap	CSG
XmNborderColor XmCBorderColor	Black Pixel	CSG
XmNborderPixmap XmCPixmap	XmUNSPECIFIED_PIXMAP Pixmap	CSG
XmNborderWidth XmCBorderWidth	0 Dimension	CSG
XmNcolormap XmCColormap	XtCopyFromParent Colormap	CG
XmNdepth XmCDepth	XtCopyFromParent int	CG
XmNdestroyCallback XmCCallback	NULL XtCallbackList	C
XmNheight XmCHeight	0 Dimension	CSG
XmNmappedWhenManaged XmCMappedWhenManaged	True Boolean	CSG
XmNscreen XmCScreen	XtCopyScreen Pointer	CG
XmNsensitive XmCSensitive	True Boolean	CSG

Name	Default	Access
Class	Type	
XmNtranslations	NULL	CSG
XmCTranslations	XtTranslations	
XmNwidth	0	CSG
XmCWidth	Dimension	
XmNx	0	CSG
XmCPosition	Position	
XmNy	0	CSG
XmCPosition	Position	

Callback Information

The following structure is returned with each callback:

typedef struct
{
    int   *reason*;
    XEvent   * *event*;
} XmAnyCallbackStruct;

reason   Indicates why the callback was invoked.

event   Points to the **XEvent** that triggered the callback or is NULL if this callback was not triggered due to an **XEvent**.

Behavior

The default behavior associated with a CascadeButton widget depends on whether the button is part of a PopupMenu system or a PulldownMenu system. The RowColumn parent determines the mouse button that is used through its **XmNrowColumnType** and **XmNwhichButton** resources.

Default PopupMenu System

Btn3Down<EnterWindow>:
> This action arms the CascadeButton and posts the associated submenu after a short delay.

Btn3Down<LeaveWindow>:
> The action that takes place depends on whether the mouse pointer has moved into the submenu associated with this CascadeButton. It if had, then this event is ignored; if not, the CascadeButton is disarmed and its submenu unposted.

<Btn3Up>: This action posts the submenu attached to the CascadeButton and enables keyboard traversal within the menu. If the CascadeButton does not have a submenu attached, then this event activates the CascadeButton and unposts the menu.

<Btn3Down>:
> This action disables traversal for the menu and returns the user to drag mode in which the menu is manipulated using the mouse. The submenu associated with this CascadeButton is posted.

<Key>Return:
> This event posts the submenu attached to the CascadeButton if keyboard traversal is enabled in the menu. If the CascadeButton does not have a submenu attached, then this event activates the CascadeButton and unposts the menu.

Default MenuBar

<Btn1Down>:
> This event arms both the CascadeButton and the MenuBar and posts the associated submenu. If the menu is already active, this event disables traversal for the menu and returns the user to the mode where the menu is manipulated using the mouse.

Btn1Down<EnterWindow>:
> This event unposts any visible MenuPanes if they are associated with a different MenuBar entry, arms the CascadeButton, and posts the associated submenu.

Btn1Down<LeaveWindow>:
> This event disarms the CascadeButton if the submenu associated with it is not currently posted or if there is no submenu associated with this CascadeButton. Otherwise, this event is ignored.

<Btn1Up>: This event posts the submenu attached to the CascadeButton and enables keyboard traversal within the menu. If the CascadeButton does not have a submenu attached, then this event activates the CascadeButton and unposts the menu.

<Key>Return:
> This event posts the submenu attached to the CascadeButton if keyboard traversal is enabled in the menu. If the CascadeButton does not have a submenu attached, the CascadeButton is activated, and unposts the menu.

Default PulldownMenu System from a MenuBar

Btn1Down<EnterWindow>:
> This event arms the CascadeButton widget, and after a short delay, posts the associated submenu.

Btn1Down<LeaveWindow>:
> The event is ignored if the mouse pointer has moved into the submenu. In all other cases, the CascadeButton is disarmed and its submenu unposted.

<Btn1Up>: This event posts the submenu attached to the CascadeButton and enables keyboard traversal within the menu. If the CascadeButton does not have a submenu attached, then this event selects the CascadeButton and unposts the menu.

<Btn1Down>:
> This event disables traversal for the menu and returns the user to the drag mode. The submenu associated with this CascadeButton is posted.

\<Key\>Return:

> This event posts the submenu attached to the CascadeButton if keyboard traversal is enabled in the menu. If the CascadeButton does not have a submenu attached, then this event activates the CascadeButton and unposts the menu.

Default Translations

The following are default translations for CascadeButton in a MenuBar:

\<BtnDown\>:	**MenuBarSelect()**
\<EnterWindow\>:	**MenuBarEnter()**
\<LeaveWindow\>:	**MenuBarLeave()**
\<BtnUp\>:	**DoSelect()**
\<Key\>Return:	**KeySelect()**
\<Key\>Escape:	**CleanupMenuBar()**

Default translations for CascadeButton in a Popup or Pulldown MenuPane are:

\<BtnDown\>:	**StartDrag()**
\<EnterWindow\>:	**DelayedArm()**
\<LeaveWindow\>:	**CheckDisarm()**
\<BtnUp\>:	**DoSelect()**
\<Key\>Return:	**KeySelect()**
\<Key\>Escape:	**MenuShellPopdownDone()**

Keyboard Traversal

The keyboard traversal translations are listed below:

<Unmap>:	**Unmap()**
<FocusOut>:	**FocusOut()**
<FocusIn>:	**FocusIn()**
<Key>space:	**Noop()**
<Key>Left:	**MenuTraverseLeft()**
<Key>Right:	**MenuTraverseRight()**
<Key>Up:	**MenuTraverseUp()**
<Key>Down:	**MenuTraverseDown()**
<Key>Home:	**Noop()**

Related Information

Core(3X), XmCascadeButtonHighlight(3X),
XmCreateCascadeButton(3X), XmCreateMenuBar(3X),
XmCreatePulldownMenu(3X), XmCreatePopupMenu(3X),
XmLabel(3X), XmPrimitive(3X), and XmRowColumn(3X).

XmCascadeButtonGadget

Purpose

The CascadeButtonGadget widget class

AES Support Level

Full-use

Synopsis

#include <Xm/CascadeBG.h>

Description

CascadeButtonGadget links two MenuPanes or an OptionMenu to a MenuPane.

It is used in menu systems and must have a RowColumn parent with its **XmNrowColumnType** resource set to **XmMENU_POPUP**, **XmMENU_PULLDOWN**, or **XmMENU_OPTION**.

It is the only gadget that can have a Pulldown MenuPane attached to it as a submenu. The submenu is displayed when this gadget is activated within a PopupMenu, a PulldownMenu, or an OptionMenu. Its visuals can include a label or pixmap and a cascading indicator when it is in a Popup or Pulldown MenuPane; or it can include only a label or a pixmap when it is in an OptionMenu.

The default behavior associated with a CascadeButtonGadget depends on the type of menu system in which it resides. By default, mouse button 1 controls the behavior of the CascadeButtonGadget if it resides in a PulldownMenu or an OptionMenu; and, mouse button 3 controls the behavior of the CascadeButtonGadget if it resides in a PopupMenu. The actual mouse button used is determined by its RowColumn parent.

A CascadeButtonGadget's visuals differ from most other button gadgets. When the button becomes armed, its visuals change from a 2-D to a 3-D look, and it displays the submenu that has been attached to it. If no submenu is attached, then it simply changes its visuals.

When a CascadeButtonGadget within a Pulldown or Popup MenuPane is armed as the result of the user moving the mouse pointer into the gadget, it does not immediately display its submenu. Instead, it waits a short time to see if the arming was temporary (that is, the user was simply passing through the gadget), or the user really wanted the submenu posted. This delay is configurable via **XmNmappingDelay**.

CascadeButtonGadget provides a single mechanism for activating the gadget from the keyboard. This mechanism is referred to as a keyboard mnemonic. If a mnemonic has been specified for the gadget, the user may activate it by simply typing the mnemonic while the CascadeButtonGadget is visible. Mnemonics are typically used to interact with a menu via the keyboard.

If a CascadeButtonGadget is in a Pulldown or Popup MenuPane and there is a submenu attached, the **XmNmarginBottom**, **XmNmarginRight**, and **XmNmarginTop** resources enlarge to accommodate **XmNcascadePixmap**.

Classes

CascadeButtonGadget inherits behavior and resources from **Object**, **RectObj**, **XmGadget**, and **XmLabelGadget** classes.

The class pointer is **xmCascadeButtonGadgetClass**.

The class name is **XmCascadeButtonGadget**.

New Resources

The following table defines a set of widget resources used by the programmer to specify data. The programmer can also set the resource values for the inherited classes to set attributes for this widget. To reference a resource by name or by class in a .Xdefaults file, remove the **XmN** or **XmC** prefix and use the remaining letters. To specify one of the defined values for a resource in a .Xdefaults file, remove the **Xm** prefix and use the remaining letters (in either lowercase or uppercase, but include any underscores between words). The codes in the access column indicate if the given resource can be set at creation time (**C**), set by using **XtSetValues** (**S**), retrieved by using **XtGetValues** (**G**), or is not applicable (**N/A**).

XmCascadeButtonGadget		
Name **Class**	**Default** **Type**	**Access**
XmNactivateCallback XmCCallback	NULL XtCallbackList	C
XmNcascadePixmap XmCPixmap	"menu_cascade" Pixmap	CSG
XmNcascadingCallback XmCCallback	NULL XtCallbackList	C
XmNmappingDelay XmCMappingDelay	100 int	CSG
XmNsubMenuId XmCMenuWidget	0 Widget	CSG

XmNactivateCallback

Specifies the list of callbacks that is called when the user activates the CascadeButtonGadget, and there is no submenu attached to pop up. The activation occurs by releasing a mouse button or by typing the mnemonic associated with the gadget. The specific mouse button depends on information in the RowColumn parent. The reason sent by the callback is **XmCR_ACTIVATE**.

XmNcascadePixmap

Specifies the cascade pixmap displayed on the right end of the gadget when a CascadeButtonGadget is used within a Popup or Pulldown MenuPane and a submenu is attached. The LabelGadget class resources **XmNmarginRight**, **XmNmarginTop**, and **XmNmarginBottom** may be modified to ensure that room is left for the cascade pixmap. The default cascade pixmap is an arrow pointing to the right.

XmNcascadingCallback

Specifies the list of callbacks that is called just prior to the mapping of the submenu associated with the CascadeButtonGadget. The reason sent by the callback is **XmCR_CASCADING**.

XmNmappingDelay

Specifies the amount of time, in milliseconds, between when a CascadeButtonGadget becomes armed and when it maps its submenu. This delay is used only when the gadget is within a Popup or Pulldown MenuPane.

XmNsubMenuId

Specifies the widget ID for the Pulldown MenuPane to be associated with this CascadeButtonGadget. The specified MenuPane is displayed when the CascadeButtonGadget becomes armed. The MenuPane must have been created with the appropriate parentage depending on the type of menu used. See **XmCreatePulldownMenu(3X)**, **XmCreatePopupMenu(3X)**, and **XmCreateOptionMenu(3X)** for more information on the menu systems.

Inherited Resources

CascadeButtonGadget inherits behavior and resources from the following superclasses. For a complete description of each resource, refer to the man page for that superclass.

XmLabelGadget Resource Set		
Name	**Default**	**Access**
Class	**Type**	
XmNalignment	XmALIGNMENT_CENTER	CSG
XmCAlignment	unsigned char	
XmNfontList	"Fixed"	CSG
XmCFontList	XmFontList	
XmNlabelInsensitivePixmap	XmUNSPECIFIED_PIXMAP	CSG
XmCLabelInsensitivePixmap	Pixmap	
XmNlabelPixmap	XmUNSPECIFIED_PIXMAP	CSG
XmCPixmap	Pixmap	
XmNlabelString	NULL	CSG
XmCXmString	XmString	
XmNlabelType	XmSTRING	CSG
XmCLabelType	unsigned char	
XmNmarginBottom	dynamic	CSG
XmCMarginBottom	short	
XmNmarginHeight	2	CSG
XmCMarginHeight	short	
XmNmarginLeft	0	CSG
XmCMarginLeft	short	
XmNmarginRight	dynamic	CSG
XmCMarginRight	short	
XmNmarginTop	dynamic	CSG
XmCMarginTop	short	
XmNmarginWidth	2	CSG
XmCMarginWidth	short	
XmNmnemonic	'\0'	CSG
XmCMnemonic	char	
XmNrecomputeSize	True	CSG
XmCRecomputeSize	Boolean	

XmGadget Resource Set		
Name	**Default**	**Access**
Class	**Type**	
XmNhelpCallback	NULL	C
XmCCallback	XtCallbackList	
XmNhighlightOnEnter	False	CSG
XmCHighlightOnEnter	Boolean	
XmNhighlightThickness	0	CSG
XmCHighlightThickness	short	
XmNshadowThickness	2	CSG
XmCShadowThickness	short	
XmNtraversalOn	False	CSG
XmCTraversalOn	Boolean	
XmNuserData	NULL	CSG
XmCUserData	caddr_t	

RectObj Resource Set		
Name **Class**	**Default** **Type**	**Access**
XmNancestorSensitive XmCSensitive	XtCopyFromParent Boolean	CSG
XmNborderWidth XmCBorderWidth	1 Dimension	CSG
XmNheight XmCHeight	0 Dimension	CSG
XmNsensitive XmCSensitive	True Boolean	CSG
XmNwidth XmCWidth	0 Dimension	CSG
XmNx XmCPosition	0 Position	CSG
XmNy XmCPosition	0 Position	CSG

Object Resource Set		
Name **Class**	**Default** **Type**	**Access**
XmNdestroyCallback XmCCallback	NULL XtCallbackList	C

Callback Information

The following structure is returned with each callback:

typedef struct
{
    int   *reason*;
    XEvent   * *event*;
} XmAnyCallbackStruct;

reason   Indicates why the callback was invoked.

event   Points to the **XEvent** that triggered the callback or is NULL if this callback was not triggered by an **XEvent**.

Behavior

The default behavior associated with a CascadeButtonGadget depends on whether the button is part of a PopupMenu system, a Pulldown MenuPane in a MenuBar, or an OptionMenu system. The RowColumn parent determines the mouse button which is used through its **XmNrowColumnType** and **XmNwhichButton** resources.

Default PopupMenu System

Btn3Down<EnterWindow>:
    This action arms the CascadeButtonGadget and posts the associated submenu after a short delay.

Btn3Down<LeaveWindow>:
    The action that takes place depends on whether the mouse pointer has moved into the submenu associated with this CascadeButtonGadget. If it has, this event is ignored; if not, the CascadeButtonGadget is disarmed and its submenu unposted.

<Btn3Up>: This action posts the submenu attached to the CascadeButtonGadget and enables keyboard traversal within the menu. If the CascadeButtonGadget does not have a submenu attached, then this event activates the CascadeButtonGadget and unposts the menu.

<Btn3Down>:

This action disables traversal for the menu and returns the user to drag mode, in which the menu is manipulated using the mouse. The submenu associated with this CascadeButtonGadget is posted.

<Key>Return:

This event posts the submenu attached to the CascadeButtonGadget if keyboard traversal is enabled in the menu. If the CascadeButtonGadget does not have a submenu attached, then this event activates the CascadeButtonGadget and unposts the menu.

Default Pulldown MenuPane from a MenuBar or from an OptionMenu

Btn1Down<EnterWindow>:

This event arms the CascadeButtonGadget, and after a short delay, posts the associated submenu.

Btn1Down<LeaveWindow>:

The event is ignored if the mouse pointer has moved into the submenu. In all other cases, the CascadeButtonGadget is disarmed and its submenu unposted.

<Btn1Up>: This event posts the submenu attached to the CascadeButtonGadget and enables keyboard traversal within the menu. If the CascadeButtonGadget does not have a submenu attached, then this event activates the CascadeButtonGadget and unposts the menu.

\<Btn1Down\>:

> This event disables traversal for the menu and returns the user to the drag mode. The submenu associated with this CascadeButtonGadget is posted.

\<Key\>Return:

> This event posts the submenu attached to the CascadeButtonGadget if keyboard traversal is enabled in the menu. If the CascadeButtonGadget does not have a submenu attached, then this event activates the CascadeButtonGadget and unposts the menu.

Default OptionMenu

\<Btn1Down\>:

> This event arms the CascadeButtonGadget and posts the associated submenu.

\<Key\>Return:

> This event posts the associated submenu and enables traversal within the menu.

Keyboard Traversal

For information on keyboard traversal, see the man page for **XmRowColumn(3X)** and its sections on behavior and default translations.

Related Information

Object(3X), RectObj(3X), XmCascadeButtonHighlight(3), XmCreateCascadeButtonGadget(3X), XmCreatePulldownMenu(3X), XmCreatePopupMenu(3X), XmCreateOptionMenu(3X), XmGadget(3X), XmLabelGadget(3X), and XmRowColumn(3X).

XmCascadeButtonHighlight

Purpose

A CascadeButton and CascadeButtonGadget function that sets the highlight state.

AES Support Level

Full-use

Synopsis

#include <Xm/CascadeB.h>
#include <Xm/CascadeBG.h>

void XmCascadeButtonHighlight (*cascadeButton, highlight*)
    Widget   *cascadeButton*;
    Boolean   *highlight*;

Description

XmCascadeButtonHighlight either draws or erases the shadow highlight around the CascadeButton or the CascadeButtonGadget.

cascadeButton

> Specifies the CascadeButton or CascadeButtonGadget to be highlighted or unhighlighted.

highlight   Specifies whether to highlight (True) or to unhighlight (False).

For a complete definition of CascadeButton or CascadeButtonGadget and their associated resources, see **XmCascadeButton(3X)** or **XmCascadeButtonGadget(3X)**.

Related Information

XmCascadeButton(3X) and **XmCascadeButtonGadget(3X)**.

XmClipboardCancelCopy

Purpose

A clipboard function that cancels a copy to the clipboard.

AES Support Level

Full-use

Synopsis

#include <Xm/Xm.h>
#include <Xm/CutPaste.h>

void XmClipboardCancelCopy (*display, window, item_id*)
    Display   * *display*;
    Window   *window*;
    long   *item_id*;

Description

> **XmClipboardCancelCopy** cancels the copy to clipboard that is in progress and frees up temporary storage. When a copy is to be performed, **XmClipboardStartCopy** allocates temporary storage for the clipboard data. **XmClipboardCopy** copies the appropriate data into the the temporary storage. **XmClipboardEndCopy** copies the data to the clipboard structure and frees up the temporary storage structures. If **XmClipboardCancelCopy** is called, the **XmClipboardEndCopy** function does not have to be called. A call to **XmClipboardCancelCopy** is valid only after a call to **XmClipboardStartCopy** and before a call to **XmClipboardEndCopy**.

> *display*   Specifies a pointer to the **Display** structure that was returned in a previous call to **XOpenDisplay** or **XtDisplay**.

> *window*   Specifies a widget's window ID that relates the application window to the clipboard. The widget's window ID can be obtained by using **XtWindow**. The same application instance should pass the same window ID to each of the clipboard functions that it calls.

> *item_id*   Specifies the number assigned to this data item. This number was returned by a previous call to **XmClipboardStartCopy**.

Related Information

> **XmClipboardCopy(3X),**   **XmClipboardEndCopy(3X),**   and
> **XmClipboardStartCopy(3X).**

XmClipboardCopy

Purpose

A clipboard function that copies a data item to temporary storage for later copying to clipboard.

AES Support Level

Full-use

Synopsis

#include <Xm/Xm.h>
#include <Xm/CutPaste.h>

int **XmClipboardCopy** (*display, window, item_id, format_name, buffer, length, private_id, data_id*)
> **Display**   * *display*;
> **Window**   *window*;
> **long**   *item_id*;
> **char**   * *format_name*;
> **char**   * *buffer*;
> **unsigned long** *length*;
> **int**   *private_id*;
> **int**   * *data_id*;

Description

XmClipboardCopy copies a data item to temporary storage. The data item is moved from temporary storage to the clipboard data structure when a call to **XmClipboardEndCopy** is made. Additional calls to **XmClipboardCopy** before a call to **XmClipboardEndCopy** add additional data item formats to the same data item or append data to an existing format. Formats are described in the *Inter-Client Communications Conventions* (ICCC) manual as targets.

NOTE: Do not call **XmClipboardCopy** before a call to **XmClipboardStartCopy** has been made. The latter function allocates temporary storage required by **XmClipboardCopy**.

If the *buffer* argument is NULL, the data is considered to be passed by name. When data, that has been passed by name is later requested by another application, the application that owns the data receives a callback with a request for the data. The application that owns the data must then transfer the data to the clipboard with the **XmClipboardCopyByName** function. When a data item that was passed by name is deleted from the clipboard, the application that owns the data receives a callback stating that the data is no longer needed.

For information on the callback function, see the callback argument description for **XmClipboardStartCopy**.

display	Specifies a pointer to the **Display** structure that was returned in a previous call to **XOpenDisplay** or **XtDisplay**.
window	Specifies a widget's window ID that relates the application window to the clipboard. The widget's window ID can be obtained by using **XtWindow**. The same application instance should pass the same window ID to each of the clipboard functions that it calls.
item_id	Specifies the number assigned to this data item. This number was returned by a previous call to **XmClipboardStartCopy**.

format_name	Specifies the name of the format in which the data item is stored on the clipboard. Format is known as target in the ICCC manual.
buffer	Specifies the buffer from which the clipboard copies the data.
length	Specifies the length of the data being copied to the clipboard.
private_id	Specifies the private data that the application wants to store with the data item.
data_id	Specifies an identifying number assigned to the data item that uniquely identifies the data item and the format. This argument is required only for data that is passed by name.

Return Value

ClipboardSuccess
> The function is successful.

ClipboardLocked
> The function failed because the clipboard was locked by another application. The application can continue to call the function again with the same parameters until the lock goes away. This gives the application the opportunity to ask if the user wants to keep trying or to give up on the operation.

Related Information

XmClipboardCopyByName(3X), XmClipboardEndCopy(3X), and
XmClipboardStartCopy(3X).

XmClipboardCopyByName

Purpose

A clipboard function that copies a data item passed by name.

AES Support Level

Full-use

Synopsis

#include <Xm/Xm.h>
#include <Xm/CutPaste.h>

int XmClipboardCopyByName (*display, window, data_id, buffer, length, private_id*)
    Display   * *display*;
    Window   *window*;
    int   *data_id*;
    char   * *buffer*;
    unsigned long*length*;
    int   *private_id*;

Description

XmClipboardCopyByName copies the actual data for a data item that was previously passed by name to the clipboard. Data is considered to be passed by name when a call to **XmClipboardCopy** is made with a NULL buffer parameter. Additional calls to this function append new data to the existing data. When making additional calls to this function, the clipboard should be locked to ensure the integrity of the clipboard data. To lock the clipboard, use **XmClipboardLock**. Unlock the clipboard when copying is completed; to unlock the clipboard, use **XmClipboardUnlock**.

display   Specifies a pointer to the **Display** structure that was returned in a previous call to **XOpenDisplay** or **XtDisplay**.

window   Specifies a widget's window ID that relates the application window to the clipboard. The widget's window ID can be obtained by using **XtWindow**. The same application instance should pass the same window ID to each clipboard function it calls.

data_id   Specifies an identifying number assigned to the data item that uniquely identifies the data item and the format. This number was assigned by **XmClipboardCopy** to the data item.

buffer   Specifies the buffer from which the clipboard copies the data.

length   Specifies the number of bytes in the data item.

private_id   Specifies the private data that the application wants to store with the data item.

Return Value

ClipboardSuccess
> The function is successful.

ClipboardLocked
> The function failed because the clipboard was locked by another application. The application can continue to call the function again with the same parameters until the lock goes away. This gives the application the opportunity to ask if the user wants to keep trying or to give up on the operation.

Related Information

XmClipboardCopy(3X), **XmClipboardLock(3X)**, **XmClipboardStartCopy(3X)**, and **XmClipboardUnlock(3X)**.

XmClipboardEndCopy

Purpose

A clipboard function that ends a copy to the clipboard.

AES Support Level

Full-use

Synopsis

#include <Xm/Xm.h>
#include <Xm/CutPaste.h>

int XmClipboardEndCopy (*display, window, item_id*)
    Display   * *display*;
    Window   *window*;
    long   *item_id*;

Description

XmClipboardEndCopy locks the clipboard from access by other applications, places data in the clipboard data structure, and unlocks the clipboard. Data items copied to the clipboard by **XmClipboardCopy** are not actually entered in the clipboard data structure until the call to **XmClipboardEndCopy**.

This function also frees up temporary storage that was allocated by **XmClipboardStartCopy**, which must be called before **XmClipboardEndCopy**. The latter function should not be called if **XmClipboardCancelCopy** has been called.

display   Specifies a pointer to the **Display** structure that was returned in a previous call to **XOpenDisplay** or **XtDisplay**.

window   Specifies a widget's window ID that relates the application window to the clipboard. The widget's window ID can be obtained by using **XtWindow**. The same application instance should pass the same window ID to each clipboard functions it calls.

item_id   Specifies the number assigned to this data item. This number was returned by a previous call to **XmClipboardStartCopy**.

Return Value

ClipboardSuccess
>The function is successful.

ClipboardLocked
>The function failed because the clipboard was locked by another application. The application can continue to call the function again with the same parameters until the lock goes away. This gives the application the opportunity to ask if the user wants to keep trying or to give up on the operation.

Related Information

XmClipboardCancelCopy(3X), **XmClipboardCopy(3X)** and **XmClipboardStartCopy(3X)**.

XmClipboardEndRetrieve

Purpose

A clipboard function that ends a copy from the clipboard.

AES Support Level

Full-use

Synopsis

```
#include <Xm/Xm.h>
#include <Xm/CutPaste.h>

int XmClipboardEndRetrieve (display, window)
        Display      * display;
        Window       window;
```

Description

XmClipboardEndRetrieve suspends copying data incrementally from the clipboard. It tells the clipboard routines that the application is through copying an item from the clipboard. Until this function is called, data items can be retrieved incrementally from the clipboard by calling **XmClipboardRetrieve**. If the application calls **XmClipboardStartRetrieve**, it must call **XmClipboardEndRetrieve**. If data is not being copied incrementally, **XmClipboardStartRetrieve** and **XmClipboardEndRetrieve** do not need to be called.

display   Specifies a pointer to the **Display** structure that was returned in a previous call to **XOpenDisplay** or **XtDisplay**.

window   Specifies a widget's window ID that relates the application window to the clipboard. The widget's window ID can be obtained by using **XtWindow**. The same application instance should pass the same window ID to each of the clipboard functions that it calls.

Return Value

ClipboardSuccess

The function is successful.

ClipboardLocked

The function failed because the clipboard was locked by another application. The application can continue to call the function again with the same parameters until the lock goes away. This gives the application the opportunity to ask if the user wants to keep trying or to give up on the operation.

Related Information

XmClipboardRetrieve(3X), XmClipboardStartCopy(3X), and
XmClipboardStartRetrieve(3X).

XmClipboardInquireCount

Purpose

A clipboard function that returns the number of data item formats.

AES Support Level

Full-use

Synopsis

#include <Xm/Xm.h>
#include <Xm/CutPaste.h>

int   **XmClipboardInquireCount**   (*display,*   *window,*   *count,*
max_format_name_length)
     Display   * *display*;
     Window   *window*;
     int   * *count*;
     int   * *max_format_name_length*;

Description

XmClipboardInquireCount returns the number of data item formats available for the data item in the clipboard. This function also returns the maximum name-length for all formats in which the data item is stored.

display	Specifies a pointer to the **Display** structure that was returned in a previous call to **XOpenDisplay** or **XtDisplay**.
window	Specifies a widget's window ID that relates the application window to the clipboard. The widget's window ID can be obtained by using **XtWindow**. The same application instance should pass the same window ID to each of the clipboard functions that it calls.
count	Returns the number of data item formats available for the data item in the clipboard. If no formats are available, this argument equals zero. The count includes the formats that were passed by name.
max_format_name_length	Specifies the maximum length of all format names for the data item in the clipboard.

Return Value

ClipboardSuccess	The function is successful.
ClipboardLocked	The function failed because the clipboard was locked by another application. The application can continue to call the function again with the same parameters until the lock goes away. This gives the application the opportunity to ask if the user wants to keep trying or to give up on the operation.
ClipboardNoData	The function could not find data on the clipboard corresponding to the format requested. This could occur because the clipboard is empty; there is data on the clipboard but not in the requested format; or the data in the requested format was passed by name and is no longer available.

Related Information

XmClipboardStartCopy(3X).

XmClipboardInquireFormat

Purpose

A clipboard function that returns a specified format name.

AES Support Level

Full-use

Synopsis

```
#include <Xm/Xm.h>
#include <Xm/CutPaste.h>

int    XmClipboardInquireFormat    (display,    window,    index,
format_name_buf, buffer_len, copied_len)
        Display      * display;
        Window       window;
        int          index;
        char         * format_name_buf;
        unsigned long buffer_len;
        unsigned long * copied_len;
```

Description

XmClipboardInquireFormat returns a specified format name for the data item in the clipboard. If the name must be truncated, the function returns a warning status.

display   Specifies a pointer to the **Display** structure that was returned in a previous call to **XOpenDisplay** or **XtDisplay**.

window   Specifies a widget's window ID that relates the application window to the clipboard. The widget's window ID can be obtained by using **XtWindow**. The same application instance should pass the same window ID to each of the clipboard functions that it calls.

index   Specifies which of the ordered format names to obtain. If this index is greater than the number of formats for the data item, this function returns a zero in the *copied_len* argument.

format_name_buf
                Specifies the buffer that receives the format name.

buffer_len   Specifies the number of bytes in the format name buffer.

copied_len   Specifies the number of bytes in the string copied to the buffer. If this argument equals zero, there is no *nth* format for the data item.

Return Value

ClipboardSuccess
                The function is successful.

ClipboardLocked

The function failed because the clipboard was locked by another application. The application can continue to call the function again with the same parameters until the lock goes away. This gives the application the opportunity to ask if the user wants to keep trying or to give up on the operation.

ClipboardTruncate

The data returned is truncated because the user did not provide a buffer large enough to hold the data.

ClipboardNoData

The function could not find data on the clipboard corresponding to the format requested. This could occur because the clipboard is empty; there is data on the clipboard but not in the requested format; or the data in the requested format was passed by name and is no longer available.

Related Information

XmClipboardStartCopy(3X).

XmClipboardInquireLength

Purpose

A clipboard function that returns the length of the stored data.

AES Support Level

Full-use

Synopsis

#include <Xm/Xm.h>
#include <Xm/CutPaste.h>

int **XmClipboardInquireLength** (*display, window, format_name, length*)
Display   * *display*;
Window   *window*;
char   * *format_name*;
unsigned long* *length*;

Description

XmClipboardInquireLength returns the length of the data stored under a specified format name for the clipboard data item. If no data is found for the specified format, or if there is no item on the clipboard, this function returns a value of zero.

Any format passed by name is assumed to have the *length* passed in a call to **XmClipboardCopy**, even though the data has not yet been transferred to the clipboard in that format.

display	Specifies a pointer to the **Display** structure that was returned in a previous call to **XOpenDisplay** or **XtDisplay**.
window	Specifies a widget's window ID that relates the application window to the clipboard. The widget's window ID can be obtained by using **XtWindow**. The same application instance should pass the same window ID to each of the clipboard functions that it calls.
format_name	Specifies the name of the format for the data item.
length	Specifies the length of the next data item in the specified format. This argument equals zero if no data is found for the specified format, or if there is no item on the clipboard.

Return Value

ClipboardSuccess

The function is successful.

ClipboardLocked

The function failed because the clipboard was locked by another application. The application can continue to call the function again with the same parameters until the lock goes away. This gives the application the opportunity to ask if the user wants to keep trying or to give up on the operation.

ClipboardNoData

The function could not find data on the clipboard corresponding to the format requested. This could occur because the clipboard is empty; there is data on the clipboard but not in the requested format; or the data in the requested format was passed by name and is no longer available.

Related Information

XmClipboardCopy(3X) and **XmClipboardStartCopy(3X)**.

XmClipboardInquirePendingItems

Purpose

A clipboard function that returns a list of *data_id*/*private_id* pairs.

AES Support Level

Full-use

Synopsis

#include <Xm/Xm.h>
#include <Xm/CutPaste.h>

int XmClipboardInquirePendingItems (*display, window, format_name, item_list, count*)
    Display   * *display*;
    Window   *window*;
    char   * *format_name*;
    XmClipboardPendingList* *item_list*;
    unsigned long   * *count*;

Description

XmClipboardInquirePendingItems returns a list of *data_id/private_id* pairs for the specified format name. A data item is considered pending if the application originally passed it by name, the application has not yet copied the data, and the item has not been deleted from the clipboard. The application is responsible for freeing the memory provided by this function to store the list.

This function is used by an application when exiting, to determine if the data that is passed by name should be sent to the clipboard.

display	Specifies a pointer to the **Display** structure that was returned in a previous call to **XOpenDisplay** or **XtDisplay**.
window	Specifies a widget's window ID that relates the application window to the clipboard. The widget's window ID can be obtained by using **XtWindow**. The same application instance should pass the same window ID to each of the clipboard functions that it calls.
format_name	Specifies a string that contains the name of the format for which the list of data ID/private ID pairs is to be obtained.
item_list	Specifies the address of the array of data ID/private ID pairs for the specified format name. This argument is a type **XmClipboardPendingList**. The application is responsible for freeing the memory provided by this function for storing the list.
item_count	Specifies the number of items returned in the list. If there is no data for the specified format name, or if there is no item on the clipboard, this argument equals zero.

Return Value

ClipboardSuccess
> The function is successful.

ClipboardLocked
> The function failed because the clipboard was locked by another application. The application can continue to call the function again with the same parameters until the lock goes away. This gives the application the opportunity to ask if the user wants to keep trying or to give up on the operation.

Related Information

XmClipboardStartCopy(3X).

XmClipboardLock

Purpose

A clipboard function that locks the clipboard

AES Support Level

Full-use

Synopsis

#include <Xm/Xm.h>
#include <Xm/CutPaste.h>

int XmClipboardLock (*display, window*)
    Display   * *display*;
    Window   *window*;

Description

XmClipboardLock locks the clipboard from access by another application until **XmClipboardUnlock** is called. All clipboard functions lock and unlock the clipboard to prevent simultaneous access. This function allows the application to keep the clipboard data from changing between calls to the **Inquire** and other clipboard functions. The application does not need to lock the clipboard between calls to **XmClipboardStartCopy** and **XmClipboardEndCopy** or to **XmClipboardStartRetrieve** and **XmClipboardEndRetrieve**.

The application should lock the clipboard before multiple calls to **XmClipboardCopyByName** and should unlock the clipboard after completion.

If the clipboard is already locked by another application, **XmClipboardLock** returns an error status. Multiple calls to this function by the same application increases the lock level.

display   Specifies a pointer to the **Display** structure that was returned in a previous call to **XOpenDisplay** or **XtDisplay**.

window   Specifies a widget's window ID that relates the application window to the clipboard. The widget's window ID can be obtained by using **XtWindow**. The same application instance should pass the same window ID to each of the clipboard functions that it calls.

Return Value

ClipboardSuccess
>The function is successful.

ClipboardLocked
>The function failed because the clipboard was locked by another application. The application can continue to call the function again with the same parameters until the lock goes away. This gives the application the opportunity to ask if the user wants to keep trying or to give up on the operation.

Related Information

XmClipboardCopyByName(3X), XmClipboardEndCopy(3X), XmClipboardEndRetrieve(3X), XmClipboardStartCopy(3X), XmClipboardStartRetrieve(3X), and XmClipboardUnlock(3X).

XmClipboardRegisterFormat

Purpose

A clipboard function that registers a new format.

AES Support Level

Full-use

Synopsis

#include <Xm/Xm.h>
#include <Xm/CutPaste.h>

int XmClipboardRegisterFormat (*display, format_name, format_length*)
    Display   * *display*;
    char   * *format_name*;
    unsigned long *format_length*;

Description

XmClipboardRegisterFormat registers a new format. Each format stored
on the clipboard should have a length associated with it; this length must be
known to the clipboard routines. Formats are known as targets in the ICCC
manual. All of the formats specified by the ICCCM conventions are
preregistered. Any other format that the application wants to use must

either be 8-bit data or be registered via this routine. Failure to register the length of the data results in incompatible applications across platforms having different byte-swapping orders.

display	Specifies a pointer to the **Display** structure that was returned in a previous call to **XOpenDisplay** or **XtDisplay**.
format_name	Specifies the string name for the new format (target).
format_length	Specifies the format length in bits (8, 16, or 32).

Return Value

ClipboardBadFormat
> The *format_name* must not be NULL, and the *format_length* must be 8, 16, or 32.

ClipboardSuccess The function is successful.

ClipboardLocked The function failed because the clipboard was locked by another application. The application can continue to call the function again with the same parameters until the lock goes away. This gives the application the opportunity to ask if the user wants to keep trying or to give up on the operation.

Related Information

XmClipboardStartCopy(3X).

XmClipboardRetrieve

Purpose

A clipboard function that retrieves a data item from the clipboard.

AES Support Level

Full-use

Synopsis

```
#include <Xm/Xm.h>
#include <Xm/CutPaste.h>

int XmClipboardRetrieve (display, window, format_name, buffer, length,
num_bytes, private_id)
        Display       * display;
        Window        window;
        char          * format_name;
        char          * buffer;
        unsigned long length;
        unsigned long * num_bytes;
        int           * private_id;
```

Description

XmClipboardRetrieve retrieves the current data item from clipboard storage. It returns a warning if the clipboard is locked; if there is no data on the clipboard; or if the data needs to be truncated because the buffer length is too short.

Between a call to XmClipboardStartRetrieve and XmClipboardEndRetrieve, multiple calls to XmClipboardRetrieve with the same format name result in data being incrementally copied from the clipboard until the data in that format has all been copied.

The return value ClipboardTruncate from calls to XmClipboardRetrieve indicates that more data remains to be copied in the given format. It is recommended that any calls to the Inquire functions that the application needs to make to effect the copy from the clipboard be made between the call to ClipboardStartRetrieve and the first call to XmClipboardRetrieve. That way, the application does not need to call XmClipboardLock and XmClipboardUnlock. Applications do not need to use XmClipboardStartRetrieve and XmClipboardEndRetrieve, in which case XmClipboardRetrieve works as it did before.

display   Specifies a pointer to the Display structure that was returned in a previous call to XOpenDisplay or XtDisplay.

window   Specifies a widget's window ID that relates the application window to the clipboard. The widget's window ID can be obtained by using XtWindow. The same application instance should pass the same window ID to each of the clipboard functions that it calls.

format_name   Specifies the name of a format in which the data is stored on the clipboard.

buffer   Specifies the buffer to which the application wants the clipboard to copy the data.

length   Specifies the length of the application buffer.

num_bytes   Specifies the number of bytes of data copied into the application buffer.

private_id   Specifies the private data stored with the data item by the application that placed the data item on the clipboard. If the application did not store private data with the data item, this argument returns zero.

Return Value

ClipboardSuccess
> The function is successful.

ClipboardLocked
> The function failed because the clipboard was locked by another application. The application can continue to call the function again with the same parameters until the lock goes away. This gives the application the opportunity to ask if the user wants to keep trying or to give up on the operation.

ClipboardTruncate
> The data returned is truncated because the user did not provide a buffer large enough to hold the data.

ClipboardNoData
> The function could not find data on the clipboard corresponding to the format requested. This could occur because the clipboard is empty; there is data on the clipboard but not in the requested format; or the data in the requested format was passed by name and is no longer available.

Related Information

XmClipboardEndRetrieve(3X), XmClipboardLock(3X), XmClipboardStartCopy(3X), XmClipboardStartRetrieve(3X), and XmClipboardUnlock(3X).

XmClipboardStartCopy

Purpose

A clipboard function that sets up a storage and data structure.

AES Support Level

Full-use

Synopsis

#include <Xm/Xm.h>
#include <Xm/CutPaste.h>

int XmClipboardStartCopy (*display, window, clip_label, timestamp, widget, callback, item_id*)
Display	* *display*;
Window	*window*;
XmString	*clip_label*;
Time	*timestamp*;
Widget	*widget*;
VoidProc	*callback*;
long	* *item_id*;

Description

XmClipboardStartCopy sets up storage and data structures to receive clipboard data. An application calls this function during a cut or copy operation. The data item that these structures receive then becomes the next data item in the clipboard.

Copying a large piece of data to the clipboard can take a long time. It is possible that, once copied, no application will ever request that data. The Motif Toolkit provides a mechanism so that an application does not need to actually pass data to the clipboard until the data has been requested by some application.

Instead, the application passes format and length information in **XmClipboardCopy** to the clipboard functions, along with a widget ID and a callback function address that is passed in **XmClipboardStartCopy**. The widget ID is needed for communications between the clipboard functions in the application that owns the data and the clipboard functions in the application that requests the data.

The callback functions are responsible for copying the actual data to the clipboard via **XmClipboardCopyByName**. The callback function is also called if the data item is removed from the clipboard, and the actual data is therefore no longer needed.

display	Specifies a pointer to the **Display** structure that was returned in a previous call to **XOpenDisplay** or **XtDisplay**.
window	Specifies a widget's window ID that relates the application window to the clipboard. The widget's window ID can be obtained by using **XtWindow**. The same application instance should pass the same window ID to each of the clipboard functions that it calls.
clip_label	Specifies the label to be associated with the data item. This argument is used to identify the data item, for example, in a clipboard viewer. An example of a label is the name of the application that places the data in the clipboard.
timestamp	Specifies the time of the event that triggered the copy.

widget   Specifies the ID of the widget that receives messages requesting data previously passed by name. This argument must be present in order to pass data by name. Any valid widget ID in your application can be used for this purpose and all the message handling is taken care of by the cut and paste functions.

callback   Specifies the address of the callback function that is called when the clipboard needs data that was originally passed by name. This is also the callback to receive the **delete** message for items that were originally passed by name. This argument must be present in order to pass data by name.

item_id   Specifies the number assigned to this data item. The application uses this number in calls to **XmClipboardCopy**, **XmClipboardEndCopy**, and **XmClipboardCancelCopy**.

For more information on passing data by name, see **XmClipboardCopy(3X)** and **XmClipboardCopyByName(3X)**.

The *widget* and *callback* arguments must be present in order to pass data by name. The callback format is as follows:

function name
    Widget   *widget*;
    int   * *data_id*;
    int   * *private*;
    int   * *reason*;

widget   Specifies the ID of the widget passed to this function.

data_id   Specifies the identifying number returned by **XmClipboardCopy**, which identifies the pass-by-name data.

private   Specifies the private information passed to **XmClipboardCopy**.

      reason   Specifies   the   reason,   which   is   either
                                 XmCR_CLIPBOARD_DATA_DELETE   or
                                 XmCR_CLIPBOARD_DATA_REQUEST.

Return Value

ClipboardSuccess

The function is successful.

ClipboardLocked

The function failed because the clipboard was locked by another application. The application can continue to call the function again with the same parameters until the lock goes away. This gives the application the opportunity to ask if the user wants to keep trying or to give up on the operation.

Related Information

XmClipboardCancelCopy(3X), XmClipboardCopy(3X),
XmClipboardCopyByName(3X), XmClipboardEndCopy(3X),
XmClipboardEndRetrieve(3X), XmClipboardInquireCount(3X),
XmClipboardInquireFormat(3X), XmClipboardInquireLength(3X),
XmClipboardInquirePendingItems(3X), XmClipboardLock(3X),
XmClipboardRegisterFormat(3X), XmClipboardRetrieve(3X),
XmClipboardStartRetrieve(3X), XmClipboardUndoCopy(3X),
XmClipboardUnlock(3X), and XmClipboardWithdrawFormat(3X).

XmClipboardStartRetrieve

Purpose

A clipboard function that starts a copy from the clipboard.

AES Support Level

Full-use

Synopsis

```
#include <Xm/Xm.h>
#include <Xm/CutPaste.h>

int XmClipboardStartRetrieve (display, window, timestamp)
    Display     * display;
    Window      window;
    Time        timestamp;
```

Description

XmClipboardStartRetrieve tells the clipboard routines that the application is ready to start copying an item from the clipboard. The clipboard is locked by this routine and stays locked until **XmClipboardEndRetrieve** is called. Between a call to **XmClipboardStartRetrieve** and **XmClipboardEndRetrieve**, multiple calls to **XmClipboardRetrieve** with the same format name result in data being incrementally copied from the clipboard until the data in that format has all been copied.

The return value **ClipboardTruncate** from calls to **XmClipboardRetrieve** indicates that more data remains to be copied in the given format. It is recommended that any calls to the **Inquire** functions that the application needs to make to effect the copy from the clipboard be made between the call to **XmClipboardStartRetrieve** and the first call to **XmClipboardRetrieve**. That way, the application does not need to call **XmClipboardLock** and **XmClipboardUnlock**. Applications do not need to use **XmClipboardStartRetrieve** and **XmClipboardEndRetrieve**, in which case **XmClipboardRetrieve** works as it did before.

display   Specifies a pointer to the **Display** structure that was returned in a previous call to **XOpenDisplay** or **XtDisplay**.

window   Specifies a widget's window ID that relates the application window to the clipboard. The widget's window ID can be obtained by using **XtWindow**. The same application instance should pass the same window ID to each of the clipboard functions that it calls.

timestamp   Specifies the time of the event that triggered the copy.

Return Value

ClipboardSuccess
> The function is successful.

ClipboardLocked
> The function failed because the clipboard was locked by another application. The application can continue to call the function again with the same parameters until the lock goes away. This gives the application the opportunity to ask if the user wants to keep trying or to give up on the operation.

Related Information

XmClipboardEndRetrieve(3X), XmClipboardInquireCount(3X), XmClipboardInquireFormat(3X), XmClipboardInquireLength(3X), XmClipboardInquirePendingItems(3X), XmClipboardLock(3X), XmClipboardRetrieve(3X), XmClipboardStartCopy(3X), and **XmClipboardUnlock(3X).**

XmClipboardUndoCopy

Purpose

A clipboard function that deletes the last item placed on the clipboard.

AES Support Level

Full-use

Synopsis

> **#include <Xm/Xm.h>**
> **#include <Xm/CutPaste.h>**
>
> **int XmClipboardUndoCopy** (*display, window*)
> **Display**   * *display*;
> **Window**   *window*;

Description

XmClipboardUndoCopy deletes the last item placed on the clipboard if the item was placed there by an application with the passed *display* and *window* arguments. Any data item deleted from the clipboard by the original call to **XmClipboardCopy** is restored. If the *display* or *window* IDs do not match the last copied item, no action is taken, and this function has no effect.

display	Specifies a pointer to the **Display** structure that was returned in a previous call to **XOpenDisplay** or **XtDisplay**.
window	Specifies a widget's window ID that relates the application window to the clipboard. The widget's window ID can be obtained by using **XtWindow**. The same application instance should pass the same window ID to each clipboard function it calls.

Return Value

ClipboardSuccess

The function is successful.

ClipboardLocked

The function failed because the clipboard was locked by another application. The application can continue to call the function again with the same parameters until the lock goes away. This gives the application the opportunity to ask if the user wants to keep trying or to give up on the operation.

Related Information

XmClipboardLock(3X) and **XmClipboardStartCopy(3X)**.

XmClipboardUnlock

Purpose

A clipboard function that unlocks the clipboard

AES Support Level

Full-use

Synopsis

#include <Xm/Xm.h>
#include <Xm/CutPaste.h>

int XmClipboardUnlock (*display, window, remove_all_locks*)
     Display   * *display*;
     Window   *window*;
     Boolean   *remove_all_locks*;

Description

XmClipboardUnlock unlocks the clipboard, enabling it to be accessed by other applications.

If multiple calls to **XmClipboardLock** have occurred, then the same number of calls to **XmClipboardUnlock** is necessary to unlock the clipboard, unless *remove_all_locks* is set to True.

The application should lock the clipboard before multiple calls to **XmClipboardCopyByName** and should unlock the clipboard after completion.

display   Specifies a pointer to the **Display** structure that was returned in a previous call to **XOpenDisplay** or **XtDisplay**.

window   Specifies a widget's window ID that relates the application window to the clipboard. The widget's window ID can be obtained by using **XtWindow**. The same application instance should pass the same window ID to each of the clipboard functions that it calls.

remove_all_locks
                 When True, indicates that all nested locks should be removed. When False, indicates that only one level of lock should be removed.

Return Value

ClipboardSuccess
                 The function is successful.

ClipboardLocked
                 The function failed because the clipboard was locked by another application. The application can continue to call the function again with the same parameters until the lock goes away. This gives the application the opportunity to ask if the user wants to keep trying or to give up on the operation.

Related Information

XmClipboardCancelCopy(3X), XmClipboardCopy(3X),
XmClipboardCopyByName(3X), XmClipboardEndCopy(3X),
XmClipboardEndRetrieve(3X), XmClipboardInquireCount(3X),
XmClipboardInquireFormat(3X), XmClipboardInquireLength(3X),
XmClipboardInquirePendingItems(3X), XmClipboardLock(3X),
XmClipboardRegisterFormat(3X), XmClipboardRetrieve(3X),
XmClipboardStartCopy(3X), XmClipboardStartRetrieve(3X),
XmClipboardUndoCopy(3X), and XmClipboardWithdrawFormat(3X).

XmClipboardWithdrawFormat

Purpose

A clipboard function that indicates that the application no longer wants to supply a data item.

AES Support Level

Full-use

Synopsis

#include <Xm/Xm.h>
#include <Xm/CutPaste.h>

int XmClipboardWithdrawFormat (*display, window, data_id*)
    Display   * *display*;
    Window   *window*;
    int   *data_id*;

Description

XmClipboardWithdrawFormat indicates that the application will no longer supply a data item to the clipboard that the application had previously passed by name.

display	Specifies a pointer to the **Display** structure that was returned in a previous call to **XOpenDisplay** or **XtDisplay**.
window	Specifies a widget's window ID that relates the application window to the clipboard. The widget's window ID can be obtained by using **XtWindow**. The same application instance should pass the same window ID to each of the clipboard functions that it calls.
data_id	Specifies an identifying number assigned to the data item that uniquely identifies the data item and the format. This was assigned to the item when it was originally passed by **XmClipboardCopy**.

Return Value

ClipboardSuccess
> The function is successful.

ClipboardLocked
> The function failed because the clipboard was locked by another application. The application can continue to call the function again with the same parameters until the lock goes away. This gives the application the opportunity to ask if the user wants to keep trying or to give up on the operation.

Related Information

XmClipboardCopy(3X) and XmClipboardStartCopy(3X).

XmCommand

Purpose

The Command widget class

AES Support Level

Full-use

Synopsis

#include <Xm/Command.h>

Description

Command is a special-purpose composite widget for command entry that provides a built-in command-history mechanism. Command includes a command-line text-input field, a command-line prompt, and a command-history list region.

One additional **WorkArea** child may be added to the Command after creation.

Whenever a command is entered, it is automatically added to the end of the command-history list and made visible. This does not change the selected item in the list, if there is one.

Many of the new resources specified for Command are actually SelectionBox resources that have been renamed for clarity and ease of use.

Classes

XmCommand inherits behavior and resources from **Core**, **Composite**, **Constraint**, **XmManager**, **XmBulletinBoard**, and **XmSelectionBox** classes.

The class pointer is **xmCommandWidgetClass**.

The class name is **XmCommand**.

New Resources

The following table defines a set of widget resources used by the programmer to specify data. The programmer can also set the resource values for the inherited classes to set attributes for this widget. To reference a resource by name or by class in a .Xdefaults file, remove the **XmN** or **XmC** prefix and use the remaining letters. To specify one of the defined values for a resource in a .Xdefaults file, remove the **Xm** prefix and use the remaining letters (in either lowercase or uppercase, but include any underscores between words). The codes in the access column indicate if the given resource can be set at creation time (**C**), set by using **XtSetValues** (**S**), retrieved by using **XtGetValues** (**G**), or is not applicable (**N/A**).

XmCommand Resource Set		
Name	**Default**	**Access**
Class	**Type**	
XmNcommand	NULL	CSG
XmCTextString	XmString	
XmNcommandChangedCallback	NULL	C
XmCCallback	XtCallbackList	
XmNcommandEnteredCallback	NULL	C
XmCCallback	XtCallbackList	
XmNhistoryItems	NULL	CSG
XmCItems	XmStringTable	
XmNhistoryItemCount	0	CSG
XmCItemCount	int	
XmNhistoryMaxItems	100	CSG
XmCMaxItems	int	
XmNhistoryVisibleItemCount	8	CSG
XmCVisibleItemCount	int	
XmNpromptString	">"	CSG
XmCXmString	XmString	

XmNcommand

Contains the current command-line text. This is the **XmNtextString** resource in SelectionBox, renamed for Command. This resource can also be modified via **XmCommandSetValue** and **XmCommandAppendValue** functions. The command area is a Text widget.

XmNcommandChangedCallback

Specifies the list of callbacks that is called when the value of the command changes. The callback reason is **XmCR_COMMAND_CHANGED**. This is equivalent to the **XmNvalueChangedCallback** of the Text widget, except that an **XmCommandCallbackStructure** is returned, loaded with the **XmString**.

XmNcommandEnteredCallback

Specifies the list of callbacks that is called when a command is entered in the Command. The callback reason is **XmCR_COMMAND_ENTERED**. An **XmCommandCallback** structure is returned.

XmNhistoryItems

Lists **XmString** items that make up the contents of the history list. This is the **XmNlistItems** resource in SelectionBox, renamed for Command.

XmNhistoryItemCount

Specifies the number of **XmStrings** in **XmNhistoryItems**. This is the **XmNlistItemCount** resource in SelectionBox, renamed for Command.

XmNhistoryMaxItems

Specifies the maximum number of items allowed in the history list. Once this number is reached, the first list item is removed from the list for each new item added to the list, that is, for each command entered.

XmNhistoryVisibleItemCount

Specifies the number of items in the history list that should be visible at one time. In effect, it sets the height (in lines) of the history list window. This is the **XmNvisibleItemCount** resource in SelectionBox, renamed for Command.

XmNpromptString

Prompts for the command line. This is the **XmNselectionLabelString** resource in SelectionBox, renamed for Command.

Inherited Resources

Command inherits behavior and resources from the following superclasses. For a complete description of each resource, refer to the man page for that superclass.

XmSelectionBox Resource Set		
Name	**Default**	**Access**
Class	**Type**	
XmNapplyCallback	NULL	N/A
XmCCallback	XtCallbackList	
XmNapplyLabelString	"Apply"	N/A
XmCApplyLabelString	XmString	
XmNcancelCallback	NULL	N/A
XmCCallback	XtCallbackList	
XmNcancelLabelString	"Cancel"	N/A
XmCXmString	XmString	
XmNdialogType	XmDIALOG_COMMAND	G
XmCDialogType	unsigned char	
XmNhelpLabelString	"Help"	N/A
XmCXmString	XmString	
XmNlistItemCount	0	N/A
XmCItemCount	int	
XmNlistItems	NULL	N/A
XmCItems	XmStringList	
XmNlistLabelString	NULL	N/A
XmCXmString	XmString	
XmNlistVisibleItemCount	8	N/A
XmCVisibleItemCount	int	
XmNminimizeButtons	False	N/A
XmCminimizeButtons	Boolean	
XmNmustMatch	False	N/A
XmCMustMatch	Boolean	
XmNnoMatchCallback	NULL	N/A
XmCCallback	XtCallbackList	
XmNokCallback	NULL	N/A
XmCCallback	XtCallbackList	

Name	Default	Access
Class	Type	
XmNokLabelString	"OK"	N/A
XmCXmString	XmString	
XmNselectionLabelString	"Selection"	CSG
XmCXmString	XmString	
XmNtextAccelerators	see description	C
XmCTextAccelerators	XtTranslations	
XmNtextColumns	20	CSG
XmCTextColumns	int	
XmNtextValue	NULL	N/A
XmCTextValue	XmString	

XmBulletinBoard Resource Set		
Name **Class**	**Default** **Type**	**Access**
XmNallowOverlap XmCAllowOverlap	True Boolean	N/A
XmNautoUnmanage XmCAutoUnmanage	False Boolean	CSG
XmNbuttonFontList XmCButtonFontList	NULL XmFontList	N/A
XmNcancelButton XmCWidget	NULL Widget	N/A
XmNdefaultButton XmCWidget	NULL Widget	N/A
XmNdefaultPosition XmCDefaultPosition	False Boolean	CSG
XmNdialogStyle XmCDialogStyle	dynamic unsigned char	CSG
XmNdialogTitle XmCXmString	NULL XmString	CSG
XmNfocusCallback XmCCallback	NULL XtCallbackList	C
XmNlabelFontList XmCLabelFontList	NULL XmFontList	CSG
XmNmapCallback XmCCallback	NULL XtCallbackList	C
XmNmarginHeight XmCMarginHeight	10 short	CSG
XmNmarginWidth XmCMarginWidth	10 short	CSG
XmNnoResize XmCNoResize	False Boolean	CSG

Name Class	Default Type	Access
XmNresizePolicy XmCResizePolicy	XmRESIZE_NONE unsigned char	CSG
XmNshadowType XmCShadowType	XmSHADOW_OUT unsigned char	CSG
XmNtextFontList XmCTextFontList	NULL XmFontList	CSG
XmNtextTranslations XmCTranslations	NULL XtTranslations	C
XmNunmapCallback XmCCallback	NULL XtCallbackList	C

XmManager Resource Set		
Name	**Default**	**Access**
Class	**Type**	
XmNbottomShadowColor	dynamic	CSG
XmCForeground	Pixel	
XmNbottomShadowPixmap	XmUNSPECIFIED_PIXMAP	CSG
XmCBottomShadowPixmap	Pixmap	
XmNforeground	dynamic	CSG
XmCForeground	Pixel	
XmNhelpCallback	NULL	C
XmCCallback	XtCallbackList	
XmNhighlightColor	Black	CSG
XmCForeground	Pixel	
XmNhighlightPixmap	dynamic	CSG
XmCHighlightPixmap	Pixmap	
XmNshadowThickness	dynamic	CSG
XmCShadowThickness	short	
XmNtopShadowColor	dynamic	CSG
XmCBackground	Pixel	
XmNtopShadowPixmap	XmUNSPECIFIED_PIXMAP	CSG
XmCTopShadowPixmap	Pixmap	
XmNuserData	NULL	CSG
XmCUserData	caddr_t	

Composite Resource Set		
Name	**Default**	**Access**
Class	**Type**	
XmNinsertPosition	NULL	CSG
XmCInsertPosition	XmRFunction	

Core Resource Set		
Name	**Default**	**Access**
Class	**Type**	
XmNaccelerators	NULL	CSG
XmCAccelerators	XtTranslations	
XmNancestorSensitive	True	G
XmCSensitive	Boolean	
XmNbackground	dynamic	CSG
XmCBackground	Pixel	
XmNbackgroundPixmap	XmUNSPECIFIED_PIXMAP	CSG
XmCPixmap	Pixmap	
XmNborderColor	Black	CSG
XmCBorderColor	Pixel	
XmNborderPixmap	XmUNSPECIFIED_PIXMAP	CSG
XmCPixmap	Pixmap	
XmNborderWidth	0	CSG
XmCBorderWidth	Dimension	
XmNcolormap	XtCopyFromParent	CG
XmCColormap	Colormap	
XmNdepth	XtCopyFromParent	CG
XmCDepth	int	
XmNdestroyCallback	NULL	C
XmCCallback	XtCallbackList	
XmNheight	0	CSG
XmCHeight	Dimension	
XmNmappedWhenManaged	True	CSG
XmCMappedWhenManaged	Boolean	
XmNscreen	XtCopyScreen	CG
XmCScreen	Pointer	
XmNsensitive	True	CSG
XmCSensitive	Boolean	

Name	Default	Access
Class	Type	
XmNtranslations	NULL	CSG
XmCTranslations	XtTranslations	
XmNwidth	0	CSG
XmCWidth	Dimension	
XmNx	0	CSG
XmCPosition	Position	
XmNy	0	CSG
XmCPosition	Position	

Callback Information

The following structure is returned with each callback.

typedef struct
{
    int   *reason*;
    XEvent   * *event*;
    XmString *value*;
    int   *length*;
} **XmCommandCallbackStruct**;

reason   Indicates why the callback was invoked

event   Points to the **XEvent** that triggered the callback

value   Specifies the **XmString** in the CommandArea

length   Specifies the size of the command in **XmString**

Behavior

Command behavior is summarized below.

<Key>: When any change is made to the text edit widget, the callbacks for **XmNcommandChangedCallback** are called.

<Key>Return:
When the Return key is pressed, the callbacks for **XmNcommandEnteredCallback** and **XmNcommandChangedCallback** are called.

<Key>Up or **<Key>Down**:
When the up-arrow or down-arrow key is pressed within the Text subwidget of Command, the text value is replaced with the previous or next item in the List subwidget. The selected item in the list is also changed to the previous or the next item. The callbacks for **XmNcommandChangedCallback** are called.

<DoubleClick>:
When an item in the List subwidget is double clicked, that item is selected and added to the end of the list in one action. The callbacks for **XmNcommandEnteredCallback** and **XmNcommandChangedCallback** are called.

<Key>F1: When the **Function Key 1** is pressed, the callbacks for **XmNhelpCallback** are called.

<FocusIn>: When a **FocusIn** *event* is generated on the widget window, the callbacks for **XmNfocusCallback** are called.

<MapWindow>:
When a Command that is the child of a DialogShell is mapped, the callbacks for **XmNmapCallback** are invoked. When a Command that is not the child of a DialogShell is mapped, the callbacks are not invoked.

<UnmapWindow>:
When a Command that is the child of a Dialogshell is unmapped, the callbacks for **XmNunmapCallback** are invoked. When a Command that is not the child of a DialogShell is unmapped, the callbacks are not invoked.

Default Translations

Command inherits default translations from SelectionBox.

Default Accelerators

The default accelerator translations added to descendants of a BulletinBoard if the parent of the BulletinBoard is a DialogShell are:

#override
<Key>F1:   **Help()**
<Key>Return: **Return()**
<Key>KP_Enter: **Return()**

Default Text Accelerators

The default text accelerators inherited from SelectionBox are:

#override
<Key>Up: **UpOrDown(0)**
<Key>Down: **UpOrDown(1)**
<Key>F1:   **Help()**
<Key>Return: **Return()**
<Key>KP_Enter: **Return()**

Keyboard Traversal

For information on keyboard traversal, see the man page for **XmManager(3X)** and its sections on behavior and default translations.

Related Information

Composite(3X), Constraint(3X), Core(3X), XmBulletinBoard(3X),
XmCommandAppendValue(3X), XmCommandError(3X),
XmCommandGetChild(3X), XmCommandSetValue(3X),
XmCreateCommand(3X), XmManager(3X), and XmSelectionBox(3X).

XmCommandAppendValue

Purpose

A Command function that appends the passed XmString to the end of the string displayed in the command area of the widget.

AES Support Level

Full-use

Synopsis

#include <Xm/Command.h>

void XmCommandAppendValue (*widget, command*)
  Widget   *widget*;
  XmString   *command*;

Description

XmCommandAppendValue appends the passed **XmString** to the end of the string displayed in the command area of the Command widget.

widget   Specifies the Command widget ID

command Specifies the passed **XmString**

For a complete definition of Command and its associated resources, see **XmCommand(3X)**.

Related Information

XmCommand(3X).

XmCommandError

Purpose

A Command function that displays an error message

AES Support Level

Full-use

Synopsis

#include <Xm/Command.h>

void XmCommandError (*widget, error*)
  Widget   *widget*;
  XmString   *error*;

Description

XmCommandError displays an error message in the history area of the Command widget. The **XmString** error is displayed until the next command entered occurs.

widget Specifies the Command widget ID.

error Specifies the passed **XmString**.

For a complete definition of Command and its associated resources, see **XmCommand(3X)**.

Related Information

XmCommand(3X).

XmCommandGetChild

Purpose

A Command function that is used to access a component.

AES Support Level

Full-use

Synopsis

#include <Xm/Command.h>

Widget XmCommandGetChild (*widget, child*)
 Widget   *widget*;
 unsigned char   *child*;

Description

XmCommandGetChild is used to access a component within a Command. The parameters given to the function are the Command widget and a value indicating which child to access.

widget   Specifies the Command widget ID.

child   Specifies a component within the Command. The following are legal values for this parameter:

- **XmDIALOG_COMMAND_TEXT**.
- **XmDIALOG_PROMPT_LABEL**.
- **XmDIALOG_HISTORY_LIST**.

For a complete definition of Command and its associated resources, see **XmCommand(3X)**.

Return Value

Returns the widget ID of the specified Command child.

Related Information

XmCommand(3X).

XmCommandSetValue

Purpose

A Command function that replaces a displayed string

AES Support Level

Full-use

Synopsis

#include <Xm/Command.h>

void XmCommandSetValue (*widget, command*)
   Widget   *widget*;
   XmString   *command*;

Description

XmCommandSetValue replaces the string displayed in the command area of the Command widget with the passed **XmString**.

widget   Specifies the Command widget ID.

command Specifies the passed **XmString**.

For a complete definition of Command and its associated resources, see **XmCommand(3X)**.

Related Information

XmCommand(3X).

XmCreateArrowButton

Purpose

The ArrowButton widget creation function

AES Support Level

Full-use

Synopsis

#include <Xm/ArrowB.h>

Widget XmCreateArrowButton (*parent, name, arglist, argcount*)
    Widget   *parent*;
    String   *name*;
    ArgList   *arglist*;
    Cardinal *argcount*;

Description

XmCreateArrowButton creates an instance of an ArrowButton widget and returns the associated widget ID.

parent   Specifies the parent widget ID

name   Specifies the name of the created widget

arglist   Specifies the argument list

argcount Specifies the number of attribute/value pairs in the argument list (*arglist*)

For a complete definition of ArrowButton and its associated resources, see **XmArrowButton(3X)**.

Return Value

Returns the ArrowButton widget ID.

Related Information

XmArrowButton(3X).

XmCreateArrowButtonGadget

Purpose

The ArrowButtonGadget creation function.

AES Support Level

Full-use

Synopsis

#include <Xm/ArrowB.h>

Widget XmCreateArrowButtonGadget (*parent, name, arglist, argcount*)
    Widget   *parent*;
    String   *name*;
    ArgList   *arglist*;
    Cardinal *argcount*;

Description

XmCreateArrowButtonGadget creates an instance of an ArrowButtonGadget widget and returns the associated widget ID.

parent   Specifies the parent widget ID

name   Specifies the name of the created widget

arglist   Specifies the argument list

argcount   Specifies the number of attribute/value pairs in the argument list (*arglist*)

For a complete definition of ArrowButtonGadget and its associated resources, see **XmArrowButtonGadget(3X)**.

Return Value

Returns the ArrowButtonGadget widget ID.

Related Information

XmArrowButtonGadget(3X).

XmCreateBulletinBoard

Purpose

The BulletinBoard widget creation function

AES Support Level

Full-use

Synopsis

#include <Xm/BulletinB.h>

Widget XmCreateBulletinBoard (*parent, name, arglist, argcount*)
  Widget *parent*;
  String *name*;
  ArgList *arglist*;
  Cardinal *argcount*;

Description

XmCreateBulletinBoard creates an instance of a BulletinBoard widget and returns the associated widget ID.

parent   Specifies the parent widget ID

name   Specifies the name of the created widget

arglist   Specifies the argument list

argcount Specifies the number of attribute/value pairs in the argument list (*arglist*)

For a complete definition of BulletinBoard and its associated resources, see **XmBulletinBoard(3X)**.

Return Value

Returns the BulletinBoard widget ID.

Related Information

XmBulletinBoard(3X).

XmCreateBulletinBoardDialog

Purpose

The BulletinBoard BulletinBoardDialog convenience creation function.

AES Support Level

Full-use

Synopsis

#include <Xm/BulletinB.h>

Widget XmCreateBulletinBoardDialog (*parent, name, arglist, argcount*)
   Widget   *parent*;
   String   *name*;
   ArgList   *arglist*;
   Cardinal *argcount*;

Description

XmCreateBulletinBoardDialog is a convenience creation function that creates a DialogShell and an unmanaged BulletinBoard child of the DialogShell. A BulletinBoardDialog is used for interactions not supported by the standard dialog set. This function does not automatically create any labels, buttons, or other dialog components. Such components should be added by the application after the BulletinBoardDialog is created.

Use **XtManageChild** to pop up the BulletinBoardDialog (passing the BulletinBoard as the widget parameter); use **XtUnmanageChild** to pop it down.

parent   Specifies the parent widget ID

name   Specifies the name of the created widget

arglist   Specifies the argument list

argcount Specifies the number of attribute/value pairs in the argument list (*arglist*)

For a complete definition of BulletinBoard and its associated resources, see **XmBulletinBoard(3X)**.

Return Value

Returns the BulletinBoard widget ID.

Related Information

XmBulletinBoard(3X).

XmCreateCascadeButton

Purpose

The CascadeButton widget creation function

AES Support Level

Full-use

Synopsis

#include <Xm/CascadeB.h>

Widget XmCreateCascadeButton (*parent, name, arglist, argcount*)
    Widget   *parent*;
    String   *name*;
    ArgList   *arglist*;
    Cardinal *argcount*;

Description

XmCreateCascadeButton creates an instance of a CascadeButton widget and returns the associated widget ID.

parent   Specifies the parent widget ID. The parent must be a RowColumn widget.

name   Specifies the name of the created widget.

arglist   Specifies the argument list.

argcount   Specifies the number of attribute/value pairs in the argument list (*arglist*).

For a complete definition of CascadeButton and its associated resources, see **XmCascadeButton(3X)**.

Return Value

Returns the CascadeButton widget ID.

Related Information

XmCascadeButton(3X).

XmCreateCascadeButtonGadget

Purpose

The CascadeButtonGadget creation function.

AES Support Level

Full-use

Synopsis

#include <Xm/CascadeBG.h>

Widget XmCreateCascadeButtonGadget (*parent, name, arglist, argcount*)
    Widget   *parent*;
    String   *name*;
    ArgList   *arglist*;
    Cardinal   *argcount*;

Description

XmCreateCascadeButtonGadget creates an instance of a CascadeButtonGadget and returns the associated widget ID.

parent   Specifies the parent widget ID. The parent must be a RowColumn widget.

name   Specifies the name of the created widget.

arglist   Specifies the argument list.

argcount Specifies the number of attribute/value pairs in the argument list (*arglist*).

For a complete definition of CascadeButtonGadget and its associated resources, see **XmCascadeButtonGadget(3X)**.

Return Value

Returns the CascadeButtonGadget widget ID.

Related Information

XmCascadeButtonGadget(3X).

XmCreateCommand

Purpose

The Command widget creation function

AES Support Level

Full-use

Synopsis

#include <Xm/Command.h>

Widget XmCreateCommand (*parent, name, arglist, argcount*)
    Widget   *parent*;
    String   *name*;
    ArgList   *arglist*;
    Cardinal *argcount*;

Description

XmCreateCommand creates an instance of a Command widget and returns the associated widget ID.

parent   Specifies the parent widget ID

name   Specifies the name of the created widget

arglist   Specifies the argument list

argcount Specifies the number of attribute/value pairs in the argument list (*arglist*)

For a complete definition of Command and its associated resources, see **XmCommand(3X)**.

Return Value

Returns the Command widget ID.

Related Information

XmCommand(3X).

XmCreateDialogShell

Purpose

The DialogShell widget creation function

AES Support Level

Full-use

Synopsis

#include <Xm/DialogS.h>

Widget XmCreateDialogShell (*parent, name, arglist, argcount*)
    Widget   *parent*;
    String   *name*;
    ArgList   *arglist*;
    Cardinal   *argcount*;

Description

XmCreateDialogShell creates an instance of a DialogShell widget and returns the associated widget ID.

parent   Specifies the parent widget ID

name   Specifies the name of the created widget

arglist   Specifies the argument list

argcount Specifies the number of attribute/value pairs in the argument list (*arglist*)

For a complete definition of DialogShell and its associated resources, see **XmDialogShell(3X)**.

Return Value

Returns the DialogShell widget ID.

Related Information

XmDialogShell(3X).

XmCreateDrawingArea

Purpose

The DrawingArea widget creation function

AES Support Level

Full-use

Synopsis

#include <Xm/DrawingA.h>

Widget XmCreateDrawingArea (*parent, name, arglist, argcount*)
    Widget   *parent*;
    String   *name*;
    ArgList   *arglist*;
    Cardinal   *argcount*;

Description

XmCreateDrawingArea creates an instance of a DrawingArea widget and returns the associated widget ID.

parent   Specifies the parent widget ID

name   Specifies the name of the created widget

arglist   Specifies the argument list

argcount Specifies the number of attribute/value pairs in the argument list (*arglist*)

For a complete definition of DrawingArea and its associated resources, see **XmDrawingArea(3X)**.

Return Value

Returns the DrawingArea widget ID.

Related Information

XmDrawingArea(3X).

XmCreateDrawnButton

Purpose

The DrawnButton widget creation function

AES Support Level

Full-use

Synopsis

#include <Xm/DrawnB.h>

Widget XmCreateDrawnButton (*parent, name, arglist, argcount*)
    Widget   *parent*;
    String   *name*;
    ArgList   *arglist*;
    Cardinal *argcount*;

Description

XmCreateDrawnButton creates an instance of a DrawnButton widget and returns the associated widget ID.

parent   Specifies the parent widget ID

name   Specifies the name of the created widget

arglist   Specifies the argument list

argcount Specifies the number of attribute/value pairs in the argument list (*arglist*)

For a complete definition of DrawnButton and its associated resources, see **XmDrawnButton(3X)**.

Return Value

Returns the DrawnButton widget ID.

Related Information

XmDrawnButton(3X).

XmCreateErrorDialog

Purpose

The MessageBox ErrorDialog convenience creation function.

AES Support Level

Full-use

Synopsis

#include <Xm/MessageB.h>

Widget XmCreateErrorDialog (*parent, name, arglist, argcount*)
    Widget   *parent*;
    String   *name*;
    ArgList   *arglist*;
    Cardinal *argcount*;

Description

XmCreateErrorDialog is a convenience creation function that creates a DialogShell and an unmanaged MessageBox child of the DialogShell. An ErrorDialog warns the user of an invalid or potentially dangerous condition. It includes a symbol, a message, and three buttons. The default symbol is an octagon with a diagonal slash. The default button labels are **OK**, **Cancel**, and **Help**.

Use **XtManageChild** to pop up the ErrorDialog (passing the MessageBox as the widget parameter); use **XtUnmanageChild** to pop it down.

parent   Specifies the parent widget ID

name   Specifies the name of the created widget

arglist   Specifies the argument list

argcount Specifies the number of attribute/value pairs in the argument list (*arglist*)

For a complete definition of MessageBox and its associated resources, see **XmMessageBox(3X)**.

Return Value

Returns the MessageBox widget ID.

Related Information

XmMessageBox(3X).

XmCreateFileSelectionBox

Purpose

The FileSelectionBox widget creation function

AES Support Level

Full-use

Synopsis

#include <Xm/FileSB.h>

Widget XmCreateFileSelectionBox (*parent, name, arglist, argcount*)
    Widget   *parent*;
    String   *name*;
    ArgList   *arglist*;
    Cardinal   *argcount*;

Description

XmCreateFileSelectionBox creates an unmanaged FileSelectionBox. A FileSelectionBox is used to select a file and includes the following:

- An editable text field for the directory mask
- A scrolling list of filenames

- An editable text field for the selected file
- Labels for the list and text fields
- Four buttons

The default button labels are **OK, Filter, Cancel**, and **Help**. One additional **WorkArea** child may be added to the FileSelectionBox after creation.

If the parent of the FileSelectionBox is a DialogShell, use **XtManageChild** to pop up the FileSelectionDialog (passing the FileSelectionBox as the widget parameter); use **XtUnmanageChild** to pop it down.

parent Specifies the parent widget ID

name Specifies the name of the created widget

arglist Specifies the argument list

argcount Specifies the number of attribute/value pairs in the argument list (*arglist*)

For a complete definition of FileSelectionBox and its associated resources, see **XmFileSelectionBox(3X)**.

Return Value

Returns the FileSelectionBox widget ID.

Related Information

XmFileSelectionBox(3X).

XmCreateFileSelectionDialog

Purpose

The FileSelectionBox FileSelectionDialog convenience creation function.

AES Support Level

Full-use

Synopsis

#include <Xm/FileSB.h>

Widget XmCreateFileSelectionDialog (*parent, name, arglist, argcount*)
    Widget   *parent*;
    String   *name*;
    ArgList   *arglist*;
    Cardinal *argcount*;

Description

XmCreateFileSelectionDialog is a convenience creation function that creates a DialogShell and an unmanaged FileSelectionBox child of the DialogShell. A FileSelectionDialog selects a file. It includes the following:

- An editable text field for the directory mask

- A scrolling list of filenames
- An editable text field for the selected file
- Labels for the list and text fields
- Four buttons

The default button labels are **OK**, **Filter**, **Cancel**, and **Help**. One additional **WorkArea** child may be added to the FileSelectionBox after creation.

Use **XtManageChild** to pop up the FileSelectionDialog (passing the FileSelectionBox as the widget parameter); use **XtUnmanageChild** to pop it down.

parent   Specifies the parent widget ID

name   Specifies the name of the created widget

arglist   Specifies the argument list

argcount Specifies the number of attribute/value pairs in the argument list (*arglist*)

For a complete definition of FileSelectionBox and its associated resources, see **XmFileSelectionBox(3X)**.

Return Value

Returns the FileSelectionBox widget ID.

Related Information

XmFileSelectionBox(3X).

XmCreateForm

Purpose

The Form widget creation function

AES Support Level

Full-use

Synopsis

#include <Xm/Form.h>

Widget XmCreateForm (*parent, name, arglist, argcount*)
    Widget   *parent*;
    String   *name*;
    ArgList   *arglist*;
    Cardinal *argcount*;

Description

XmCreateForm creates an instance of a Form widget and returns the associated widget ID.

parent   Specifies the parent widget ID

name   Specifies the name of the created widget

arglist   Specifies the argument list

argcount Specifies the number of attribute/value pairs in the argument list (*arglist*)

For a complete definition of Form and its associated resources, see **XmForm(3X)**.

Return Value

Returns the Form widget ID.

Related Information

XmForm(3X).

XmCreateFormDialog

Purpose

A Form FormDialog convenience creation function

AES Support Level

Full-use

Synopsis

#include <Xm/Form.h>

Widget XmCreateFormDialog (*parent, name, arglist, argcount*)
      Widget   *parent*;
      String   *name*;
      ArgList   *arglist*;
      Cardinal *argcount*;

Description

XmCreateFormDialog is a convenience creation function that creates a DialogShell and an unmanaged Form child of the DialogShell. A FormDialog is used for interactions not supported by the standard dialog set. This function does not automatically create any labels, buttons, or other dialog components. Such components should be added by the application after the FormDialog is created.

Use **XtManageChild** to pop up the FormDialog (passing the Form as the widget parameter); use **XtUnmanageChild** to pop it down.

parent   Specifies the parent widget ID

name   Specifies the name of the created widget

arglist   Specifies the argument list

argcount   Specifies the number of attribute/value pairs in the argument list (*arglist*)

For a complete definition of Form and its associated resources, see **XmForm(3X)**.

Return Value

Returns the Form widget ID.

Related Information

XmForm(3X).

XmCreateFrame

Purpose

The Frame widget creation function

AES Support Level

Full-use

Synopsis

#include <Xm/Frame.h>

Widget XmCreateFrame (*parent, name, arglist, argcount*)
    Widget   *parent*;
    String   *name*;
    ArgList   *arglist*;
    Cardinal   *argcount*;

Description

XmCreateFrame creates an instance of a Frame widget and returns the associated widget ID.

parent   Specifies the parent widget ID

name Specifies the name of the created widget

arglist Specifies the argument list

argcount Specifies the number of attribute/value pairs in the argument list (*arglist*)

For a complete definition of Frame and its associated resources, see **XmFrame(3X)**.

Return Value

Returns the Frame widget ID.

Related Information

XmFrame(3X).

XmCreateInformationDialog

Purpose

The MessageBox InformationDialog convenience creation function.

AES Support Level

Full-use

Synopsis

#include <Xm/MessageB.h>

Widget XmCreateInformationDialog (*parent, name, arglist, argcount*)
      Widget   *parent*;
      String   *name*;
      ArgList   *arglist*;
      Cardinal   *argcount*;

Description

XmCreateInformationDialog is a convenience creation function that creates a DialogShell and an unmanaged MessageBox child of the DialogShell. An InformationDialog gives the user information, such as the status of an action. It includes a symbol, a message, and three buttons. The default symbol is a lowercase **i**. The default button labels are **OK**, **Cancel**, and **Help**.

Use **XtManageChild** to pop up the InformationDialog (passing the MessageBox as the widget parameter); use **XtUnmanageChild** to pop it down.

parent   Specifies the parent widget ID

name   Specifies the name of the created widget

arglist   Specifies the argument list

argcount Specifies the number of attribute/value pairs in the argument list (*arglist*)

For a complete definition of MessageBox and its associated resources, see **XmMessageBox(3X)**.

Return Value

Returns the MessageBox widget ID.

Related Information

XmMessageBox(3X).

XmCreateLabel

Purpose

The Label widget creation function

AES Support Level

Full-use

Synopsis

#include <Xm/Label.h>

Widget XmCreateLabel (*parent, name, arglist, argcount*)
    Widget   *parent*;
    String   *name*;
    ArgList   *arglist*;
    Cardinal *argcount*;

Description

XmCreateLabel creates an instance of a Label widget and returns the associated widget ID.

parent   Specifies the parent widget ID

name   Specifies the name of the created widget

arglist   Specifies the argument list

argcount Specifies the number of attribute/value pairs in the argument list (*arglist*)

For a complete definition of Label and its associated resources, see **XmLabel(3X)**.

Return Value

Returns the Label widget ID.

Related Information

XmLabel(3X).

XmCreateLabelGadget

Purpose

The LabelGadget creation function

AES Support Level

Full-use

Synopsis

#include <Xm/LabelG.h>

Widget XmCreateLabelGadget (*parent, name, arglist, argcount*)
    Widget   *parent*;
    String   *name*;
    ArgList   *arglist*;
    Cardinal   *argcount*;

Description

XmCreateLabelGadget creates an instance of a LabelGadget widget and returns the associated widget ID.

parent   Specifies the parent widget ID

name   Specifies the name of the created widget

arglist   Specifies the argument list

argcount Specifies the number of attribute/value pairs in the argument list (*arglist*)

For a complete definition of LabelGadget and its associated resources, see **XmLabelGadget(3X)**.

Return Value

Returns the LabelGadget widget ID.

Related Information

XmLabelGadget(3X).

XmCreateList

Purpose

The List widget creation function

AES Support Level

Full-use

Synopsis

#include <Xm/List.h>

Widget XmCreateList (*parent, name, arglist, argcount*))
Widget	*parent*;
String	*name*;
ArgList	*arglist*;
Cardinal	*argcount*;

Description

XmCreateList creates an instance of a List widget and returns the associated widget ID.

parent   Specifies the parent widget ID

name   Specifies the name of the created widget

arglist   Specifies the argument list

argcount Specifies the number of attribute/value pairs in the argument list (*arglist*)

For a complete definition of List and its associated resources, see **XmList(3X)**.

Return Value

Returns the List widget ID.

Related Information

XmList(3X).

XmCreateMainWindow

Purpose

The MainWindow widget creation function

AES Support Level

Full-use

Synopsis

#include <Xm/MainW.h>

Widget XmCreateMainWindow (*parent, name, arglist, argcount*)
    Widget   *parent*;
    String   *name*;
    ArgList   *arglist*;
    Cardinal   *argcount*;

Description

XmCreateMainWindow creates an instance of a MainWindow widget and returns the associated widget ID.

parent   Specifies the parent widget ID

name   Specifies the name of the created widget

arglist   Specifies the argument list

argcount Specifies the number of attribute/value pairs in the argument list (*arglist*)

For a complete definition of MainWindow and its associated resources, see **XmMainWindow(3X)**.

Return Value

Returns the MainWindow widget ID.

Related Information

XmMainWindow(3X).

XmCreateMenuBar

Purpose

A RowColumn widget convenience creation function

AES Support Level

Full-use

Synopsis

#include <Xm/RowColumn.h>

Widget XmCreateMenuBar (*parent, name, arglist, argcount*)
    Widget   *parent*;
    String   *name*;
    ArgList   *arglist*;
    Cardinal *argcount*;

Description

XmCreateMenuBar creates an instance of a RowColumn widget of type **XmMENU_BAR** and returns the associated widget ID.

It is provided as a convenience function for creating RowColumn widgets configured to operate as a MenuBar and is not implemented as a separate widget class.

The MenuBar widget is generally used for building a Pulldown menu system. Typically, a MenuBar is created and placed along the top of the application window, and several CascadeButtons are inserted as the children. Each of the CascadeButtons has a Pulldown MenuPane associated with it. These Pulldown MenuPanes must have been created as children of the MenuBar. The user interacts with the MenuBar by using either the mouse or the keyboard.

The MenuBar displays a 3-D shadow along its border. The application controls the shadow attributes using the visual-related resources supported by **XmManager**.

The MenuBar widget is homogeneous in that it accepts only children that are a subclass of **XmCascadeButton**. Attempting to insert a child of a different class results in a warning message.

If the MenuBar does not have enough room to fit all of its subwidgets on a single line, the MenuBar attempts to wrap the remaining entries onto additional lines if allowed by the geometry manager of the parent widget.

parent   Specifies the parent widget ID

name   Specifies the name of the created widget

arglist   Specifies the argument list

argcount Specifies the number of attribute/value pairs in the argument list (*arglist*)

For a complete definition of RowColumn and its associated resources, see **XmRowColumn(3X)**.

Return Value

Returns the RowColumn widget ID.

Related Information

XmCascadeButton(3X), XmCreatePulldownMenu(3X),
XmManager(3X), and XmRowColumn(3X).

XmCreateMenuShell

Purpose

The MenuShell widget creation function

AES Support Level

Full-use

Synopsis

#include <Xm/MenuShell.h>

Widget XmCreateMenuShell (*parent, name, arglist, argcount*)
    Widget   *parent*;
    String   *name*;
    ArgList   *arglist*;
    Cardinal   *argcount*;

Description

XmCreateMenuShell creates an instance of a MenuShell widget and returns the associated widget ID.

parent   Specifies the parent widget ID

name   Specifies the name of the created widget

arglist   Specifies the argument list

argcount Specifies the number of attribute/value pairs in the argument list
(*arglist*)

For a complete definition of MenuShell and its associated resources, see
XmMenuShell(3X).

Return Value

Returns the MenuShell widget ID.

Related Information

XmMenuShell(3X).

XmCreateMessageBox

Purpose

The MessageBox widget creation function

AES Support Level

Full-use

Synopsis

#include <Xm/MessageB.h>

Widget XmCreateMessageBox (*parent, name, arglist, argcount*)
    Widget   *parent*;
    String   *name*;
    ArgList   *arglist*;
    Cardinal *argcount*;

Description

XmCreateMessageBox creates an unmanaged MessageBox. A MessageBox is used for common interaction tasks, which include giving information, asking questions, and reporting errors. It includes an optional symbol, a message, and three buttons.

By default, there is no symbol. The default button labels are **OK**, **Cancel**, and **Help**.

If the parent of the MessageBox is a Dialogshell, use **XtManageChild** to pop up the MessageBox (passing the MessageBox as the widget parameter); use **XtUnmanageChild** to pop it down.

parent   Specifies the parent widget ID

name   Specifies the name of the created widget

arglist   Specifies the argument list

argcount Specifies the number of attribute/value pairs in the argument list (*arglist*)

For a complete definition of MessageBox and its associated resources, see **XmMessageBox(3X)**.

Return Value

Returns the MessageBox widget ID.

Related Information

XmMessageBox(3X).

XmCreateMessageDialog

Purpose

The MessageBox MessageDialog convenience creation function.

AES Support Level

Full-use

Synopsis

```
#include <Xm/MessageB.h>

Widget XmCreateMessageDialog (parent, name, arglist, argcount)
        Widget      parent;
        String      name;
        ArgList     arglist;
        Cardinal    argcount;
```

Description

XmCreateMessageDialog is a convenience creation function that creates a DialogShell and an unmanaged MessageBox child of the DialogShell. A MessageDialog is used for common interaction tasks, which include giving information, asking questions, and reporting errors. It includes a symbol, a message, and three buttons. By default, there is no symbol. The default button labels are **OK**, **Cancel**, and **Help**.

Use **XtManageChild** to pop up the MessageDialog (passing the MessageBox as the widget parameter); use **XtUnmanageChild** to pop it down.

parent   Specifies the parent widget ID

name   Specifies the name of the created widget

arglist   Specifies the argument list

argcount Specifies the number of attribute/value pairs in the argument list (*arglist*)

For a complete definition of MessageBox and its associated resources, see **XmMessageBox(3X)**.

Return Value

Returns the MessageBox widget ID.

Related Information

XmMessageBox(3X).

XmCreateOptionMenu

Purpose

A RowColumn widget convenience creation function

AES Support Level

Full-use

Synopsis

#include <Xm/RowColumn.h>

Widget XmCreateOptionMenu (*parent, name, arglist, argcount*)
    Widget   *parent*;
    String   *name*;
    ArgList   *arglist*;
    Cardinal   *argcount*;

Description

XmCreateOptionMenu creates an instance of a RowColumn widget of type **XmMENU_OPTION** and returns the associated widget ID.

It is provided as a convenience function for creating a RowColumn widget configured to operate as an OptionMenu and is not implemented as a separate widget class.

The OptionMenu widget is a specialized RowColumn manager composed of a label, a selection area, and a single Pulldown MenuPane. When an application creates an OptionMenu widget, it supplies the label string and the Pulldown MenuPane. In order to succeed, there must be a valid **XmNsubMenuId** resource set when calling this function. When the OptionMenu is created, the Pulldown MenuPane must have been created as a child of the OptionMenu's parent and must be specified. The LabelGadget and the selection area (a CascadeButtonGadget) are created by the OptionMenu.

An OptionMenu is laid out with the label displayed on the left side of the widget and the selection area on the right side. The selection area has a dual purpose; it displays the label of the last item selected from the associated Pulldown MenuPane, and it provides the means for posting the Pulldown MenuPane.

The OptionMenu typically does not display any 3-D visuals around itself or the internal LabelGadget. By default, the internal CascadeButtonGadget has a visible 3-D shadow. The application may change this by getting the CascadeButtonGadget ID using **XmOptionButtonGadget**, and then calling **XtSetValues** using the standard visual-related resources.

The Pulldown MenuPane is posted by moving the mouse pointer over the selection area and pressing the mouse button defined by OptionMenu's **XmNwhichButton** resource. The Pulldown MenuPane is posted and positioned so that the last selected item is directly over the selection area. The mouse is then used to arm the desired menu item. When the mouse button is released, the armed menu item is selected and the label within the selection area is changed to match that of the selected item. By default, mouse button 1 is used to interact with an OptionMenu. The default can be changed via the RowColumn resource **XmNwhichButton**.

The OptionMenu also operates by using the keyboard interface mechanism. If the application has established a mnemonic with the OptionMenu, typing the mnemonic causes the Pulldown MenuPane to be posted with traversal enabled. The standard traversal keys can then be used to move within the MenuPane. Selection can occur as the result of pressing the Return key or typing a mnemonic or accelerator for one of the menu items.

An application may use the **XmNmenuHistory** resource to indicate which item in the Pulldown MenuPane should be treated as the current choice and have its label displayed in the selection area. By default, the first item in the Pulldown MenuPane is used.

parent Specifies the parent widget ID

name Specifies the name of the created widget

arglist Specifies the argument list

argcount Specifies the number of attribute/value pairs in the argument list (*arglist*)

For a complete definition of RowColumn and its associated resources, see **XmRowColumn(3X)**.

Return Value

Returns the RowColumn widget ID.

Related Information

XmCascadeButtonGadget(3X), **XmCreatePulldownMenu(3X)**, **XmLabelGadget(3X)**, and **XmRowColumn(3X)**.

XmCreatePanedWindow

Purpose

The PanedWindow widget creation function.

AES Support Level

Full-use

Synopsis

#include <Xm/PanedW.h>

Widget XmCreatePanedWindow (*parent, name, arglist, argcount*)
    Widget   *parent*;
    String   *name*;
    ArgList   *arglist*;
    Cardinal   *argcount*;

Description

XmCreatePanedWindow creates an instance of a PanedWindow widget and returns the associated widget ID.

parent   Specifies the parent widget ID

name   Specifies the name of the created widget

arglist   Specifies the argument list

argcount Specifies the number of attribute/value pairs in the argument list (*arglist*)

For a complete definition of PanedWindow and its associated resources, see **XmPanedWindow(3X)**.

Return Value

Returns the PanedWindow widget ID.

Related Information

XmPanedWindow(3X).

XmCreatePopupMenu

Purpose

A RowColumn widget convenience creation function

AES Support Level

Full-use

Synopsis

#include <Xm/RowColumn.h>

Widget XmCreatePopupMenu (*parent, name, arglist, argcount*)
      Widget   *parent*;
      String   *name*;
      ArgList   *arglist*;
      Cardinal   *argcount*;

Description

XmCreatePopupMenu creates an instance of a RowColumn widget of type **XmMENU_POPUP** and returns the associated widget ID. When using this function to create the Popup MenuPane, a MenuShell widget is automatically created as the parent of the MenuPane. The parent of the MenuShell widget is the widget indicated by the *parent* parameter.

XmCreatePopupMenu is provided as a convenience function for creating RowColumn widgets configured to operate as Popup MenuPanes and is not implemented as a separate widget class.

The PopupMenu is used as the first MenuPane within a PopupMenu system; all other MenuPanes are of the Pulldown type. A Popup MenuPane displays a 3-D shadow, unless the feature is disabled by the application. The shadow appears around the edge of the MenuPane.

The Popup MenuPane must be created as the child of a MenuShell widget in order to function properly when it is incorporated into a menu. If the application uses this convenience function for creating a Popup MenuPane, then the MenuShell is automatically created as the real parent of the MenuPane. If the application does not use this convenience function to create the RowColumn to function as a Popup MenuPane, then it is the application's responsibility to create the MenuShell widget.

To access the PopupMenu, the application must first position the widget using the **XmMenuPosition** function and then manage it using **XtManageChild**.

parent   Specifies the parent widget ID

name   Specifies the name of the created widget

arglist   Specifies the argument list

argcount Specifies the number of attribute/value pairs in the argument list (*arglist*)

For a complete definition of RowColumn and its associated resources, see **XmRowColumn(3X)**.

Return Value

Returns the RowColumn widget ID.

Related Information

XmMenuPosition(3X), XmMenuShell(3X), and XmRowColumn(3X).

XmCreatePromptDialog

Purpose

The SelectionBox PromptDialog convenience creation function.

AES Support Level

Full-use

Synopsis

#include <Xm/SelectioB.h>

Widget XmCreatePromptDialog (*parent, name, arglist, argcount*)
    Widget   *parent*;
    String   *name*;
    ArgList   *arglist*;
    Cardinal   *argcount*;

Description

XmCreatePromptDialog is a convenience creation function that creates a DialogShell and an unmanaged SelectionBox child of the DialogShell. A PromptDialog prompts the user for text input. It includes a message, a text input region, and three managed buttons. The default button labels are **OK**,

Cancel, and **Help**. An additional button, with **Apply** as the default label, is created unmanaged; it may be explicitly managed if needed. One additional **WorkArea** child may be added to the SelectionBox after creation.

Use **XtManageChild** to pop up the PromptDialog (passing the SelectionBox as the widget parameter); use **XtUnmanageChild** to pop it down.

parent   Specifies the parent widget ID

name   Specifies the name of the created widget

arglist   Specifies the argument list

argcount   Specifies the number of attribute/value pairs in the argument list (*arglist*)

For a complete definition of SelectionBox and its associated resources, see **XmSelectionBox(3X)**.

Return Value

Returns the SelectionBox widget ID.

Related Information

XmSelectionBox(3X).

XmCreatePulldownMenu

Purpose

A RowColumn widget convenience creation function

AES Support Level

Full-use

Synopsis

#include <Xm/RowColumn.h>

Widget XmCreatePulldownMenu (*parent, name, arglist, argcount*)
    Widget   *parent*;
    String   *name*;
    ArgList   *arglist*;
    Cardinal   *argcount*;

Description

XmCreatePulldownMenu creates an instance of a RowColumn widget of type **XmMENU_PULLDOWN** and returns the associated widget ID. When using this function to create the Pulldown MenuPane, a MenuShell widget is automatically created as the parent of the MenuPane. If the widget specified by the *parent* parameter is a Popup or a Pulldown

MenuPane, then the MenuShell widget is created as a child of the *parent*'s MenuShell; otherwise, it is created as a child of the specified *parent* widget.

XmCreatePulldownMenu is provided as a convenience function for creating RowColumn widgets configured to operate as Pulldown MenuPanes and is not implemented as a separate widget class.

A Pulldown MenuPane displays a 3-D shadow, unless the feature is disabled by the application. The shadow appears around the edge of the MenuPane.

A Pulldown MenuPane is used when creating submenus that are to be attached to a CascadeButton or a CascadeButtonGadget. This is the case for all MenuPanes that are part of a PulldownMenu system (a MenuBar), the MenuPane associated with an OptionMenu, and any MenuPanes that cascade from a Popup MenuPane. Pulldown MenuPanes, that are to be associated with an OptionMenu must be created before the OptionMenu is created.

The Pulldown MenuPane must be attached to a CascadeButton or CascadeButtonGadget that resides in a MenuBar, a Popup MenuPane, a Pulldown MenuPane, or an OptionMenu. This is done by using the button resource **XmNsubMenuId**.

A MenuShell widget is required between the Pulldown MenuPane and its parent. If the application uses this convenience function for creating a Pulldown MenuPane, then the MenuShell is automatically created as the real parent of the MenuPane; otherwise, it is the application's responsibility to create the MenuShell widget.

To function correctly when incorporated into a menu, the Pulldown MenuPane's hierarchy must be considered; this hierarchy depends the type of menu system that is being built as follows:

- If the Pulldown MenuPane is to be pulled down from a MenuBar, its *parent* must be the MenuBar.

- If the Pulldown MenuPane is to be pulled down from a Popup or another Pulldown MenuPane, its *parent* must be that Popup or Pulldown MenuPane.

- If the Pulldown MenuPane is to be pulled down from an OptionMenu, its *parent* must be the same as the OptionMenu parent.

parent   Specifies the parent widget ID

name   Specifies the name of the created widget

arglist Specifies the argument list

argcount Specifies the number of attribute/value pairs in the argument list (*arglist*)

For a complete definition of RowColumn and its associated resources, see **XmRowColumn(3X)**.

Return Value

Returns the RowColumn widget ID.

Related Information

XmCascadeButton(3X), XmCascadeButtonGadget(3X), XmCreateOptionMenu(3X), XmCreatePopupMenu(3X), XmCreatePulldownMenu(3X), XmMenuShell(3X), and **XmRowColumn(3X)**.

XmCreatePushButton

Purpose

The PushButton widget creation function

AES Support Level

Full-use

Synopsis

#include <Xm/PushB.h>

Widget XmCreatePushButton (*parent, name, arglist, argcount*)
    Widget   *parent*;
    String   *name*;
    ArgList   *arglist*;
    Cardinal   *argcount*;

Description

XmCreatePushButton creates an instance of a PushButton widget and returns the associated widget ID.

parent   Specifies the parent widget ID

name   Specifies the name of the created widget

arglist   Specifies the argument list

argcount Specifies the number of attribute/value pairs in the argument list (*arglist*)

For a complete definition of PushButton and its associated resources, see **XmPushButton(3X)**.

Return Value

Returns the PushButton widget ID.

Related Information

XmPushButton(3X).

XmCreatePushButtonGadget

Purpose

The PushButtonGadget creation function

AES Support Level

Full-use

Synopsis

#include <Xm/PushBG.h>

Widget XmCreatePushButtonGadget (*parent, name, arglist, argcount*)
    Widget   *parent*;
    String   *name*;
    ArgList   *arglist*;
    Cardinal *argcount*;

Description

XmCreatePushButtonGadget creates an instance of a PushButtonGadget widget and returns the associated widget ID.

parent   Specifies the parent widget ID

name   Specifies the name of the created widget

arglist   Specifies the argument list

argcount Specifies the number of attribute/value pairs in the argument list (*arglist*)

For a complete definition of PushButtonGadget and its associated resources, see **XmPushButtonGadget(3X)**.

Return Value

Returns the PushButtonGadget widget ID.

Related Information

XmPushButtonGadget(3X).

XmCreateQuestionDialog

Purpose

The MessageBox QuestionDialog convenience creation function.

AES Support Level

Full-use

Synopsis

#include <Xm/MessageB.h>

Widget XmCreateQuestionDialog (*parent, name, arglist, argcount*)
    Widget   *parent*;
    String   *name*;
    ArgList   *arglist*;
    Cardinal   *argcount*;

Description

XmCreateQuestionDialog is a convenience creation function that creates a
DialogShell and an unmanaged MessageBox child of the DialogShell. A
QuestionDialog is used to get the answer to a question from the user. It

includes a symbol, a message, and three buttons. The default symbol is a question mark. The default button labels are **OK**, **Cancel**, and **Help**.

Use **XtManageChild** to pop up the QuestionDialog (passing the MessageBox as the widget parameter); use **XtUnmanageChild** to pop it down.

parent   Specifies the parent widget ID

name   Specifies the name of the created widget

arglist   Specifies the argument list

argcount Specifies the number of attribute/value pairs in the argument list (*arglist*)

For a complete definition of MessageBox and its associated resources, see **XmMessageBox(3X)**.

Return Value

Returns the MessageBox widget ID.

Related Information

XmMessageBox(3X).

XmCreateRadioBox

Purpose

A RowColumn widget convenience creation function

AES Support Level

Full-use

Synopsis

#include <Xm/RowColumn.h>

Widget XmCreateRadioBox (*parent, name, arglist, argcount*)
    Widget   *parent*;
    String   *name*;
    ArgList   *arglist*;
    Cardinal *argcount*;

Description

XmCreateRadioBox creates an instance of a RowColumn widget of type **XmWORK_AREA** and returns the associated widget ID. Typically, this is a composite widget that contains multiple ToggleButtonGadgets. The RadioBox arbitrates and ensures that at most one ToggleButtonGadget is on at any time.

The ToggleButtons are forced to have the resources **XmNindicatorType** set to **XmONE_OF_MANY** and **XmNvisibleWhenOff** set to True.

It is provided as a convenience function for creating RowColumn widgets.

parent   Specifies the parent widget ID

name   Specifies the name of the created widget

arglist   Specifies the argument list

argcount Specifies the number of attribute/value pairs in the argument list (*arglist*)

For a complete definition of RowColumn and its associated resources, see **XmRowColumn(3X)**.

Return Value

Returns the RowColumn widget ID.

Related Information

XmRowColumn(3X).

XmCreateRowColumn

Purpose

The RowColumn widget creation function

AES Support Level

Full-use

Synopsis

#include <Xm/RowColumn.h>

Widget XmCreateRowColumn (*parent, name, arglist, argcount*)
    Widget   *parent*;
    String   *name*;
    ArgList   *arglist*;
    Cardinal   *argcount*;

Description

XmCreateRowColumn creates an instance of a RowColumn widget and returns the associated widget ID. If **XmNrowColumnType** is not specified, then it is created with **XmWORK_AREA**, which is the default.

If this function is used to create a Popup Menu of type **XmMENU_POPUP** or a Pulldown Menu of type **XmMENU_PULLDOWN**, a MenuShell widget is not automatically created as the parent of the MenuPane. The application must first create the MenuShell by using either **XmCreateMenuShell** or the standard toolkit create function.

parent   Specifies the parent widget ID

name   Specifies the name of the created widget

arglist   Specifies the argument list

argcount Specifies the number of attribute/value pairs in the argument list (*arglist*)

For a complete definition of RowColumn and its associated resources, see **XmRowColumn(3X)**.

Return Value

Returns the RowColumn widget ID.

Related Information

XmCreateMenuShell(3X), **XmCreatePopupMenu(3X)**, **XmCreatePulldownMenu(3X)**, and **XmRowColumn(3X)**.

XmCreateScale

Purpose

The Scale widget creation function

AES Support Level

Full-use

Synopsis

#include <Xm/Scale.h>

Widget XmCreateScale (*parent, name, arglist, argcount*)
    Widget   *parent*;
    String   *name*;
    ArgList   *arglist*;
    Cardinal *argcount*;

Description

XmCreateScale creates an instance of a Scale widget and returns the associated widget ID.

parent   Specifies the parent widget ID

name   Specifies the name of the created widget

arglist   Specifies the argument list

argcount Specifies the number of attribute/value pairs in the argument list (*arglist*)

For a complete definition of Scale and its associated resources, see **XmScale(3X)**.

Return Value

Returns the Scale widget ID.

Related Information

XmScale(3X).

XmCreateScrollBar

Purpose

The ScrollBar widget creation function

AES Support Level

Full-use

Synopsis

#include <Xm/ScrollBar.h>

Widget XmCreateScrollBar (*parent, name, arglist, argcount*)
    Widget   *parent*;
    String   *name*;
    ArgList   *arglist*;
    Cardinal *argcount*;

Description

XmCreateScrollBar creates an instance of a ScrollBar widget and returns the associated widget ID.

parent   Specifies the parent widget ID

name   Specifies the name of the created widget

arglist   Specifies the argument list

argcount Specifies the number of attribute/value pairs in the argument list (*arglist*)

For a complete definition of ScrollBar and its associated resources, see **XmScrollBar(3X)**.

Return Value

Returns the ScrollBar widget ID.

Related Information

XmScrollBar(3X).

XmCreateScrolledList

Purpose

The List ScrolledList convenience creation function.

AES Support Level

Full-use

Synopsis

#include <Xm/List.h>

Widget XmCreateScrolledList (*parent, name, arglist, argcount*))
    Widget   *parent*;
    String   *name*;
    ArgList   *arglist*;
    Cardinal   *argcount*;

Description

XmCreateScrolledList creates an instance of a List widget that is contained within a ScrolledWindow. All ScrolledWindow subarea widgets are automatically created by this function. The ID returned by this function is that of the List widget. Use this ID for all normal List operations, as well as those that are relevant for the ScrolledList widget.

Other aspects of the appearance and behavior of the ScrolledList should be controlled by using the ScrolledWindow widget resources. For instance, an application writer who wishes to specify the *x,y* location of a ScrolledList within a larger manager should set the **XmNx** and **XmNy** resources of the ScrolledWindow rather than of the List widget.

To obtain the ID of the ScrolledWindow widget associated with the ScrolledList, use the Xt Intrinsics **XtParent** function. The name of the ScrolledWindow created by this function is formed by concatenating the letters **SW** onto the end of the *name* specified in the parameter list.

parent   Specifies the parent widget ID

name   Specifies the name of the created widget

arglist   Specifies the argument list

argcount Specifies the number of attribute/value pairs in the argument list
            (*arglist*)

For a complete definition of List and its associated resources, see **XmList(3X)**.

Return Value

Returns the List widget ID.

Related Information

XmList(3X) and **XmScrolledWindow(3X)**.

XmCreateScrolledText

Purpose

The Text ScrolledText convenience creation function.

AES Support Level

Full-use

Synopsis

#include <Xm/Text.h>

Widget XmCreateScrolledText (*parent, name, arglist, argcount*)
    Widget   *parent*;
    String   *name*;
    ArgList   *arglist*;
    Cardinal   *argcount*;

Description

XmCreateScrolledText creates an instance of a Text widget that is contained within a ScrolledWindow. All ScrolledWindow subarea widgets are automatically created by this function. The ID returned by this function is that of the Text widget. Use this ID for all normal Text operations, as well as those that are relevant for the ScrolledText widget.

The Text widget defaults to single-line text edit; therefore, no ScrollBars are displayed. The Text resource **XmNeditMode** must be set to **XmMULTI-LINE-EDIT** to display the ScrollBars.

Other aspects of the appearance and behavior of the ScrolledText should be controlled by using the ScrolledWindow widget resources. For instance, if an application writer wishes to specify the *x,y* location of a ScrolledText within a larger manager, set the **XmNx** and **XmNy** resources of the ScrolledWindow rather than of the Text widget.

To obtain the ID of the ScrolledWindow widget associated with the ScrolledText, use the Xt Intrinsics **XtParent** function. The name of the ScrolledWindow created by this function is formed by concatenating the letters **SW** onto the end of the *name* specified in the parameter list.

parent   Specifies the parent widget ID

name   Specifies the name of the created widget

arglist   Specifies the argument list

argcount Specifies the number of attribute/value pairs in the argument list (*arglist*)

For a complete definition of Text and its associated resources, see **XmText(3X)**.

Return Value

Returns the Text widget ID.

Related Information

XmScrolledWindow(3X) and **XmText(3X)**.

XmCreateScrolledWindow

Purpose

The ScrolledWindow widget creation function.

AES Support Level

Full-use

Synopsis

#include <Xm/ScrolledW.h>

Widget XmCreateScrolledWindow (*parent, name, arglist, argcount*)
    Widget   *parent*;
    String   *name*;
    ArgList   *arglist*;
    Cardinal *argcount*;

Description

XmCreateScrolledWindow creates an instance of a ScrolledWindow widget and returns the associated widget ID.

parent   Specifies the parent widget ID

name   Specifies the name of the created widget

arglist   Specifies the argument list

argcount Specifies the number of attribute/value pairs in the argument list
(*arglist*)

For a complete definition of ScrolledWindow and its associated resources,
see **XmScrolledWindow(3X)**.

Return Value

Returns the ScrolledWindow widget ID.

Related Information

XmScrolledWindow(3X).

XmCreateSelectionBox

Purpose

The SelectionBox widget creation function

AES Support Level

Full-use

Synopsis

#include <Xm/SelectioB.h>

Widget XmCreateSelectionBox (*parent, name, arglist, argcount*)
    Widget   *parent*;
    String   *name*;
    ArgList   *arglist*;
    Cardinal   *argcount*;

Description

XmCreateSelectionBox creates an unmanaged SelectionBox. A SelectionBox is used to get a selection from a list of alternatives from the user and includes the following:

- A scrolling list of alternatives

- An editable text field for the selected alternative
- Labels for the list and text field
- Three buttons

The default button labels are **OK**, **Cancel**, and **Help**. An **Apply** button is created unmanaged and may be explicitly managed as needed. One additional **WorkArea** child may be added to the SelectionBox after creation.

parent   Specifies the parent widget ID

name   Specifies the name of the created widget

arglist   Specifies the argument list

argcount Specifies the number of attribute/value pairs in the argument list (*arglist*)

For a complete definition of SelectionBox and its associated resources, see **XmSelectionBox(3X)**.

Return Value

Returns the SelectionBox widget ID.

Related Information

XmSelectionBox(3X)

XmCreateSelectionDialog

Purpose

The SelectionBox SelectionDialog convenience creation function.

AES Support Level

Full-use

Synopsis

#include <Xm/SelectioB.h>

Widget XmCreateSelectionDialog (*parent, name, arglist, argcount*)
 Widget *parent*;
 String *name*;
 ArgList *arglist*;
 Cardinal *argcount*;

Description

XmCreateSelectionDialog is a convenience creation function that creates a DialogShell and an unmanaged SelectionBox child of the DialogShell. A SelectionDialog offers the user a choice from a list of alternatives and gets a selection. It includes the following:

- A scrolling list of alternatives
- An editable text field for the selected alternative

- Labels for the text field
- Three buttons

The default button labels are **OK**, **Cancel**, and **Help**. One additional **WorkArea** child may be added to the SelectionBox after creation.

Use **XtManageChild** to pop up the SelectionDialog (passing the SelectionBox as the widget parameter); use **XtUnmanageChild** to pop it down.

parent   Specifies the parent widget ID

name   Specifies the name of the created widget

arglist   Specifies the argument list

argcount Specifies the number of attribute/value pairs in the argument list (*arglist*)

For a complete definition of SelectionBox and its associated resources, see **XmSelectionBox(3X)**.

Return Value

Returns the SelectionBox widget ID.

Related Information

XmSelectionBox(3X).

XmCreateSeparator

Purpose

The Separator widget creation function.

AES Support Level

Full-use

Synopsis

#include <Xm/Separator.h>

Widget XmCreateSeparator (*parent, name, arglist, argcount*)
    Widget   *parent*;
    String   *name*;
    ArgList   *arglist*;
    Cardinal   *argcount*;

Description

XmCreateSeparator creates an instance of a Separator widget and returns the associated widget ID.

parent   Specifies the parent widget ID

> *name*　　Specifies the name of the created widget
>
> *arglist*　　Specifies the argument list
>
> *argcount* Specifies the number of attribute/value pairs in the argument list (*arglist*)

For a complete definition of Separator and its associated resources, see **XmSeparator(3X)**.

Return Value

Returns the Separator widget ID.

Related Information

XmSeparator(3X).

XmCreateSeparatorGadget

Purpose

The SeparatorGadget creation function.

AES Support Level

Full-use

Synopsis

#include <Xm/SeparatoG.h>

Widget XmCreateSeparatorGadget (*parent, name, arglist, argcount*)
    Widget   *parent*;
    String   *name*;
    ArgList   *arglist*;
    Cardinal   *argcount*;

Description

XmCreateSeparatorGadget creates an instance of a SeparatorGadget widget and returns the associated widget ID.

parent   Specifies the parent widget ID

name   Specifies the name of the created widget

arglist   Specifies the argument list

argcount Specifies the number of attribute/value pairs in the argument list (*arglist*)

For a complete definition of SeparatorGadget and its associated resources, see **XmSeparatorGadget(3X)**.

Return Value

Returns the SeparatorGadget widget ID.

Related Information

XmSeparatorGadget(3X).

XmCreateText

Purpose

The Text widget creation function

AES Support Level

Full-use

Synopsis

#include <Xm/Text.h>

Widget XmCreateText (*parent, name, arglist, argcount*)
    Widget   *parent*;
    String   *name*;
    ArgList   *arglist*;
    Cardinal   *argcount*;

Description

XmCreateText creates an instance of a Text widget and returns the associated widget ID.

parent   Specifies the parent widget ID

name	Specifies the name of the created widget
arglist	Specifies the argument list
argcount	Specifies the number of attribute/value pairs in the argument list (*arglist*)

For a complete definition of Text and its associated resources, see **XmText(3X)**.

Return Value

Returns the Text widget ID.

Related Information

XmText(3X).

XmCreateToggleButton

Purpose

The ToggleButton widget creation function

AES Support Level

Full-use

Synopsis

#include <Xm/ToggleB.h>

Widget XmCreateToggleButton (*parent, name, arglist, argcount*)
    Widget   *parent*;
    String   *name*;
    ArgList   *arglist*;
    Cardinal *argcount*;

Description

XmCreateToggleButton creates an instance of a ToggleButton widget and returns the associated widget ID.

parent   Specifies the parent widget ID

name   Specifies the name of the created widget

arglist   Specifies the argument list

argcount Specifies the number of attribute/value pairs in the argument list (*arglist*)

For a complete definition of ToggleButton and its associated resources, see **XmToggleButton(3X)**.

Return Value

Returns the ToggleButton widget ID.

Related Information

XmToggleButton(3X).

XmCreateToggleButtonGadget

Purpose

The ToggleButtonGadget creation function.

AES Support Level

Full-use

Synopsis

#include <Xm/ToggleBG.h>

Widget XmCreateToggleButtonGadget (*parent, name, arglist, argcount*)
    Widget   *parent*;
    String   *name*;
    ArgList   *arglist*;
    Cardinal *argcount*;

Description

XmCreateToggleButtonGadget creates an instance of a ToggleButtonGadget and returns the associated widget ID.

parent   Specifies the parent widget ID

name   Specifies the name of the created widget

arglist   Specifies the argument list

argcount Specifies the number of attribute/value pairs in the argument list (*arglist*)

For a complete definition of ToggleButtonGadget and its associated resources, see **XmToggleButtonGadget(3X)**.

Return Value

Returns the ToggleButtonGadget widget ID.

Related Information

XmToggleButtonGadget(3X).

XmCreateWarningDialog

Purpose

A MessageBox WarningDialog convenience creation function.

AES Support Level

Full-use

Synopsis

#include <Xm/MessageB.h>

Widget XmCreateWarningDialog (*parent, name, arglist, argcount*)
    Widget   *parent*;
    String   *name*;
    ArgList   *arglist*;
    Cardinal   *argcount*;

Description

XmCreateWarningDialog is a convenience creation function that creates a DialogShell and an unmanaged MessageBox child of the DialogShell. A WarningDialog warns uses of action consequences and gives them a choice of resolutions. It includes a symbol, a message, and three buttons. The default symbol is an exclamation point. The default button labels are **OK**, **Cancel**, and **Help**.

Use **XtManageChild** to pop up the WarningDialog (passing the MessageBox as the widget parameter); use **XtUnmanageChild** to pop it down.

parent   Specifies the parent widget ID

name   Specifies the name of the created widget

arglist   Specifies the argument list

argcount Specifies the number of attribute/value pairs in the argument list (*arglist*)

For a complete definition of MessageBox and its associated resources, see **XmMessageBox(3X)**.

Return Value

Returns the MessageBox widget ID.

Related Information

XmMessageBox(3X).

XmCreateWorkingDialog

Purpose

The MessageBox WorkingDialog convenience creation function.

AES Support Level

Full-use

Synopsis

#include <Xm/MessageB.h>

Widget XmCreateWorkingDialog (*parent, name, arglist, argcount*)
    Widget   *parent*;
    String   *name*;
    ArgList   *arglist*;
    Cardinal   *argcount*;

Description

XmCreateWorkingDialog is a convenience creation function that creates a DialogShell and an unmanaged MessageBox child of the DialogShell. A WorkingDialog informs uses that there is a time-consuming operation in progress and allows them cancel the operation. It includes a symbol, a message, and three buttons. The default symbol is an hourglass. The default button labels are **OK**, **Cancel**, and **Help**.

Use **XtManageChild** to pop up the WorkingDialog (passing the MessageBox as the widget parameter); use **XtUnmanageChild** to pop it down.

parent   Specifies the parent widget ID

name   Specifies the name of the created widget

arglist   Specifies the argument list

argcount Specifies the number of attribute/value pairs in the argument list (*arglist*)

For a complete definition of MessageBox and its associated resources, see **XmMessageBox(3X)**.

Return Value

Returns the MessageBox widget ID.

Related Information

XmMessageBox(3X).

XmDestroyPixmap

Purpose

A pixmap caching function that removes a pixmap from the pixmap cache.

AES Support Level

Full-use

Synopsis

#include <Xm/Xm.h>

Boolean XmDestroyPixmap (*screen, pixmap*)
    Screen   * *screen*;
    Pixmap   *pixmap*;

Description

XmDestroyPixmap removes pixmaps that are no longer used. Pixmaps are completely freed only when there is no further reference to them.

screen   Specifies the display screen for which the pixmap was requested

pixmap   Specifies the pixmap to be destroyed

Return Value

Returns True when successful; returns False if there is no matching screen and pixmap in the pixmap cache.

Related Information

XmInstallImage(3X), **XmUninstallImage(3X)**, and **XmGetPixmap(3X)**.

XmDialogShell

Purpose

The DialogShell widget class

AES Support Level

Full-use

Synopsis

#include <Xm/DialogS.h>

Description

Modal and modeless dialogs use DialogShell as the Shell parent. DialogShell widgets cannot be iconified. Instead, all secondary DialogShell widgets associated with an ApplicationShell widget are iconified and de-iconified as a group with the primary widget.

The client indirectly manipulates DialogShell via the convenience interfaces during creation, and it can directly manipulate its BulletinBoard-derived child. Much of the functionality of DialogShell assumes that its child is a BulletinBoard subclass, although it can potentially stand alone.

Classes

DialogShell inherits behavior and resources from **Core**, **Composite**, **Shell**, **WMShell**, **VendorShell**, and **TransientShell** classes.

The class pointer is **xmDialogShellWidgetClass**.

The class name is **XmDialogShell**.

New Resources

DialogShell defines no new resources but overrides the **XmNdeleteResponse** resource in the **VendorShell** class.

Inherited Resources

DialogShell inherits behavior and resources from the following superclasses. For a complete description of each resource, refer to the man page for that superclass.

The following table defines a set of widget resources used by the programmer to specify data. The programmer can also set the resource values for the inherited classes to set attributes for this widget. To reference a resource by name or by class in a .Xdefaults file, remove the **XmN** or **XmC** prefix and use the remaining letters. To specify one of the defined values for a resource in a .Xdefaults file, remove the **Xm** prefix and use the remaining letters (in either lowercase or uppercase, but include any underscores between words). The codes in the access column indicate if the given resource can be set at creation time (**C**), set by using **XtSetValues** (**S**), retrieved by using **XtGetValues** (**G**), or is not applicable (**N/A**).

TransientShell Resource Set		
Name	**Default**	**Access**
Class	**Type**	
XmNsaveUnder	True	CSG
XmCSaveUnder	Boolean	
XmNtransient	True	CSG
XmCTransient	Boolean	

VendorShell Resource Set		
Name	**Default**	**Access**
Class	**Type**	
XmNdeleteResponse	XmUNMAP	CSG
XmCDeleteResponse	unsigned char	
XmNkeyboardFocusPolicy	XmEXPLICIT	CSG
XmCKeyboardFocusPolicy	unsigned char	
XmNmwmDecorations	-1	CSG
XmCMwmDecorations	int	
XmNmwmFunctions	-1	CSG
XmCMwmFunctions	int	
XmNmwmInputMode	-1	CSG
XmCMwmInputMode	int	
XmNmwmMenu	NULL	CSG
XmCMwmMenu	String	

WMShell Resource Set		
Name **Class**	**Default** **Type**	**Access**
XmNheightInc XmCHeightInc	-1 int	CSG
XmNiconMask XmCIconMask	NULL Pixmap	CSG
XmNiconPixmap XmCIconPixmap	NULL Pixmap	CSG
XmNiconWindow XmCIconWindow	NULL Window	CSG
XmNiconX XmCIconX	-1 int	CSG
XmNiconY XmCIconY	-1 int	CSG
XmNinitialState XmCInitialState	1 int	CSG
XmNinput XmCInput	True Boolean	CSG
XmNmaxAspectX XmCMaxAspectX	-1 int	CSG
XmNmaxAspectY XmCMaxAspectY	-1 int	CSG
XmNmaxHeight XmCMaxHeight	-1 int	CSG
XmNmaxWidth XmCMaxWidth	-1 int	CSG
XmNminAspectX XmCMinAspectX	-1 int	CSG
XmNminAspectY XmCMinAspectY	-1 int	CSG

Name	Default	Access
Class	Type	
XmNminHeight	-1	CSG
XmCMinHeight	int	
XmNminWidth	-1	CSG
XmCMinWidth	int	
XmNtitle	NULL	CSG
XmCTitle	char *	
XmNtransient	False	CSG
XmCTransient	Boolean	
XmNwaitForWm	True	CSG
XmCWaitForWm	Boolean	
XmNwidthInc	-1	CSG
XmCWidthInc	int	
XmNwindowGroup	None	CSG
XmCWindowGroup	XID	
XmNwmTimeout	fivesecond	CSG
XmCWmTimeout	int	

Shell Resource Set		
Name	**Default**	**Access**
Class	**Type**	
XmNallowShellResize	False	CSG
XmCAllowShellResize	Boolean	
XmNcreatePopupChildProc	NULL	CSG
XmCCreatePopupChildProc	XmCreatePopupChildProc	
XmNgeometry	NULL	CSG
XmCGeometry	String	
XmNoverrideRedirect	False	CSG
XmCOverrideRedirect	Boolean	
XmNpopdownCallback	NULL	C
XmCCallback	XtCallbackList	
XmNpopupCallback	NULL	C
XmCCallback	XtCallbackList	
XmNsaveUnder	False	CSG
XmCSaveUnder	Boolean	

Composite Resource Set		
Name	**Default**	**Access**
Class	**Type**	
XmNinsertPosition	NULL	CSG
XmCInsertPosition	XmRFunction	

Core Resource Set		
Name	**Default**	**Access**
Class	**Type**	
XmNaccelerators	NULL	CSG
XmCAccelerators	XtTranslations	
XmNancestorSensitive	ShellAncestorSensitive	G
XmCSensitive	Boolean	
XmNbackground	White	CSG
XmCBackground	Pixel	
XmNbackgroundPixmap	XmUNSPECIFIED_PIXMAP	CSG
XmCPixmap	Pixmap	
XmNborderColor	Black	CSG
XmCBorderColor	Pixel	
XmNborderPixmap	XmUNSPECIFIED_PIXMAP	CSG
XmCPixmap	Pixmap	
XmNborderWidth	1	CSG
XmCBorderWidth	Dimension	
XmNcolormap	ShellColormap	CG
XmCColormap	Colormap	
XmNdepth	ShellDepth	CG
XmCDepth	int	
XmNdestroyCallback	NULL	C
XmCCallback	XtCallbackList	
XmNheight	0	CSG
XmCHeight	Dimension	
XmNmappedWhenManaged	True	CSG
XmCMappedWhenManaged	Boolean	
XmNscreen	XtCopyScreen	CG
XmCScreen	Pointer	
XmNsensitive	True	CSG
XmCSensitive	Boolean	

Name	Default	Access
Class	Type	
XmNtranslations	NULL	CSG
XmCTranslations	XtTranslations	
XmNwidth	0	CSG
XmCWidth	Dimension	
XmNx	0	CSG
XmCPosition	Position	
XmNy	0	CSG
XmCPosition	Position	

Related Information

Composite(3X), Core(3X), Shell(3X), TransientShell(3X), WMShell(3X), VendorShell(3X), and **XmCreateDialogShell(3X).**

XmDrawingArea

Purpose

The DrawingArea widget class

AES Support Level

Full-use

Synopsis

#include <Xm/DrawingA.h>

Description

DrawingArea is an empty widget that is easily adaptable to a variety of purposes. It does no drawing and defines no behavior except for invoking callbacks. Callbacks notify the application when graphics need to be drawn (exposure events or widget resize) and when the widget receives input from the keyboard or mouse. Applications are responsible for defining appearance and behavior as needed in response to DrawingArea callbacks.

DrawingArea is also a composite widget and subclass of **XmManager** that supports minimal geometry management for multiple widget or gadget children.

Classes

DrawingArea inherits behavior and resources from the **Core**, **Composite**, **Constraint**, and **XmManager** classes.

The class pointer is **xmDrawingAreaWidgetClass**.

The class name is **XmDrawingArea**.

New Resources

The following table defines a set of widget resources used by the programmer to specify data. The programmer can also set the resource values for the inherited classes to set attributes for this widget. To reference a resource by name or by class in a .Xdefaults file, remove the **XmN** or **XmC** prefix and use the remaining letters. To specify one of the defined values for a resource in a .Xdefaults file, remove the **Xm** prefix and use the remaining letters (in either lowercase or uppercase, but include any underscores between words). The codes in the access column indicate if the given resource can be set at creation time (**C**), set by using **XtSetValues** (**S**), retrieved by using **XtGetValues** (**G**), or is not applicable (**N/A**).

XmDrawingArea Resource Set		
Name **Class**	**Default** **Type**	**Access**
XmNexposeCallback XmCCallback	NULL XtCallbackList	C
XmNinputCallback XmCCallback	NULL XtCallbackList	C
XmNmarginHeight XmCMarginHeight	10 short	CSG
XmNmarginWidth XmCMarginWidth	10 short	CSG
XmNresizeCallback XmCCallback	NULL XtCallbackList	C
XmNresizePolicy XmCResizePolicy	XmRESIZE_ANY unsigned char	CSG

XmNexposeCallback

Specifies the list of callbacks that is called when DrawingArea receives an exposure event. The callback reason is **XmCR_EXPOSE**. The callback structure also includes the exposure event.

XmNinputCallback

Specifies the list of callbacks that is called when the DrawingArea receives a keyboard or mouse event (key or button, up or down). The callback reason is **XmCR_INPUT**. The callback structure also includes the input event.

XmNmarginHeight

Specifies the minimum spacing in pixels between the top or bottom edge of DrawingArea and any child widget.

XmNmarginWidth

Specifies the minimum spacing in pixels between the left or right edge of DrawingArea and any child widget.

XmNresizeCallback

> Specifies the list of callbacks that is called when the DrawingArea is resized. The callback reason is **XmCR_RESIZE**.

XmNresizePolicy

> Controls the policy for resizing DrawingArea widgets. Possible values include **XmRESIZE_NONE** (fixed size), **XmRESIZE_ANY** (shrink or grow as needed), and **XmRESIZE_GROW** (grow only).

Inherited Resources

DrawingArea inherits behavior and resources from the following superclasses. For a complete description of each resource, refer to the man page for that superclass.

XmManager Resource Set		

Name
    Class
	Default
	    Type
		Access

XmNbottomShadowColor
    XmCForeground
	dynamic
	    Pixel
		CSG

XmNbottomShadowPixmap
    XmCBottomShadowPixmap
	XmUNSPECIFIED_PIXMAP
	    Pixmap
		CSG

XmNforeground
    XmCForeground
	dynamic
	    Pixel
		CSG

XmNhelpCallback
    XmCCallback
	NULL
	    XtCallbackList
		C

XmNhighlightColor
    XmCForeground
	Black
	    Pixel
		CSG

XmNhighlightPixmap
    XmCHighlightPixmap
	dynamic
	    Pixmap
		CSG

XmNshadowThickness
    XmCShadowThickness
	0
	    short
		CSG

XmNtopShadowColor
    XmCBackground
	dynamic
	    Pixel
		CSG

XmNtopShadowPixmap
    XmCTopShadowPixmap
	XmUNSPECIFIED_PIXMAP
	    Pixmap
		CSG

XmNuserData
    XmCUserData
	NULL
	    caddr_t
		CSG

Composite Resource Set		

Name
    Class
	Default
	    Type
		Access

XmNinsertPosition
    XmCInsertPosition
	NULL
	    XmRFunction
		CSG

Core Resource Set		
Name	**Default**	**Access**
Class	**Type**	
XmNaccelerators	NULL	CSG
XmCAccelerators	XtTranslations	
XmNancestorSensitive	True	G
XmCSensitive	Boolean	
XmNbackground	dynamic	CSG
XmCBackground	Pixel	
XmNbackgroundPixmap	XmUNSPECIFIED_PIXMAP	CSG
XmCPixmap	Pixmap	
XmNborderColor	Black	CSG
XmCBorderColor	Pixel	
XmNborderPixmap	XmUNSPECIFIED_PIXMAP	CSG
XmCPixmap	Pixmap	
XmNborderWidth	0	CSG
XmCBorderWidth	Dimension	
XmNcolormap	XtCopyFromParent	CG
XmCColormap	Colormap	
XmNdepth	XtCopyFromParent	CG
XmCDepth	int	
XmNdestroyCallback	NULL	C
XmCCallback	XtCallbackList	
XmNheight	0	CSG
XmCHeight	Dimension	
XmNmappedWhenManaged	True	CSG
XmCMappedWhenManaged	Boolean	
XmNscreen	XtCopyScreen	CG
XmCScreen	Pointer	
XmNsensitive	True	CSG
XmCSensitive	Boolean	

Name	Default	Access
Class	Type	
XmNtranslations	NULL	CSG
XmCTranslations	XtTranslations	
XmNwidth	0	CSG
XmCWidth	Dimension	
XmNx	0	CSG
XmCPosition	Position	
XmNy	0	CSG
XmCPosition	Position	

Callback Information

The following structure is returned with each callback.

typedef struct
{
   int   *reason*;
  XEvent   * *event*;
  Window   *window*;
} **XmDrawingAreaCallbackStruct**;

reason   Indicates why the callback was invoked

event   Points to the **XEvent** that triggered the callback

window   Is set to the widget window

Behavior

DrawingArea behavior is summarized below.

\<KeyDown\>, \<KeyUp\>, \<BtnDown\>, \<BtnUp\>:
　　The callbacks for **XmNinputCallback** are called when a keyboard key or mouse button is pressed or released.

\<Expose\>:　The callbacks for **XmNexposeCallback** are called when the widget receives an exposure event.

\<Widget Resize\>:
　　The callbacks for **XmNresizeCallback** are called when the widget is resized.

Default Translations

The following are DrawingArea's default translations:

\<Btn1Down\>:	**Arm()**
\<Btn1Up\>:	**Activate()**
\<EnterWindow\>:	**Enter()**
\<FocusIn\>:	**FocusIn()**

Keyboard Traversal

For information on keyboard traversal, see the man page for **XmManager(3X)** and its sections on behavior and default translations.

Related Information

Composite(3X), Constraint(3X), Core(3X), XmCreateDrawingArea(3X), and **XmManager(3X)**.

XmDrawnButton

Purpose

The DrawnButton widget class

AES Support Level

Full-use

Synopsis

#include <Xm/DrawnB.h>

Description

The DrawnButton widget consists of an empty widget window surrounded by a shadow border. It provides the application developer with a graphics area that can have PushButton input semantics.

Callback types are defined for widget exposure and resize to allow the application to redraw or reposition its graphics. If the DrawnButton widget has a highlight and shadow thickness, the application should not draw in that area. To avoid drawing in the highlight and shadow area, create the graphics context with a clipping rectangle for drawing in the widget. The clipping rectangle should take into account the size of the widget's highlight thickness and shadow.

Classes

DrawnButton inherits behavior and resources from **Core**, **XmPrimitive**, and **XmLabel** Classes.

The class pointer is **xmDrawnButtonWidgetClass**.

The class name is **XmDrawnButton**.

New Resources

The following table defines a set of widget resources used by the programmer to specify data. The programmer can also set the resource values for the inherited classes to set attributes for this widget. To reference a resource by name or by class in a .Xdefaults file, remove the **XmN** or **XmC** prefix and use the remaining letters. To specify one of the defined values for a resource in a .Xdefaults file, remove the **Xm** prefix and use the remaining letters (in either lowercase or uppercase, but include any underscores between words). The codes in the access column indicate if the given resource can be set at creation time (**C**), set by using **XtSetValues** (**S**), retrieved by using **XtGetValues** (**G**), or is not applicable (**N/A**).

XmDrawnButton Resource Set		
Name **Class**	**Default** **Type**	**Access**
XmNactivateCallback XmCCallback	NULL XtCallbackList	C
XmNarmCallback XmCCallback	NULL XtCallbackList	C
XmNdisarmCallback XmCCallback	NULL XtCallbackList	C
XmNexposeCallback XmCCallback	NULL XtCallbackList	C
XmNpushButtonEnabled XmCPushButtonEnabled	False Boolean	CSG
XmNresizeCallback XmCCallback	NULL XtCallbackList	C
XmNshadowType XmCShadowType	XmSHADOW_ETCHED_IN unsigned char	CSG

XmNactivateCallback

Specifies the list of callbacks that is called when the widget becomes selected. The reason sent by the callback is **XmCR_ACTIVATE**.

XmNarmCallback

Specifies the list of callbacks that is called when the widget becomes armed. The reason sent by the callback is **XmCR_ARM**.

XmNdisarmCallback

Specifies the list of callbacks that is called when the widget becomes disarmed. The reason sent by the callback is **XmCR_DISARM**.

XmNexposeCallback

Specifies the list of callbacks that is called when the widget receives an exposure event. The reason sent by the callback is **XmCR_EXPOSE**.

XmNpushButtonEnabled
  Enables or disables the three-dimensional shadow drawing as in PushButton.

XmNresizeCallback
  Specifies the list of callbacks that is called when the widget receives a resize event. The reason sent by the callback is **XmCR_RESIZE**. The event returned for this callback is NULL.

XmNshadowType
  Describes the drawing style for the DrawnButton. This resource can have the following values:

- **XmSHADOW_IN** — draws the DrawnButton that the shadow appears inset. This means that the bottom shadow visuals and top shadow visuals are reversed.

- **XmSHADOW_OUT** — draws the DrawnButton that the shadow appears outset.

- **XmSHADOW_ETCHED_IN** — draws the DrawnButton using a double line. This gives the effect of a line etched into the window. The thickness of the double line is equal to the value of **XmNshadowThickness**.

- **XmSHADOW_ETCHED_OUT** — draws the DrawnButton using a double line. This gives the effect of a line coming out of the window. The thickness of the double line is equal to the value of **XmNshadowThickness**.

Inherited Resources

DrawnButton inherits behavior and resources from the following superclasses. For a complete description of each resource, refer to the man page for that superclass.

XmLabel Resource Set		

Name
    Class
	Default
	        Type
		Access

XmNaccelerator
    XmCAccelerator
	NULL
	        String
		CSG

XmNacceleratorText
    XmCAcceleratorText
	NULL
	        XmString
		CSG

XmNalignment
    XmCAlignment
	XmALIGNMENT_CENTER
	        unsigned char
		CSG

XmNfontList
    XmCFontList
	"Fixed"
	        XmFontList
		CSG

XmNlabelInsensitivePixmap
    XmCLabelInsensitivePixmap
	XmUNSPECIFIED_PIXMAP
	        Pixmap
		CSG

XmNlabelPixmap
    XmCPixmap
	XmUNSPECIFIED_PIXMAP
	        Pixmap
		CSG

XmNlabelString
    XmCXmString
	'\0'
	        XmString
		CSG

XmNlabelType
    XmCLabelType
	XmSTRING
	        unsigned char
		CSG

XmNmarginBottom
    XmCMarginBottom
	0
	        short
		CSG

XmNmarginHeight
    XmCMarginHeight
	dynamic
	        short
		CSG

XmNmarginLeft
    XmCMarginLeft
	0
	        short
		CSG

XmNmarginRight
    XmCMarginRight
	0
	        short
		CSG

XmNmarginTop
    XmCMarginTop
	0
	        short
		CSG

XmNmarginWidth
    XmCMarginWidth
	dynamic
	        short
		CSG

Name	Default	Access
Class	Type	
XmNmnemonic	'\0'	CSG
XmCMnemonic	char	
XmNrecomputeSize	True	CSG
XmCRecomputeSize	Boolean	

XmPrimitive Resource Set		
Name	Default	Access
Class	Type	
XmNbottomShadowColor	dynamic	CSG
XmCForeground	Pixel	
XmNbottomShadowPixmap	XmUNSPECIFIED_PIXMAP	CSG
XmCBottomShadowPixmap	Pixmap	
XmNforeground	dynamic	CSG
XmCForeground	Pixel	
XmNhelpCallback	NULL	C
XmCCallback	XtCallbackList	
XmNhighlightColor	Black	CSG
XmCForeground	Pixel	
XmNhighlightOnEnter	False	CSG
XmCHighlightOnEnter	Boolean	
XmNhighlightPixmap	dynamic	CSG
XmCHighlightPixmap	Pixmap	
XmNhighlightThickness	0	CSG
XmCHighlightThickness	short	
XmNshadowThickness	2	CSG
XmCShadowThickness	short	
XmNtopShadowColor	dynamic	CSG
XmCBackground	Pixel	

Name	Default	Access
Class	Type	
XmNtopShadowPixmap	XmUNSPECIFIED_PIXMAP	CSG
XmCTopShadowPixmap	Pixmap	
XmNtraversalOn	False	CSG
XmCTraversalOn	Boolean	
XmNuserData	NULL	CSG
XmCUserData	caddr_t	

Core Resource Set		
Name	Default	Access
Class	Type	
XmNaccelerators	NULL	CSG
XmCAccelerators	XtTranslations	
XmNancestorSensitive	True	G
XmCSensitive	Boolean	
XmNbackground	dynamic	CSG
XmCBackground	Pixel	
XmNbackgroundPixmap	XmUNSPECIFIED_PIXMAP	CSG
XmCPixmap	Pixmap	
XmNborderColor	Black	CSG
XmCBorderColor	Pixel	
XmNborderPixmap	XmUNSPECIFIED_PIXMAP	CSG
XmCPixmap	Pixmap	
XmNborderWidth	0	CSG
XmCBorderWidth	Dimension	
XmNcolormap	XtCopyFromParent	CG
XmCColormap	Colormap	
XmNdepth	XtCopyFromParent	CG
XmCDepth	int	

Name	Default	Access
Class	Type	
XmNdestroyCallback	NULL	C
XmCCallback	XtCallbackList	
XmNheight	0	CSG
XmCHeight	Dimension	
XmNmappedWhenManaged	True	CSG
XmCMappedWhenManaged	Boolean	
XmNscreen	XtCopyScreen	CG
XmCScreen	Pointer	
XmNsensitive	True	CSG
XmCSensitive	Boolean	
XmNtranslations	NULL	CSG
XmCTranslations	XtTranslations	
XmNwidth	0	CSG
XmCWidth	Dimension	
XmNx	0	CSG
XmCPosition	Position	
XmNy	0	CSG
XmCPosition	Position	

Callback Information

The following structure is returned with each callback:

typedef struct
{
    int   *reason*;
    XEvent * *event*;
    Window *window*;
} **XmDrawnButtonCallbackStruct;**

reason   Indicates why the callback was invoked.

event   Points to the **XEvent** that triggered the callback. NULL is returned by the *event* for **XmNresizeCallback**. This event will be NULL for the **XmNactivateCallback** if the callback was triggered when Primitive's resource **XmNtraversalOn** was True or if the callback was accessed through the **ArmAndActivate** action routine.

window Is set to the window ID in which the event occurred.

Behavior

<Btn1Down>:
    A selection on the DrawnButton causes its shadow to be drawn in the selected state if the **XmNpushButtonEnabled** flag is set to **True**. The callbacks for **XmNarmCallback** are also called.

<Btn1Up>: If **<Btn1Up>** occurs when the pointer is within the DrawnButton, the shadows are redrawn in the unselected state if the **XmNpushButtonEnabled** flag is set to True. The callbacks for **XmNactivateCallback** are called, followed by callbacks for **XmdisarmCallback**.

    If **<Btn1Up>** occurs when the pointer is outside the DrawnButton, the callbacks for **XmNdisarmCallback** are called.

<Leave Window>:

If the mouse button is pressed and the cursor leaves the DrawnButtons window, the shadow is redrawn to its unselected state if the **XmNpushButtonEnabled** flag is set to True.

<Enter Window>:

If the mouse button is pressed and the cursor reenters the DrawnButton window, the shadow is drawn in the same manner as when the button was first selected.

Default Translations

<Btn1Down>:	**Arm()**
<Btn1Up>:	**Activate()**
	Disarm()
<Key>Return:	**ArmAndActivate()**
<Key>space:	**ArmAndActivate()**
<EnterWindow>:	**Enter()**
<LeaveWindow>:	**Leave()**

Keyboard Traversal

For information on keyboard traversal, see the man page for **XmPrimitive(3X)** and its sections on behavior and default translations.

Related Information

Core(3X), **XmCreateDrawnButton**, **XmLabel(3X)**, **XmPrimitive(3X)**, **XmPushButton**, and **XmSeparator(3X)**.

XmFileSelectionBox

Purpose

The FileSelectionBox widget class

AES Support Level

Full-use

Synopsis

#include <Xm/FileSB.h>

Description

FileSelectionBox traverses through directories, views the files in them, and then selects a file.

A FileSelectionBox has four main areas:

- A directory mask that includes a filter label and a directory-mask input field used to specify the directory that is to be examined
- A scrollable list of filenames
- A text input field for directly typing in a filename
- A group of PushButtons, labeled **OK**, **Filter**, **Cancel**, and **Help**

One additional **WorkArea** child may be added to the FileSelectionBox after creation.

The user can select a file by scrolling through the list of filenames and selecting the desired file or by entering the filename directly into the text edit area. Selecting a file from the list will cause that filename to appear in the file selection text edit area.

The user may select a new file as many times as desired. The application is not notified until the user selects the **OK** PushButton or presses the return key while the selection text edit area has the keyboard focus.

FileSelectionBox initiates a file search when any of the following occurs:

- The function **XtSetValues** is used to change the directory mask.

- The user activates the **Filter** PushButton.

- The application calls **XmFileSelectionDoSearch**.

- The user presses the return key while the directory mask input field has the keyboard focus.

This may be useful when an application creates a new file and wants to incorporate it into the file list.

Classes

FileSelectionBox inherits behavior and resources from **Core**, **Composite**, **Constraint**, **XmManager**, **XmBulletinBoard**, and **XmSelectionBox**.

The class pointer is **xmFileSelectionBoxWidgetClass**. The class name is **XmFileSelectionBox**.

New Resources

The following table defines a set of widget resources used by the programmer to specify data. The programmer can also set the resource values for the inherited classes to set attributes for this widget. To reference a resource by name or by class in a .Xdefaults file, remove the **XmN** or **XmC** prefix and use the remaining letters. To specify one of the defined values for a resource in a .Xdefaults file, remove the **Xm** prefix and use the remaining letters (in either lowercase or uppercase, but include any underscores between words). The codes in the access column indicate if the given resource can be set at creation time (**C**), set by using **XtSetValues** (**S**), retrieved by using **XtGetValues** (**G**), or is not applicable (**N/A**).

XmFileSelectionBox Resource Set		
Name **Class**	**Default** **Type**	**Access**
XmNdirMask XmCDirMask	"*" XmString	CSG
XmNdirSpec XmCDirSpec	NULL XmString	CSG
XmNfileSearchProc XmCFileSearchProc	see below XtProc	CSG
XmNfilterLabelString XmCFilterLabelString	"File Filter" XmString	CSG
XmNlistUpdated XmCListUpdated	True Boolean	CSG

XmNdirMask

Specifies the directory mask used in determining the files to be displayed in the list box.

XmNdirSpec

Specifies the full file specification. This resource overrides the **XmNtextString** resource in SelectionBox.

XmNfileSearchProc

Specifies a directory search procedure to replace the default file search procedure. FileSelectionBox's default file-search procedure fulfills the needs of most applications. Because it is impossible to cover the requirements of all applications, you can replace the default search procedure.

The file search procedure is called with two arguments: the **XmFileSelectionCallbackStruct** structure and the FileSelectionBox widget. The callback structure contains all required information to conduct a directory search, including the current file search mask. Once called, the search routine must generate a new list of files and update the file selection widget by using **XtSetValues**.

The following attributes must be set: **XmNitems**, **XmNitemsCount**, **XmNlistUpdated**, and **XmNdirSpec**. Set **XmNitems** to the new list of files. If there are no files, set this attribute to NULL. This sets the **XmNitems** attribute associated with SelectionBox.

If there are no files, set **XmNitemsCount** to zero. This sets the **XmNitemsCount** associated with SelectionBox. Always set **XmNlistUpdated** to True when you use a search procedure to update the file list, even if there are no files. Setting **XmNdirSpec** is optional, but recommended. Set this attribute to the full file specification of the directory searched. The directory specification is displayed above the list box.

XmNfilterLabelString
Specifies the string value for the label located above the **DIR_MASK** text entry field.

XmNlistUpdated
Specifies an attribute that is set only by the file search procedure. Set to True, if the file list has been updated.

Inherited Resources

FileSelectionBox inherits behavior and resources from the following superclasses. For a complete description of each resource, refer to the man page for that superclass.

XmSelectionBox Resource Set		
Name	**Default**	**Access**
Class	**Type**	
XmNapplyCallback	NULL	C
XmCCallback	XtCallbackList	
XmNapplyLabelString	"Filter"	CSG
XmCApplyLabelString	XmString	
XmNcancelCallback	NULL	C
XmCCallback	XtCallbackList	
XmNcancelLabelString	"Cancel"	CSG
XmCXmString	XmString	
XmNdialogType	XmDIALOG_FILE_SELECTION	CG
XmCDialogType	unsigned char	
XmNhelpLabelString	"Help"	CSG
XmCXmString	XmString	
XmNlistItemCount	0	CSG
XmCItemCount	int	
XmNlistItems	NULL	CSG
XmCItems	XmStringList	
XmNlistLabelString	"Files"	CSG
XmCXmString	XmString	
XmNlistVisibleItemCount	8	CSG
XmCVisibleItemCount	int	
XmNminimizeButtons	False	CSG
XmCMinimizeButtons	Boolean	
XmNmustMatch	False	CSG
XmCMustMatch	Boolean	
XmNnoMatchCallback	NULL	C
XmCCallback	XtCallbackList	
XmNokCallback	NULL	C
XmCCallback	XtCallbackList	

Name Class	Default Type	Access

XmNokLabelString
    XmCXmString
	"OK"
	    XmString
		CSG

XmNselectionLabelString
    XmCXmString
	"Selection"
	    XmString
		CSG

XmNtextAccelerators
    XmCTextAccelerators
	see description
	    XtTranslations
		C

XmNtextColumns
    XmCTextColumns
	31
	    int
		CSG

XmNtextString
    XmCTextString
	NULL
	    XmString
		CSG

XmBulletinBoard Resource Set		

Name
    Class
	Default
	    Type
		Access

XmNallowOverlap
    XmCAllowOverlap
	True
	    Boolean
		CSG

XmNautoUnmanage
    XmCAutoUnmanage
	False
	    Boolean
		CSG

XmNbuttonFontList
    XmCButtonFontList
	NULL
	    XmFontList
		CSG

XmNcancelButton
    XmCWidget
	Cancel button
	    Widget
		SG

XmNdefaultButton
    XmCWidget
	OK button
	    Widget
		SG

XmNdefaultPosition
    XmCDefaultPosition
	True
	    Boolean
		CSG

XmNdialogStyle
    XmCDialogStyle
	dynamic
	    unsigned char
		CSG

XmNdialogTitle
    XmCXmString
	NULL
	    XmString
		CSG

XmNfocusCallback
    XmCCallback
	NULL
	    XtCallbackList
		C

XmNlabelFontList
    XmCLabelFontList
	NULL
	    XmFontList
		CSG

XmNmapCallback
    XmCCallback
	NULL
	    XtCallbackList
		C

XmNmarginHeight
    XmCMarginHeight
	10
	    short
		CSG

XmNmarginWidth
    XmCMarginWidth
	10
	    short
		CSG

XmNnoResize
    XmCNoResize
	False
	    Boolean
		CSG

Name Class	Default Type	Access

XmNresizePolicy
  XmCResizePolicy
	XmRESIZE_ANY
	  unsigned char
		CSG

XmNshadowType
  XmCShadowType
	XmSHADOW_OUT
	  unsigned char
		CSG

XmNtextFontList
  XmCTextFontList
	NULL
	  XmFontList
		CSG

XmNtextTranslations
  XmCTranslations
	NULL
	  XtTranslations
		C

XmNunmapCallback
  XmCCallback
	NULL
	  XtCallbackList
		C

XmManager Resource Set		
Name **Class**	**Default** **Type**	**Access**
XmNbottomShadowColor XmCForeground	dynamic Pixel	CSG
XmNbottomShadowPixmap XmCBottomShadowPixmap	XmUNSPECIFIED_PIXMAP Pixmap	CSG
XmNforeground XmCForeground	dynamic Pixel	CSG
XmNhelpCallback XmCCallback	NULL XtCallbackList	C
XmNhighlightColor XmCForeground	Black Pixel	CSG
XmNhighlightPixmap XmCHighlightPixmap	dynamic Pixmap	CSG
XmNshadowThickness XmCShadowThickness	dynamic short	CSG
XmNtopShadowColor XmCBackground	dynamic Pixel	CSG
XmNtopShadowPixmap XmCTopShadowPixmap	XmUNSPECIFIED_PIXMAP Pixmap	CSG
XmNuserData XmCUserData	NULL caddr_t	CSG

Composite Resource Set		
Name **Class**	**Default** **Type**	**Access**
XmNinsertPosition XmCInsertPosition	NULL XmRFunction	CSG

Core Resource Set		
Name	**Default**	**Access**
Class	**Type**	
XmNaccelerators	NULL	CSG
XmCAccelerators	XtTranslations	
XmNancestorSensitive	True	G
XmCSensitive	Boolean	
XmNbackground	dynamic	CSG
XmCBackground	Pixel	
XmNbackgroundPixmap	XmUNSPECIFIED_PIXMAP	CSG
XmCPixmap	Pixmap	
XmNborderColor	Black	CSG
XmCBorderColor	Pixel	
XmNborderPixmap	XmUNSPECIFIED_PIXMAP	CSG
XmCPixmap	Pixmap	
XmNborderWidth	0	CSG
XmCBorderWidth	Dimension	
XmNcolormap	XtCopyFromParent	CG
XmCColormap	Colormap	
XmNdepth	XtCopyFromParent	CG
XmCDepth	int	
XmNdestroyCallback	NULL	C
XmCCallback	XtCallbackList	
XmNheight	0	CSG
XmCHeight	Dimension	
XmNmappedWhenManaged	True	CSG
XmCMappedWhenManaged	Boolean	
XmNscreen	XtCopyScreen	CG
XmCScreen	Pointer	
XmNsensitive	True	CSG
XmCSensitive	Boolean	

Name	Default	Access
Class	Type	
XmNtranslations	NULL	CSG
XmCTranslations	XtTranslations	
XmNwidth	0	CSG
XmCWidth	Dimension	
XmNx	0	CSG
XmCPosition	Position	
XmNy	0	CSG
XmCPosition	Position	

Callback Information

The following structure is returned with each callback:

```
typedef struct
{
    int         reason;
    XEvent      * event;
    XmString    value;
    int         length;
    XmString    mask;
    int         mask_length;
} XmFileSelectionBoxCallbackStruct;
```

reason   Indicates why the callback was invoked

event   Points to the **XEvent** that triggered the callback

value   Specifies the value of the current **XmNdirSpec**

length   Specifies the number of bytes of the structure pointed to by *value mask*   Specifies the current value of **XmNdirMask**

mask_length Specifies the number of bytes of the structure pointed to by *mask*

Behavior

FileSelectionBox inherits behavior from SelectionBox and BulletinBoard and also has the following behavior.

<Apply Button Activated>:
> A new file search begins when the apply button is activated.

Default Translations

FileSelectionBox inherits SelectionBox's default translations. See the man page for **XmSelectionBox(3X)**.

Default Accelerators

The following are the default accelerator translations added to descendants of a BulletinBoard if the parent of the BulletinBoard is a DialogShell:

#override
<Key>F1:   **Help()**
<Key>Return: **Return()**
<Key>KP_Enter: **Return()**

Default Text Accelerators

The following are the default text accelerators inherited from SelectionBox:

#override
<Key>Up:	**UpOrDown(0)**
<Key>Down:	**UpOrDown(1)**
<Key>F1:	**Help()**
<Key>Return:	**Return()**
<Key>KP_Enter:	**Return()**

Keyboard Traversal

For information on keyboard traversal, see the man page for **XmManager(3X)** and its sections on behavior and default translations.

Related Information

Composite(3X), Constraint(3X), Core(3X), XmBulletinBoard(3X), XmCreateFileSelectionBox(3X), XmCreateFileSelectionDialog(3X), XmFileSelectionBoxGetChild(3X), XmFileSelectionDoSearch(3X), XmManager(3X), and XmSelectionBox(3X),

XmFileSelectionBoxGetChild

Purpose

A FileSelectionBox function that is used to access a component.

AES Support Level

Full-use

Synopsis

#include <Xm/FileSB.h>

Widget XmFileSelectionBoxGetChild (*widget, child*)
    Widget   *widget*;
    unsigned char*child*;

Description

XmFileSelectionBoxGetChild is used to access a component within a FileSelectionBox. The parameters given to the function are the FileSelectionBox widget and a value indicating which child to access.

widget   Specifies the FileSelectionBox widget ID.

child   Specifies a component within the FileSelectionBox. The following are legal values for this parameter:

- **XmDIALOG_APPLY_BUTTON.**
- **XmDIALOG_CANCEL_BUTTON.**
- **XmDIALOG_DEFAULT_BUTTON.**
- **XmDIALOG_FILTER_LABEL.**
- **XmDIALOG_FILTER_TEXT.**
- **XmDIALOG_HELP_BUTTON.**
- **XmDIALOG_LIST.**
- **XmDIALOG_LIST_LABEL.**
- **XmDIALOG_OK_BUTTON.**
- **XmDIALOG_SELECTION_LABEL.**
- **XmDIALOG_TEXT.**

For a complete definition of FileSelectionBox and its associated resources, see **XmFileSelectionBox(3X)**.

Return Value

Returns the widget ID of the specified FileSelectionBox child.

Related Information

XmFileSelectionBox(3X).

XmFileSelectionDoSearch

Purpose

A FileSelectionBox function that initiates a directory search.

AES Support Level

Full-use

Synopsis

#include <Xm/FileSB.h>

void XmFileSelectionDoSearch (*widget, dirmask*)
    Widget   *widget*;
    XmString   *dirmask*;

Description

XmFileSelectionDoSearch initiates a directory search. If the *dirmask* parameter is not NULL, the directory mask is updated before the search is initiated.

widget   Specifies the FileSelectionBox widget ID.

dirmask   Specifies the directory mask used in determining the files displayed in the FileSelectionBox list. This sets the **XmNdirMask** attribute associated with the function **XmCreateFileSelectionBox**. This is an optional attribute. If you do not specify a directory mask, the current directory mask is used.

For a complete definition of FileSelectionBox and its associated resources, see **XmFileSelectionBox(3X)**.

Related Information

XmFileSelectionBox(3X).

XmForm

Purpose

The Form widget class

AES Support Level

Full-use

Synopsis

#include <Xm/Form.h>

Description

Form is a container widget with no input semantics of its own. Constraints are placed on children of the Form to define attachments for each of the child's four sides. These attachments can be to the Form, to another child widget or gadget, to a relative position within the Form, or to the initial position of the child. The attachments determine the layout behavior of the Form when resizing occurs.

Classes

Form inherits behavior and resources from **Core**, **Composite**, **Constraint**, **XmManager**, and **XmBulletinBoard** classes.

The class pointer is **xmFormWidgetClass**.

The class name is **XmForm**.

New Resources

The following table defines a set of widget resources used by the programmer to specify data. The programmer can also set the resource values for the inherited classes to set attributes for this widget. To reference a resource by name or by class in a .Xdefaults file, remove the **XmN** or **XmC** prefix and use the remaining letters. To specify one of the defined values for a resource in a .Xdefaults file, remove the **Xm** prefix and use the remaining letters (in either lowercase or uppercase, but include any underscores between words). The codes in the access column indicate if the given resource can be set at creation time (**C**), set by using **XtSetValues** (**S**), retrieved by using **XtGetValues** (**G**), or is not applicable (**N/A**).

XmForm Resource Set		
Name Class	Default Type	Access
XmNfractionBase XmCMaxValue	100 int	CSG
XmNhorizontalSpacing XmCSpacing	0 int	CSG
XmNrubberPositioning XmCRubberPositioning	False Boolean	CSG
XmNverticalSpacing XmCSpacing	0 int	CSG

XmNfractionBase

> Specifies the denominator used in calculating the relative position of a child widget using **XmATTACH_POSITION** constraints.

XmNhorizontalSpacing

> Specifies the offset for right and left attachments.

XmNrubberPositioning

> Indicates the default attachment for a child of the Form. If this Boolean resource is set to False, then the left and top of the child defaults to being attached to the left and top side of the Form. If this resource is set to True, then the child defaults to being attached to its initial position in the Form.

XmNverticalSpacing

> Specifies the offset for top and bottom attachments.

XmForm Constraint Resource Set		
Name **Class**	**Default** **Type**	**Access**
XmNbottomAttachment XmCAttachment	XmATTACH_NONE unsigned char	CSG
XmNbottomOffset XmCOffset	0 int	CSG
XmNbottomPosition XmCAttachment	0 int	CSG
XmNbottomWidget XmCWidget	NULL Widget	CSG
XmNleftAttachment XmCAttachment	XmATTACH_NONE unsigned char	CSG
XmNleftOffset XmCOffset	0 int	CSG
XmNleftPosition XmCAttachment	0 int	CSG
XmNleftWidget XmCWidget	NULL Widget	CSG
XmNresizable XmCBoolean	True Boolean	CSG
XmNrightAttachment XmCAttachment	XmATTACH_NONE unsigned char	CSG
XmNrightOffset XmCOffset	0 int	CSG
XmNrightPosition XmCAttachment	0 int	CSG
XmNrightWidget XmCWidget	NULL Widget	CSG
XmNtopAttachment XmCAttachment	XmATTACH_NONE unsigned char	CSG

Name	Default	Access
Class	Type	
XmNtopOffset	0	CSG
XmCOffset	int	
XmNtopPosition	0	CSG
XmCAttachment	int	
XmNtopWidget	NULL	CSG
XmCWidget	Widget	

XmNbottomAttachment

Specifies attachment of the bottom side of the child. It can have the following data values:

- **XmATTACH_NONE** — do not attach this side

- **XmATTACH_FORM** — attach the bottom side of the child to the bottom side of the Form

- **XmATTACH_OPPOSITE_FORM** — attach the bottom side of the child to the top side of the Form

- **XmATTACH_WIDGET** — attach the bottom side of the child to the top side of the widget or gadget specified in the **XmNbottomWidget** resource

- **XmATTACH_OPPOSITE_WIDGET** — attach the bottom side of the child to the bottom side of the widget or gadget specified in the **XmNbottomWidget** resource

- **XmATTACH_POSITION** — attach the bottom side of the child to a relative position in the Form. This position is specified by the **XmNbottomPosition** resource

- **XmATTACH_SELF** — attach the bottom of the child to its initial position in the Form

XmNbottomOffset

Specifies the constant offset between the bottom side of the child and the object to which it is attached. This resource is ignored if **XmNbottomAttachment** is set to **XmATTACH_POSITION**. The relationship established remains, regardless of any resizing operations that occur.

XmNbottomPosition

Determines the relative position of the bottom side of the child. The relative position is a fraction of the height of the Form. The fraction is equal to the value of this resource divided by the value of **XmNfractionBase**. This resource is used only if **XmNbottomAttachment** is set to **XmATTACH_POSITION**.

XmNbottomWidget

Specifies the widget or gadget to which the bottom side of the child is attached. This resource is used if **XmNbottomAttachment** is set to **XmATTACH_WIDGET** or **XmATTACH_OPPOSITE_WIDGET**.

XmNleftAttachment

Specifies attachment of the left side of the child. It can have the following data values:

- **XmATTACH_NONE** — do not attach this side

- **XmATTACH_FORM** — attach the left side of the child to the left side of the Form

- **XmATTACH_OPPOSITE_FORM** — attach the left side of the child to the right side of the Form

- **XmATTACH_WIDGET** — attach the left side of the child to the right side of the widget or gadget specified in the **XmNleftWidget** resource

- **XmATTACH_OPPOSITE_WIDGET** — attach the left side of the child to the left side of the widget or gadget specified in the **XmNleftWidget** resource

- **XmATTACH_POSITION** — attach the left side of the child to a relative position in the Form. This position is specified by the **XmNleftPosition** resource

- **XmATTACH_SELF** — attach the left side of the child to its initial position in the Form

XmNleftOffset

Specifies the constant offset between the left side of the child and the object to which it is attached. This resource is ignored if **XmNleftAttachment** is set to **XmATTACH_POSITION**. The relationship established remains, regardless of any resizing operations that occur.

XmNleftPosition

Determines the relative position of the left side of the child. The relative position is a fractional value of the width of the Form. The fractional value is equal to the value of this resource divided by the value of **XmNfractionBase**. This resource is used only if **XmNleftAttachment** is set to **XmATTACH_POSITION**.

XmNleftWidget

Specifies the widget or gadget to which the left side of the child is attached. This resource is used if **XmNleftAttachment** is set to either **XmATTACH_WIDGET** or **XmATTACH_OPPOSITE_WIDGET**.

XmNresizable

Specifies whether a child widget can be resized by the Form. The default value is True.

XmNrightAttachment

Specifies attachment of the right side of the child. It can have the following data values:

- **XmATTACH_NONE** — do not attach this side

- **XmATTACH_FORM** — attach the right side of the child to the right side of the Form

- **XmATTACH_OPPOSITE_FORM** — attach the right side of the child to the left side of the Form

- **XmATTACH_WIDGET** — attach the right side of the child to the left side of the widget or gadget specified in the **XmNrightWidget** resource

- **XmATTACH_OPPOSITE_WIDGET** — attach the right side of the child to the right side of the widget or gadget specified in the **XmNrightWidget** resource

- **XmATTACH_POSITION** — attach the right side of the child to a relative position in the Form. This position is specified by the **XmNrightPosition** resource

- **XmATTACH_SELF** — attach the right side of the child to its initial position in the Form

XmNrightOffset

Specifies the constant offset between the right side of the child and the object to which it is attached. This resource is ignored if **XmNrightAttachment** is set to **XmATTACH_POSITION**. The relationship established remains, regardless of any resizing operations that occur.

XmNrightPosition

Determines the relative position of the right side of the child. The relative position is a fractional value of the width of the Form. The fractional value is equal to the value of this resource divided by the value of **XmNfractionBase**. This resource is used only if **XmNrightAttachment** is set to **XmATTACH_POSITION**.

XmNrightWidget

Specifies the widget or gadget to which the right side of the child is attached. This resource is used if **XmNrightAttachment** is set to **XmATTACH_WIDGET** or **XmATTACH_OPPOSITE_WIDGET**.

XmNtopAttachment

Specifies attachment of the top side of the child. It can have the following data values:

- **XmATTACH_NONE** — do not attach this side
- **XmATTACH_FORM** — attach the top side of the child to the top side of the Form
- **XmATTACH_OPPOSITE_FORM** — attach the top side of the child to the bottom side of the Form
- **XmATTACH_WIDGET** — attach the top side of the child to the bottom side of the widget or gadget specified in the **XmNtopWidget** resource
- **XmATTACH_OPPOSITE_WIDGET** — attach the top side of the child to the top side of the widget or gadget specified in the **XmNtopWidget** resource
- **XmATTACH_POSITION** — attach the top side of the child to a relative position in the Form. This position is specified by the **XmNtopPosition** resource
- **XmATTACH_SELF** — attach the top side of the child to its initial position in the Form

XmNtopOffset

Specifies the constant offset between the top side of the child and the object to which it is attached. This resource is ignored if **XmNtopAttachment** is set to **XmATTACH_POSITION**. The relationship established remains, regardless of any resizing operations that occur.

XmNtopPosition

Determines the relative position of the top side of the child. The relative position is a fractional value of the height of the Form. The fractional value is equal to the value of this resource divided by the value of **XmNfractionBase**. This resource is used only if **XmNtopAttachment** is set to **XmATTACH_POSITION**.

XmNtopWidget
> Specifies the widget or gadget to which the top side of the child is attached. This resource is used if **XmNtopAttachment** is set to either **XmATTACH_WIDGET** or **XmATTACH_OPPOSITE_WIDGET**.

Inherited Resources

Form inherits behavior and resources from the following superclasses. For a complete description of each resource, refer to the man page for that superclass.

XmBulletinBoard Resource Set		
Name	**Default**	**Access**
Class	**Type**	
XmNallowOverlap	True	N/A
XmCAllowOverlap	Boolean	
XmNautoUnmanage	True	N/A
XmCAutoUnmanage	Boolean	
XmNbuttonFontList	NULL	N/A
XmCButtonFontList	XmFontList	
XmNcancelButton	NULL	N/A
XmCWidget	Widget	
XmNdefaultButton	NULL	N/A
XmCWidget	Widget	
XmNdefaultPosition	True	N/A
XmCDefaultPosition	Boolean	
XmNdialogStyle	dynamic	N/A
XmCDialogStyle	unsigned char	
XmNdialogTitle	NULL	N/A
XmCXmString	XmString	
XmNfocusCallback	NULL	C
XmCCallback	XtCallbackList	
XmNlabelFontList	NULL	N/A
XmCLabelFontList	XmFontList	
XmNmapCallback	NULL	C
XmCCallback	XtCallbackList	
XmNmarginHeight	10	N/A
XmCMarginHeight	short	
XmNmarginWidth	10	N/A
XmCMarginWidth	short	
XmNnoResize	False	N/A
XmCNoResize	Boolean	

Name
    Class
	Default
	    Type
		Access

XmNresizePolicy
    XmCResizePolicy
	XmRESIZE_ANY
	    unsigned char
		CSG

XmNshadowType
    XmCShadowType
	XmSHADOW_OUT
	    unsigned char
		N/A

XmNtextFontList
    XmCTextFontList
	NULL
	    XmFontList
		N/A

XmNtextTranslations
    XmCTranslations
	NULL
	    XtTranslations
		N/A

XmNunmapCallback
    XmCCallback
	NULL
	    XtCallbackList
		C

XmManager Resource Set		
Name	**Default**	**Access**
Class	**Type**	
XmNbottomShadowColor	dynamic	CSG
XmCForeground	Pixel	
XmNbottomShadowPixmap	XmUNSPECIFIED_PIXMAP	CSG
XmCBottomShadowPixmap	Pixmap	
XmNforeground	dynamic	CSG
XmCForeground	Pixel	
XmNhelpCallback	NULL	C
XmCCallback	XtCallbackList	
XmNhighlightColor	Black	CSG
XmCForeground	Pixel	
XmNhighlightPixmap	dynamic	CSG
XmCHighlightPixmap	Pixmap	
XmNshadowThickness	0	N/A
XmCShadowThickness	short	
XmNtopShadowColor	dynamic	CSG
XmCBackground	Pixel	
XmNtopShadowPixmap	XmUNSPECIFIED_PIXMAP	CSG
XmCTopShadowPixmap	Pixmap	
XmNuserData	NULL	CSG
XmCUserData	caddr_t	

Composite Resource Set		
Name	**Default**	**Access**
Class	**Type**	
XmNinsertPosition	NULL	CSG
XmCInsertPosition	XmRFunction	

Core Resource Set		
Name	**Default**	**Access**
Class	**Type**	
XmNaccelerators	NULL	CSG
XmCAccelerators	XtTranslations	
XmNancestorSensitive	True	G
XmCSensitive	Boolean	
XmNbackground	dynamic	CSG
XmCBackground	Pixel	
XmNbackgroundPixmap	XmUNSPECIFIED_PIXMAP	CSG
XmCPixmap	Pixmap	
XmNborderColor	Black	CSG
XmCBorderColor	Pixel	
XmNborderPixmap	XmUNSPECIFIED_PIXMAP	CSG
XmCPixmap	Pixmap	
XmNborderWidth	0	CSG
XmCBorderWidth	Dimension	
XmNcolormap	XtCopyFromParent	CG
XmCColormap	Colormap	
XmNdepth	XtCopyFromParent	CG
XmCDepth	int	
XmNdestroyCallback	NULL	C
XmCCallback	XtCallbackList	
XmNheight	0	CSG
XmCHeight	Dimension	
XmNmappedWhenManaged	True	CSG
XmCMappedWhenManaged	Boolean	
XmNscreen	XtCopyScreen	CG
XmCScreen	Pointer	
XmNsensitive	True	CSG
XmCSensitive	Boolean	

Name	Default	Access
Class	Type	
XmNtranslations	NULL	CSG
XmCTranslations	XtTranslations	
XmNwidth	0	CSG
XmCWidth	Dimension	
XmNx	0	CSG
XmCPosition	Position	
XmNy	0	CSG
XmCPosition	Position	

Behavior

Form inherits BulletinBoard's behavior.

Default Translations

Form inherits BulletinBoard's default translations.

Keyboard Traversal

For information on keyboard traversal, see the man page for **XmManager(3X)** and its sections on behavior and default translations.

Related Information

Composite(3X), Constraint(3X), Core(3X), XmBulletinBoard(3X), XmCreateForm, XmCreateFormDialog(3X), and XmManager(3X).

XmFrame

Purpose

The Frame widget class

AES Support Level

Full-use

Synopsis

#include <Xm/Frame.h>

Description

Frame is a very simple manager used to enclose a single child in a border drawn by Frame. It uses the Manager class resources for border drawing and performs geometry management so that its size always matches its child's size plus the margins defined for it.

Frame is most often used to enclose other managers when the application developer desires the manager to have the same border appearance as the primitive widgets. Frame can also be used to enclose primitive widgets that do not support the same type of border drawing. This gives visual consistency when you develop applications using diverse widget sets.

If the Frame's parent is a Shell widget, then **XmNshadowType** is set to **XmSHADOW_OUT** and Manager's resource **XmNshadowThickness** is set to one by default.

Classes

Frame inherits behavior and resources from the **Core**, **Composite**, **Constraint**, and **XmManager** classes.

The class pointer is **xmFrameWidgetClass**.

The class name is **XmFrame**.

New Resources

The following table defines a set of widget resources used by the programmer to specify data. The programmer can also set the resource values for the inherited classes to set attributes for this widget. To reference a resource by name or by class in a .Xdefaults file, remove the **XmN** or **XmC** prefix and use the remaining letters. To specify one of the defined values for a resource in a .Xdefaults file, remove the **Xm** prefix and use the remaining letters (in either lowercase or uppercase, but include any underscores between words). The codes in the access column indicate if the given resource can be set at creation time (**C**), set by using **XtSetValues** (**S**), retrieved by using **XtGetValues** (**G**), or is not applicable (**N/A**).

XmFrame Resource Set		
Name	**Default**	**Access**
Class	**Type**	
XmNmarginWidth	0	CSG
XmCMarginWidth	short	
XmNmarginHeight	0	CSG
XmCMarginHeight	short	
XmNshadowType	XmSHADOW_ETCHED_IN	CSG
XmCShadowType	unsigned char	

XmNmarginWidth

Specifies the padding space on the left and right sides between Frame's child and Frame's shadow drawing.

XmNmarginHeight
>Specifies the padding space on the top and bottom sides between Frame's child and Frame's shadow drawing.

XmNshadowType
>Describes the drawing style for Frame. This resource can have the following values:

- **XmSHADOW_IN** — draws Frame so that it appears inset. This means that the bottom shadow visuals and top shadow visuals are reversed.

- **XmSHADOW_OUT** — draws Frame so that it appears outset.

- **XmSHADOW_ETCHED_IN** — draws Frame using a double line giving the effect of a line etched into the window. The thickness of the double line is equal to the value of **XmNshadowThickness**. This is the default if Frame's parent is a Shell widget.

- **XmSHADOW_ETCHED_OUT** — draws Frame using a double line giving the effect of a line coming out of the window. The thickness of the double line is equal to the value of **XmNshadowThickness**. This is the default except when Frame's parent is a Shell widget.

Inherited Resources

Frame inherits behavior and resources from the following superclasses. For a complete description of each resource, refer to the man page for that superclass.

XmManager Resource Set		
Name	**Default**	**Access**
Class	**Type**	
XmNbottomShadowColor	dynamic	CSG
XmCForeground	Pixel	
XmNbottomShadowPixmap	XmUNSPECIFIED_PIXMAP	CSG
XmCBottomShadowPixmap	Pixmap	
XmNforeground	dynamic	CSG
XmCForeground	Pixel	
XmNhelpCallback	NULL	C
XmCCallback	XtCallbackList	
XmNhighlightColor	Black	CSG
XmCForeground	Pixel	
XmNhighlightPixmap	dynamic	CSG
XmCHighlightPixmap	Pixmap	
XmNshadowThickness	dynamic	CSG
XmCShadowThickness	short	
XmNtopShadowColor	dynamic	CSG
XmCBackground	Pixel	
XmNtopShadowPixmap	XmUNSPECIFIED_PIXMAP	CSG
XmCTopShadowPixmap	Pixmap	
XmNuserData	NULL	CSG
XmCUserData	caddr_t	

Composite Resource Set		
Name	**Default**	**Access**
Class	**Type**	
XmNinsertPosition	NULL	CSG
XmCInsertPosition	XmRFunction	

Core Resource Set		
Name **Class**	**Default** **Type**	**Access**
XmNaccelerators XmCAccelerators	NULL XtTranslations	CSG
XmNancestorSensitive XmCSensitive	True Boolean	G
XmNbackground XmCBackground	dynamic Pixel	CSG
XmNbackgroundPixmap XmCPixmap	XmUNSPECIFIED_PIXMAP Pixmap	CSG
XmNborderColor XmCBorderColor	Black Pixel	CSG
XmNborderPixmap XmCPixmap	XmUNSPECIFIED_PIXMAP Pixmap	CSG
XmNborderWidth XmCBorderWidth	0 Dimension	CSG
XmNcolormap XmCColormap	XtCopyFromParent Colormap	CG
XmNdepth XmCDepth	XtCopyFromParent int	CG
XmNdestroyCallback XmCCallback	NULL XtCallbackList	C
XmNheight XmCHeight	0 Dimension	CSG
XmNmappedWhenManaged XmCMappedWhenManaged	True Boolean	CSG
XmNscreen XmCScreen	XtCopyScreen Pointer	CG
XmNsensitive XmCSensitive	True Boolean	CSG

Name	Default	Access
Class	**Type**	
XmNtranslations	NULL	CSG
XmCTranslations	XtTranslations	
XmNwidth	0	CSG
XmCWidth	Dimension	
XmNx	0	CSG
XmCPosition	Position	
XmNy	0	CSG
XmCPosition	Position	

Default Translations

<EnterWindow>:	**Enter()**
<FocusIn>:	**FocusIn()**
<Btn1Down>:	**Arm()**
<Btn1Up>:	**Activate()**

Related Information

Composite(3X), Constraint(3X), Core(3X), XmCreateFrame(3X), and **XmManager(3X).**

XmGadget

Purpose

The Gadget widget class

AES Support Level

Full-use

Synopsis

#include <Xm/Xm.h>

Description

Gadget is a widget class used as a supporting superclass for other gadget classes. It handles shadow-border drawing and highlighting, traversal activation and deactivation, and various callback lists needed by gadgets.

The color and pixmap resources defined by XmManager are directly used by gadgets. If **XtSetValues** is used to change one of the resources for a manager widget, then all of the gadget children within the manager also change.

Classes

Gadget inherits behavior and resources from **Object** and **RectObj** classes.

The class pointer is **xmGadgetClass**.

The class name is **XmGadget**.

New Resources

The following table defines a set of widget resources used by the programmer to specify data. The programmer can also set the resource values for the inherited classes to set attributes for this widget. To reference a resource by name or by class in a .Xdefaults file, remove the **XmN** or **XmC** prefix and use the remaining letters. To specify one of the defined values for a resource in a .Xdefaults file, remove the **Xm** prefix and use the remaining letters (in either lowercase or uppercase, but include any underscores between words). The codes in the access column indicate if the given resource can be set at creation time (**C**), set by using **XtSetValues** (**S**), retrieved by using **XtGetValues** (**G**), or is not applicable (**N/A**).

XmGadget Resource Set		
Name	**Default**	**Access**
Class	**Type**	
XmNhelpCallback	NULL	C
XmCCallback	XtCallbackList	
XmNhighlightOnEnter	False	CSG
XmCHighlightOnEnter	Boolean	
XmNhighlightThickness	0	CSG
XmCHighlightThickness	short	
XmNshadowThickness	2	CSG
XmCShadowThickness	short	
XmNtraversalOn	False	CSG
XmCTraversalOn	Boolean	
XmNuserData	NULL	CSG
XmCUserData	caddr_t	

XmNhelpCallback

Specifies the list of callbacks that is called when the help key sequence is pressed. The reason sent by the callback is **XmCR_HELP.**

XmNhighlightOnEnter

Specifies whether to draw border highlighting. This resource is ignored if **XmNtraversalOn** is True.

XmNhighlightThickness

Specifies the thickness of the highlighting rectangle.

XmNshadowThickness

Specifies the size of the drawn border shadow.

XmNtraversalOn

Specifies traversal activation for this gadget.

XmNuserData

Allows the application to attach any necessary specific data to the gadget. This is an internally unused resource.

Inherited Resources

Gadget inherits the following resources from the named superclass. For a complete description of each resource, refer to the man page for that superclass.

RectObj Resource Set		
Name **Class**	**Default** **Type**	**Access**
XmNancestorSensitive XmCSensitive	XtCopyFromParent Boolean	CSG
XmNborderWidth XmCBorderWidth	0 Dimension	CSG
XmNheight XmCHeight	0 Dimension	CSG
XmNsensitive XmCSensitive	True Boolean	CSG
XmNwidth XmCWidth	0 Dimension	CSG
XmNx XmCPosition	0 Position	CSG
XmNy XmCPosition	0 Position	CSG

Object Resource Set		
Name **Class**	**Default** **Type**	**Access**
XmNdestroyCallback XmCCallback	NULL XtCallbackList	C

Behavior

Gadgets cannot have translations associated with them. Because of this, a Gadget's behavior is determined by the Manager widget into which the Gadget is placed. The following types of events are caught by a Manager widget and forwarded to a Gadget:

- ButtonPress
- ButtonRelease
- EnterNotify
- LeaveNotify
- FocusIn
- FocusOut
- MotionNotify

Refer to **XmManager(3X)** for a discussion of the translations supported by all Manager widgets.

Related Information

Object(3X), **RectObj(3X)**, and **XmManager(3X)**.

XmGetAtomName

Purpose

A function that returns the string representation for an atom.

AES Support Level

Full-use

Synopsis

#include <Xm/Xm.h>
#include <X11/AtomMgr.h>

String XmGetAtomName (*display, atom*)
    Display   * *display*;
    Atom   * *atom*;

Description

XmGetAtomName returns the string representation for an atom. It mirrors the **Xlib** interfaces for atom management but provides client-side caching. When and where caching is provided in **Xlib**, the routines will become pseudonyms for the **Xlib** routines.

display   Specifies the connection to the X server

atom   Specifies the atom for the property name you want returned

Return Value

Returns a string.

XmGetMenuCursor

Purpose

A RowColumn function that returns the cursor ID for the current menu cursor.

AES Support Level

Full-use

Synopsis

Cursor XmGetMenuCursor (*display*)
    Display   * *display*;

Description

XmGetMenuCursor queries the menu cursor currently being used by this client on the specified display and returns the cursor ID.

display   Specifies the display whose menu cursor is to be queried

For a complete definition of the menu cursor resource, see **XmRowColumn(3X)**.

Return Value

Returns the cursor ID for the current menu cursor or the value None if a cursor is not yet defined. A cursor will not be defined if the application makes this call before the client has created any menus on the specified display.

Related Information

XmRowColumn(3X).

XmGetPixmap

Purpose

A pixmap caching function that generates a pixmap, stores it in a pixmap cache, and returns the pixmap.

AES Support Level

Full-use

Synopsis

#include <Xm/Xm.h>

Pixmap XmGetPixmap (*screen, image_name, foreground, background*)
    Screen   * *screen*;
    char   * *image_name*;
    Pixel   *foreground*;
    Pixel   *background*;

Description

XmGetPixmap uses the parameter data to perform a lookup in the pixmap cache to see if a pixmap has already been generated that matches the data.

If one is found, a reference count is incremented and the pixmap is returned. Applications should use **XmDestroyPixmap** when the pixmap is no longer needed.

If a pixmap is not found, *image_name* is used to perform a lookup in the image cache. If an image is found, it is used to generate the pixmap, which is then cached and returned.

If an image is not found, the *image_name* is used as a filename, and a search is made for an **X10** or **X11** bitmap file. If it is found, the file is read, converted into an image, and cached in the image cache. The image is then used to generate a pixmap, which is cached and returned.

Several paths are searched to find the file. The user can specify an environment variable **XBMLANGPATH**, which is used to generate one set of paths. See **XtInitialize(3X)** for an explanation of using this environment variable. If **XBMLANGPATH** is not set, the following path names are searched:

> **/usr/lib/X11/%L/bitmaps/%N/%B**
> **/usr/lib/X11/%L/bitmaps/%B**
> **/usr/lib/X11/bitmaps/%B**
> **/usr/include/X11/bitmaps/%B**

Parameter descriptions are listed below:

screen   Specifies the display screen on which the pixmap is to be drawn and is used to ensure that the pixmap matches the visual required for the screen

image_name Specifies the name of the image to be used to generate the pixmap

foreground Combines the image with the *foreground* color to create the pixmap if the image referenced is a bit-per-pixel image

background Combines the image with the *background* color to create the pixmap if the image referenced is a bit-per-pixel image

Return Value

Returns a pixmap when successful; returns **XmUNSPECIFIED_PIXMAP** if the image corresponding to the *image_name* cannot be found.

Related Information

XmDestroyPixmap(3X),   **XmInstallImage(3X),**   and **XmUninstallImage(3X).**

XmInstallImage

Purpose

A pixmap caching function that adds an image to the pixmap cache.

AES Support Level

Full-use

Synopsis

#include <Xm/Xm.h>

Boolean XmInstallImage (*image, image_name*)
    XImage   * *image*;
    char   * *image_name*;

Description

XmInstallImage stores an image in an image cache that can later be used to generate a pixmap. Part of the installation process is to extend the resource converter used to reference these images. The resource converter is given the image name so that the image can be referenced in a .Xdefaults file. Since an image can be referenced by a widget through its pixmap resources, it is up to the application to ensure that the image is installed before the widget is created.

image   Points to the image structure to be installed. The installation process does not make a local copy of the image. Therefore, the application should not destroy the image until it is uninstalled from the caching functions.

image_name Specifies a string that the application uses to name the image. After installation, this name can be used in .Xdefaults for referencing the image. A local copy of the name is created by the image caching functions.

The image caching functions provide a set of eight preinstalled images. These names can be used within a **.Xdefaults** file for generating pixmaps for the resource for which they are provided.

Image Name	Description
background	A tile of solid background
25_foreground	A tile of 25% foreground, 75% background
50_foreground	A tile of 50% foreground, 50% background
75_foreground	A tile of 75% foreground, 25% background
horizontal	A tile of horizontal lines of the two colors
vertical	A tile of vertical lines of the two colors
slant_right	A tile of slanting lines of the two colors
slant_left	A tile of slanting lines of the two colors

Return Value

Returns True when successful; returns False if NULL *image*, NULL *image_name*, or duplicate *image_name* are used as parameter values.

Related Information

XmUninstallImage(3X), **XmGetPixmap(3X)**, and **XmDestroyPixmap(3X)**.

XmInternAtom

Purpose

A function that returns an atom for a given name

AES Support Level

Full-use

Synopsis

#include <Xm/Xm.h>
#include <X11/AtomMgr.h>

Atom **XmInternAtom** (*display, name, only_if_exists*)
    Display   * *display*;
    String   *name*;
    Boolean   *only_if_exists*;

Description

XmInternAtom returns an atom for a given name. It mirrors the **Xlib** interfaces for atom management, but provides client-side caching. When and where caching is provided in **Xlib**, the routines will become pseudonyms for the **Xlib** routines.

display   Specifies the connection to the X server

name   Specifies the name associated with the atom you want returned

only_if_exists

      Specifies a Boolean value that indicates whether **XInternAtom** creates the atom

Return Value

Returns an atom.

XmIsMotifWMRunning

Purpose

A function that specifies if the window manager is running.

AES Support Level

Full-use

Synopsis

#include <X11/Shell.h>

Boolean XmIsMotifWMRunning (*shell*)
    Widget   *shell*;

Description

XmIsMotifWMRunning lets a user know if the Motif Window Manager is running on a screen that contains a specific widget hierarchy. This function first sees whether the **MOTIF_WM_INFO** property is present on the root window of the shell's screen. If it is, its window field is used to query for the presence of the specified window as a child of root.

shell   Specifies the shell whose screen will be tested for **mwm**'s presence.

Return Value

Returns True if MWM is running.

XmLabel

Purpose

The Label widget class

AES Support Level

Full-use

Synopsis

#include <Xm/Label.h>

Description

Label is an instantiable widget and is also used as a superclass for other button widgets, such as PushButton and ToggleButton. The Label widget does not accept any button or key input, and the help callback is the only callback defined. Label also receives enter and leave events.

Label can contain either text or a pixmap. Label text is a compound string. Refer to the *OSF/ Motif Programmer's Guide* for more information on compound strings. The text can be multidirectional, multiline, and/or multifont. When a Label is insensitive, its text is stippled, or the user-supplied insensitive pixmap is displayed.

Label supports both accelerators and mnemonics primarily for use in Label subclass widgets that are contained in menus. Mnemonics are available in a menu system when the button is visible. Accelerators in a menu system are accessible even when the button is not visible. The Label widget displays the mnemonic by underlining the first matching character in the text string. The accelerator is displayed as a text string to the right of the label text or pixmap.

Label consists of many margin fields surrounding the text or pixmap. These margin fields are resources that may be set by the user, but Label subclasses also modify some of these fields. The subclasses tend to modify the **XmNmarginLeft**, **XmNmarginRight**, **XmNmarginTop**, and **XmNmarginBottom** resources and leave the **XmNmarginWidth** and **XmNmarginHeight** resources as set by the application.

Classes

Label inherits behavior and resources from **Core** and **XmPrimitive** Classes.

The class pointer is **xmLabelWidgetClass**.

The class name is **XmLabel**.

New Resources

The following table defines a set of widget resources used by the programmer to specify data. The programmer can also set the resource values for the inherited classes to set attributes for this widget. To reference a resource by name or by class in a .Xdefaults file, remove the **XmN** or **XmC** prefix and use the remaining letters. To specify one of the defined values for a resource in a .Xdefaults file, remove the **Xm** prefix and use the remaining letters (in either lowercase or uppercase, but include any underscores between words). The codes in the access column indicate if the given resource can be set at creation time (**C**), set by using **XtSetValues** (**S**), retrieved by using **XtGetValues** (**G**), or is not applicable (**N/A**).

XmLabel Resource Set		
Name Class	Default Type	Access
XmNaccelerator XmCAccelerator	NULL String	CSG
XmNacceleratorText XmCAcceleratorText	NULL XmString	CSG
XmNalignment XmCAlignment	XmALIGNMENT_CENTER unsigned char	CSG
XmNfontList XmCFontList	"Fixed" XmFontList	CSG
XmNlabelInsensitivePixmap XmCLabelInsensitivePixmap	XmUNSPECIFIED_PIXMAP Pixmap	CSG
XmNlabelPixmap XmCPixmap	XmUNSPECIFIED_PIXMAP Pixmap	CSG
XmNlabelString XmCXmString	NULL XmString	CSG
XmNlabelType XmCLabelType	XmSTRING unsigned char	CSG
XmNmarginBottom XmCMarginBottom	0 short	CSG
XmNmarginHeight XmCMarginHeight	2 short	CSG
XmNmarginLeft XmCMarginLeft	0 short	CSG
XmNmarginRight XmCMarginRight	0 short	CSG
XmNmarginTop XmCMarginTop	0 short	CSG
XmNmarginWidth XmCMarginWidth	2 short	CSG

Name	Default	Access
Class	Type	
XmNmnemonic	'\0'	CSG
XmCMnemonic	char	
XmNrecomputeSize	True	CSG
XmCRecomputeSize	Boolean	

XmNaccelerator

Sets the accelerator on a button widget in a menu, which activates a visible or invisible button from the keyboard. This resource is a string that describes a set of modifiers and the key which may be used to select the button. The format of this string is identical to that used by the translations manager, with the exception that only a single event may be specified and only **KeyPress** events are allowed.

Accelerators for buttons are supported only for certain buttons in certain menu widgets, namely for PushButton and ToggleButton in Pulldown and Popup MenuPanes.

XmNacceleratorText

Specifies the text displayed for the accelerator. The text is displayed to the right of the label string or pixmap. Accelerator text for buttons is displayed only for PushButtons and ToggleButtons in Pulldown and Popup Menus.

XmNalignment

Specifies the label alignment for text or pixmap.

- **XmALIGNMENT_CENTER** (center alignment) — causes the centers of the lines of text to be vertically aligned in the center of the widget window. For a pixmap, its center is vertically aligned with the center of the widget window.

- **XmALIGNMENT_END** (right alignment) — causes the right sides of the lines of text to be vertically aligned with the right edge of the widget window. For a pixmap, its right side is vertically aligned with the right edge of the widget window.

- **XmALIGNMENT_BEGINNING** (left alignment) — causes the left sides of the lines of text to be vertically aligned with the left edge of the widget window. For a pixmap, its left side is vertically aligned with the left edge of the widget window.

XmNfontList

Specifies the font of the text used in the widget.

XmNlabelInsensitivePixmap

Specifies a pixmap used as the button face if **XmNlabelType** is **XmPIXMAP** and the button is insensitive.

XmNlabelPixmap

Specifies the pixmap when **XmNlabelType** is **XmPIXMAP**.

XmNlabelString

Specifies the compound string when the **XmNlabelType** is **XmSTRING**.

XmNlabelType

Specifies the label type.

- **XmSTRING** — text displays **XmNlabelString**.

- **XmPIXMAP** — icon data in pixmap displays **XmNlabelInsensitivePixmap**.

XmNmarginBottom

Specifies the amount of spacing that is to be left, after the bottom margin (**XmNmarginHeight**) of the widget, before the label is drawn. This may be modified by Label's subclasses. For example, CascadeButton may increase this field to make room for the cascade pixmap.

XmNmarginHeight

Specifies the amount of blank space between the bottom edge of the top shadow and the label, and the top edge of the bottom shadow and the label.

XmNmarginLeft

Specifies the amount of spacing that is to be left after the left margin (**XmNmarginWidth**) of the widget before the label is drawn. This may be modified by Label's subclasses. For example, ToggleButton may increase this field to make room for the toggle indicator and for spacing between the indicator and label.

XmNmarginRight

Specifies the amount of spacing that is to be left after the right margin (**XmNmarginWidth**) of the widget before the label is drawn. This may be modified by Label's subclasses. For example, CascadeButton may increase this field to make room for the cascade pixmap.

XmNmarginTop

Specifies the amount of spacing that is to be left after the top margin (**XmNmarginHeight**) of the widget before the label is drawn. This may be modified by Label's subclasses. For example, CascadeButton may increase this field to make room for the cascade pixmap.

XmNmarginWidth

Specifies the amount of blank space between the right edge of the left shadow and the label, and the left edge of the right shadow and the label.

XmNmnemonic

Provides the user with alternate means of selecting a button. The buttons must be visible for mnemonics to work. Buttons, which are in a MenuBar, a Popup MenuPane, or a Pulldown MenuPane, can have a mnemonic.

This resource contains a single character. The first character in the label string that exactly matches the mnemonic is underlined when the button is displayed.

When a mnemonic is specified for a MenuBar button, the user activates the mnemonic by pressing the **meta** key and the specified mnemonic key simultaneously. All other mnemonics are activated by pressing the specified mnemonic. Mnemonics are case insensitive; the character underlined can be a modified key, but the key pressed should always be unmodified.

XmNrecomputeSize

Specifies a Boolean value that indicates whether the widget attempts to be big enough to contain the label. If True, an **XtSetValues** with a new label string or pixmap, accelerator text, margins, font, or label type causes the widget to shrink or expand to exactly fit the new label string or pixmap. If False, the widget never attempts to change size on its own.

Inherited Resources

Label inherits behavior and resources from the following superclasses. For a complete description of each resource, refer to the man page for that superclass.

XmPrimitive Resource Set		

Name
     Class
	Default
	     Type
		Access

XmNbottomShadowColor
   XmCForeground
	dynamic
	   Pixel
		CSG

XmNbottomShadowPixmap
   XmCBottomShadowPixmap
	XmUNSPECIFIED_PIXMAP
	   Pixmap
		CSG

XmNforeground
   XmCForeground
	dynamic
	   Pixel
		CSG

XmNhelpCallback
   XmCCallback
	NULL
	   XtCallbackList
		C

XmNhighlightColor
   XmCForeground
	Black
	   Pixel
		CSG

XmNhighlightOnEnter
   XmCHighlightOnEnter
	False
	   Boolean
		CSG

XmNhighlightPixmap
   XmCHighlightPixmap
	dynamic
	   Pixmap
		CSG

XmNhighlightThickness
   XmCHighlightThickness
	0
	   short
		CSG

XmNshadowThickness
   XmCShadowThickness
	0
	   short
		CSG

XmNtopShadowColor
   XmCBackground
	dynamic
	   Pixel
		CSG

XmNtopShadowPixmap
   XmCTopShadowPixmap
	XmUNSPECIFIED_PIXMAP
	   Pixmap
		CSG

XmNtraversalOn
   XmCTraversalOn
	False
	   Boolean
		CSG

XmNuserData
   XmCUserData
	NULL
	   caddr_t
		CSG

Core Resource Set		
Name	**Default**	**Access**
Class	**Type**	
XmNaccelerators	NULL	CSG
XmCAccelerators	XtTranslations	
XmNancestorSensitive	True	G
XmCSensitive	Boolean	
XmNbackground	dynamic	CSG
XmCBackground	Pixel	
XmNbackgroundPixmap	XmUNSPECIFIED_PIXMAP	CSG
XmCPixmap	Pixmap	
XmNborderColor	Black	CSG
XmCBorderColor	Pixel	
XmNborderPixmap	XmUNSPECIFIED_PIXMAP	CSG
XmCPixmap	Pixmap	
XmNborderWidth	0	CSG
XmCBorderWidth	Dimension	
XmNcolormap	XtCopyFromParent	CG
XmCColormap	Colormap	
XmNdepth	XtCopyFromParent	CG
XmCDepth	int	
XmNdestroyCallback	NULL	C
XmCCallback	XtCallbackList	
XmNheight	0	CSG
XmCHeight	Dimension	
XmNmappedWhenManaged	True	CSG
XmCMappedWhenManaged	Boolean	
XmNscreen	XtCopyScreen	CG
XmCScreen	Pointer	
XmNsensitive	True	CSG
XmCSensitive	Boolean	

Name	Default	Access
Class	Type	
XmNtranslations	NULL	CSG
XmCTranslations	XtTranslations	
XmNwidth	0	CSG
XmCWidth	Dimension	
XmNx	0	CSG
XmCPosition	Position	
XmNy	0	CSG
XmCPosition	Position	

Callback Information

The following structure is returned with each callback:

```
typedef struct
{
    int          reason;
    XEvent       * event;
} XmAnyCallbackStruct;
```

reason   Indicates why the callback was invoked. For this callback, *reason* is set to **XmCR_HELP**.

event   Points to the **XEvent** that triggered the callback.

Default Translations

```
<EnterWindow>:  Enter()
<LeaveWindow>:  Leave()
```

Keyboard Traversal

For information on keyboard traversal, see the man page for
XmPrimitive(3X) and its sections on behavior and default translations.

Related Information

Core(3X), XmCreateLabel(3X), and XmPrimitive(3X).

XmLabelGadget

Purpose

The LabelGadget widget class

AES Support Level

Full-use

Synopsis

#include <Xm/LabelG.h>

Description

LabelGadget is an instantiable widget and is also used as a superclass for other button gadgets, such as PushButtonGadget and ToggleButtonGadget. The LabelGadget widget does not accept any button or key input, and the help callback is the only callback defined. LabelGadget also receives enter and leave events.

LabelGadget can contain either text or a pixmap. LabelGadget text is a compound string. The text can be multidirectional, multiline, and/or multifont. When a LabelGadget is insensitive, its text is stippled, or the user supplied insensitive pixmap is displayed.

LabelGadget supports both accelerators and mnemonics primarily for use in LabelGadget subclass widgets that are contained in menus. Mnemonics are available in a menu system when the button is visible. Accelerators in a menu system are accessible even when the button is not visible. The LabelGadget displays the mnemonic by underlining the first matching character in the text string. The accelerator is displayed as a text string to the right of the label text or pixmap.

LabelGadget consists of many margin fields surrounding the text or pixmap. These margin fields are resources that may be set by the user, but LabelGadget subclasses also modify some of these fields. The subclasses tend to modify the **XmNmarginLeft**, **XmNmarginRight**, **XmNmarginTop**, and **XmNmarginBottom** resources and leave the **XmNmarginWidth** and **XmNmarginHeight** resources as set by the application.

Classes

LabelGadget inherits behavior and resources from **Object**, **RectObj** and **XmGadget** classes.

The class pointer is **xmLabelGadgetClass**.

The class name is **XmLabelGadget**.

New Resources

The following table defines a set of widget resources used by the programmer to specify data. The programmer can also set the resource values for the inherited classes to set attributes for this widget. To reference a resource by name or by class in a .Xdefaults file, remove the **XmN** or **XmC** prefix and use the remaining letters. To specify one of the defined values for a resource in a .Xdefaults file, remove the **Xm** prefix and use the remaining letters (in either lowercase or uppercase, but include any underscores between words). The codes in the access column indicate if the given resource can be set at creation time (**C**), set by using **XtSetValues** (**S**), retrieved by using **XtGetValues** (**G**), or is not applicable (**N/A**).

XmLabelGadget Resource Set		
Name	**Default**	**Access**
Class	**Type**	
XmNaccelerator	NULL	CSG
XmCAccelerator	String	
XmNacceleratorText	NULL	CSG
XmCAcceleratorText	XmString	
XmNalignment	XmALIGNMENT_CENTER	CSG
XmCAlignment	unsigned char	
XmNfontList	"Fixed"	CSG
XmCFontList	XmFontList	
XmNlabelInsensitivePixmap	XmUNSPECIFIED_PIXMAP	CSG
XmCLabelInsensitivePixmap	Pixmap	
XmNlabelPixmap	XmUNSPECIFIED_PIXMAP	CSG
XmCPixmap	Pixmap	
XmNlabelString	NULL	CSG
XmCXmString	XmString	
XmNlabelType	XmSTRING	CSG
XmCLabelType	unsigned char	
XmNmarginBottom	0	CSG
XmCMarginBottom	short	
XmNmarginHeight	2	CSG
XmCMarginHeight	short	
XmNmarginLeft	0	CSG
XmCMarginLeft	short	
XmNmarginRight	0	CSG
XmCMarginRight	short	
XmNmarginTop	0	CSG
XmCMarginTop	short	
XmNmarginWidth	2	CSG
XmCMarginWidth	short	

Name	Default	Access
Class	Type	
XmNmnemonic	'\0'	CSG
XmCMnemonic	char	
XmNrecomputeSize	True	CSG
XmCRecomputeSize	Boolean	

XmNaccelerator

Sets the accelerator on a button widget in a menu, which activates a visible or invisible button from the keyboard. This resource is a string that describes a set of modifiers and the key that may be used to select the button. The format of this string is identical to that used by the translations manager, with the exception that only a single event may be specified and only **KeyPress** events are allowed.

Accelerators for buttons are supported only for certain buttons in certain menu gadgets, namely for PushButtonGadget and ToggleButtonGadget in Pulldown and Popup menus.

XmNaccelerator Text

Specifies the text displayed for the accelerator. The text is displayed to the right of the label string or pixmap. Accelerator text for buttons is displayed only for PushButtonGadgets and ToggleButtonGadgets in Pulldown and Popup Menus.

XmNalignment

Specifies the label alignment for text or pixmap.

- **XmALIGNMENT_CENTER** (center alignment) — causes the centers of the lines of text to be vertically aligned in the center of the parent window. For a pixmap, its center is vertically aligned with the center of the widget window.

- **XmALIGNMENT_END** (right alignment) — causes the right sides of the lines of text to be vertically aligned with the right edge of the parent window. For a pixmap, its right side is vertically aligned with the right edge of the widget window.

- **XmALIGNMENT_BEGINNING** (left alignment) — causes the left sides of the lines of text to be vertically aligned with the left edge of the parent window. For a pixmap, its left side is vertically aligned with the left edge of the widget window.

XmNfontList

Specifies the font of the text used in the gadget.

XmNlabelInsensitivePixmap

Specifies a pixmap used as the button face if **XmNlabelType** is **XmPIXMAP** and the button is insensitive.

XmNlabelPixmap

Specifies the pixmap when **XmNlabelType** is **XmPIXMAP**.

XmNlabelString

Specifies the compound string when **XmNlabelType** is **XmSTRING**.

XmNlabelType

Specifies the label type.

- **XmSTRING** — text displays **XmNlabelString**

- **XmPIXMAP** — icon data in pixmap displays **XmNlabelPixmap** or **XmNlabelInsensitivePixmap**

XmNmarginBottom

Specifies the amount of spacing that is to be left, after the bottom margin (**XmNmarginHeight**) of the gadget, before the label is drawn. This may be modified by LabelGadget's subclasses. For example, CascadeButtonGadget may increase this field to make room for the cascade pixmap.

XmNmarginHeight
> Specifies the amount of blank space between the bottom edge of the top shadow and the label, and the top edge of the bottom shadow and the label.

XmNmarginLeft
> Specifies the amount of spacing that is to be left after the left margin (**XmNmarginWidth**) of the gadget before the label is drawn. This may be modified by LabelGadget's subclasses. For example, ToggleButtonGadget may increase this field to make room for the toggle indicator and for spacing between the indicator and label.

XmNmarginRight
> Specifies the amount of spacing that is to be left after the right margin (**XmNmarginWidth**) of the gadget before the label is drawn. This may be modified by LabelGadget's subclasses. For example, CascadeButtonGadget may increase this field to make room for the cascade pixmap.

XmNmarginTop
> Specifies the amount of spacing that is to be left after the top margin (**XmNmarginHeight**) of the gadget before the label is drawn. This may be modified by LabelGadget's subclasses. For example, CascadeButtonGadget may increase this field to make room for the cascade pixmap.

XmNmarginWidth
> Specifies the amount of blank space between the right edge of the left shadow and the label, and the left edge of the right shadow and the label.

XmNmnemonic
> Provides the user with alternate means for selecting a button. The buttons must be visible for mnemonics to work. Buttons that are in either a Popup MenuPane, a Pulldown MenuPane, or an Option menu are allowed to have a mnemonic.
>
> This resource contains a single character. The first character in the label string that exactly matches the mnemonic is underlined when the button is displayed.

Mnemonics are activated by pressing the specified mnemonic. Mnemonics are case insensitive; the character underlined can be a modified key, but the key pressed should always be unmodified.

XmNrecomputeSize

Specifies a Boolean value that indicates whether the gadget attempts to be big enough to contain the label. If True, an **XtSetValues** with a new label string or pixmap, accelerator text, margins, font, or label type causes the gadget to shrink or expand to exactly fit the new label string or pixmap. If False, the gadget never attempts to change size on its own.

Inherited Resources

LabelGadget inherits behavior and resources from the following superclasses. For a complete description of each resource, refer to the man page for that superclass.

XmGadget Resource Set		
Name	**Default**	**Access**
Class	**Type**	
XmNhelpCallback	NULL	C
XmCCallback	XtCallbackList	
XmNhighlightOnEnter	False	CSG
XmCHighlightOnEnter	Boolean	
XmNhighlightThickness	0	CSG
XmCHighlightThickness	short	
XmNshadowThickness	0	CSG
XmCShadowThickness	short	
XmNtraversalOn	False	CSG
XmCTraversalOn	Boolean	
XmNuserData	NULL	CSG
XmCUserData	caddr_t	

RectObj Resource Set		
Name	**Default**	**Access**
Class	**Type**	
XmNancestorSensitive	XtCopyFromParent	CSG
XmCSensitive	Boolean	
XmNborderWidth	0	CSG
XmCBorderWidth	Dimension	
XmNheight	0	CSG
XmCHeight	Dimension	
XmNsensitive	True	CSG
XmCSensitive	Boolean	
XmNwidth	0	CSG
XmCWidth	Dimension	
XmNx	0	CSG
XmCPosition	Position	
XmNy	0	CSG
XmCPosition	Position	

Object Resource Set		
Name	**Default**	**Access**
Class	**Type**	
XmNdestroyCallback	NULL	C
XmCCallback	XtCallbackList	

Keyboard Traversal

For information on keyboard traversal, see the man page for **XmGadget(3X)** and its sections on behavior and default translations.

Related Information

Object(3X), **RectObj(3X)**, **XmCreateLabelGadget(3X)**,
XmFontListCreate(3X), and **XmGadget(3X)**.

XmList

Purpose

The List widget class

AES Support Level

Full-use

Synopsis

#include <Xm/List.h>

Description

List allows a user to select one or more items from a group of choices. Items are selected from the list in a variety of ways, using both the pointer and the keyboard.

List operates on an array of strings that are defined by the application. Each string becomes an item in List, with the first string becoming the item in position 1, the second string becoming the item in position 2, and so on.

The size of List is set by specifying the number of items that are visible. If selection scrolling ability through a large set of choices is desired, use the **XmCreateScrolledList** convenience function.

To select items, move the pointer or cursor to the desired item and press the mouse button or the key defined as Select. There are several styles of selection behavior, and they all highlight the selected item or items by displaying them in inverse colors. An appropriate callback is invoked to notify the application of the user's choice. The application then takes whatever action is required for the specified selection.

Classes

List inherits behavior and resources from **Core** and **XmPrimitive** classes.

The class pointer is **xmListWidgetClass**.

The class name is **XmList**.

New Resources

The following table defines a set of widget resources used by the programmer to specify data. The programmer can also set the resource values for the inherited classes to set attributes for this widget. To reference a resource by name or by class in a .Xdefaults file, remove the **XmN** or **XmC** prefix and use the remaining letters. To specify one of the defined values for a resource in a .Xdefaults file, remove the **Xm** prefix and use the remaining letters (in either lowercase or uppercase, but include any underscores between words). The codes in the access column indicate if the given resource can be set at creation time (**C**), set by using **XtSetValues** (**S**), retrieved by using **XtGetValues** (**G**), or is not applicable (**N/A**).

XmList Resource Set		
Name **Class**	**Default** **Type**	**Access**
XmNautomaticSelection XmCAutomaticSelection	False Boolean	CSG
XmNbrowseSelectionCallback XmCCallback	NULL XtCallbackList	C
XmNdefaultActionCallback XmCCallback	NULL XtCallbackList	C
XmNextendedSelectionCallback XmCCallback	NULL XtCallbackList	C
XmNfontList XmCFontList	"fixed" XmFontList	CSG
XmNitemCount XmCItemCount	0 int	CSG
XmNitems XmCItems	NULL XmStringTable	CSG
XmNlistMarginHeight XmCListMarginHeight	0 Dimension	CSG
XmNlistMarginWidth XmCListMarginWidth	0 Dimension	CSG
XmNlistSpacing XmCListSpacing	0 short	CSG
XmNmultipleSelectionCallback XmCCallback	NULL XtCallbackList	C
XmNselectedItemCount XmCSelectedItemCount	0 int	CSG
XmNselectedItems XmCSelectedItems	NULL XmStringTable	CSG
XmNselectionPolicy XmCSelectionPolicy	XmBROWSE_SELECT unsigned char	CSG

Name	Default	Access
Class	Type	
XmNsingleSelectionCallback	NULL	C
XmCCallback	XtCallbackList	
XmNvisibleItemCount	1	CSG
XmCVisibleItemCount	int	

XmNautomaticSelection

Invokes **XmNsingleSelectionCallback** when the user moves into a new item if the value is True and the selection mode is either **XmBROWSE_SELECT** or **XmEXTENDED_SELECT**. If False, no selection callbacks are invoked until the user releases the mouse button. See the Behavior section for further details on the interaction of this resource with the selection modes.

XmNbrowseSelectionCallback

Specifies a list of callbacks that is called when an item is selected in the browse selection mode. The reason is **XmCR_BROWSE_SELECT**.

XmNdefaultActionCallback

Specifies a list of callbacks that is called when an item is double clicked. The reason is **XmCR_DEFAULT_ACTION**.

XmNextendedSelectionCallback

Specifies a list of callbacks that is called when items are selected using the extended selection mode. The reason is **XmCR_EXTENDED_SELECT**.

XmNfontList

Specifies the font list associated with the list items. This is used in conjunction with the **XmNvisibleItemsCount** resource to determine the height of the List widget.

XmNitemCount
> Specifies the total number of items. This number must match
> **XmNitems**. It is automatically updated by the list whenever
> an element is added to or deleted from the list.

XmNitems Points to an array of compound strings that are to be displayed
as the list items.

XmNlistMarginHeight
> Specifies the height of the margin between the list border and
> the items.

XmNlistMarginWidth
> Specifies the width of the margin between the list border and
> the items.

XmNlistSpacing
> Specifies the spacing between list items. When keyboard
> traversal is enabled, this spacing increases by the value of the
> **XmNhighlightThickness** parameter in Primitive.

XmNmultipleSelectionCallback
> Specifies a list of callbacks that is called when an item is
> selected in multiple selection mode. The reason is
> **XmCR_MULTIPLE_SELECT**.

XmNselectedItemCount
> Specifies the number of strings in the selected items list.

XmNselectedItems
> Points to an array of compound strings that represents the list
> items that are currently selected, either by the user or by the
> application.

XmNselectionPolicy
> Defines the interpretation of the selection action. This can be
> one of the following:
>
> - **XmSINGLE_SELECT** — allows only single selections
>
> - **XmMULTIPLE_SELECT** — allows multiple selections

- **XmEXTENDED_SELECT** — allows extended selections
- **XmBROWSE_SELECT** — allows PM "drag and browse" functionality

XmNsingleSelectionCallback
Specifies a list of callbacks that is called when an item is selected in single selection mode. The reason is **XmCR_SINGLE_SELECT**.

XmNvisibleItemCount
Specifies the number of items that can fit in the visible space of the list work area. The List uses this value to determine its height.

XmScrolledList Resource Set		
Name Class	**Default** Type	**Access**
XmNhorizontalScrollBar XmCHorizontalScrollBar	NULL Widget	CSG
XmNlistSizePolicy XmCListSizePolicy	XmVARIABLE unsigned char	CG
XmNscrollBarDisplayPolicy XmCScrollBarDisplayPolicy	XmAS_NEEDED unsigned char	CSG
XmNscrollBarPlacement XmCScrollBarPlacement	XmBOTTOM_RIGHT unsigned char	CSG
XmNscrolledWindowMarginHeight XmCScrolledWindowMarginHeight	0 Dimension	CSG
XmNscrolledWindowMarginWidth XmCScrolledWindowMarginWidth	0 Dimension	CSG
XmNspacing XmCSpacing	4 Dimension	CSG
XmNverticalScrollBar XmCVerticalScrollBar	NULL Widget	CSG

XmNhorizontalScrollBar

Specifies the widget ID of the horizontal ScrollBar. This widget is created automatically by the **XmCreateScrolledList** convenience function.

XmNlistSizePolicy

Controls the reaction of the List when an item grows horizontally beyond the current size of the list work area. If the value is **XmCONSTANT**, the list viewing area does not grow, and a horizontal ScrollBar is added. If this resource is set to **XmVARIABLE**, List grows to match the size of the longest item, and no horizontal ScrollBar appears.

When the value of this resource is **XmRESIZE_IF_POSSIBLE**, the List attempts to grow or shrink to match the width of the widest item. If it cannot grow to match the widest size, a horizontal ScrollBar is added if the longest item is wider than the list viewing area.

The size policy must be set at the time the List widget is created. It cannot be changed at a later time through **XtSetValues**.

XmNscrollBarDisplayPolicy

Specifies the ScrollBar display policy. When this resource is set to **XmAS_NEEDED**, the vertical ScrollBar is displayed only when the number of items in the List exceeds the number of visible items. If **XmNlistSizePolicy** is **XmCONSTANT** or **XmRESIZE_IF_POSSIBLE**, the horizontal ScrollBar is displayed only if there is an item that is wider than the current width of the list. When this resource is set to **XmSTATIC**, the vertical ScrollBar is always displayed. The horizontal ScrollBar is always displayed if **XmNlistSizePolicy** is set to **XmCONSTANT** or **XmRESIZE_IF_POSSIBLE**.

XmNscrollBarPlacement

Specifies the positioning of the ScrollBars in relation to the visible items. The following are the values:

- **XmTOP_LEFT** — The horizontal ScrollBar is placed above the visible items and the vertical ScrollBar to the left of the visible items.

- **XmBOTTOM_LEFT** — The horizontal ScrollBar is placed below the visible items and the vertical ScrollBar to the left of the visible items.

- **XmTOP_RIGHT** — The horizontal ScrollBar is placed above the visible items and the vertical ScrollBar to the right of the visible items.

- **XmBOTTOM_RIGHT** — The horizontal ScrollBar is placed below the visible items and the vertical ScrollBar to the right of the visible items.

XmNscrolledWindowMarginHeight
Specifies the margin height on the top and bottom of the ScrolledWindow.

XmNscrolledWindowMargin Width
Specifies the margin width on the right and left sides of the ScrolledWindow.

XmNspacing
Specifies the distance between the ScrollBars from the visible items.

XmNverticalScrollBar
Specifies the widget ID of the vertical ScrollBar. This widget is created automatically by the **XmCreateScrolledList** convenience function.

Inherited Resources

List inherits behavior and resources from the following superclasses. For a complete description of each resource, refer to the man page for that superclass.

XmPrimitive Resource Set		
Name Class	**Default** Type	**Access**
XmNbottomShadowColor XmCForeground	dynamic Pixel	CSG
XmNbottomShadowPixmap XmCBottomShadowPixmap	XmUNSPECIFIED_PIXMAP Pixmap	CSG
XmNforeground XmCForeground	dynamic Pixel	CSG
XmNhelpCallback XmCCallback	NULL XtCallbackList	C
XmNhighlightColor XmCForeground	Black Pixel	CSG
XmNhighlightOnEnter XmCHighlightOnEnter	False Boolean	CSG
XmNhighlightPixmap XmCHighlightPixmap	dynamic Pixmap	CSG
XmNhighlightThickness XmCHighlightThickness	0 short	CSG
XmNshadowThickness XmCShadowThickness	2 short	CSG
XmNtopShadowColor XmCBackground	dynamic Pixel	CSG
XmNtopShadowPixmap XmCTopShadowPixmap	XmUNSPECIFIED_PIXMAP Pixmap	CSG
XmNtraversalOn XmCTraversalOn	False Boolean	CSG
XmNuserData XmCUserData	NULL caddr_t	CSG

Core Resource Set		

Name
    Class
	Default
	    Type
		Access

XmNaccelerators
    XmCAccelerators
	NULL
	    XtTranslations
		CSG

XmNancestorSensitive
    XmCSensitive
	True
	    Boolean
		G

XmNbackground
    XmCBackground
	dynamic
	    Pixel
		CSG

XmNbackgroundPixmap
    XmCPixmap
	XmUNSPECIFIED_PIXMAP
	    Pixmap
		CSG

XmNborderColor
    XmCBorderColor
	Black
	    Pixel
		CSG

XmNborderPixmap
    XmCPixmap
	XmUNSPECIFIED_PIXMAP
	    Pixmap
		CSG

XmNborderWidth
    XmCBorderWidth
	0
	    Dimension
		CSG

XmNcolormap
    XmCColormap
	XtCopyFromParent
	    Colormap
		CG

XmNdepth
    XmCDepth
	XtCopyFromParent
	    int
		CG

XmNdestroyCallback
    XmCCallback
	NULL
	    XtCallbackList
		C

XmNheight
    XmCHeight
	0
	    Dimension
		CSG

XmNmappedWhenManaged
    XmCMappedWhenManaged
	True
	    Boolean
		CSG

XmNscreen
    XmCScreen
	XtCopyScreen
	    Pointer
		CG

XmNsensitive
    XmCSensitive
	True
	    Boolean
		CSG

Name	Default	Access
Class	Type	
XmNtranslations	NULL	CSG
XmCTranslations	XtTranslations	
XmNwidth	0	CSG
XmCWidth	Dimension	
XmNx	0	CSG
XmCPosition	Position	
XmNy	0	CSG
XmCPosition	Position	

Callback Information

List defines a new callback structure. The application must first look at the reason field and use only the structure members that are valid for that particular reason, because not all fields are relevant for every possible reason. The callback structure is defined as follows:

```
typedef struct
{
    int          reason;
    XEvent       * event;
    XmString     item;
    int          item_length;
    int          item_position;
    XmString     * selected_items;
    int          selected_item_count;
    int          selection_type;
} XmListCallbackStruct;
```

reason	Indicates why the callback was invoked.
event	Points to the **XEvent** that triggered the callback. It can be NULL.
item	Is the item selected by this action. *selected_items* points to a temporary storage space that is reused after the callback is finished. Therefore, if an application needs to save the selected list, it should copy the list into its own data space.
item_length	Is the length of the item when the selection action occurred.
item_position	Is the position in the List of the selected item.
selected_items	Points to the list of items selected at the time of the *event* that caused the callback. *selected_items* points to a temporary storage space that is reused after the callback is finished. Therefore, if an application needs to save the selected list, it should copy the list into its own data space.

selected_items_count
Is the number of items in the *selected_items* list.

selection_type	Indicates that the most recent extended selection was the initial selection (**XmINITIAL**), a modification of an existing selection (**XmMODIFICATION**), or an additional noncontiguous selection (**XmADDITION**).

The following table describes the reasons for which the individual callback structure fields are valid:

Reason	Valid Fields
XmCR_SINGLE_SELECT	*reason, event, item, item_length, item_position*
XmCR_DEFAULT_ACTION	*reason, event, item, item_length, item_position*
XmCR_BROWSE_SELECT	*reason, event, item, item_length, item_position*
XmCR_MULTIPLE_SELECT	*reason, event, item, selected_items, selected_item_count*
XmCR_EXTENDED_SELECT	*reason, event, item, selected_items, selected_item_count, selection_type*

Behavior

List provides several methods for selecting its items. The general selection model is as follows:

The user moves the pointer to the item to be selected, either by using the mouse to move the pointer over the desired item, or, in keyboard traversal mode, moving the active highlight to the desired item with the up and down arrow keys. The item is selected by clicking the select button on the mouse (usually the left mouse button), or by pressing the select key on the keyboard (usually the Space key). Each of the selection modes provides some variation of the above behavior. Note that the keyboard selection interface is active only when traversal is enabled for the List widget.

The selection mode is set by the **XmNselectionPolicy** resource and is modified by the **XmNautomaticSelection** resource. The behavior of the various modes are defined below:

XmSINGLE_SELECT (Single Selection):

Move the mouse pointer or keyboard highlight until it is over the desired item and press the select button or key. The item inverts its foreground and background colors to indicate that it is the selected object. Any previously selected items are unselected (returned to their normal visual state). When the button or key is released, **XmNsingleSelectionCallback** is invoked.

XmBROWSE_SELECT (Browse Selection):

When using the mouse, press the select button; the item under the pointer is highlighted. While the button is held down, drag the selection by moving the pointer. When the select button is released, the object under the pointer becomes the selected item and the **XmNbrowseSelectionCallback** is invoked.

If **XmNautomaticSelection** is True, the **XmNbrowseSelectionCallback** is invoked when the select button is pressed. For each subsequent item entered while the select button is held down, the callback is invoked when the pointer moves into the item. No selection callback is invoked when the button is released.

When selecting through the keyboard and **XmNautomaticSelection** is False, browse selection is no different from single-selection mode. However, when **XmNautomaticSelection** is True, the callback is invoked for each element that is selected. Both the keyboard highlight and the selection highlight move as the user moves through the list.

XmMULTIPLE_SELECT (Multiple Selection):

Move the mouse pointer or keyboard highlight until it is over the desired item and press the select button or key. The item inverts its foreground and background colors to indicate that it is a selected object. Any previously selected items are not affected by this action. When the button or key is released, the **XmNmultipleSelectionCallback** is invoked. To unselect an item in this mode, move to a selected item and press the select button or key. The **XmNmultipleSelectionCallback** is invoked with the updated selection list.

XmEXTENDED_SELECT (Extended Selection):

This mode selects a contiguous range of objects with one action. Press the select button on the first item of the range. This begins a new selection process, which deselects any previous selection in the list. That item's colors are inverted to show its inclusion in the selection. While pressing the button, drag the cursor through other items in the List. As the pointer moves through the list, the colors of all items between the initial item and the item currently under the pointer are inverted to show that they are included in the selection. When the button is released, the **XmNextendedSelectionCallback** is invoked and contains a list of all selected items. The *selection_type* field is set to **XmINITIAL**.

Modify a selection by pressing and holding the shift key, moving to the new endpoint, and pressing the select button. The items between the initial start point and the new end point are selected. The rest of the selection process proceeds as above. Any previous selections are not unselected. When the select button is released, the **XmNextendedSelectionCallback** is invoked and contains a list of all selected items, both new and previous. The *selection_type* field is to **XmMODIFICATION**.

Items can be added to or deleted from a selected range by using the CTRL key. To add an additional range to an existing selection, move to the first item of the new group, press and hold the CTRL key, and then press the select button. The color of the item under the pointer inverts; any previous selections are unaffected. This item becomes the initial item for the new selection range. If the pointer is dragged through additional items while the CTRL key and select button are held down, those items' colors invert as described above. When the select button is released, the **XmNextendedSelectionCallback** is invoked and contains a list of all selected items, both new and previous. The *selection_type* field is set to **XmADDITION**.

To delete an item or a range of items from an existing selection, move to the first item to be deselected, press and hold the CTRL key, and then press the select button. The item under the pointer returns to its normal visual state to indicate that it is no longer in the selection. This item becomes the initial item for the range to be deselected. If the pointer is dragged through additional selected items while the CTRL key and select button are held down, those items are deselected. Any other selections are unaffected. When the select button is released, the **XmNextendedSelectionCallback** is invoked and contains a list of remaining selected items, both new and previous. The *selection_type* field is set to **XmADDITION**.

A range of items can also be deselected by setting the initial item for the range as described above, then moving to the end of the range, and pressing the select button while holding the Shift key down. All items between the two endpoints are deselected. When the button is released, the **XmNextendedSelectionCallback** is issued as described above.

If the **XmNautomaticSelection** resource is set to True, the **XmNextendedSelectionCallback** is invoked when the select button is pressed. For each subsequent item the user selects or deselects, the callback is invoked when the pointer is moved into the item. The *selection_type* field is set to reflect the current action. No selection callback is invoked when the button is released.

Keyboard selection in extended selection mode is accomplished by moving the keyboard highlight to the start of the desired range and pressing the select key. The selection callback is invoked with a *selection_type* value of **XmINITIAL**. Then, using the arrow keys, move the keyboard highlight to the end of the range, hold down the Shift key, and press the select key. The **XmNextendedSelectionCallback** is invoked with a value of **XmMODIFICATION**. Select additional ranges by moving to the beginning of a range, pressing the select key while holding down the CTRL key, and then moving to the end of the range and pressing the select key while holding the Shift key. Erase previously selected elements by moving to them and pressing the select key while holding down the CTRL key. In all cases, callbacks are issued as described above.

When using the keyboard with the **XmNautomaticSelection** resource set to True, the **XmNextendedSelectionCallback** is invoked when the select button is pressed. For each subsequent item the user selects, the callback is invoked when the pointer is moved into the item if there are modifier keys in use. For example, start the selection by pressing the select key, and then extend it by using the arrow keys while holding down the Shift key. The *selection_type* field is set to reflect the current action. There is no selection callback invoked when the button is released.

XmDEFAULT-ACTION (Double Click)

If an object is double clicked, the **XmNdefaultActionCallback** is invoked. The item's colors invert to indicate that it is selected.

Default Translations

The following are the default Translations for XmList:

Button1<Motion>:   **ListButtonMotion()**
Shift Ctrl ¯Meta<Btn1Down>: ListShiftCtrlSelect()
Shift Ctrl ¯Meta<Btn1Up>:   ListShiftCtrlUnSelect()
Shift Ctrl ¯Meta<KeyDown>space:ListKbdShiftCtrlSelect()
Shift Ctrl ¯Meta<KeyUp>space:ListKbdShiftCtrlUnSelect()
Shift Ctrl ¯Meta<KeyDown>Select:ListKbdShiftCtrlSelect()
Shift Ctrl ¯Meta<KeyUp>Select:ListKbdShiftCtrlUnSelect()
Shift ¯Ctrl ¯Meta<Btn1Down>: ListShiftSelect()
Shift ¯Ctrl ¯Meta<Btn1Up>:   ListShiftUnSelect()
Shift ¯Ctrl ¯Meta<KeyDown>space:ListKbdShiftSelect()
Shift ¯Ctrl ¯Meta<KeyUp>space:ListKbdShiftUnSelect()
Shift ¯Ctrl ¯Meta<KeyDown>Select:ListKbdShiftSelect()
Shift ¯Ctrl ¯Meta<KeyUp>Select:ListKbdShiftUnSelect()
Ctrl ¯Shift ¯Meta<Btn1Down>: ListCtrlSelect()
Ctrl ¯Shift ¯Meta<Btn1Up>:   ListCtrlUnSelect()
Ctrl ¯Shift ¯Meta<KeyDown>space:ListKbdCtrlSelect()
Ctrl ¯Shift ¯Meta<KeyUp>space:ListKbdCtrlUnSelect()
Ctrl ¯Shift ¯Meta<KeyDown>Select:ListKbdCtrlSelect()
Ctrl ¯Shift ¯Meta<KeyUp>Select:ListKbdCtrlUnSelect()
¯Shift ¯Ctrl ¯Meta<Btn1Down>: ListElementSelect()
¯Shift ¯Ctrl ¯Meta<Btn1Up>:   ListElementUnSelect()
¯Shift ¯Ctrl ¯Meta<KeyDown>space:ListKbdSelect()

˜Shift ˜Ctrl ˜Meta<KeyUp>space:ListKbdUnSelect()
˜Shift ˜Ctrl ˜Meta<KeyDown>Select:ListKbdSelect()
˜Shift ˜Ctrl ˜Meta<KeyUp>Select:ListKbdUnSelect()
Shift Ctrl ˜Meta<Key>Up: **ListShiftCtrlPrevElement()**
Shift Ctrl ˜Meta<Key>Down: **ListShiftCtrlNextElement()**
Shift ˜Ctrl ˜Meta<Key>Up: **ListShiftPrevElement()**
Shift ˜Ctrl ˜Meta<Key>Down: **ListShiftNextElement()**
˜Shift Ctrl ˜Meta<Key>Up: **ListCtrlPrevElement()**
˜Shift Ctrl ˜Meta<Key>Down: **ListCtrlNextElement()**
˜Shift ˜Ctrl ˜Meta<Key>Up: **ListPrevElement()**
˜Shift ˜Ctrl ˜Meta<Key>Down: **ListNextElement()**
<Enter>:   **ListEnter()**
<Leave>:   **ListLeave()**
<FocusIn>:   **ListFocusIn()**
<FocusOut>:   **ListFocusOut()**
<Unmap>:   **PrimitiveUnmap()**
Shift<Key>Tab: **PrimitivePrevTabGroup()**
<Key>Tab: **PrimitiveNextTabGroup()**
<Key>Home: **PrimitiveTraverseHome()**

Keyboard Traversal

For those actions not inherited from **XmPrimitive(3X)**, keyboard traversal is described in the behavior section of this man page.

Related Information

Core(3X), XmCreateList(3X), XmCreateScrolledList(3X),
XmListAddItem(3X), XmListAddItemUnselected(3X),
XmListDeleteItem(3X), XmListDeletePos(3X),
XmListDeselectItem(3X), XmListDeselectAllItems(3X),
XmListSelectItem(3X), XmListSetHorizPos(3X), XmListSetItem(3X),
XmListSetPos(3X), XmListSetBottomItem(3X),
XmListSetBottomPos(3X), XmListSelectPos(3X),
XmListDeselectPos(3X), and XmListItemExists(3X), and
XmPrimitive(3X).

XmListAddItem

Purpose

A List function that adds an item to the list

AES Support Level

Full-use

Synopsis

#include <Xm/List.h>

void XmListAddItem (*widget, item, position*)
    Widget   *widget*;
    XmString *item*;
    int   *position*;

Description

XmListAddItem adds an item to the list at the given position. The position specifies the location of the new item in the list. Position 1 is the first element, position 2 is the second, and so on. If the position argument is zero, the item is added after the last item in the list. When the item is inserted into the list, it is compared with the current **XmNselectedItems** list. If the new item matches an item on the selected list, it appears selected.

widget   Specifies the ID of the List from whose list an item is added.

item   Specifies the item to be added to the list.

position Specifies the placement of the item within the list in terms of its cell position. It uses an insert mode/cell number scheme with a 1 specifying the top-entry position and a zero specifying the bottom entry for adding an item to the bottom of the list.

For a complete definition of List and its associated resources, see **XmList(3X)**.

Related Information

XmList(3X).

XmListAddItemUnselected

Purpose

A List function that adds an item to the list

AES Support Level

Full-use

Synopsis

#include <Xm/List.h>

void XmListAddItemUnselected (*widget, item, position*)
    Widget   *widget*;
    XmString *item*;
    int   *position*;

Description

XmListAddItemUnselected adds an item to the list at the given position. The position specifies the location of the new item in the list. Position 1 is the first element, position 2 is the second, and so on. If the position argument is zero, the item is added after the last item in the list.

widget   Specifies the ID of the List from whose list an item is added.

item   Specifies the item to be added to the list.

position Specifies the placement of the item within the list in terms of its cell position. It uses an insert mode/cell number scheme with a 1 specifying the top-entry position and a zero specifying the bottom entry position.

For a complete definition of List and its associated resources, see **XmList(3X)**.

Related Information

XmList(3X).

Related Information

XmList(3X).

XmListDeletePos

Purpose

A List function that deletes an item from a list at a specified position.

AES Support Level

Full-use

Synopsis

#include <Xm/List.h>

void XmListDeletePos (*widget, position*)
    Widget   *widget*;
    int   *position*;

Description

XmListDeletePos deletes an item at a specified position. A position argument of zero deletes the last item in the list. A warning message appears if the position does not exist.

widget   Specifies the ID of the List from whose list an item is to be deleted.

position   Identifies the position of the item to be deleted.

For a complete definition of List and its associated resources, see **XmList(3X)**.

For a complete definition of List and its associated resources, see
XmList(3X).

Related Information

XmList(3X).

XmListDeselectItem

Purpose

A List function that deselects the specified item from the selected list.

AES Support Level

Full-use

Synopsis

#include <Xm/List.h>

void XmListDeselectItem (*widget, item*)
    Widget   *widget*;
    XmString *item*;

Description

XmListDeselectItem unhighlights and removes the specified item from the selected list.

widget   Specifies the ID of the List from whose list an item is deselected

item   Specifies the item to be deselected from the list

For a complete definition of List and its associated resources, see **XmList(3X)**.

Related Information

XmList(3X).

XmListItemExists

Purpose

A List function that checks if a specified item is in the list.

AES Support Level

Full-use

Synopsis

#include <Xm/List.h>

Boolean XmListItemExists (*widget, item*)
    Widget   *widget*;
    XmString *item*;

Description

XmListItemExists is a Boolean function that checks if a specified item is present in the list.

widget   Specifies the ID of the List widget

item   Specifies the item whose presence is checked

For a complete definition of List and its associated resources, see **XmList(3X)**.

Description

XmListSelectItem highlights and adds the specified item to the current selected list.

widget   Specifies the ID of the List widget from whose list an item is selected

item   Specifies the item to be added to the List widget

notify   Specifies a Boolean value that when True invokes the selection callback for the current mode. From an application interface view, calling this function with *notify* True is indistinguishable from a user-initiated selection action.

For a complete definition of List and its associated resources, see **XmList(3X)**.

Related Information

XmList(3X).

XmListSelectPos

Purpose

A List function that selects an item at a specified position in the list.

AES Support Level

Full-use

Synopsis

#include <Xm/List.h>

void XmListSelectPos (*widget, position, notify*)
    Widget   *widget*;
    int   *position*;
    Boolean   *notify*;

For a complete definition of List and its associated resources, see
XmList(3X).

Related Information

XmList(3X).

XmListSetBottomPos

Purpose

A List function that makes a specified item the last visible position in the list.

AES Support Level

Full-use

Synopsis

#include <Xm/List.h>

void **XmListSetBottomPos** (*widget, position*)
    Widget   *widget*;
    int   *position*;

widget   Specifies the ID of the List widget

position   Identifies the specified position

For a complete definition of List and its associated resources, see **XmList(3X)**.

Related Information

XmList(3X).

XmListSetItem

Purpose

A List function that makes an existing item the first visible item in the list.

AES Support Level

Full-use

Synopsis

#include <Xm/List.h>

void XmListSetItem (*widget, item*)
    Widget   *widget*;
    XmString *item*;

Description

XmListSetItem makes an existing item the first visible item in the list. The item can be any valid item in the list.

widget   Specifies the ID of the List widget from whose list an item is made the first visible

item   Specifies the item

For a complete definition of List and its associated resources, see **XmList(3X)**.

Related Information

XmList(3X).

XmMainWindow

Purpose

The MainWindow widget class

AES Support Level

Full-use

Synopsis

#include <Xm/MainW.h>

Description

MainWindow provides a standard layout for the primary window of an application. This layout includes a MenuBar, a CommandWindow, a work region, and ScrollBars. Any or all of these areas are optional. The work region and ScrollBars in the MainWindow behave identically to the work region and ScrollBars in the ScrolledWindow widget. The user can think of the MainWindow as an extended ScrolledWindow with an optional MenuBar and optional CommandWindow.

XmNmainWindowMarginHeight

Specifies the margin height on the top and bottom of MainWindow. This resource overrides any setting of the ScrolledWindow resource **XmNscrolledWindowMarginHeight**.

XmNmainWindowMarginWidth

Specifies the margin width on the right and left sides of MainWindow. This resource overrides any setting of the ScrolledWindow resource **XmNscrolledWindowMarginWidth**.

XmNmenuBar

Specifies the widget to be laid out as the MenuBar. This widget must have been previously created and managed as a child of MainWindow.

XmNshowSeparator

Displays separators between the components of the MainWindow when set to True. If set to False, no separators are displayed.

Inherited Resources

MainWindow inherits behavior and resources from the following superclasses. For a complete description of each resource, refer to the man page for that superclass.

XmScrolledWindow Resource Set		
Name Class	**Default** Type	**Access**
XmNclipWindow XmCClipWindow	NULL Widget	G
XmNhorizontalScrollBar XmCHorizontalScrollBar	NULL Widget	CSG
XmNscrollBarDisplayPolicy XmCScrollBarDisplayPolicy	XmSTATIC unsigned char	CG
XmNscrollBarPlacement XmCScrollBarPlacement	XmBOTTOM_RIGHT unsigned char	CSG
XmNscrolledWindowMarginHeight XmCScrolledWindowMarginHeight	0 Dimension	CSG
XmNscrolledWindowMarginWidth XmCScrolledWindowMarginWidth	0 Dimension	CSG
XmNscrollingPolicy XmCScrollingPolicy	XmAPPLICATION_DEFINED unsigned char	CG
XmNspacing XmCSpacing	4 int	CSG
XmNverticalScrollBar XmCVerticalScrollBar	NULL Widget	CSG
XmNvisualPolicy XmCVisualPolicy	XmVARIABLE unsigned char	CG
XmNworkWindow XmCWorkWindow	NULL Widget	CSG

Core Resource Set		
Name	**Default**	**Access**
Class	**Type**	
XmNaccelerators	NULL	CSG
XmCAccelerators	XtTranslations	
XmNancestorSensitive	True	G
XmCSensitive	Boolean	
XmNbackground	dynamic	CSG
XmCBackground	Pixel	
XmNbackgroundPixmap	XmUNSPECIFIED_PIXMAP	CSG
XmCPixmap	Pixmap	
XmNborderColor	Black	CSG
XmCBorderColor	Pixel	
XmNborderPixmap	XmUNSPECIFIED_PIXMAP	CSG
XmCPixmap	Pixmap	
XmNborderWidth	0	CSG
XmCBorderWidth	Dimension	
XmNcolormap	XtCopyFromParent	CG
XmCColormap	Colormap	
XmNdepth	XtCopyFromParent	CG
XmCDepth	int	
XmNdestroyCallback	NULL	C
XmCCallback	XtCallbackList	
XmNheight	0	CSG
XmCHeight	Dimension	
XmNmappedWhenManaged	True	CSG
XmCMappedWhenManaged	Boolean	
XmNscreen	XtCopyScreen	CG
XmCScreen	Pointer	
XmNsensitive	True	CSG
XmCSensitive	Boolean	

Name	Default	Access
Class	Type	
XmNtranslations	NULL	CSG
XmCTranslations	XtTranslations	
XmNwidth	0	CSG
XmCWidth	Dimension	
XmNx	0	CSG
XmCPosition	Position	
XmNy	0	CSG
XmCPosition	Position	

Behavior

MainWindow inherits behavior from ScrolledWindow.

Keyboard Traversal

For information on keyboard traversal, see the man page for **XmManager(3X)** and its sections on behavior and default translations.

Related Information

Composite(3X), **Constraint(3X)**, **Core(3X)**, **XmCreateMainWindow(3X)**, **XmMainWindowSep1(3X)**, **XmMainWindowSep2(3X)**, **XmMainWindowSetAreas(3X)**, **XmManager(3X)**, and **XmScrolledWindow(3X)**,

XmMainWindowSep1

Purpose

A MainWindow function that returns the widget ID of the first Separator widget.

AES Support Level

Full-use

Synopsis

#include <Xm/MainW.h>

Widget XmMainWindowSep1 (*widget*)
    Widget   *widget*;

Description

XmMainWindowSep1 returns the widget ID of the first Separator widget in the MainWindow. The first Separator widget is located between the MenuBar and the Command widget. This Separator is visible only when **XmNshowSeparator** is True.

widget   Specifies the MainWindow widget ID

For a complete definition of MainWindow and its associated resources, see **XmMainWindow(3X)**.

Return Value

Returns the widget ID of the first Separator.

Related Information

XmMainWindow(3X).

XmMainWindowSep2

Purpose

A MainWindow function that returns the widget ID of the second Separator widget.

AES Support Level

Full-use

Synopsis

#include <Xm/MainW.h>

Widget XmMainWindowSep2 (*widget*)
   Widget   *widget*;

Description

XmMainWindowSep2 returns the widget ID of the second Separator widget in the MainWindow. The second Separator widget is located between the Command widget and the ScrolledWindow. This Separator is visible only when **XmNshowSeparator** is True.

widget   Specifies the MainWindow widget ID

For a complete definition of MainWindow and its associated resources, see **XmMainWindow(3X)**.

Return Value

Returns the widget ID of the second Separator.

Related Information

XmMainWindow(3X).

XmMainWindowSetAreas

Purpose

A MainWindow function that identifies manageable children for each area.

AES Support Level

Full-use

Synopsis

#include <Xm/MainW.h>

void XmMainWindowSetAreas (*widget, menu_bar, command_window, horizontal_scrollbar,*
                 vertical_scrollbar, work_region)
       Widget   *widget*;
       Widget   *menu_bar*;
       Widget   *command_window*;
       Widget   *horizontal_scrollbar*;
       Widget   *vertical_scrollbar*;
       Widget   *work_region*;

Description

XmMainWindowSetAreas identifies which of the valid children for each area (such as the MenuBar and work region) are to be actively managed by MainWindow. This function also sets up or adds the MenuBar, work window, command window, and ScrollBar widgets to the application's main window widget.

Each area is optional; therefore, the user can pass NULL to one or more of the following arguments. The window manager provides the title bar.

widget　　　　Specifies the MainWindow widget ID.

menu_bar　　　Specifies the widget ID for the MenuBar to be associated with the MainWindow widget. Set this ID only after creating an instance of the MainWindow widget. The attribute name associated with this argument is **XmNmenuBar**.

command_window
　　　　　　　Specifies the widget ID for the command window to be associated with the MainWindow widget. Set this ID only after creating an instance of the MainWindow widget. The attribute name associated with this argument is **XmNcommandWindow**.

horizontal_scrollbar
　　　　　　　Specifies the ScrollBar widget ID for the horizontal ScrollBar to be associated with the MainWindow widget. Set this ID only after creating an instance of the MainWindow widget. The attribute name associated with this argument is **XmNhorizontalScrollBar**.

vertical_scrollbar
　　　　　　　Specifies the ScrollBar widget ID for the vertical ScrollBar to be associated with the MainWindow widget. Set this ID only after creating an instance of the MainWindow widget. The attribute name associated with this argument is **XmNverticalScrollBar**.

work_region   Specifies the widget ID for the work window to be associated with the MainWindow widget. Set this ID only after creating an instance of the MainWindow widget. The attribute name associated with this argument is **XmNworkWindow**.

For a complete definition of MainWindow and its associated resources, see **XmMainWindow(3X)**.

Related Information

XmMainWindow(3X).

XmManager

Purpose

The Manager widget class

AES Support Level

Full-use

Synopsis

#include <Xm/Xm.h>

Description

Manager is a widget class used as a supporting superclass for other widget classes. It supports the visual resources, graphics contexts, and traversal resources necessary for the graphics and traversal mechanisms.

Classes

Manager inherits behavior and resources from **Core**, **Composite**, and **Constraint** classes.

The class pointer is **xmManagerWidgetClass**.

The class name is **XmManager**.

New Resources

The following table defines a set of widget resources used by the programmer to specify data. The programmer can also set the resource values for the inherited classes to set attributes for this widget. To reference a resource by name or by class in a .Xdefaults file, remove the **XmN** or **XmC** prefix and use the remaining letters. To specify one of the defined values for a resource in a .Xdefaults file, remove the **Xm** prefix and use the remaining letters (in either lowercase or uppercase, but include any underscores between words). The codes in the access column indicate if the given resource can be set at creation time (**C**), set by using **XtSetValues** (**S**), retrieved by using **XtGetValues** (**G**), or is not applicable (**N/A**).

XmManager Resource Set		

Name
    Class
	Default
	    Type
		Access

XmNbottomShadowColor
    XmCForeground
	dynamic
	    Pixel
		CSG

XmNbottomShadowPixmap
    XmCBottomShadowPixmap
	XmUNSPECIFIED_PIXMAP
	    Pixmap
		CSG

XmNforeground
    XmCForeground
	dynamic
	    Pixel
		CSG

XmNhelpCallback
    XmCCallback
	NULL
	    XtCallbackList
		C

XmNhighlightColor
    XmCForeground
	Black
	    Pixel
		CSG

XmNhighlightPixmap
    XmCHighlightPixmap
	dynamic
	    Pixmap
		CSG

XmNshadowThickness
    XmCShadowThickness
	0
	    short
		CSG

XmNtopShadowColor
    XmCBackground
	dynamic
	    Pixel
		CSG

XmNtopShadowPixmap
    XmCTopShadowPixmap
	XmUNSPECIFIED_PIXMAP
	    Pixmap
		CSG

XmNuserData
    XmCUserData
	NULL
	    caddr_t
		CSG

XmNbottomShadowColor

Specifies the color to use to draw the bottom and right sides of the border shadow. This color is used if the **XmNbottomShadowPixmap** resource is NULL.

XmNbottomShadowPixmap

Specifies the pixmap to use to draw the bottom and right sides of the border shadow.

XmNforeground

Specifies the foreground drawing color used by manager widgets.

XmNhelpCallback

Specifies the list of callbacks that are called when the help key sequence is pressed. The reason sent by this callback is **XmCR_HELP**. No translation is bound to this resource. It is up to the application to install a translation for help.

XmNhighlightColor

Specifies the color of the highlighting rectangle. This color is used if the highlight pixmap resource is **XmUNSPECIFIED_PIXMAP**.

XmNhighlightPixmap

Specifies the pixmap used to draw the highlighting rectangle.

XmNshadowThickness

Specifies the thickness of the drawn border shadow.

XmNtopShadowColor

Specifies the color to use to draw the top and left sides of the border shadow. This color is used if the **XmNtopShadowPixmap** resource is NULL.

XmNtopShadowPixmap

Specifies the pixmap to use to draw the top and left sides of the border shadow.

XmNuserData

Allows the application to attach any necessary specific data to the widget. This is an internally unused resource.

Dynamic Color Defaults

The foreground, background, top shadow, and bottom shadow resources are dynamically defaulted. If no color data is specified, the colors are automatically generated. On a monochrome system, a black and white color scheme is generated. On a color system, four colors are generated, which display the correct shading for the 3-D visuals.

If the background is the only color specified for a widget, the top shadow, bottom shadow, and foreground colors are generated to give the 3-D appearance. The color generation works best with non-saturated colors. Using pure red, green, or blue yields poor results.

Colors are generated at creation only. Resetting the background through **XtSetValues** does not regenerate the other colors.

Inherited Resources

Manager inherits the following resources from the named superclasses. For a complete description of each resource, refer to the man page for that superclass.

Composite Resource Set		
Name	**Default**	**Access**
Class	**Type**	
XmNinsertPosition	NULL	CSG
XmCInsertPosition	XmRFunction	

Core Resource Set		
Name	**Default**	**Access**
Class	**Type**	
XmNaccelerators	NULL	CSG
XmCAccelerators	XtTranslations	
XmNancestorSensitive	True	G
XmCSensitive	Boolean	
XmNbackground	dynamic	CSG
XmCBackground	Pixel	
XmNbackgroundPixmap	XmUNSPECIFIED_PIXMAP	CSG
XmCPixmap	Pixmap	
XmNborderColor	Black	CSG
XmCBorderColor	Pixel	
XmNborderPixmap	XmUNSPECIFIED_PIXMAP	CSG
XmCPixmap	Pixmap	
XmNborderWidth	0	CSG
XmCBorderWidth	Dimension	
XmNcolormap	XtCopyFromParent	CG
XmCColormap	Colormap	
XmNdepth	XtCopyFromParent	CG
XmCDepth	int	
XmNdestroyCallback	NULL	C
XmCCallback	XtCallbackList	
XmNheight	0	CSG
XmCHeight	Dimension	
XmNmappedWhenManaged	True	CSG
XmCMappedWhenManaged	Boolean	
XmNscreen	XtCopyScreen	CG
XmCScreen	Pointer	
XmNsensitive	True	CSG
XmCSensitive	Boolean	

Name	Default	Access
Class	Type	
XmNtranslations	NULL	CSG
XmCTranslations	XtTranslations	
XmNwidth	0	CSG
XmCWidth	Dimension	
XmNx	0	CSG
XmCPosition	Position	
XmNy	0	CSG
XmCPosition	Position	

Behavior

The following set of translations are used by Manager widgets that have Gadget children. Since Gadgets cannot have translations associated with them, it is the responsibility of the Manager widget to intercept the events of interest and pass them to the appropriate Gadget child.

Shift<Key>Tab:

Moves the focus to the first item contained within the previous tab group. If the beginning of the tab group list is reached, it wraps to the end of the tab group list.

<Key>Tab: Moves the focus to the first item contained within the next tab group. If the current tab group is the last entry in the tab group list, it will wrap to the beginning of the tab group list.

<Key>Up or **<Key>Left**:

Moves the keyboard focus to the previous Manager widget or gadget within the current tab group. The previous widget or gadget is the previous entry in the tab group's list of children. Wrapping occurs, if necessary.

<Key>Down or **<Key>Right**:

Moves the Keyboard focus to the next Manager widget or gadget within the current tab group. The previous widget or gadget is the next entry in the tab group's list of children. Wrapping occurs, if necessary.

<Key>Home:

Moves the keyboard focus to the first Manager widget or gadget in the current tab group.

Default Translations

The following are translations used by all Manager widgets.

<EnterWindow>:	**ManagerEnter()**
<FocusOut>:	**ManagerFocusOut()**
<FocusIn>:	**ManagerFocusIn()**

The following are the translations necessary to provide gadget event processing:

<Key>space:	**ManagerGadgetSelect()**
<Key>Return:	**ManagerGadgetSelect()**
Shift<Key>Tab:	**ManagerGadgetPrevTabGroup()**
<Key>Tab:	**ManagerGadgetNextTabGroup()**
<Key>Up:	**ManagerGadgetTraversePrev()**
<Key>Down:	**ManagerGadgetTraverseNext()**
<Key>Left:	**ManagerGadgetTraversePrev()**
<Key>Right:	**ManagerGadgetTraverseNext()**
<Key>Home:	**ManagerGadgetTraverseHome()**

Related Information

Composite(3X), **Constraint(3X)**, **Core(3X)**, and **XmGadget3X)**.

XmMenuPosition

Purpose

A RowColumn function that positions a Popup MenuPane

AES Support Level

Full-use

Synopsis

#include <Xm/RowColumn.h>

void XmMenuPosition (*menu, event*)
    Widget   *menu*;
    XButtonPressedEvent* *event*;

Description

XmMenuPosition positions a Popup MenuPane using the information in the specified event. Unless an application is positioning the MenuPane itself, it must first invoke this function before managing the PopupMenu. The x_root and y_root values in the specified event are used to determine the menu position.

menu   Specifies the PopupMenu to be positioned

event   Specifies the event passed to the action procedure which manages the PopupMenu

For a complete definition of RowColumn and its associated resources, see **XmRowColumn(3X)**.

Related Information

XmRowColumn(3X).

XmMenuShell

Purpose

The MenuShell widget class

AES Support Level

Full-use

Synopsis

#include <Xm/MenuShell.h>

Description

The MenuShell widget is a custom OverrideShell widget. An OverrideShell widget bypasses **mwm** when displaying itself. It is designed specifically to contain Popup or Pulldown MenuPanes.

Most application writers will never encounter this widget if they use the menu-system convenience functions, **XmCreatePopupMenu** or **XmCreatePulldown Menu**, to create a Popup or Pulldown MenuPane. The convenience functions automatically create a MenuShell widget as the parent of the MenuPane. However, if the convenience functions are not used, the application programmer must create the required MenuShell. In this case, it is important to note that the type of parent of the MenuShell depends on the type of menu system being built.

- If the MenuShell is for the top-level Popup MenuPane, the MenuShell must be created as a child of the widget from which the Popup MenuPane is popped up.

- If the MenuShell is for a MenuPane that is pulled down from a Popup or another Pulldown MenuPane, the MenuShell must be created as a child of the Popup or Pulldown MenuPane's parent MenuShell.

- If the MenuShell is for a MenuPane that is pulled down from a MenuBar, then the MenuShell must be created as a child of the MenuBar.

- If the MenuShell is for a Pulldown MenuPane in an OptionMenu, the MenuShell must have the same parent as the OptionMenu.

Classes

MenuShell inherits behavior and resources from **Core**, **Composite**, **Shell**, and **OverrideShell** classes.

The class pointer is **xmMenuShellWidgetClass**.

The class name is **XmMenuShell**.

New Resources

MenuShell defines no new resources, but overrides the **XmNallowShellResize** resource in Shell.

Inherited Resources

MenuShell inherits behavior and resources from the following superclasses. For a complete description of each resource, refer to the man page for that superclass. The following tables define a set of widget resources used by the programmer to specify data. The programmer can set the resource values for these inherited classes to set attributes for this widget. To reference a resource by name or by class in a .Xdefaults file, remove the **XmN** or **XmC** prefix and use the remaining letters. To specify one of the defined values for a resource in a .Xdefaults file, remove the **Xm** prefix and use the remaining letters (in either lowercase or uppercase, but include any underscores between words). The codes in the access column indicate if the given resource can be set at creation time (**C**), set by using **XtSetValues** (**S**), retrieved by using **XtGetValues** (**G**), or is not applicable (**N/A**).

Shell Resource Set		
Name **Class**	**Default** **Type**	**Access**
XmNallowShellResize XmCAllowShellResize	True Boolean	G
XmNancestorSensitive XmCSensitive	ShellAncestorSensitive Boolean	G
XmNcreatePopupChildProc XmCCreatePopupChildProc	NULL XmCreatePopupChildProc	CSG
XmNdepth XmCDepth	ShellDepth int	CSG
XmNgeometry XmCGeometry	NULL caddr_t	CSG
XmNoverrideRedirect XmCOverrideRedirect	True Boolean	CSG
XmNpopdownCallback XmCCallback	NULL caddr_t	C
XmNpopupCallback XmCCallback	NULL caddr_t	C
XmNsaveUnder XmCSaveUnder	True Boolean	CSG

Composite Resource Set		
Name	**Default**	**Access**
Class	**Type**	
XmNinsertPosition	NULL	CSG
XmCInsertPosition	XmRFunction	

Core Resource Set		
Name	**Default**	**Access**
Class	**Type**	
XmNaccelerators	NULL	CSG
XmCAccelerators	XtTranslations	
XmNancestorSensitive	ShellAncestorSensitive	CSG
XmCSensitive	Boolean	
XmNbackground	White	CSG
XmCBackground	Pixel	
XmNbackgroundPixmap	XmUNSPECIFIED_PIXMAP	CSG
XmCPixmap	Pixmap	
XmNborderColor	Black	CSG
XmCBorderColor	Pixel	
XmNborderPixmap	XmUNSPECIFIED_PIXMAP	CSG
XmCPixmap	Pixmap	
XmNborderWidth	1	CSG
XmCBorderWidth	Dimension	
XmNcolormap	ShellColormap	CG
XmCColormap	Colormap	
XmNdepth	ShellDepth	CG
XmCDepth	int	
XmNdestroyCallback	NULL	C
XmCCallback	XtCallbackList	
XmNheight	0	CSG
XmCHeight	Dimension	
XmNmappedWhenManaged	True	CSG
XmCMappedWhenManaged	Boolean	
XmNscreen	XtCopyScreen	CG
XmCScreen	Pointer	
XmNsensitive	True	CSG
XmCSensitive	Boolean	

Name	Default	Access
Class	Type	
XmNtranslations	NULL	CSG
XmCTranslations	XtTranslations	
XmNwidth	0	CSG
XmCWidth	Dimension	
XmNx	0	CSG
XmCPosition	Position	
XmNy	0	CSG
XmCPosition	Position	

Behavior

The mouse button that is used depends upon the resources
XmNrowColumnType and **XmNwhichButton** in the menu's top level
RowColumn widget.

Default PopupMenu System

<Btn3Down>:

> If this event has not already been processed by another menu
> component, then this action disables keyboard traversal for the
> menus and returns the user to drag mode.

<Btn3Up>: If this event has not already been processed by another menu
component, then all visible MenuPanes are unposted.

<Key>Escape:

> If this event has not already been processed by another menu
> component, then all visible MenuPanes are unposted.

Default PulldownMenu System or OptionMenu System

<Btn1Down>:

If this event has not already been processed by another menu component, then this action disables keyboard traversal for the menus and returns the user to drag mode.

<Btn1Up>: If this event has not already been processed by another menu component, then all visible MenuPanes are unposted.

<Key>Escape:

If this event has not already been processed by another menu component, then all visible MenuPanes are unposted.

Default Translations

The default translations for MenuShell are:

<BtnDown>:	**ClearTraversal()**
<Key>Escape:	**MenuShellPopdownDone()**
<BtnUp>:	**MenuShellPopdownDone()**

Related Information

Composite(3X), Core(3X), OverrideShell(3X), Shell(3X), XmCreateMenuShell(3X), XmCreatePopupMenu(3X), XmCreatePulldown(3X), and XmRowColumn(3X).

XmMessageBox

Purpose

The MessageBox widget class

AES Support Level

Full-use

Synopsis

#include <Xm/MessageB.h>

Description

MessageBox is a dialog class used for creating simple message dialogs. Convenience dialogs based on MessageBox are provided for several common interaction tasks, which include giving information, asking questions, and reporting errors.

A MessageBox dialog is typically transient in nature, displayed for the duration of a single interaction. MessageBox is a subclass of XmBulletinBoard and depends on it for much of its general dialog behavior.

A MessageBox can contain a message symbol, a message, and up to three standard default PushButtons: **OK, Cancel**, and **Help**. It is laid out with the symbol in the top left, the message in the top and center-to-right side, and the PushButtons on the bottom. The help button is positioned to the right of the other push buttons. You can localize the default symbols and button labels for MessageBox convenience dialogs.

Button label defaults are easily modified by including the new values in any of the app-defaults file locations supported by Xt Intrinsics. Changing the defaults for MessageBox symbols is more complicated, since the Xt Intrinsics do not support specification of pixmaps by name in resource files.

At initialization, MessageBox looks for the following bitmap files:

- xm_error
- xm_information
- xm_question
- xm_working
- xm_warning

See **XmGetPixmap(3X)** for a list of the paths that are searched for these files.

Classes

MessageBox inherits behavior and resources from **Core, Composite, Constraint, XmManager**, and **XmBulletinBoard**.

The class pointer is **xmMessageBoxWidgetClass**.

The class name is **XmMessageBox**.

New Resources

The following table defines a set of widget resources used by the programmer to specify data. The programmer can also set the resource values for the inherited classes to set attributes for this widget. To reference a resource by name or by class in a .Xdefaults file, remove the **XmN** or **XmC** prefix and use the remaining letters. To specify one of the defined values for a resource in a .Xdefaults file, remove the **Xm** prefix and use the remaining letters (in either lowercase or uppercase, but include any underscores between words). The codes in the access column indicate if the given resource can be set at creation time (**C**), set by using **XtSetValues** (**S**), retrieved by using **XtGetValues** (**G**), or is not applicable (**N/A**).

XmMessageBox Resource Set		
Name	**Default**	**Access**
Class	**Type**	
XmNcancelCallback	NULL	C
XtCallbackList	XtCallbackList	
XmNcancelLabelString	"Cancel"	CSG
XmCXmString	XmString	
XmNdefaultButtonType	XmDIALOG_OK_BUTTON	CSG
XmCDefaultButtonType	unsigned char	
XmNdialogType	XmDIALOG_MESSAGE	CSG
XmCDialogType	unsigned char	
XmNhelpLabelString	"Help"	CSG
XmCXmString	XmString	
XmNmessageAlignment	XmALIGNMENT_BEGINNING	CSG
XmCAlignment	unsigned char	
XmNmessageString	NULL	CSG
XmCXmString	XmString	
XmNminimizeButtons	False	CSG
XmCMinimizeButtons	Boolean	
XmNokCallback	NULL	C
XtCallbackList	XtCallbackList	
XmNokLabelString	"OK"	CSG
XmCXmString	XmString	
XmNsymbolPixmap	dynamic	CSG
XmCPixmap	Pixmap	

XmNcancelCallback

Specifies the list of callbacks that is called when the user clicks on the cancel button. The reason sent by the callback is **XmCR_CANCEL**.

XmNcancelLabelString

Specifies the string label for the cancel button.

XmNdefaultButtonType

> Specifies the default PushButton. The following are valid types:

- **XmDIALOG_CANCEL_BUTTON.**

- **XmDIALOG_OK_BUTTON.**

- **XmDIALOG_HELP_BUTTON.**

XmNdialogType

> Specifies the type of MessageBox dialog, which determines the default message symbol. The following are the possible values for this resource:

- **XmDIALOG_ERROR** — indicates an ErrorDialog.

- **XmDIALOG_INFORMATION** — indicates an InformationDialog.

- **XmDIALOG_MESSAGE** — indicates a MessageDialog. This is the default MessageBox dialog type. The default message symbol is NULL.

- **XmDIALOG_QUESTION** — indicates a QuestionDialog.

- **XmDIALOG_WARNING** — indicates a WarningDialog.

-

XmDIALOG_WORKING — indicates a WorkingDialog.

> If this resource is changed via **XtSetValues**, the symbol bitmap is modified to the new **XmdialogType** bitmap unless **XmNsymbolPixmap** is also being set in **XtSetValues**.

XmNhelpLabelString

> Specifies the string label for the help button.

XmNmessageAlignment

Controls the alignment of the message Label. Possible values include the following:

- **XmALIGNMENT_BEGINNING** — the default

- **XmALIGNMENT_CENTER**

- **XmALIGNMENT_END**

XmNmessageString

Specifies the string to be used as the message.

XmNminimizeButtons

Sets the buttons to the width of the widest button and height of the tallest button if False. If True, button width and height are set to the preferred size of each button.

XmNokCallback

Specifies the list of callbacks that is called when the user clicks on the OK button. The reason sent by the callback is **XmCR_OK**.

XmNokLabelString

Specifies the string label for the OK button.

XmNsymbolPixmap

Specifies the pixmap label to be used as the message symbol.

Inherited Resources

MessageBox inherits behavior and resources from the following superclasses. For a complete description of each resource, refer to the man page for that superclass.

XmBulletinBoard Resource Set		
Name	**Default**	**Access**
Class	Type	
XmNallowOverlap	True	N/A
XmCAllowOverlap	Boolean	
XmNautoUnmanage	True	CSG
XmCAutoUnmanage	Boolean	
XmNbuttonFontList	NULL	CSG
XmCButtonFontList	XmFontList	
XmNcancelButton	Cancel button	G
XmCWidget	Widget	
XmNdefaultButton	OK button	G
XmCWidget	Widget	
XmNdefaultPosition	True	CSG
XmCDefaultPosition	Boolean	
XmNdialogStyle	dynamic	CSG
XmCDialogStyle	unsigned char	
XmNdialogTitle	NULL	CSG
XmCXmString	XmString	
XmNfocusCallback	NULL	C
XmCCallback	XtCallbackList	
XmNlabelFontList	NULL	CSG
XmCLabelFontList	XmFontList	
XmNmapCallback	NULL	C
XmCCallback	XtCallbackList	
XmNmarginHeight	10	CSG
XmCMarginHeight	short	
XmNmarginWidth	10	CSG
XmCMarginWidth	short	
XmNnoResize	False	CSG
XmCNoResize	Boolean	

Name Class	Default Type	Access
XmNresizePolicy XmCResizePolicy	XmRESIZE_ANY unsigned char	CSG
XmNshadowType XmCShadowType	XmSHADOW_OUT unsigned char	CSG
XmNtextFontList XmCTextFontList	NULL XmFontList	N/A
XmNtextTranslations XmCTranslations	NULL XtTranslations	N/A
XmNunmapCallback XmCCallback	NULL XtCallbackList	C

XmManager Resource Set		
Name	**Default**	**Access**
Class	**Type**	
XmNbottomShadowColor	dynamic	CSG
XmCForeground	Pixel	
XmNbottomShadowPixmap	XmUNSPECIFIED_PIXMAP	CSG
XmCBottomShadowPixmap	Pixmap	
XmNforeground	dynamic	CSG
XmCForeground	Pixel	
XmNhelpCallback	NULL	C
XmCCallback	XtCallbackList	
XmNhighlightColor	Black	CSG
XmCForeground	Pixel	
XmNhighlightPixmap	dynamic	CSG
XmCHighlightPixmap	Pixmap	
XmNshadowThickness	dynamic	CSG
XmCShadowThickness	short	
XmNtopShadowColor	dynamic	CSG
XmCBackground	Pixel	
XmNtopShadowPixmap	XmUNSPECIFIED_PIXMAP	CSG
XmCTopShadowPixmap	Pixmap	
XmNuserData	NULL	CSG
XmCUserData	caddr_t	

Composite Resource Set		
Name	**Default**	**Access**
Class	**Type**	
XmNinsertPosition	NULL	CSG
XmCInsertPosition	XmRFunction	

Core Resource Set		
Name	**Default**	**Access**
Class	**Type**	
XmNaccelerators	NULL	CSG
XmCAccelerators	XtTranslations	
XmNancestorSensitive	True	G
XmCSensitive	Boolean	
XmNbackground	dynamic	CSG
XmCBackground	Pixel	
XmNbackgroundPixmap	XmUNSPECIFIED_PIXMAP	CSG
XmCPixmap	Pixmap	
XmNborderColor	Black	CSG
XmCBorderColor	Pixel	
XmNborderPixmap	XmUNSPECIFIED_PIXMAP	CSG
XmCPixmap	Pixmap	
XmNborderWidth	0	CSG
XmCBorderWidth	Dimension	
XmNcolormap	XtCopyFromParent	CG
XmCColormap	Colormap	
XmNdepth	XtCopyFromParent	CG
XmCDepth	int	
XmNdestroyCallback	NULL	C
XmCCallback	XtCallbackList	
XmNheight	0	CSG
XmCHeight	Dimension	
XmNmappedWhenManaged	True	CSG
XmCMappedWhenManaged	Boolean	
XmNscreen	XtCopyScreen	CG
XmCScreen	Pointer	
XmNsensitive	True	CSG
XmCSensitive	Boolean	

Name	Default	Access
Class	Type	
XmNtranslations	NULL	CSG
XmCTranslations	XtTranslations	
XmNwidth	0	CSG
XmCWidth	Dimension	
XmNx	0	CSG
XmCPosition	Position	
XmNy	0	CSG
XmCPosition	Position	

Callback Information

The following structure is returned with each callback:

typedef struct
{
    int   *reason*;
    XEvent   * *event*;
} **XmAnyCallbackStruct;**

reason   Indicates why the callback was invoked

event   Points to the **XEvent** that triggered the callback

Behavior

Following is a summary of the behavior of MessageBox.

<Ok Button Activated>:
        When the ok PushButton is activated, the callbacks for
        XmNokCallback are called.

<Cancel Button Activated>:
> When the cancel PushButton is activated, the callbacks for **XmNcancelCallback** are called.

<Help Button Activated> or **<Key>F1**:
> When the help button or **Function key 1** is pressed, the callbacks for **XmNhelpCallback** are called.

<Default Button Activated>:
> When the default button is pressed, the activate callbacks of the default PushButton are called.

<FocusIn>: When a **FocusIn** event is generated on the widget window, the callbacks for **XmNfocusCallback** are called.

<MapWindow>:
> When a **MapWindow** event is generated on the widget window, the callbacks for **XmNmapCallback** are called.

<UnmapWindow>:
> When a **UnmapWindow** event is generated on the widget window, the callbacks for **XmNunmapCallback** are called.

Default Accelerators

The default accelerator translations added to descendants of a BulletinBoard if the parent of the BulletinBoard is a DialogShell are:

#override
<Key>F1:   **Help()**
<Key>Return: **Return()**
<Key>KP_Enter: **Return()**

Keyboard Traversal

For information on keyboard traversal, see the man page for **XmManager(3X)** and its sections on behavior and default translations.

Related Information

Composite(3X), Constraint(3X), Core(3X), XmBulletinBoard(3X),
XmCreateErrorDialog(3X), XmCreateInformationDialog(3X),
XmCreateMessageBox(3X), XmCreateMessageDialog(3X),
XmCreateQuestionDialog(3X), XmCreateWarningDialog(3X),
XmCreateWorkingDialog(3X), XmManager(3X), and
XmMessageBoxGetChild(3X).

XmMessageBoxGetChild

Purpose

A MessageBox function that is used to access a component.

AES Support Level

Full-use

Synopsis

#include <Xm/MessageB.h>

Widget XmMessageBoxGetChild (*widget, child*)
    Widget *widget*;
    unsigned char*child*;

Description

XmMessageBoxGetChild is used to access a component within a MessageBox. The parameters given to the function are the MessageBox widget and a value indicating which child to access.

widget   Specifies the MessageBox widget ID.

child   Specifies a component within the MessageBox. The following are legal values for this parameter:

- **XmDIALOG_CANCEL_BUTTON**
- **XmDIALOG_DEFAULT_BUTTON**
- **XmDIALOG_HELP_BUTTON**
- **XmDIALOG_MESSAGE_LABEL**
- **XmDIALOG_OK_BUTTON**
- **XmDIALOG_SEPARATOR**
- **XmDIALOG_SYMBOL_LABEL**

For a complete definition of MessageBox and its associated resources, see **XmMessageBox(3X)**.

Return Value

Returns the widget ID of the specified MessageBox child.

Related Information

XmMessageBox(3X).

XmOptionButtonGadget

Purpose

A RowColumn function that obtains the widget ID for the CascadeButtonGadget in an OptionMenu.

AES Support Level

Full-use

Synopsis

#include <Xm/RowColumn.h>

Widget XmOptionButtonGadget (*option_menu*)
  Widget *option_menu*;

Description

XmOptionButtonGadget provides the application with the means for obtaining the widget ID for the internally created CascadeButtonGadget. Once the application has obtained the widget ID, it can adjust the visuals for the CascadeButtonGadget, if desired.

When an application creates an instance of the OptionMenu widget, the widget creates two internal gadgets. One is a LabelGadget that is used to display RowColumn's **XmNlabelString** resource. The other is a CascadeButtonGadget that displays the current selection and provides the means for posting the OptionMenu's submenu.

option_menu Specifies the OptionMenu widget ID

For a complete definition of RowColumn and its associated resources, see **XmRowColumn(3X)**.

Return Value

Returns the widget ID for the internal button.

Related Information

XmCreateOptionMenu(3X), **XmCascadeButtonGadget(3X)**, **XmOptionLabelGadget(3X)**, and **XmRowColumn(3X)**.

XmOptionLabelGadget

Purpose

A RowColumn function that obtains the widget ID for the LabelGadget in an OptionMenu.

AES Support Level

Full-use

Synopsis

#include <Xm/RowColumn.h>

Widget XmOptionLabelGadget (*option_menu*)
    Widget   *option_menu*;

Description

XmOptionLabelGadget provides the application with the means for obtaining the widget ID for the internally created LabelGadget. Once the application has obtained the widget ID, it can adjust the visuals for the LabelGadget, if desired.

When an application creates an instance of the OptionMenu widget, the widget creates two internal gadgets. One is a LabelGadget that is used to display RowColumn's **XmNlabelString** resource. The other is a CascadeButtonGadget that displays the current selection and provides the means for posting the OptionMenu's submenu.

option_menu Specifies the OptionMenu widget ID

For a complete definition of RowColumn and its associated resources, see **XmRowColumn(3X)**.

Return Value

Returns the widget ID for the internal label.

Related Information

XmCreateOptionMenu(3X), XmLabelGadget(3X), XmOptionButtonGadget(3X), and XmRowColumn(3X).

XmPanedWindow

Purpose

The PanedWindow widget class

AES Support Level

Full-use

Synopsis

#include <Xm/PanedW.h>

Description

PanedWindow is a composite widget that lays out children in a vertically tiled format. Children appear in top-to-bottom fashion, with the first child inserted appearing at the top of the PanedWindow and the last child inserted appearing at the bottom. The PanedWindow grows to match the width of its widest child and all other children are forced to this width. The height of the PanedWindow is equal to the sum of the heights of all its children, the spacing between them, and the size of the top and bottom margins.

The end user can also adjust the size of the panes. To facilitate this adjustment, a pane control sash is created for most children. The sash appears as a square box positioned on the bottom of the pane that it controls. The user can adjust the size of a pane by using the mouse.

The PanedWindow is also a constraint widget, which means that it creates and manages a set of constraints for each child. You can specify a minimum and maximum size for each pane. The PanedWindow does not allow a pane to be resized below its minimum size or beyond its maximum size. Also, when the minimum size of a pane is equal to its maximum size, no control sash is presented for that pane or for the lowest pane.

Classes

PanedWindow inherits behavior and resources from the **Core**, **Composite**, **Constraint**, and **XmManager** classes.

The class pointer is **xmPanedWindowWidgetClass**.

The class name is **XmPanedWindow**.

New Resources

The following table defines a set of widget resources used by the programmer to specify data. The programmer can also set the resource values for the inherited classes to set attributes for this widget. To reference a resource by name or by class in a .Xdefaults file, remove the **XmN** or **XmC** prefix and use the remaining letters. To specify one of the defined values for a resource in a .Xdefaults file, remove the **Xm** prefix and use the remaining letters (in either lowercase or uppercase, but include any underscores between words). The codes in the access column indicate if the given resource can be set at creation time (**C**), set by using **XtSetValues** (**S**), retrieved by using **XtGetValues** (**G**), or is not applicable (**N/A**).

XmPanedWindow Resource Set		
Name **Class**	**Default** **Type**	**Access**
XmNmarginHeight XmCMarginHeight	3 short	CSG
XmNmarginWidth XmCMarginWidth	3 short	CSG
XmNrefigureMode XmCBoolean	True Boolean	CSG
XmNsashHeight XmCSashHeight	10 Dimension	CSG
XmNsashIndent XmCSashIndent	-10 Position	CSG
XmNsashShadowThickness XmCShadowThickness	2 int	CSG
XmNsashWidth XmCSashWidth	10 Dimension	CSG
XmNseparatorOn XmCSeparatorOn	True Boolean	CSG
XmNspacing XmCSpacing	8 int	CSG

XmNmarginHeight

Specifies the distance between the top and bottom edges of the PanedWindow and its children.

XmNmarginWidth

Specifies the distance between the left and right edges of the PanedWindow and its children.

XmNrefigureMode

Determines whether the panes' positions are recomputed and repositioned when programmatic changes are being made to the PanedWindow. Setting this resource to True resets the children to their appropriate positions.

XmNsashHeight

Specifies the height of the sash.

XmNsashIndent

Specifies the horizontal placement of the sash along each pane. A positive value causes the sash to be offset from the left side of the PanedWindow, and a negative value causes the sash to be offset from the right side of the PanedWindow. If the offset is greater than the width of the PanedWindow minus the width of the sash, the sash is placed flush against the left-hand side of the PanedWindow.

XmNsashShadowThickness

Specifies the thickness of the shadows of the sashes.

XmNsashWidth

Specifies the width of the sash.

XmNseparatorOn

Determines whether a separator is created between each of the panes. Setting this resource to True creates a Separator at the midpoint between each of the panes.

XmNspacing

Specifies the distance between each child pane.

XmPanedWIndow Constraint Resource Set		
Name	**Default**	**Access**
Class	**Type**	
XmNallowResize	False	CSG
XmCBoolean	Boolean	
XmNmaximum	1000	CSG
XmRInt	int	
XmNminimum	1	CSG
XmCMin	int	
XmNskipAdjust	False	CSG
XmCBoolean	Boolean	

XmNallowResize

> Allows an application to specify whether the PanedWindow should allow a pane to request to be resized. This flag has an effect only after the PanedWindow and its children have been realized. If this flag is set to True, the PanedWindow tries to honor requests to alter the height of the pane. If False, it always denies pane requests to resize.

XmNmaximum

> Allows an application to specify the maximum size to which a pane may be resized. This value must be greater than the specified minimum.

XmNminimum

> Allows an application to specify the minimum size to which a pane may be resized. This value must be greater than 0.

XmNskipAdjust

> When set to True, this Boolean resource allows an application to specify that the PanedWindow should not automatically resize this pane.

Inherited Resources

PanedWindow inherits behavior and resources from the following superclasses. For a complete description of each resource, refer to the man page for that superclass.

XmManager Resource Set		
Name Class	**Default** Type	**Access**
XmNbottomShadowColor XmCForeground	dynamic Pixel	CSG
XmNbottomShadowPixmap XmCBottomShadowPixmap	XmUNSPECIFIED_PIXMAP Pixmap	CSG
XmNforeground XmCForeground	dynamic Pixel	CSG
XmNhelpCallback XmCCallback	NULL XtCallbackList	C
XmNhighlightColor XmCForeground	Black Pixel	CSG
XmNhighlightPixmap XmCHighlightPixmap	dynamic Pixmap	CSG
XmNshadowThickness XmCShadowThickness	0 short	N/A
XmNtopShadowColor XmCBackground	dynamic Pixel	CSG
XmNtopShadowPixmap XmCTopShadowPixmap	XmUNSPECIFIED_PIXMAP Pixmap	CSG
XmNuserData XmCUserData	NULL caddr_t	CSG

Core Resource Set		
Name **Class**	**Default** **Type**	**Access**
XmNaccelerators XmCAccelerators	NULL XtTranslations	CSG
XmNancestorSensitive XmCSensitive	True Boolean	G
XmNbackground XmCBackground	dynamic Pixel	CSG
XmNbackgroundPixmap XmCPixmap	XmUNSPECIFIED_PIXMAP Pixmap	CSG
XmNborderColor XmCBorderColor	Black Pixel	CSG
XmNborderPixmap XmCPixmap	XmUNSPECIFIED_PIXMAP Pixmap	CSG
XmNborderWidth XmCBorderWidth	0 Dimension	CSG
XmNcolormap XmCColormap	XtCopyFromParent Colormap	CG
XmNdepth XmCDepth	XtCopyFromParent int	CG
XmNdestroyCallback XmCCallback	NULL XtCallbackList	C
XmNheight XmCHeight	0 Dimension	CSG
XmNmappedWhenManaged XmCMappedWhenManaged	True Boolean	CSG
XmNscreen XmCScreen	XtCopyScreen Pointer	CG
XmNsensitive XmCSensitive	True Boolean	CSG

Name	Default	Access
Class	Type	
XmNtranslations	NULL	CSG
XmCTranslations	XtTranslations	
XmNwidth	0	CSG
XmCWidth	Dimension	
XmNx	0	CSG
XmCPosition	Position	
XmNy	0	CSG
XmCPosition	Position	

Behavior

Shift<Btn1Down>:

> **(in sash)**: Activates the interactive placement of the pane's borders. It changes the pointer cursor from a crosshair to an upward pointing arrow to indicate that the upper pane is being adjusted (usually the pane to which the sash is attached). All panes below the sash that can be adjusted are adjusted.

<Btn1Down>:

> **(in sash)**: Activates the interactive placement of the pane's borders. It changes the pointer cursor from a crosshair to a double headed arrow to indicate that the pane to be adjusted is the pane to which the sash is attached and the first pane below it that can be adjusted. Unlike pane adjustment using **Shift Btn1Down** or **CTRL Btn1Down**, only two panes are affected. If one of the panes reaches its minimum or maximum size, adjustment stops instead of finding the next adjustable pane.

CTRL <Btn1Down>:
> **(in sash)**: Activates the interactive placement of the pane's borders. It changes the pointer cursor from a crosshair to a downward pointing arrow to indicate that the lower pane is being adjusted (usually the pane below the pane to which the sash is attached). All panes above the sash that can be adjusted are adjusted.

Shift Button1<PtrMoved>:
> If the button press occurs within the sash, the motion events draw a series of track lines to illustrate what the heights of the panes would be if the Commit action were invoked. This action determines which pane below the upper pane can be adjusted and makes the appropriate adjustments.

Button1<PtrMoved>:
> If the button press occurs within the sash, the motion events draw a series of track lines to illustrate what the heights of the panes would be if the Commit action were invoked. This action adjusts as needed (and possible) the upper and lower panes selected when the Btn1Down action is invoked.

CTRL Button1<PtrMoved>:
> If the button press occurs within the sash, the motion events draw a series of track lines to illustrate what the heights of the panes would be if the Commit action were invoked. This action determines which pane above the lower pane can be adjusted and makes the appropriate adjustments.

Any<BtnUp>:
> Commits to any action taken since the interactive placement was activated. The sashes and the pane boundaries are moved to the committed positions of the panes.

Default Translations

The following are default translations for PanedWindow:

Shift<Btn1Down>: SashAction(Start, UpperPane)
<Btn1Down>:   SashAction(Start, ThisBorderOnly)
CTRL<Btn1Down>:SashAction(Start, LowerPane)
Shift<Btn1Motion>:SashAction(Move, Upper)
<Btn1Motion>:   SashAction(Move, ThisBorder)
CTRL<Btn1Motion>:SashAction(Move, Lower)
Any<BtnUp>:   SashAction(Commit)
<EnterWindow>: enter()
<LeaveWindow>: leave()

Keyboard Traversal

For information on keyboard traversal, see the man page for **XmManager(3X)** and its sections on behavior and default translations.

Related Information

Composite(3X),   **Constraint(3X),**   **Core(3X),**
XmCreatePanedWindow(3X), and **XmManager(3X)**.

XmPrimitive

Purpose

The Primitive widget class

AES Support Level

Full-use

Synopsis

#include <Xm/Xm.h>

Description

Primitive is a widget class used as a supporting superclass for other widget classes. It handles border drawing and highlighting, traversal activation and deactivation, and various callback lists needed by Primitive widgets.

Classes

Primitive inherits behavior and resources from **Core** class.

The class pointer is **xmPrimitiveWidgetClass**.

The class name is **XmPrimitive**.

New Resources

The following table defines a set of widget resources used by the programmer to specify data. The programmer can also set the resource values for the inherited classes to set attributes for this widget. To reference a resource by name or by class in a .Xdefaults file, remove the **XmN** or **XmC** prefix and use the remaining letters. To specify one of the defined values for a resource in a .Xdefaults file, remove the **Xm** prefix and use the remaining letters (in either lowercase or uppercase, but include any underscores between words). The codes in the access column indicate if the given resource can be set at creation time (**C**), set by using **XtSetValues** (**S**), retrieved by using **XtGetValues** (**G**), or is not applicable (**N/A**).

XmPrimitive Resource Set		

Name
    Class
	Default
	    Type
		Access

XmNbottomShadowColor
    XmCForeground
	dynamic
	    Pixel
		CSG

XmNbottomShadowPixmap
    XmCBottomShadowPixmap
	XmUNSPECIFIED_PIXMAP
	    Pixmap
		CSG

XmNforeground
    XmCForeground
	dynamic
	    Pixel
		CSG

XmNhelpCallback
    XmCCallback
	NULL
	    XtCallbackList
		C

XmNhighlightColor
    XmCForeground
	Black
	    Pixel
		CSG

XmNhighlightOnEnter
    XmCHighlightOnEnter
	False
	    Boolean
		CSG

XmNhighlightPixmap
    XmCHighlightPixmap
	dynamic
	    Pixmap
		CSG

XmNhighlightThickness
    XmCHighlightThickness
	0
	    short
		CSG

XmNshadowThickness
    XmCShadowThickness
	2
	    short
		CSG

XmNtopShadowColor
    XmCBackground
	dynamic
	    Pixel
		CSG

XmNtopShadowPixmap
    XmCTopShadowPixmap
	XmUNSPECIFIED_PIXMAP
	    Pixmap
		CSG

XmNtraversalOn
    XmCTraversalOn
	False
	    Boolean
		CSG

XmNuserData
    XmCUserData
	NULL
	    caddr_t
		CSG

XmNbottomShadowColor

Specifies the pixmap to use to draw the top and left sides of the border shadow.

XmNbottomShadowPixmap
> Specifies the pixmap to use to draw the bottom and right sides of the border shadow.

XmNforeground
> Specifies the foreground drawing color used by Primitive widgets.

XmNhelpCallback
> Specifies the list of callbacks that is called when the help key sequence is pressed. The reason sent by the callback is **XmCR_HELP**. No translation is bound to this resource. It is up to the application to install a translation for help.

XmNhighlightColor
> Specifies the color of the highlighting rectangle. This color is used if the highlight pixmap resource is **XmUNSPECIFIED_PIXMAP**.

XmNhighlightOnEnter
> Specifies if the highlighting rectangle is drawn when the cursor moves into the widget. If this resource is True and **XmNtraversalOn** is False, then the rectangle highlights the window when the cursor is moved into it. This resource is ignored if the **XmNtraversalOn** resource is set to True.

XmNhighlightPixmap
> Specifies the pixmap used to draw the highlighting rectangle.

XmNhighlightThickness
> Specifies the thickness of the highlighting rectangle.

XmNshadowThickness
> Specifies the size of the drawn border shadow.

XmNtopShadowColor
> Specifies the pixmap to use to draw the top and left sides of the border shadow. This color is used if the **XmNtopShadowPixmap** resource is NULL.

XmNtopShadowPixmap
> Specifies the pixmap to use to draw the top and left sides of the border shadow.

XmNtraversalOn
> Specifies if traversal is activated for this widget.

XmNuserData
> Allows the application to attach any necessary specific data to the widget. It is an internally unused resource.

Dynamic Color Defaults

The foreground, background, top shadow, and bottom shadow resources are dynamically defaulted. If no color data is specified, the colors are automatically generated. On a monochrome system, a black and white color scheme is generated. On a color system, four colors are generated, which display the correct shading for the 3-D visuals.

If the background is the only color specified for a widget, the top shadow, bottom shadow, and foreground colors are generated to give the 3-D appearance. The color generation works best with non-saturated colors. Using pure red, green, or blue yields poor results.

Colors are generated at creation only. Resetting the background through **XtSetValues** does not regenerate the other colors.

Inherited Resources

Primitive inherits behavior and resources from the following superclass. For a complete description of each resource, refer to the man page for that superclass.

Core Resource Set		
Name	**Default**	**Access**
Class	**Type**	
XmNaccelerators	NULL	CSG
XmCAccelerators	XtTranslations	
XmNancestorSensitive	True	G
XmCSensitive	Boolean	
XmNbackground	dynamic	CSG
XmCBackground	Pixel	
XmNbackgroundPixmap	XmUNSPECIFIED_PIXMAP	CSG
XmCPixmap	Pixmap	
XmNborderColor	Black	CSG
XmCBorderColor	Pixel	
XmNborderPixmap	XmUNSPECIFIED_PIXMAP	CSG
XmCPixmap	Pixmap	
XmNborderWidth	0	CSG
XmCBorderWidth	Dimension	
XmNcolormap	XtCopyFromParent	CG
XmCColormap	Colormap	
XmNdepth	XtCopyFromParent	CG
XmCDepth	int	
XmNdestroyCallback	NULL	C
XmCCallback	XtCallbackList	
XmNheight	0	CSG
XmCHeight	Dimension	
XmNmappedWhenManaged	True	CSG
XmCMappedWhenManaged	Boolean	
XmNscreen	XtCopyScreen	CG
XmCScreen	Pointer	
XmNsensitive	True	CSG
XmCSensitive	Boolean	

Name	Default	Access
Class	Type	
XmNtranslations	NULL	CSG
XmCTranslations	XtTranslations	
XmNwidth	0	CSG
XmCWidth	Dimension	
XmNx	0	CSG
XmCPosition	Position	
XmNy	0	CSG
XmCPosition	Position	

Behavior

Shift<Key>Tab:

Moves the focus to the first item contained within the previous tab group. If the beginning of the tab group list is reached, it wraps to the end of the tab group list.

<Key>Tab: Moves the focus to the first item contained within the next tab group. If the current tab group is the last entry in the tab group list, it wraps to the beginning of the tab group list.

<Key>Up or **<Key>Left**:

Moves the keyboard focus to the previous Primitive widget or gadget within the current tab group. The previous widget or gadget is the one which is the previous entry in the tab group's list of children. Wrapping occurs, if necessary.

<Key>Down or **<Key>Right**:

> Moves the Keyboard focus to the next Primitive widget or gadget within the current tab group. The previous widget or gadget is the one which is the next entry in the tab group's list of children. Wrapping occurs, if necessary.

<Key>Home:

> Moves the keyboard focus to the first Primitive widget or gadget in the current tab group.

Default Translations

The following are the default translations for Primitive:

<FocusIn>:	**PrimitiveFocusIn()**
<FocusOut>:	**PrimitiveFocusOut()**
<Unmap>:	**PrimitiveUnmap()**
Shift<Key>Tab:	**PrimitivePrevTabGroup()**
<Key>Tab:	**PrimitiveNextTabGroup()**
<Key>Up:	**PrimitiveTraversePrev()**
<Key>Down:	**PrimitiveTraverseNext()**
<Key>Left:	**PrimitiveTraversePrev()**
<Key>Right:	**PrimitiveTraverseNext()**
<Key>Home:	**PrimitiveTraverseHome()**

Related Information

Core(3X).

XmPushButton

Purpose

The PushButton widget class

AES Support Level

Full-use

Synopsis

#include <Xm/PushB.h>

Description

PushButton issues commands within an application. It consists of a text label or pixmap surrounded by a border shadow. When PushButton is selected, the shadow moves to give the appearance that it has been pressed in. When PushButton is unselected, the shadow moves to give the appearance that it is out.

The behavior of PushButton differs, depending on the active mouse button. The active mouse button may be determined by the parent widget. Normally, mouse button 1 is used to arm and activate the PushButton. However, if the PushButton resides within a menu, then the mouse button used is determined by the RowColumn resources **XmNrowColumnType** and **XmNwhichButton**.

Thickness for a second shadow may be specified by using the **XmNshowAsDefault** resource. If it has a non-zero value, the Label's resources **XmNmarginBottom**, **XmNmarginTop**, **XmNmarginRight**, and **XmNmarginLeft** may be modified to accommodate the second shadow.

Classes

PushButton inherits behavior and resources from **Core**, **XmPrimitive**, and **XmLabel** Classes.

The class pointer is **xmPushButtonWidgetClass**.

The class name is **XmPushButton**.

New Resources

The following table defines a set of widget resources used by the programmer to specify data. The programmer can also set the resource values for the inherited classes to set attributes for this widget. To reference a resource by name or by class in a .Xdefaults file, remove the **XmN** or **XmC** prefix and use the remaining letters. To specify one of the defined values for a resource in a .Xdefaults file, remove the **Xm** prefix and use the remaining letters (in either lowercase or uppercase, but include any underscores between words). The codes in the access column indicate if the given resource can be set at creation time (**C**), set by using **XtSetValues** (**S**), retrieved by using **XtGetValues** (**G**), or is not applicable (**N/A**).

XmPushButton Resource Set		
Name	**Default**	**Access**
Class	**Type**	
XmNactivateCallback	NULL	C
XmCCallback	XtCallbackList	
XmNarmCallback	NULL	C
XmCCallback	XtCallbackList	
XmNarmColor	dynamic	CSG
XmCArmColor	Pixel	
XmNarmPixmap	XmUNSPECIFIED_PIXMAP	CSG
XmCArmPixmap	Pixmap	
XmNdisarmCallback	NULL	C
XmCCallback	XtCallbackList	
XmNfillOnArm	True	CSG
XmCFillOnArm	Boolean	
XmNshowAsDefault	0	CSG
XmCShowAsDefault	short	

XmNactivateCallback

> Specifies the list of callbacks that is called when PushButton is activated. PushButton is activated when the user presses and releases the active mouse button while the pointer is inside that widget. Activating the PushButton also disarms it. For this callback the reason is **XmCR_ACTIVATE**.

XmNarmCallback

> Specifies the list of callbacks that is called when PushButton is armed. PushButton is armed when the user presses the active mouse button while the pointer is inside that widget. For this callback the reason is **XmCR_ARM**.

XmNarmColor

Specifies the color with which to fill the armed button. **XmNfillOnArm** must be set to True for this resource to have an effect. The default for a color display is a color between the background and the bottom shadow color. For a monochrome display, the default is set to the foreground color, and any text in the label appears in the background color when the button is armed.

XmNarmPixmap

Specifies the pixmap to be used as the button face if **XmNlabeltype** is **XmPIXMAP** and PushButton is armed. This resource is disabled when the PushButton is in a menu.

XmNdisarmCallback

Specifies the list of callbacks that is called when PushButton is disarmed. PushButton is disarmed when the user presses and releases the active mouse button while the pointer is inside that widget. For this callback, the reason is **XmCR_DISARM.**

XmNfillOnArm

Forces the PushButton to fill the background of the button with the color specified by **XmNarmColor** when the button is armed and when this resource is set to True. If False, only the top and bottom shadow colors are switched. When the PushButton is in a menu, this resource is ignored and assumed to be False.

XmNshowAsDefault

Specifies a shadow thickness for a second shadow to be drawn around the PushButton to visually mark it as a default button. The space between the shadow and the default shadow is equal to the sum of both shadows. The default value is zero. When this value is not zero, the Label resources **XmNmarginLeft,** **XmNmarginRight,** **XmNmarginBottom,** and **XmNmarginTop** may be modified to accommodate the second shadow. This resource is disabled when the PushButton is in a menu.

Inherited Resources

PushButton inherits behavior and resources from the following superclasses. For a complete description of each resource, refer to the man page for that superclass.

XmLabel Resource Set		

Name
   Class
	Default
	   Type
		Access

XmNaccelerator
   XmCAccelerator
	NULL
	   String
		CSG

XmNacceleratorText
   XmCAcceleratorText
	NULL
	   XmString
		CSG

XmNalignment
   XmCAlignment
	XmALIGNMENT_CENTER
	   unsigned char
		CSG

XmNfontList
   XmCFontList
	"Fixed"
	   XmFontList
		CSG

XmNlabelInsensitivePixmap
   XmCLabelInsensitivePixmap
	XmUNSPECIFIED_PIXMAP
	   Pixmap
		CSG

XmNlabelPixmap
   XmCPixmap
	XmUNSPECIFIED_PIXMAP
	   Pixmap
		CSG

XmNlabelString
   XmCXmString
	NULL
	   XmString
		CSG

XmNlabelType
   XmCLabelType
	XmSTRING
	   unsigned char
		CSG

XmNmarginBottom
   XmCMarginBottom
	dynamic
	   short
		CSG

XmNmarginHeight
   XmCMarginHeight
	2
	   short
		CSG

Name Class	Default Type	Access
XmNmarginLeft XmCMarginLeft	dynamic short	CSG
XmNmarginRight XmCMarginRight	dynamic short	CSG
XmNmarginTop XmCMarginTop	dynamic short	CSG
XmNmarginWidth XmCMarginWidth	2 short	CSG
XmNmnemonic XmCMnemonic	'\0' char	CSG
XmNrecomputeSize XmCRecomputeSize	True Boolean	CSG

XmPrimitive Resource Set		

Name
    Class
	Default
	    Type
		Access

XmNbottomShadowColor
    XmCForeground
	dynamic
	    Pixel
		CSG

XmNbottomShadowPixmap
    XmCBottomShadowPixmap
	XmUNSPECIFIED_PIXMAP
	    Pixmap
		CSG

XmNforeground
    XmCForeground
	dynamic
	    Pixel
		CSG

XmNhelpCallback
    XmCCallback
	NULL
	    XtCallbackList
		C

XmNhighlightColor
    XmCForeground
	Black
	    Pixel
		CSG

XmNhighlightOnEnter
    XmCHighlightOnEnter
	False
	    Boolean
		CSG

XmNhighlightPixmap
    XmCHighlightPixmap
	dynamic
	    Pixmap
		CSG

XmNhighlightThickness
    XmCHighlightThickness
	0
	    short
		CSG

XmNshadowThickness
    XmCShadowThickness
	2
	    short
		CSG

XmNtopShadowColor
    XmCBackground
	dynamic
	    Pixel
		CSG

XmNtopShadowPixmap
    XmCTopShadowPixmap
	XmUNSPECIFIED_PIXMAP
	    Pixmap
		CSG

XmNtraversalOn
    XmCTraversalOn
	False
	    Boolean
		CSG

XmNuserData
    XmCUserData
	NULL
	    caddr_t
		CSG

Core Resource Set		
Name **Class**	**Default** **Type**	**Access**
XmNaccelerators XmCAccelerators	NULL XtTranslations	CSG
XmNancestorSensitive XmCSensitive	True Boolean	G
XmNbackground XmCBackground	dynamic Pixel	CSG
XmNbackgroundPixmap XmCPixmap	XmUNSPECIFIED_PIXMAP Pixmap	CSG
XmNborderColor XmCBorderColor	Black Pixel	CSG
XmNborderPixmap XmCPixmap	XmUNSPECIFIED_PIXMAP Pixmap	CSG
XmNborderWidth XmCBorderWidth	0 Dimension	CSG
XmNcolormap XmCColormap	XtCopyFromParent Colormap	CG
XmNdepth XmCDepth	XtCopyFromParent int	CG
XmNdestroyCallback XmCCallback	NULL XtCallbackList	C
XmNheight XmCHeight	0 Dimension	CSG
XmNmappedWhenManaged XmCMappedWhenManaged	True Boolean	CSG
XmNscreen XmCScreen	XtCopyScreen Pointer	CG
XmNsensitive XmCSensitive	True Boolean	CSG

Name	Default	Access
Class	Type	
XmNtranslations	NULL	CSG
XmCTranslations	XtTranslations	
XmNwidth	0	CSG
XmCWidth	Dimension	
XmNx	0	CSG
XmCPosition	Position	
XmNy	0	CSG
XmCPosition	Position	

Callback Information

The following structure is returned with each callback:

```
typedef struct
{
    int        reason;
    XEvent     * event;
} XmAnyCallbackStruct;
```

reason   Indicates why the callback was invoked.

event   Points to the **XEvent** that triggered the callback. This event is NULL for the **XmNactivateCallback** if the callback was triggered when Primitive's resource **XmNtraversalOn** was True or if the callback was accessed through the **ArmAndActivate** action routine.

Behavior

PushButton is associated with the default behavior unless it is part of a menu system. In a menu system, the RowColumn parent determines which mouse button is used.

Default Behavior

<Btn1Down>:

> This action causes the PushButton to be armed. The shadow is drawn in the armed state, and the button is filled with the color specified by **XmNarmColor** if **XmNfillOnArm** is set to True. The callbacks for **XmNarmCallback** are also called.

<Btn1Up>: **(in button):** This action redraws the shadow in the unarmed state. The background color reverts to the unarmed color if **XmNfillOnArm** is set to True. The callbacks for **XmNactivateCallback** are called, followed by callbacks for **XmNdisarmCallback**.

> **(outside of button):** This action causes the callbacks for **XmNdisarmCallback** to be called.

<Leave Window>:

> If the button is pressed and the cursor leaves the widget's window, the shadow is redrawn in its unarmed state, and the background color reverts to the unarmed color if **XmNfillOnArm** is set to True.

<Enter Window>:

> If the button is pressed and the cursor leaves and reenters the widget's window, the shadow is drawn in the armed state, and the button is filled with the color specified by **XmNarmColor** if **XmNfillOnArm** is set to True.

Default PopupMenu System

<Btn3Down>:

> This action disables keyboard traversal for the menu and returns the user to drag mode, which is the mode in which the menu is manipulated by using the mouse. The shadow is drawn in the armed state, and the callbacks for **XmNarmCallback** are called.

<Btn3Up>: This action causes the PushButton to be activated and the menu to be unposted. The callbacks for **XmNactivateCallback** are called, followed by callbacks for **XmNdisarmCallback**.

<Leave Window>:

> If button 3 is pressed and the cursor leaves the widget's window, the PushButton is redrawn with no shadow. The callbacks for **XmNdisarmCallback** are called. If keyboard traversal is enabled in the menu, then this event is ignored.

<Enter Window>:

> If button 3 is pressed and the cursor enters the widget's window, the shadow is drawn in the armed state. The callbacks for **XmNarmCallback** are called. If keyboard traversal is enabled in the menu, then this event is ignored.

<Key>Return:

> If keyboard traversal is enabled in the menu, then this event causes the PushButton to be activated and the menu to be unposted. The callbacks for **XmNactivateCallback** are called, followed by callbacks for **XmNdisarmCallback**.

Default PulldownMenu and OptionMenu System

<Btn1Down>:

> This action disables keyboard traversal for the menu and returns the user to drag mode, which is the mode in which the menu is manipulated by using the mouse. The shadow is drawn in the armed state, and the callbacks for **XmNarmCallback** are called.

<Btn1Up>: This action causes the PushButton to be activated and the menu to be unposted. The callbacks for **XmNactivateCallback** are called, followed by callbacks for **XmNdisarmCallback**.

<Leave Window>:

> If mouse button 1 is pressed and the cursor leaves the widget's window, the PushButton is redrawn with no shadow. The callbacks for **XmNdisarmCallback** are called. If keyboard traversal is enabled in the menu, then this event is ignored.

<Enter Window>:

If mouse button 1 is pressed and the cursor enters the widget's window, the shadow is drawn in the armed state. The callbacks for **XmNarmCallback** are called. If keyboard traversal is enabled in the menu, then this event is ignored.

<Key>Return:

If keyboard traversal is enabled in the menu, then this event causes the PushButton to be activated and the menu to be unposted. The callbacks for **XmNactivateCallback** are called, followed by callbacks for **XmNdisarmCallback**.

Default Translations

When not in a menu system, the following are PushButton's default translations:

<Btn1Down>:	**Arm()**
<Btn1Up>:	**Activate()**
	Disarm()
<Key>Return:	**ArmAndActivate()**
<Key>space:	**ArmAndActivate()**
<EnterWindow>:	**Enter()**
<LeaveWindow>:	**Leave()**

When in a menu system, the following are PushButton's default translations:

<BtnDown>:	**BtnDown()**
<BtnUp>:	**BtnUp()**
<EnterWindow>:	**Enter()**
<LeaveWindow>:	**Leave()**
<Key>Return:	**KeySelect()**
<Key>Escape:	**MenuShellPopdownDone()**

Keyboard Traversal

For information on keyboard traversal outside a menu system, see the man page for **XmPrimitive(3X)** and its sections on behavior and default translations. In a menu system, the following keyboard traversal translations are defined:

\<Unmap>:	**Unmap()**
\<FocusOut>:	**FocusOut()**
\<FocusIn>:	**FocusIn()**
\<Key>space:	**Noop()**
\<Key>Left:	**MenuTraverseLeft()**
\<Key>Right:	**MenuTraverseRight()**
\<Key>Up:	**MenuTraverseUp()**
\<Key>Down:	**MenuTraverseDown()**
\<Key>Home:	**Noop()**

Related Information

Core(3X), XmCreatePushButton(3X), XmLabel(3X), XmPrimitive(3X), and XmRowColumn(3X).

XmPushButtonGadget

Purpose

The PushButtonGadget widget class

AES Support Level

Full-use

Synopsis

#include <Xm/PushBG.h>

Description

PushButtonGadget issues commands within an application. It consists of a text label or icon surrounded by a border shadow. When PushButtonGadget is selected, the shadow moves to give the appearance that the PushButtonGadget has been pressed in. When PushButtonGadget is unselected, the shadow moves to give the appearance that the PushButtonGadget is out.

The behavior of PushButtonGadget differs, depending on the active mouse button. The active mouse button may be determined by the parent widget. Normally, mouse button 1 is used to arm and activate the PushButtonGadget. However, if the PushButtonGadget resides within a menu, then the mouse button used is determined by the RowColumn resources **XmNrowColumnType** and **XmNwhichButton**.

Thickness for a second shadow may be specified by using the **XmNshowAsDefault** resource. If it has a non-zero value, the Label's resources **XmNmarginLeft**, **XmNmarginRight**, **XmNmarginTop**, and **XmNmarginBottom** may be modified to accommodate the second shadow.

Classes

PushButtonGadget inherits behavior and resources from **Object**, **RectObj**, **XmGadget** and **XmLabelGadget** classes.

The class pointer is **xmPushButtonGadgetClass**.

The class name is **XmPushButtonGadget**.

New Resources

The following table defines a set of widget resources used by the programmer to specify data. The programmer can also set the resource values for the inherited classes to set attributes for this widget. To reference a resource by name or by class in a .Xdefaults file, remove the **XmN** or **XmC** prefix and use the remaining letters. To specify one of the defined values for a resource in a .Xdefaults file, remove the **Xm** prefix and use the remaining letters (in either lowercase or uppercase, but include any underscores between words). The codes in the access column indicate if the given resource can be set at creation time (**C**), set by using **XtSetValues** (**S**), retrieved by using **XtGetValues** (**G**), or is not applicable (**N/A**).

XmPushButtonGadget		
Name Class	**Default** Type	**Access**
XmNactivateCallback XmCCallback	NULL XtCallbackList	C
XmNarmCallback XmCCallback	NULL caddr_t	C
XmNarmColor XmCArmColor	dynamic Pixel	CSG
XmNarmPixmap XmCArmPixmap	XmUNSPECIFIED_PIXMAP Pixmap	CSG
XmNdisarmCallback XmCCallback	NULL caddr_t	C
XmNfillOnArm XmCFillOnArm	True Boolean	CSG
XmNshowAsDefault XmCShowAsDefault	0 short	CSG

XmNactivateCallback

Specifies the list of callbacks that is called when the PushButtonGadget is activated. It is activated when the user presses and releases the active mouse button while the pointer is inside the PushButtonGadget. Activating PushButtonGadget also disarms it. For this callback the reason is **XmCR_ACTIVATE**.

XmNarmCallback

Specifies the list of callbacks that is called when PushButtonGadget is armed. It is armed when the user presses the active mouse button while the pointer is inside the PushButtonGadget. For this callback the reason is **XmCR_ARM**.

XmNarmColor

Specifies the color with which to fill the armed button. **XmNfillOnArm** must be set to True for this resource to have an effect. The default for a color display is a color between the background and the bottom shadow color. For a monochrome display, the default is set to the foreground color, and any text in the label appears in the background color when the button is armed.

XmNarmPixmap

Specifies the pixmap to be used as the button face if **XmNlabeltype** is **XmPIXMAP** and PushButtonGadget is armed. This resource is disabled when the PushButtonGadget is in a menu.

XmNdisarmCallback

Specifies the list of callbacks that is called when the PushButtonGadget is disarmed. PushButtonGadget is disarmed when the user presses and releases the active mouse button while the pointer is inside that gadget. For this callback, the reason is **XmCR_DISARM**.

XmNfillOnArm

Forces the PushButtonGadget to fill the background of the button with the color specified by **XmNarmColor** when the button is armed and when this resource is set to True. If False, only the top and bottom shadow colors are switched. When the PushButtonGadget is in a menu, this resource is ignored and assumed to be False.

XmNshowAsDefault

Specifies a shadow thickness for a second shadow to be drawn around the PushButtonGadget to visually mark it as a default button. The space between the shadow and the default shadow is equal to the sum of both shadows. The default value is zero. When this value is not zero, the Label resources **XmNmarginLeft**, **XmNmarginRight**, **XmNmarginTop**, and **XmNmarginbottom** may be modified to accommodate the second shadow. This resource is disabled when the PushButtonGadget is in a menu.

Inherited Resources

PushButtonGadget inherits behavior and resources from the following superclasses. For a complete description of each resource, refer to the man page for that superclass.

XmLabelGadget Resource Set		
Name **Class**	**Default** **Type**	**Access**
XmNaccelerator XmCAccelerator	NULL String	CSG
XmNacceleratorText XmCAcceleratorText	NULL XmString	CSG
XmNalignment XmCAlignment	XmALIGNMENT_CENTER unsigned char	CSG
XmNfontList XmCFontList	"Fixed" XmFontList	CSG
XmNlabelInsensitivePixmap XmCLabelInsensitivePixmap	XmUNSPECIFIED_PIXMAP Pixmap	CSG
XmNlabelPixmap XmCPixmap	XmUNSPECIFIED_PIXMAP Pixmap	CSG
XmNlabelString XmCXmString	NULL XmString	CSG
XmNlabelType XmCLabelType	XmSTRING unsigned char	CSG
XmNmarginBottom XmCMarginBottom	0 short	CSG
XmNmarginHeight XmCMarginHeight	2 short	CSG

Name	Default	Access
Class	Type	
XmNmarginLeft	0	CSG
XmCMarginLeft	short	
XmNmarginRight	0	CSG
XmCMarginRight	short	
XmNmarginTop	0	CSG
XmCMarginTop	short	
XmNmarginWidth	2	CSG
XmCMarginWidth	short	
XmNmnemonic	'\0'	CSG
XmCMnemonic	char	
XmNrecomputeSize	True	CSG
XmCRecomputeSize	Boolean	

XmGadget Resource Set		
Name	**Default**	**Access**
Class	Type	
XmNhelpCallback	NULL	C
XmCCallback	XtCallbackList	
XmNhighlightOnEnter	False	CSG
XmCHighlightOnEnter	Boolean	
XmNhighlightThickness	0	CSG
XmCHighlightThickness	short	
XmNshadowThickness	2	CSG
XmCShadowThickness	short	
XmNtraversalOn	False	CSG
XmCTraversalOn	Boolean	
XmNuserData	NULL	CSG
XmCUserData	caddr_t	

RectObj Resource Set		
Name **Class**	**Default** **Type**	**Access**
XmNancestorSensitive XmCSensitive	XtCopyFromParent Boolean	CSG
XmNborderWidth XmCBorderWidth	1 Dimension	CSG
XmNheight XmCHeight	0 Dimension	CSG
XmNsensitive XmCSensitive	True Boolean	CSG
XmNwidth XmCWidth	0 Dimension	CSG
XmNx XmCPosition	0 Position	CSG
XmNy XmCPosition	0 Position	CSG

Object Resource Set		
Name **Class**	**Default** **Type**	**Access**
XmNdestroyCallback XmCCallback	NULL XtCallbackList	C

Callback Information

The following structure is returned with each callback:

typedef struct
{
    int   *reason*;
    XEvent   * *event*;
} XmAnyCallbackStruct;

reason   Indicates why the callback was invoked.

event   Points to the **XEvent** that triggered the callback. This event is NULL for the **XmNactivateCallback** if the callback was triggered when Primitive's resource **XmNtraversalOn** was True or if the callback was accessed through the **ArmAndActivate** action routine.

Behavior

PushButtonGadget is associated with the default behavior unless it is part of a menu system. In a menu system, the RowColumn parent determines which mouse button is used.

Default Behavior

<Btn1Down>:

    This action causes the PushButtonGadget to be armed. The shadow is drawn in the armed state, and the button is filled with the color specified by **XmNarmColor** if **XmNfillOnArm** is set to True. The callbacks for **XmNarmCallback** are also called.

<Btn1Up>: **(in button)**: This action redraws the shadow in the unarmed state. The background color reverts to the unarmed color if **XmNfillOnArm** is set to True. The callbacks for **XmNactivateCallback** are called, followed by callbacks for **XmNdisarmCallback**.

(outside of button): This action causes the callbacks for **XmNdisarmCallback** to be called.

<Leave Window>:

If the button is pressed and the cursor leaves the gadget's window, the shadow is redrawn in its unarmed state, and the background color reverts to the unarmed color if **XmNfillOnArm** is set to True.

<Enter Window>:

If the button is pressed and the cursor leaves and reenters the gadget's window, the shadow is drawn in the armed state, and the button is filled with the color specified by **XmNarmColor** if **XmNfillOnArm** is set to True.

Default PopupMenu System

<Btn3Down>:

This action disables keyboard traversal for the menu and returns the user to drag mode, which is the mode in which the menu is manipulated by using the mouse. The shadow is drawn in the armed state, and the callbacks for **XmNarmCallback** are called.

<Btn3Up>: This action causes the PushButtonGadget to be activated and the menu to be unposted. The callbacks for **XmNactivateCallback** are called, followed by callbacks for **XmNdisarmCallback**.

<Leave Window>:

If button 3 is pressed and the cursor leaves the widget's window, the PushButtonGadget is redrawn with no shadow. The callbacks for **XmNdisarmCallback** are called. If keyboard traversal is enabled in the menu, then this event is ignored.

<Enter Window>:

If button 3 is pressed and the cursor enters the widget's window, the shadow is drawn in the armed state. The callbacks for **XmNarmCallback** are called. If keyboard traversal is enabled in the menu, then this event is ignored.

<Key>Return:

If keyboard traversal is enabled in the menu, then this event causes the PushButtonGadget to be activated and the menu to be unposted. The callbacks for **XmNactivateCallback** are called, followed by callbacks for **XmNdisarmCallback**.

Default PulldownMenu System and OptionMenu System

<Btn1Down>:

This action disables keyboard traversal for the menu and returns the user to drag mode, which is the mode in which the menu is manipulated by using the mouse. The shadow is drawn in the armed state, and the callbacks for **XmNarmCallback** are called.

<Btn1Up>: This action causes the PushButtonGadget to be activated and the menu to be unposted. The callbacks for **XmNactivateCallback** are called, followed by callbacks for **XmNdisarmCallback**.

<Leave Window>:

If mouse button 1 is pressed and the cursor leaves the widget's window, the PushButtonGadget is redrawn with no shadow. The callbacks for **XmNdisarmCallback** are called. If keyboard traversal is enabled in the menu, then this event is ignored.

<Enter Window>:

If mouse button 1 is pressed and the cursor enters the widget's window, the shadow is drawn in the armed state. The callbacks for **XmNarmCallback** are called. If keyboard traversal is enabled in the menu, then this event is ignored.

<Key>Return:
> If keyboard traversal is enabled in the menu, then this event causes the PushButtonGadget to be activated and the menu to be unposted. The callbacks for **XmNactivateCallback** are called, followed by callbacks for **XmNdisarmCallback**.

Keyboard Traversal

For information on keyboard traversal outside of menu systems, see the man page for **XmGadget(3X)** and its sections on behavior and default translations. For information on keyboard traversal inside of menu systems, see **XmRowColumn(3X)**.

Related Information

Object(3X), **RectObj(3X)**, **XmCreatePushButtonGadget(3X)**, **XmGadget(3X)**, **XmLabelGadget(3X)**, and **XmRowColumn(3X)**.

XmRemoveTabGroup

Purpose

A function that removes a tab group

AES Support Level

Full-use

Synopsis

#include <Xm/Xm.h>

void XmRemoveTabGroup (*tab_group*)
    Widget   *tab_group*;

Description

XmRemoveTabGroup removes a Manager or Primitive widget from the list of tab groups associated with a particular widget hierarchy.

tab_group
        Specifies the Manager or Primitive widget ID.

Related Information

XmAddTabGroup(3X), **XmManager(3X)**, and **XmPrimitive(3X)**.

XmResolvePartOffsets

Purpose

A function that allows writing of upward-compatible applications and widgets.

AES Support Level

Full-use

Synopsis

#include <Xm/XmP.h>

void **XmResolvePartOffsets** (*widget_class, offset*)
  WidgetClass *widget_class*;
  XmOffsetPtr * *offset*;

Description

The use of offset records requires one extra global variable per widget class. The variable consists of a pointer to an array of offsets into the widget record for each part of the widget structure. The **XmResolvePartOffsets** function allocates the offset records needed by an application to guarantee upward-compatible applications and widgets. These offset records are used by the widget to access all of the widget's variables. A widget needs to take the following steps:

- Instead of creating a resource list, the widget creates an offset resource list. To help you accomplish this, use the **XmPartResource** structure and the **XmPartOffset** macro. The **XmPartResource** data structure looks just like a resource list, but instead of having one integer for its offset, it has two shorts. This is put into the class record as if it were a normal resource list. Instead of using **XtOffset** for the offset, it uses **XmPartOffset**.

- Instead of putting the widget size in the class record, the widget puts the widget part in the same field.

- Instead of putting **XtVersion** in the class record, the widget puts **XtVersionDontCheck** in the class record.

- The widget defines a variable to point to the offset record. This can be part of the widget's class record or a separate global variable.

- In class initialization, the widget calls **XmResolvePartOffsets**, passing it the offset address and the class record. This does several things:

  - Adds the superclass (which, by definition, has already been initialized) size field to the part size field

  - Allocates an array based upon the number of superclasses

  - Fills in the offsets of all the widget parts with the appropriate values, determined by examining the size fields of all superclass records

  - Uses the part offset array to modify the offset entries in the resource list to be real offsets, in place

- Instead of accessing fields directly, the widget must always go through the offset table. You can define macros for each field to make this easier. Assume an integer field ''xyz'':

#define BarXyz(w) (*(int *)(((char *) w) + offset[BarIndex] + \
                   XtOffset(BarPart,xyz)))

The **XmField** macro helps you access these fields. Because the **XmPartOffset** and **XmField** macros concatenate things together, you must ensure that there is no space before or after the part argument. For example, the following macros do not work because of the space before or after the part (Label) argument:

XmField(w, offset, Label, text, char *)

XmPartOffset(Label, text).

Therefore, you must not have any spaces before or after the part (Label) argument, as illustrated here:

XmField(w, offset,Label, text, char *)

The parameters for **XmResolvePartOffsets** are defined below:

widget_class Specifies the widget class pointer for the created widget

offset　　　　Specifies the offset record

XmRowColumn

Purpose

The RowColumn widget class

AES Support Level

Full-use

Synopsis

#include <Xm/RowColumn.h>

Description

The RowColumn widget is a general purpose RowColumn manager capable of containing any widget type as a child. In general, it requires no special knowledge about how its children function and provides nothing beyond support for several different layout styles. However, it can be configured as a menu, in which case, it expects only certain children, and it configures to a particular layout. The menus supported are: MenuBar, Pulldown or Popup MenuPanes, and OptionMenu.

The type of layout performed is controlled by how the application has set the various layout resources. It can be configured to lay out its children in either rows or columns. In addition, the application can specify how the children are laid out, as follows:

the children are packed tightly together (not into organized rows and columns)

each child is placed in an identically-sized box (producing a symmetrical look)

a specific layout (the current x and y positions of the children control their location)

In addition, the application has control over both the spacing that occurs between each row and column and the margin spacing present between the edges of the RowColumn widget and any children that are placed against it.

In most cases, the RowColumn widget has no 3-D visuals associated with it; if an application wishes to have a 3-D shadow placed around this widget, it can create the RowColumn as a child of a Frame widget.

Classes

RowColumn inherits behavior and resources from **Core**, **Composite**, **Constraint**, and **XmManager** classes.

The class pointer is **xmRowColumnWidgetClass**.

The class name is **XmRowColumn**.

New Resources

The following table defines a set of widget resources used by the programmer to specify data. The programmer can also set the resource values for the inherited classes to set attributes for this widget. To reference a resource by name or by class in a .Xdefaults file, remove the **XmN** or **XmC** prefix and use the remaining letters. To specify one of the defined values for a resource in a .Xdefaults file, remove the **Xm** prefix and use the remaining letters (in either lowercase or uppercase, but include any underscores between words). The codes in the access column indicate if the given resource can be set at creation time (**C**), set by using **XtSetValues** (**S**), retrieved by using **XtGetValues** (**G**), or is not applicable (**N/A**).

XmRowColumn Resource Set		
Name	**Default**	**Access**
Class	**Type**	
XmNadjustLast	True	CSG
XmCAdjustLast	Boolean	
XmNadjustMargin	True	CSG
XmCAdjustMargin	Boolean	
XmNentryAlignment	dynamic	CSG
XmCAlignment	unsigned char	
XmNentryBorder	dynamic	CSG
XmCEntryBorder	short	
XmNentryCallback	NULL	C
XtCCallback	XtCallbackList	
nXmNentryClass	dynamic	CSG
XmCEntryClass	WidgetClass	
XmNisAligned	True	CSG
XmCIsAligned	Boolean	
XmNisHomogeneous	dynamic	CSG
XmCIsHomogeneous	Boolean	
XmNlabelString	NULL	C
XtCString	XmString	
XmNmapCallback	NULL	C
XtCCallback	XtCallbackList	
XmNmarginHeight	dynamic	CSG
XmCMarginHeight	Dimension	

Name	Default	Access
Class	Type	
XmNmarginWidth	3	CSG
XmCMarginWidth	Dimension	
XmNmenuAccelerator	dynamic	CSG
XmCAccelerators	String	
XmNmenuHelpWidget	NULL	CSG
XmCMenuWidget	Widget	
XmNmenuHistory	NULL	CSG
XmCMenuWidget	Widget	
XmNmnemonic	dynamic	CSG
XmCMnemonic	char	
XmNnumColumns	dynamic	CSG
XmCNumColumns	short	
XmNorientation	dynamic	CSG
XmCOrientation	unsigned char	
XmNpacking	dynamic	CSG
XmCPacking	unsigned char	
XmNpopupEnabled	True	CSG
XmCPopupEnabled	Boolean	
XmNradioAlwaysOne	True	CSG
XmCRadioAlwaysOne	Boolean	
XmNradioBehavior	False	CSG
XmCRadioBehavior	Boolean	
XmNresizeHeight	True	CSG
XmCResizeHeight	Boolean	
XmNresizeWidth	True	CSG
XmCResizeWidth	Boolean	
XmNrowColumnType	XmWORK_AREA	CG
XmCRowColumnType	unsigned char	

Name	Default	Access
Class	Type	
XmNshadowThickness	dynamic	CSG
XmCShadowThickness	int	
XmNspacing	dynamic	CSG
XmCSpacing	short	
XmNsubMenuId	NULL	CG
XmCMenuWidget	Widget	
XmNunmapCallback	NULL	C
XtCCallback	XtCallbackList	
XmNwhichButton	dynamic	CSG
XmCWhichButton	unsigned int	

XmNadjustLast

Extends the last row of children to the bottom edge of RowColumn (when **XmOrientation** is **XmHORIZONTAL**) or extends the last column to the right edge of RowColumn (when **XmOrientation** is **XmVERTICAL**). This feature is disabled by setting **XmNadjustLast** to False.

XmNadjustMargin

Specifies whether the inner minor margins of all items contained within the RowColumn widget are forced to the same value. The inner minor margin corresponds to the **XmNmarginLeft**, **XmNmarginRight**, **XmNmarginTop**, and **XmNmarginBottom** resources supported by **XmLabel** and **XmLabelGadget**.

A horizontal orientation causes **XmNmarginTop** and **XmNmarginBottom** for all items in a particular row to be forced to the same value; the value is the largest margin specified for one of the Label items.

A vertical orientation causes **XmNmarginLeft** and **XmNmarginRight** for all items in a particular column to be forced to the same value; the value is the largest margin specified for one of the Label items.

This keeps all text within each row or column lined up with all other text in its row or column. If the **XmNrowColumnType** is either **XmMENU_POPUP** or **XmMENU_PULLDOWN** and this resource is True, only button children have their margins adjusted.

XmNentryAlignment

Specifies the alignment type for Label or LabelGadget children when **XmNisAligned** is enabled. The following are textual alignment types:

- **XmALIGNMENT_BEGINNING** — the default

- **XmALIGNMENT_CENTER**

- **XmALIGNMENT_END**

See the description of **XmNalignment** in the **XmLabel(3X)** man page for an explanation of these actions.

XmNentryBorder

Imposes a uniform border width upon all RowColumn's children. The default value is 0, which disables the feature.

XmNentryCallback

Disables the activation callbacks for all ToggleButton, PushButton, and CascadeButton widgets and gadgets contained within the RowColumn widget. If the application supplies this resource, the activation callbacks are then revectored to this callback. This allows an application to supply a single callback routine for handling all items contained in a RowColumn widget. The application must supply this resource when this widget is created.

If the application does not supply this resource, then the activation callbacks for each item in the RowColumn widget work as normal. The callback reason is **XmCR_ACTIVATE** and the default value is NULL. Changing this resource using the **XtSetValues** is not supported.

XmNentryClass

>Specifies the only widget class that can be added to the RowColumn widget; this resource is meaningful only when the **XmNisHomogeneous** resource is set to True. When **XmNrowColumnType** is set to **XmWORK_AREA** and **XmNradioBehavior** is True, then the default value for **XmNentryClass** is **xmToggleButtonGadgetClass**. When **XmNrowColumnType** is set to **XmMENU_BAR**, then the value of **XmNentryClass** is forced to **xmCascadeButtonWidgetClass**.

XmNisAligned

>Specifies text alignment for each item within the RowColumn widget; this applies only to items that are a subclass of **XmLabel** or **XmLabelGadget**. However, if the item is a Label widget or gadget and its parent is either a Popup MenuPane or a Pulldown MenuPane, then alignment is not performed; the Label is treated as the title within the MenuPane, and the alignment set by the application is not overridden. **XmNentryAlignment** controls the type of textual alignment.

XmNisHomogeneous

>Indicates if the RowColumn widget should enforce exact homogeneity among the items it contains; if True, then only the widgets which are of the class indicated by **XmNentryClass** are allowed as children of the RowColumn widget. This is most often used when creating a MenuBar or a RadioBox widget.

>Attempting to insert a child that is not a member of the specified class generates a warning message. The default value is False, except when creating a MenuBar or a RadioBox, when the default is True.

XmNlabelString

Points to a text string, which displays the label to the left of the selection area when **XmNrowColumnType** is set to **XmMENU_OPTION**. This resource is not meaningful for all other RowColumn types. If the application wishes to change the label after creation, it must get the LabelGadget ID (**XmOptionLabelGadget**) and call **XtSetValues** on the LabelGadget directly. The default value is no label.

XmNmapCallback

Specifies a widget-specific callback function that is invoked when the window associated with the RowColumn widget is about to be mapped. The callback reason is **XmCRMap**.

XmNmarginHeight

Specifies the amount of blank space between the top edge of the RowColumn widget and the first item in each column, and the bottom edge of the RowColumn widget and the last item in each column. The default value is three pixels.

XmNmarginWidth

Specifies the amount of blank space between the left edge of the RowColumn widget and the first item in each row, and the right edge of the RowColumn widget and the last item in each row. The default value is three pixels.

XmNmenuAccelerator

This resource is useful only when the RowColumn widget has been configured to operate as a Popup MenuPane or a MenuBar. The format of this resource is similar to the left side specification of a translation string, with the limitation that it must specify a key event. For a Popup MenuPane, when the accelerator is typed by the user, the Popup MenuPane is posted. For a MenuBar, when the accelerator is typed by the user, the first item in the MenuBar is highlighted, and traversal is enabled in the MenuBar. The default for a Popup MenuPane is **<Key>F4**. The default for a MenuBar is **<Key>F10**. The accelerator can be disabled by setting the **XmNpopupEnabled** resource to False.

XmNmenuHelpWidget

Specifies the widget ID for the CascadeButton, which is treated as the Help widget if **XmNrowColumnType** is set to **XmMENU_BAR**. The MenuBar always places the Help widget at the lower right corner. If the RowColumn widget is any type other than **XmMENU_BAR**, then this resource is not meaningful.

XmNmenuHistory

Specifies the widget ID of the last menu entry to be activated. It is also useful for specifying the current selection for an OptionMenu. If **XmNrowColumnType** is set to **XmMENU_OPTION**, then the specified menu item is positioned under the cursor when the menu is displayed.

If the RowColumn widget has the **XmNradioBehavior** resource set to True, then the widget field associated with this resource contains the widget ID of the last ToggleButton or ToggleButtonGadget to change from unselected to selected. The default value is the widget ID of the first child in the widget.

XmNmnemonic

This resource is useful only when **XmNrowColumnType** is set to **XmMENU_OPTION**. Specifies a single character which, when typed by the user, posts the associated Pulldown MenuPane. The character is underlined if it appears in the OptionMenu label, giving the user a visual cue that the character has special functionality associated with it. The default is no mnemonic.

XmNnumColumns

Specifies the number of minor dimension extensions that are made to accommodate the entries; this attribute is meaningful only when **XmNpacking** is set to **XmPACK_COLUMN**.

For vertically-oriented RowColumn widgets, this attribute indicates how many columns are built; the number of entries per column is adjusted to maintain this number of columns, if possible.

For horizontally-oriented RowColumn widgets, this attribute indicates how many rows are built.

The default value is one.

XmNorientation

Determines whether RowColumn layouts are row-major or column-major. In a column-major layout, the children of the RowColumn are laid out in columns top to bottom within the widget. In a row-major layout the children of the RowColumn are laid out in rows. **XmVERTICAL** resource value selects a column-major layout. **XmHORIZONTAL** resource value selects a row-major layout.

The default value is **XmVERTICAL**, except when creating a MenuBar, when the default is **XmHORIZONTAL**.

XmNpacking

Specifies how to pack the items contained within a RowColumn widget. This can be set to **XmPACK_TIGHT, XmPACK_COLUMN** or **XmPACK_NONE**. When a RowColumn widget packs the items it contains, it determines its major dimension using the value of the **XmNorientation** resource.

XmPACK_TIGHT indicates that given the current major dimension (for example, vertical if **XmNorientation** is **XmVERTICAL**), entries are placed one after the other until the RowColumn widget must wrap. RowColumn wraps when there is no room left for a complete child in that dimension. Wrapping occurs by beginning a new row or column in the next available space. Wrapping continues, as often as necessary, until all of the children are laid out. In the vertical dimension (columns), boxes are set to the same width; in the horizontal dimension (rows), boxes are set to the same depth. Each entry's position in the major dimension is left unaltered (for example, **XmNy** is left unchanged when **XmNorientation** is **XmVERTICAL**); its position in the minor dimension is set to the same value as the greatest entry in that particular row or column. The position in the minor dimension of any particular row or column is independent of all other rows or columns.

XmPACK_COLUMN indicates that all entries are placed in identically sized boxes. The box is based on the largest height and width values of all the children widgets. The value of the **XmNnumColumns** resource determines how many boxes are placed in the major dimension, before extending in the minor dimension.

XmPACK_NONE indicates that no packing is performed. The x and y attributes of each entry are left alone, and the RowColumn widget attempts to become large enough to enclose all entries.

The default value is **XmPACK_TIGHT** except when building an OptionMenu or a RadioBox, when the default is **XmPACK_COLUMN**.

XmNpopupEnabled

Allows the menu system to enable keyboard input (accelerators and mnemonics) defined for the Popup MenuPane and any of its submenus. The Popup MenuPane must be informed whenever its accessibility to the user changes because posting of the Popup MenuPane is controlled by the application. The default value for this resource is True (keyboard input — accelerators and mnemonics — defined for the Popup MenuPane and any of its submenus is enabled).

XmNradioAlwaysOne

Forces the active ToggleButton or ToggleButtonGadget to be automatically selected after having been unselected (if no other toggle was activated), if True. If False, the active toggle may be unselected. The default value is True. This resource is important only when **XmNradioBehavior** is True.

The application can always add and subtract toggles from RowColumn regardless of the selected/unselected state of the toggle. The application can also manage and unmanage toggle children of RowColumn at any time regardless of state. Therefore, the application can sometimes create a RowColumn that has **XmNradioAlwaysOne** set to True and none of the toggle children selected.

XmNradioBehavior

Specifies a Boolean value that when True, indicates that the RowColumn widget should enforce a RadioBox-type behavior on all of its children that are ToggleButtons or ToggleButtonGadgets.

Two ToggleButton and ToggleButtonGadget resources are forced to specified values at creation time: **XmNindicator** is forced to **XmONE_OF_MANY** and **XmNvisibleWhenOff** is forced to True.

RadioBox behavior dictates that when one toggle is selected and the user selects another, the first toggle is unselected automatically. The default value is False, except when creating a RadioBox, when the default is True.

XmNresizeHeight

Requests a new height if necessary, when set to True. When set to False, the widget does not request a new height regardless of any changes to the widget or its children.

XmNresizeWidth

Requests a new width if necessary, when set to True. When set to False, the widget does not request a new width regardless of any changes to the widget or its children.

XmNrowColumnType

Specifies the type of RowColumn widget to be created. It is a non-standard resource that cannot be changed after it is set. If an application uses any of the convenience routines, except **XmCreateRowColumn**, then this resource is automatically forced to the appropriate value by the convenience routine. If an application uses the Xt Intrinsics API to create its RowColumn widgets, then it must specify this resource itself. The set of possible settings for this resource are:

- **XmWORK_AREA** — the default

- **XmMENU_BAR**

- **XmMENU_PULLDOWN**

- **XmMENU_POPUP**

- **XmMENU_OPTION**

This resource cannot be changed after the RowColumn widget is created. Any changes attempted through **XtSetValues** are ignored.

XmNspacing

Specifies the horizontal and vertical spacing between items contained within the RowColumn widget. The default value is one pixel, except for a horizontal MenuBar, which defaults to 0 pixels.

XmNsubMenuId

Specifies the widget ID for the Pulldown MenuPane to be associated with an OptionMenu. This resource is useful only when **XmNrowColumnType** is set to **XmMENU_OPTION**. This resource must be specified at creation time for an OptionMenu to function properly; it is unused for all other RowColumn types. The default value is NULL.

XmNunmapCallback

Specifies a list of callbacks that is called after the window associated with the RowColumn widget has been unmapped. The callback reason is **XmCR_Unmap**. The default value is NULL.

Inherited Resources

RowColumn inherits behavior and resources from the following named superclasses. For a complete description of each resource, refer to the man page for that superclass.

XmManager Resource Set		
Name Class	**Default** Type	**Access**
XmNbottomShadow Color XmCForeground	dynamic Pixel	CSG
XmNbottomShadowPixmap XmCBottomShadowPixmap	XmUNSPECIFIED_PIXMAP Pixmap	CSG
XmNforeground XmCForeground	dynamic Pixel	CSG
XmNhelpCallback XmCCallback	NULL XtCallbackList	C
XmNhighlightColor XmCForeground	Black Pixel	CSG
XmNhighlightPixmap XmCHighlightPixmap	dynamic Pixmap	CSG
XmNshadowThickness XmCShadowThickness	0 short	CSG
XmNtopShadowColor XmCBackground	dynamic Pixel	CSG
XmNtopShadowPixmap XmCTopShadowPixmap	XmUNSPECIFIED_PIXMAP Pixmap	CSG
XmNuserData XmCUserData	NULL caddr_t	CSG

Composite Resource Set		
Name Class	**Default** Type	**Access**
XmNinsertPosition XmCInsertPosition	NULL XmRFunction	CSG

Core Resource Set		
Name	**Default**	**Access**
Class	**Type**	
XmNaccelerators	NULL	CSG
XmCAccelerators	XtTranslations	
XmNancestorSensitive	True	G
XmCSensitive	Boolean	
XmNbackground	dynamic	CSG
XmCBackground	Pixel	
XmNbackgroundPixmap	XmUNSPECIFIED_PIXMAP	CSG
XmCPixmap	Pixmap	
XmNborderColor	Black	CSG
XmCBorderColor	Pixel	
XmNborderPixmap	XmUNSPECIFIED_PIXMAP	CSG
XmCPixmap	Pixmap	
XmNborderWidth	dynamic	CSG
XmCBorderWidth	Dimension	
XmNcolormap	XtCopyFromParent	CG
XmCColormap	Colormap	
XmNdepth	XtCopyFromParent	CG
XmCDepth	int	
XmNdestroyCallback	NULL	C
XmCCallback	XtCallbackList	
XmNheight	16	CSG
XmCHeight	Dimension	
XmNmappedWhenManaged	True	CSG
XmCMappedWhenManaged	Boolean	
XmNscreen	XtCopyScreen	CG
XmCScreen	Pointer	
XmNsensitive	True	CSG
XmCSensitive	Boolean	

Name	Default	Access
Class	Type	
XmNtranslations	NULL	CSG
XmCTranslations	XtTranslations	
XmNwidth	16	CSG
XmCWidth	Dimension	
XmNx	0	CSG
XmCPosition	Position	
XmNy	0	CSG
XmCPosition	Position	

Callback Information

The following structure is returned with each callback:

typedef struct
{
    int   *reason*;
    XEvent   * *event*;
    Widget   *widget*;
    char   * *data*;
    char   * *callbackstruct*;
} XmRowColumnCallbackStruct;

reason   Indicates why the callback was invoked

event   Points to the **XEvent** that triggered the callback

The following fields apply only when the callback reason is **XmCR_ACTIVATE**; for all other callback reasons, these fields are set to NULL. The **XmCR_ACTIVATE** callback reason is generated only when the application has supplied an entry callback, which overrides any activation callbacks registered with the individual RowColumn items.

widget   Is set to the widget ID of the RowColumn item that was activated

data   Contains the client-data value supplied by the application when the RowColumn item's activation callback was registered

callbackstruct
               Points to the callback structure generated by the RowColumn item's activation callback

Behavior

A RowColumn widget's behavior depends on its type (MenuBar, Popup MenuPane, and so forth) and the type of menu system in which it resides (Pulldown, Popup, or Option). The specific mouse button depends on the **XmNwhichButton** resource.

Default MenuBar

<Btn1Down>:
               If the button event occurs within one of the MenuBar buttons, then the MenuBar is armed (if not already armed) and the submenu associated with the selected button is posted. The user can then move the mouse to access the MenuPanes attached to the MenuBar.

               If the button event does not occur within one of the MenuBar buttons and if the MenuBar is already armed, it is disarmed, and any visible MenuPanes are unposted; if the MenuBar is not already armed, then nothing occurs.

<Btn1Up>: If the MenuBar is armed, then this event unposts all visible MenuPanes and then disarms the menubar.

Default OptionMenu

<Btn1Down>:

> When this event occurs within the selection area, the Pulldown MenuPane is posted. If this event occurs outside of the selection area and if the MenuPane is already posted, then the Pulldown MenuPane is unposted.

<Btn1Up>: When this event occurs while the Pulldown MenuPane is posted, it is unposted.

<Return>: If this key is pressed while the focus is set to the selection area, then the Pulldown MenuPane is posted.

Default Pulldown MenuPane from a Popup MenuPane

<Btn3Down>:

> When this event occurs, the menu system disables traversal mode, and re-enters drag mode. Depending upon where the button-down event occurs, certain portions of the visible set of MenuPanes are unposted.

<Btn3Up>: When this event occurs within a gadget child of the MenuPane, the indicated child is activated. If the child is not a CascadeButton (widget or gadget), then this also results in all visible MenuPanes being unposted. If the child is a CascadeButton (widget or gadget), then this results in the associated submenu being posted and traversal being enabled. When this event occurs outside of a gadget child, then all visible MenuPanes are unposted.

<Return>: If this key is pressed while the focus is set to a gadget child of the MenuPane, then the indicated child is activated. If the child is not a CascadeButton (widget or gadget), then this also results in all visible MenuPanes being unposted. If the child is a CascadeButton (widget or gadget), then this results in the associated submenu being posted and traversal being enabled.

<Escape>: This event unposts all visible MenuPanes.

<Right>:   If the current focus item is a CascadeButtonGadget, then this posts the associated Pulldown MenuPane and highlights the first accessible item within the Pulldown MenuPane.

<Left>:   If this occurs within a MenuPane that is a submenu of another MenuPane, then this causes the last MenuPane to be unposted and the focus to move to the previous MenuPane.

<Up>:   This moves the focus to the previous menu item; the previous menu item is defined as the widget which was created prior to the one which currently has the focus. Wrapping occurs, if necessary.

<Down>:   This moves the focus to the next menu item; the next menu item is defined as the widget that was created after the one that currently has the focus. Wrapping occurs, if necessary.

Default Pulldown MenuPane from a MenuBar or from an OptionMenu

<Btn1Down>:
When this event occurs, the menu system disables traversal mode and re-enters drag mode. Depending upon where the button down event occurs, certain portions of the visible set of MenuPanes are unposted.

<Btn1Up>:   When this event occurs within a gadget child of the MenuPane, the indicated child is activated. If the child is not a CascadeButton (widget or gadget), then this also results in all visible MenuPanes being unposted. If the child is a CascadeButton (widget or gadget), then this results in the associated submenu being posted and traversal being enabled. When this event occurs outside of a gadget child, then all visible MenuPanes are unposted.

<Return>:   If this key is pressed while the focus is set to a gadget child of the MenuPane, then the indicated child is activated. If the child is not a CascadeButton (widget or gadget), then this also results in all visible MenuPanes being unposted. If the child is a CascadeButton (widget or gadget), then this results in the associated submenu being posted and traversal being enabled.

<Escape>: This event unposts all visible MenuPanes.

<Right>: If the current focus item is a CascadeButtonGadget, then this posts the associated Pulldown MenuPane and highlights the first accessible item within the Pulldown MenuPane. If the current focus item is not a CascadeButton, then the visible set of MenuPanes are unposted, and the top level Pulldown MenuPane associated with the next MenuBar item is posted.

<Left>: If this is occurs within a MenuPane that is a submenu of another MenuPane, then this event causes the last MenuPane to be unposted and the focus to move to the previous MenuPane. If this is occurs within a MenuPane that is connected directly to the MenuBar, then the visible set of MenuPanes are unposted, and the top level Pulldown MenuPane associated with the previous menubar item is posted.

<Up>: This moves the focus to the previous menu item; the previous menu item is defined as the widget that was created prior to the one that currently has the focus. Wrapping occurs, if necessary.

<Down>: This moves the focus to the next menu item; the next menu item is defined as the widget that was created after the one which currently has the focus. Wrapping occurs, if necessary.

WorkArea

<Btn1Down>

If the button press occurred in a gadget child, it is dispatched to it.

<Btn1Up> If the button press occurred in a gadget child, it is dispatched to it.

Default Translations

The following are the default translations for an OptionMenu:

\<BtnDown\>:	**PopupBtnDown()**
\<BtnUp\>:	**PopupBtnUp()**
\<Key\>Return:	**MenuGadgetReturn()**

The following are the default translations for a Popup MenuPane:

\<BtnDown\>:	**PopupBtnDown()**
\<BtnUp\>:	**PopupBtnUp()**
\<Key\>Return:	**MenuGadgetReturn()**
\<Key\>Escape:	**MenuGadgetEscape()**
\<Unmap\>:	**MenuUnmap()**
\<FocusIn\>:	**MenuFocusIn()**
\<FocusOut\>:	**MenuFocusOut()**
\<EnterWindow\>:	**MenuEnter()**
\<Key\>Left:	**MenuGadgetTraverseLeft()**
\<Key\>Right:	**MenuGadgetTraverseRight()**
\<Key\>Up:	**MenuGadgetTraverseUp()**
\<Key\>Down:	**MenuGadgetTraverseDown()**

The following are the default translations are for a Pulldown MenuPane:

\<BtnDown\>:	**PulldownBtnDown()**
\<BtnUp\>:	**PulldownBtnUp()**
\<Key\>Return:	**MenuGadgetReturn()**
\<Key\>Escape:	**MenuGadgetEscape()**
\<Unmap\>:	**MenuUnmap()**
\<FocusIn\>:	**MenuFocusIn()**
\<FocusOut\>:	**MenuFocusOut()**
\<EnterWindow\>:	**MenuEnter()**
\<Key\>Left:	**MenuGadgetTraverseLeft()**
\<Key\>Right:	**MenuGadgetTraverseRight()**
\<Key\>Up:	**MenuGadgetTraverseUp()**
\<Key\>Down:	**MenuGadgetTraverseDown()**

The following are the default translations for a MenuBar:

<BtnDown>:	**MenuBarBtnDown()**
<BtnUp>:	**MenuBarBtnUp()**
<Unmap>:	**MenuUnmap()**
<FocusIn>:	**MenuFocusIn()**
<FocusOut>:	**MenuFocusOut()**
<EnterWindow>:	**MenuEnter()**

The following are the default translations for a WorkArea:

<Btn1Down>:	**WorkAreaBtnDown()**
<Btn1Up>:	**WorkAreaBtnUp()**

Keyboard Traversal

For information on keyboard traversal in a WorkArea, see the man page for
XmManager(3X) and its sections on behavior and default translations.

Related Information

**Composite(3X), Constraint(3X), Core(3X), XmCreateRowColumn(3X),
XmCreateMenuBar(3X), XmCreateOptionMenu(3X),
XmCreatePopupMenu(3X), XmCreatePulldownMenu(3X),
XmCreateRadioBox(3X), XmGetMenuCursor(3X), XmLabel(3X),
XmManager(3X), XmOptionButtonGadget(3X),
XmOptionLabelGadget(3X), XmSetMenuCursor(3X),
XmMenuPosition(3X), and XmUpdateDisplay(3X).**

XmScale

Purpose

The Scale widget class

AES Support Level

Full-use

Synopsis

#include <Xm/Scale.h>

Description

Scale is used by an application to indicate a value from within a range of values, and it allows the user to input or modify a value from the same range.

A Scale has an elongated rectangular region similar to a ScrollBar. A slider inside this region indicates the current value along the Scale. The user can also modify the Scale's value by moving the slider within the rectangular region of the Scale. A Scale can also include a label set located outside the Scale region. These can indicate the relative value at various positions along the scale.

A Scale can be either input/output or output only. An input/output Scale's value can be set by the application and also modified by the user with the slider. An output-only Scale is used strictly as an indicator of the current value of something and cannot be modified interactively by the user. The **Core** resource **XmNsensitive** specifies whether the user can interactively modify the Scale's value.

Classes

Scale inherits behavior and resources from **Core**, **Composite**, **Constraint**, and **XmManager** classes.

The class pointer is **xmScaleWidgetClass**.

The class name is **XmScale**.

New Resources

The following table defines a set of widget resources used by the programmer to specify data. The programmer can also set the resource values for the inherited classes to set attributes for this widget. To reference a resource by name or by class in a .Xdefaults file, remove the **XmN** or **XmC** prefix and use the remaining letters. To specify one of the defined values for a resource in a .Xdefaults file, remove the **Xm** prefix and use the remaining letters (in either lowercase or uppercase, but include any underscores between words). The codes in the access column indicate if the given resource can be set at creation time (**C**), set by using **XtSetValues** (**S**), retrieved by using **XtGetValues** (**G**), or is not applicable (**N/A**).

XmScale Resource Set		
Name **Class**	**Default** **Type**	**Access**
XmNdecimalPoints XmCDecimalPoints	0 short	CSG
XmNdragCallback XmCCallback	NULL XtCallbackList	C
XmNfontList XmCFontList	"Fixed" XmFontList	CSG
XmNhighlightOnEnter XmCHighlightOnEnter	False Boolean	CSG
XmNhighlightThickness XmCHighlightThickness	0 short	CSG
XmNmaximum XmCMaximum	100 int	CSG
XmNminimum XmCMinimum	0 int	CSG
XmNorientation XmCOrientation	XmVERTICAL unsigned char	CSG
XmNprocessingDirection XmCProcessingDirection	XmMAX_ON_TOP unsigned char	CSG
XmNscaleHeight XmCScaleHeight	0 Dimension	CSG
XmNscaleWidth XmCScaleWidth	0 Dimension	CSG
XmNshowValue XmCShowValue	False Boolean	CSG

Name	Default	Access
Class	Type	
XmNtitleString	NULL	CSG
XmCTitleString	XmString	
XmNtraversalOn	False	CSG
XmCTraversalOn	Boolean	
XmNvalue	0	CSG
XmCValue	int	
XmNvalueChangedCallback	NULL	C
XmCCallback	XtCallbackList	

XmNdecimalPoints

Specifies the number of decimal points to shift the slider value when displaying it. For example, a slider value of 2,350 and an **XmdecimalPoints** value of 2 would result in a display value of 23.50.

XmNdragCallback

Specifies the list of callbacks that is called when the slider position changes as the slider is being dragged. The reason sent by the callback is **XmCR_DRAG**.

XmNfontList

Specifies the font list to use for the title text string specified by **XmNtitleString**.

XmNhighlightOnEnter

Specifies whether to draw the slider's border highlight on enter-window events. This resource is ignored if the **XmNtraversalOn** resource is set to True.

XmNhighlightThickness

Specifies the size of the slider's border drawing rectangle used for enter window and traversal highlight drawing.

XmNmaximum

Specifies the slider's maximum value.

XmNminimum

Specifies the slider's minimum value.

XmNorientation

Displays Scale vertically or horizontally. This resource can have values of **XmVERTICAL and XmHORIZONTAL.**

XmNprocessingDirection

Specifies whether the value for **XmNmaximum** is on the right or left side of **XmNminimum** for horizontal Scales or above or below **XmNminimum** for vertical Scales. This resource can have values of **XmMAX_ON_TOP, XmMAX_ON_LEFT, XmMAX_ON_BOTTOM,** and **XmMAX_ON_RIGHT.**

XmNscaleHeight

Specifies the height of the slider area. The value should be in the specified unit type (the default is pixels).

XmNscaleWidth

Specifies the width of the slider area. The value should be in the specified unit type (the default is pixels).

XmNshowValue

Specifies if a label for the current slider value should be displayed next to the slider. If it is True, the current slider value is displayed.

XmNtitleString

Specifies the title text string to appear in the Scale widget window.

XmNtraversalOn

Specifies whether the Scale's slider is to have traversal on for it.

XmNvalue Specifies the slider's current position along the scale, between minimum and maximum.

XmNvalueChangedCallback

Specifies the list of callbacks that is called when the value of the slider has changed. The reason sent by the callback is **XmCR_VALUE_CHANGED.**

Inherited Resources

Scale inherits behavior and resources from the following superclasses. For a complete description of each resource, refer to the man page for that superclass.

XmManager Resource Set		

Name
    Class
	Default
	    Type
		Access

XmNbottomShadowColor
   XmCForeground
	dynamic
	   Pixel
		CSG

XmNbottomShadowPixmap
   XmCBottomShadowPixmap
	XmUNSPECIFIED_PIXMAP
	   Pixmap
		CSG

XmNforeground
   XmCForeground
	dynamic
	   Pixel
		CSG

XmNhelpCallback
   XmCCallback
	NULL
	   XtCallbackList
		C

XmNhighlightColor
   XmCForeground
	Black
	   Pixel
		CSG

XmNhighlightPixmap
   XmCHighlightPixmap
	dynamic
	   Pixmap
		CSG

XmNshadowThickness
   XmCShadowThickness
	0
	   short
		N/A

XmNtopShadowColor
   XmCBackground
	dynamic
	   Pixel
		CSG

XmNtopShadowPixmap
   XmCTopShadowPixmap
	XmUNSPECIFIED_PIXMAP
	   Pixmap
		CSG

XmNuserData
   XmCUserData
	NULL
	   caddr_t
		CSG

Composite Resource Set		
Name **Class**	**Default** **Type**	**Access**
XmNinsertPosition XmCInsertPosition	NULL XmRFunction	CSG

Core Resource Set		
Name **Class**	**Default** **Type**	**Access**
XmNaccelerators XmCAccelerators	NULL XtTranslations	CSG
XmNancestorSensitive XmCSensitive	True Boolean	G
XmNbackground XmCBackground	dynamic Pixel	CSG
XmNbackgroundPixmap XmCPixmap	XmUNSPECIFIED_PIXMAP Pixmap	CSG
XmNborderColor XmCBorderColor	Black Pixel	CSG
XmNborderPixmap XmCPixmap	XmUNSPECIFIED_PIXMAP Pixmap	CSG
XmNborderWidth XmCBorderWidth	0 Dimension	CSG
XmNcolormap XmCColormap	XtCopyFromParent Colormap	CG
XmNdepth XmCDepth	XtCopyFromParent int	CG
XmNdestroyCallback XmCCallback	NULL XtCallbackList	C

Name	Default	Access
Class	Type	
XmNheight	0	CSG
XmCHeight	Dimension	
XmNmappedWhenManaged	True	CSG
XmCMappedWhenManaged	Boolean	
XmNscreen	XtCopyScreen	CG
XmCScreen	Pointer	
XmNsensitive	True	CSG
XmCSensitive	Boolean	
XmNtranslations	NULL	CSG
XmCTranslations	XtTranslations	
XmNwidth	0	CSG
XmCWidth	Dimension	
XmNx	0	CSG
XmCPosition	Position	
XmNy	0	CSG
XmCPosition	Position	

Callback Information

The following structure is returned with each callback.

typedef struct
{
    int   *reason*;
    XEvent * *event*;
    int   *value*;
} XmScaleCallbackStruct;

reason   Indicates why the callback was invoked

event   Points to the **XEvent** that triggered the callback

value   Is the new slider location value

Behavior

<Btn1Down>:

Activates the interactive dragging of the slider if the button is pressed anywhere inside the scale rectangle, including the slider.

Button1<PtrMoved>:

Moves the slider to the new position and calls the callbacks for **XmNdragCallback** if the button press occurs within the slider.

<Btn1Up>: Calls the callbacks for **XmNvalueChangedCallback** if the button press occurs within the scale rectangle and if the slider position was changed.

Default Translations

The following are Scale's default translations:

<Btn1Down>:   **Arm()**
<Btn1Up>:   **Activate()**
<EnterWindow>: **Enter()**
<FocusIn>:   **FocusIn()**

Keyboard Traversal

For information on keyboard traversal, see the man page for **XmManager(3X)** and its sections on behavior and default translations.

Related Information

Composite(3X), Constraint(3X), Core(3X), XmCreateScale(3X), XmManager(3X), XmScaleGetValue(3X), and XmScaleSetValue(3X).

XmScaleGetValue

Purpose

A Scale function that returns the current slider position.

AES Support Level

Full-use

Synopsis

#include <Xm/Scale.h>

void XmScaleGetValue (*widget, value_return*)
    Widget   *widget*;
    int   * *value_return*;

Description

XmScaleGetValue returns the current slider position value displayed in the scale.

widget   Specifies the Scale widget ID

value_return Returns the current slider position value

For a complete definition of Scale and its associated resources, see
XmScale(3X).

Related Information

XmScale(3X).

XmScaleSetValue

Purpose

A Scale function that sets a slider value

AES Support Level

Full-use

Synopsis

#include <Xm/Scale.h>

void XmScaleSetValue (*widget, value*)
    Widget   *widget*;
    int   *value*;

Description

XmScaleSetValue sets the slider *value* within the Scale widget.

widget   Specifies the Scale widget ID.

value   Specifies the slider position along the scale. This sets the **XmNvalue** resource.

For a complete definition of Scale and its associated resources, see
XmScale(3X).

Related Information

XmScale(3X). 11˜.

XmScrollBar

Purpose

The ScrollBar widget class

AES Support Level

Full-use

Synopsis

#include <Xm/ScrollBar.h>

Description

The ScrollBar widget allows the user to view data that is too large to be displayed all at once. ScrollBars are usually located beside or within the widget that contains the data to be viewed. When the user interacts with the ScrollBar, the data within the other widget scrolls.

A ScrollBar consists of two arrows placed at each end of a rectangle. The rectangle is called the scroll region. A smaller rectangle, called the slider, is placed within the scroll region. The data is scrolled by clicking either arrow, selecting on the scroll region, or dragging the slider. When an arrow is selected, the slider within the scroll region is moved in the direction of the arrow by an amount supplied by the application. If the mouse button is held down, the slider continues to move at a constant rate.

The ratio of the slider size to the scroll region size corresponds to the relationship between the size of the visible data and the total size of the data. For example, if 10 percent of the data is visible, the slider occupies 10 percent of the scroll region. This provides the user with a visual clue to the size of the invisible data.

Classes

ScrollBar inherits behavior and resources from the **Core** and **XmPrimitive** classes.

The class pointer is **xmScrollBarWidgetClass**.

The class name is **XmScrollBar**.

New Resources

The following table defines a set of widget resources used by the programmer to specify data. The programmer can also set the resource values for the inherited classes to set attributes for this widget. To reference a resource by name or by class in a .Xdefaults file, remove the **XmN** or **XmC** prefix and use the remaining letters. To specify one of the defined values for a resource in a .Xdefaults file, remove the **Xm** prefix and use the remaining letters (in either lowercase or uppercase, but include any underscores between words). The codes in the access column indicate if the given resource can be set at creation time (**C**), set by using **XtSetValues** (**S**), retrieved by using **XtGetValues** (**G**), or is not applicable (**N/A**).

XmScrollBar Resource Set		
Name	**Default**	**Access**
Class	**Type**	
XmNdecrementCallback	NULL	C
XmCCallback	XtCallbackList	
XmNdragCallback	NULL	C
XmCCallback	XtCallbackList	
XmNincrement	1	CSG
XmCIncrement	int	
XmNincrementCallback	NULL	C
XmCCallback	XtCallbackList	
XmNinitialDelay	250	CSG
XmCInitialDelay	int	
XmNmaximum	0	CSG
XmCMaximum	int	
XmNminimum	0	CSG
XmCMinimum	int	
XmNorientation	XmVERTICAL	CSG
XmCOrientation	unsigned char	
XmNpageDecrementCallback	NULL	CSG
XmCCallback	XtCallbackList	
XmNpageIncrement	10	C
XmCPageIncrement	int	
XmNpageIncrementCallback	NULL	C
XmCCallback	XtCallbackList	
XmNprocessingDirection	XmMAX_ON_BOTTOM	CSG
XmCProcessingDirection	unsigned char	
XmNrepeatDelay	50	CSG
XmCRepeatDelay	int	
XmNshowArrows	True	CSG
XmCShowArrows	Boolean	

Name	Default	Access
Class	Type	
XmNsliderSize	10	CSG
XmCSliderSize	int	
XmNtoBottomCallback	NULL	C
XmCCallback	XtCallbackList	
XmNtoTopCallback	NULL	C
XmCCallback	XtCallbackList	
XmNvalue	0	CSG
XmCValue	int	
XmNvalueChangedCallback	NULL	C
XmCCallback	XtCallbackList	

XmNdecrementCallback

Specifies the list of callbacks that is called when an arrow is selected which decreases the slider value by one increment. The reason sent by the callback is **XmCR_DECREMENT**.

XmNdragCallback

Specifies the list of callbacks that is called on each incremental change of position when the slider is being dragged. The reason sent by the callback is **XmCR_DRAG**.

XmNincrement

Specifies the amount to move the slider when the corresponding arrow is selected.

XmNincrementCallback

Specifies the list of callbacks that is called when an arrow that increases the slider value by one increment is selected. The reason sent by the callback is **XmCR_INCREMENT**.

XmNinitialDelay

Specifies the amount of time to wait (milliseconds) before starting continuous slider movement while an arrow or the scroll region is being pressed.

XmNmaximum

Specifies the slider's maximum value.

XmNminimum

Specifies the slider's minimum value.

XmNorientation

Specifies whether the ScrollBar is displayed vertically or horizontally. This resource can have values of **XmVERTICAL** and **XmHORIZONTAL**.

XmNpageDecrementCallback

Specifies the list of callbacks that is called when the slider area is selected and the slider value is decreased by one page increment. The reason sent by the callback is **XmCR_PAGE_DECREMENT**.

XmNpageIncrement

Specifies the amount to move the slider when selection occurs on the slide area.

XmNpageIncrementCallback

Specifies the list of callbacks that is called when the slider area is selected and the slider value is increased by one page increment. The reason sent by the callback is **XmCR_PAGE_INCREMENT**.

XmNprocessingDirection

Specifies whether the value for **XmNmaximum** should be on the right or left side of **XmNminimum** for horizontal ScrollBars or above or below **XmNminimum** for vertical ScrollBars. This resource can have values of **XmMAX_ON_TOP**, **XmMAX_ON_BOTTOM**, **XmMAX_ON_LEFT**, and **XmMAX_ON_RIGHT**.

XmNrepeatDelay

Specifies the amount of time to wait (milliseconds) between subsequent slider movements after the **XmNinitialDelay** has been processed.

XmNshowArrows

Specifies whether the arrows are displayed.

XmNsliderSize
>
> Specifies the size of the slider between the values of 0 and maximum - minimum.

XmNtoBottomCallback
>
> Specifies the list of callbacks that is called when the user selects <**Shift**> mouse button 1 down in the bottom arrow button. This callback sends as a value the maximum ScrollBar value minus the ScrollBar slider size. The slider location is not automatically repositioned. The reason sent by the callback is **XmCR_TO_BOTTOM**.

XmNtoTopCallback
>
> Specifies the list of callbacks that is called when the user selects <**Shift**> mouse button 1 down in the top arrow button. This callback sends as a value the minimum ScrollBar slider value. The slider location is not automatically repositioned. The reason sent by the callback is **XmCR_TO_TOP**.

XmNvalue   Specifies the slider's position between minimum and maximum.

XmNvalueChangedCallback
>
> Specifies the list of callbacks that is called when the slider is released while being dragged; this is in place of **XmNincrementCallback**, **XmNdecrementCallback**, **XmNpageIncrementCallback**   or **XmNpageDecrementCallback** when they do not have any callbacks attached. The reason sent by the callback is **XmCR_VALUE_CHANGED**.

Inherited Resources

ScrollBar inherits behavior and resources from the following superclasses. For a complete description of each resource, refer to the man page for that superclass.

XmPrimitive Resource Set		

Name
    Class
	Default
	    Type
		Access

XmNbottomShadowColor
    XmCForeground
	dynamic
	    Pixel
		CSG

XmNbottomShadowPixmap
    XmCBottomShadowPixmap
	XmUNSPECIFIED_PIXMAP
	    Pixmap
		CSG

XmNforeground
    XmCForeground
	dynamic
	    Pixel
		CSG

XmNhelpCallback
    XmCCallback
	NULL
	    XtCallbackList
		C

XmNhighlightColor
    XmCForeground
	Black
	    Pixel
		CSG

XmNhighlightOnEnter
    XmCHighlightOnEnter
	False
	    Boolean
		CSG

XmNhighlightPixmap
    XmCHighlightPixmap
	dynamic
	    Pixmap
		CSG

XmNhighlightThickness
    XmCHighlightThickness
	0
	    short
		CSG

XmNshadowThickness
    XmCShadowThickness
	2
	    short
		CSG

XmNtopShadowColor
    XmCBackground
	dynamic
	    Pixel
		CSG

XmNtopShadowPixmap
    XmCTopShadowPixmap
	XmUNSPECIFIED_PIXMAP
	    Pixmap
		CSG

XmNtraversalOn
    XmCTraversalOn
	False
	    Boolean
		CSG

XmNuserData
    XmCUserData
	NULL
	    caddr_t
		CSG

Core Resource Set		
Name	**Default**	**Access**
Class	**Type**	
XmNaccelerators	NULL	CSG
XmCAccelerators	XtTranslations	
XmNancestorSensitive	True	G
XmCSensitive	Boolean	
XmNbackground	dynamic	CSG
XmCBackground	Pixel	
XmNbackgroundPixmap	XmUNSPECIFIED_PIXMAP	CSG
XmCPixmap	Pixmap	
XmNborderColor	Black	CSG
XmCBorderColor	Pixel	
XmNborderPixmap	XmUNSPECIFIED_PIXMAP	CSG
XmCPixmap	Pixmap	
XmNborderWidth	0	CSG
XmCBorderWidth	Dimension	
XmNcolormap	XtCopyFromParent	CG
XmCColormap	Colormap	
XmNdepth	XtCopyFromParent	CG
XmCDepth	int	
XmNdestroyCallback	NULL	C
XmCCallback	XtCallbackList	
XmNheight	0	CSG
XmCHeight	Dimension	
XmNmappedWhenManaged	True	CSG
XmCMappedWhenManaged	Boolean	
XmNscreen	XtCopyScreen	CG
XmCScreen	Pointer	
XmNsensitive	True	CSG
XmCSensitive	Boolean	

Name	Default	Access
Class	Type	
XmNtranslations	NULL	CSG
XmCTranslations	XtTranslations	
XmNwidth	0	CSG
XmCWidth	Dimension	
XmNx	0	CSG
XmCPosition	Position	
XmNy	0	CSG
XmCPosition	Position	

Callback Information

The following structure is returned with each callback.

typedef struct
{
    int   *reason*;
    XEvent * *event*;
    int   *value*;
    int   *pixel*;
} **XmScrollBarCallbackStruct**;

reason   Indicates why the callback was invoked.

event   Points to the **XEvent** that triggered the callback.

value   Contains the new slider location value.

pixel   Is used only for **XmNtoTopCallback** and **XmNtoBottomCallback**. For horizontal ScrollBars, it contains the x coordinate of where the mouse button selection occurred. For vertical ScrollBars, it contains the y coordinate.

Behavior

<Btn1Down>:

(**in arrow**): Moves the slider one increment or decrement in the direction of the arrow and calls the callbacks for **XmNincrementCallback** or **XmNdecrementCallback**. The **XmNvalueChangedCallbacks** is called if the **XmNincrementCallbacks** or **XmNdecrementCallbacks** are empty.

(**in scroll region**): Moves the slider one page increment or page decrement depending on which side of the slider is selected and calls the callbacks for **XmNpageIncrementCallback** or **XmNpageDecrementCallback**. The **XmNvalueChangedCallbacks** is called if the **XmNpageIncrementCallbacks** or **XmNpageDecrementCallbacks** are empty.

(**in slider**): Activates the interactive dragging of the slider. If the button is held down in either the arrows or the scroll region longer than the **XmNinitialDelay** resource, then the slider is moved again by the same increment and the same callbacks are called. After the initial delay has been used, the time delay changes to the time defined by the resource **XmNrepeatDelay**.

Button1<PtrMoved>:

If the button press occurs within the slider, the subsequent motion events move the slider to the new position and the callbacks for **XmNdragCallback** are called.

<Btn1Up>: If the button press occurs within the slider and the slider position is changed, then the callbacks for **XmNvalueChangedCallback** are called.

Shift<Btn1Down>:
This mouse-button press in the top arrow button causes the callbacks for **XmNtoTopCallback** to be called.

Shift<Btn1Down>:
This mouse-button press in the bottom arrow button causes the callbacks for **XmNtoBottomCallback** to be called.

<Key>Up: For vertical ScrofllBars, pressing the up-arrow cursor key decrements the slider one unit and calls **XmNdecrementCallback**. The **XmNvalueChangedCallbacks** is called if the **XmNdecrementCallbacks** are empty.

<Key>Down:
For vertical ScrollBars, pressing the down-arrow cursor key increments the slider one unit and calls **XmNincrementCallback**. The **XmNvalueChangedCallbacks** is called if the **XmNincrementCallbacks** are empty.

<Key>Left: For horizontal ScrollBars, pressing the left-arrow cursor key decrements the slider one unit and calls **XmNdecrementCallback**. The **XmNvalueChangedCallbacks** is called if the **XmNdecrementCallbacks** are empty.

<Key>Right:
For horizontal ScrollBars, pressing the right-arrow cursor key increments the slider one unit and calls **XmNincrementCallback**. The **XmNvalueChangedCallbacks** is called if the **XmNincrementCallbacks** are empty.

Default Translations

˜Shift ˜Ctrl ˜Meta ˜Alt **\<Btn1Down\>**:	**Select()**
˜Shift ˜Ctrl ˜Meta ˜Alt **\<Btn1Up\>**:	**Release()**
˜Shift ˜Ctrl ˜Meta ˜Alt **Button1\<PtrMoved\>:Moved()**	
Shift ˜Ctrl ˜Meta ˜Alt \<Btn1Down\>:	**GoToTop()**
Shift ˜Ctrl ˜Meta ˜Alt \<Btn1Down\>:	**GoToBottom()**
˜Shift ˜Ctrl ˜Meta ˜Alt **\<Key\>Up**:	**UpOrLeft(0)**
˜Shift ˜Ctrl ˜Meta ˜Alt **\<Key\>Down**:	**DownOrRight(0)**
˜Shift ˜Ctrl ˜Meta ˜Alt **\<Key\>Left**:	**UpOrLeft(1)**
˜Shift ˜Ctrl ˜Meta ˜Alt **\<Key\>Right**:	**DownOrRight(1)**
\<EnterWindow\>:	**Enter()**
\<LeaveWindow\>:	**Leave()**

Keyboard Traversal

If the **XtNtraversalOn** resource is set to True either at create time or during a call to **XtSetValues**, the Manager superclass automatically augments the Manager widget's translations to support keyboard traversal. Refer to **XmManager(3X)** for a complete description of these translations.

Related Information

Core(3X), XmCreateScrollBar(3X), XmPrimitive(3X), XmScrollBarGetValues(3X), and XmScrollBarSetValues(3X).

XmScrollBarGetValues

Purpose

A ScrollBar function that returns the ScrollBar's increment values and changes the slider's size and position.

AES Support Level

Full-use

Synopsis

#include <Xm/ScrollBar.h>

void XmScrollBarGetValues (*widget, value_return, slider_size_return, increment_return,*
                        page_increment_return)
Widget	*widget*;
int	* *value_return*;
int	* *slider_size_return*;
int	* *increment_return*;
int	* *page_increment_return*;

Description

XmScrollBarGetValues returns the the ScrollBar's increment values and changes the slider's size and position. The scroll region is overlaid with a slider bar that is adjusted in size and position using the main ScrollBar or set slider function attributes.

widget	Specifies the ScrollBar widget ID.
value_return	Returns the ScrollBar's slider position between the **XmNminimum** and **XmNmaximum** resources to the ScrollBar widget.
slider_size_return	Returns the size of the slider as a value between zero and the absolute value of **XmNmaximum** minus **XmNminimum**. The size of the slider varies, depending on how much of the slider scroll area it represents.
increment_return	Returns the amount of button increment and decrement.

page_increment_return

Returns the amount of page increment and decrement.

For a complete definition of ScrollBar and its associated resources, see **XmScrollBar(3X)**.

Return Value

Returns the ScrollBar's increment values and changes the slider's size and position.

Related Information

XmScrollBar(3X).

XmScrollBarSetValues

Purpose

A ScrollBar function that changes ScrollBar's increment values and the slider's size and position.

AES Support Level

Full-use

Synopsis

#include <Xm/ScrollBar.h>

void XmScrollBarSetValues (*widget, value, slider_size, increment, page_increment, notify*)

Widget	*widget*;
int	*value*;
int	*slider_size*;
int	*increment*;
int	*page_increment*;
Boolean	*notify*;

Description

XmSetScrollBarValues changes the ScrollBar's increment values and the slider's size and position. The scroll region is overlaid with a slider bar that is adjusted in size and position using the main ScrollBar or set slider function attributes.

widget   Specifies the ScrollBar widget ID.

value   Specifies the ScrollBar's slider position between **XmNminimum** and **XmNmaximum**. The resource name associated with this argument is **XmNvalue**.

slider_size   Specifies the size of the slider as a value between zero and the absolute value of **XmNmaximum** minus **XmNminimum**. The size of the slider varies, depending on how much of the slider scroll area it represents. This sets the **XmNsliderSize** resource associated with ScrollBar.

increment   Specifies the amount of button increment and decrement. If this argument is not zero, the ScrollBar widget automatically adjusts the slider when an increment or decrement action occurs. This sets the **XmNincrement** resource associated with ScrollBar.

page_increment

         Specifies the amount of page increment and decrement. If this argument is not zero, the ScrollBar widget automatically adjusts the slider when an increment or decrement action occurs. This sets the **XmNpageIncrement** resource associated with ScrollBar.

notify   Specifies a Boolean value that when True, indicates a change in the ScrollBar value and also specifies that the ScrollBar widget automatically activates the **XmNvalueChangedCallback** with the recent change. If False, no change has occurred in the ScrollBar's value and **XmNvalueChangedCallback** is not activated.

For a complete definition of ScrollBar and its associated resources, see **XmScrollBar(3X)**.

Related Information

XmScrollBar(3X).

XmScrolledWindow

Purpose

The ScrolledWindow widget class

AES Support Level

Full-use

Synopsis

#include <Xm/ScrolledW.h>

Description

The ScrolledWindow widget combines one or more ScrollBar widgets and a viewing area to implement a visible window onto some other (usually larger) data display. The visible part of the window can be scrolled through the larger display by the use of ScrollBars.

To use ScrolledWindow, an application first creates a ScrolledWindow widget, any needed ScrollBar widgets, and a widget capable of displaying any desired data as the work area of ScrolledWindow. ScrolledWindow positions the work area widget and display the ScrollBars if so requested. When the buildmeuser performs some action on the ScrollBar, the application is notified through the normal ScrollBar callback interface.

ScrolledWindow can be configured to operate automatically so that it performs all scrolling and display actions with no need for application program involvement. It can also be configured to provide a minimal support framework in which the application is responsible for processing all user input and making all visual changes to the displayed data in response to that input.

When ScrolledWindow is performing automatic scrolling it creates a clipping window. Conceptually, this window becomes the viewport through which the user examines the larger underlying data area. The application simply creates the desired data, then makes that data the work area of the ScrolledWindow. When the user moves the slider to change the displayed data, the workspace is moved under the viewing area so that a new portion of the data becomes visible.

Sometimes it is impractical for an application to create a large data space and simply display it through a small clipping window. For example, in a text editor creating a single data area that consisted of a large file would involve undesirable amount of overhead. The application would want to use a ScrolledWindow (a small viewport onto some larger data), but would want to be notified when the user scrolled the viewport so it could bring in more data from storage and update the display area. For these cases the ScrolledWindow can be configured so that it provides only visual layout support. No clipping window is created, and the application must maintain the data displayed in the work area, as well as respond to user input on the ScrollBars.

Classes

ScrolledWindow inherits behavior and resources from **Core**, **Composite**, **Constraint**, and **XmManager** Classes.

The class pointer is **xmScrolledWindowWidgetClass**.

The class name is **XmScrolledWindow**.

New Resources

The following table defines a set of widget resources used by the programmer to specify data. The programmer can also set the resource values for the inherited classes to set attributes for this widget. To reference a resource by name or by class in a .Xdefaults file, remove the **XmN** or **XmC** prefix and use the remaining letters. To specify one of the defined values for a resource in a .Xdefaults file, remove the **Xm** prefix and use the remaining letters (in either lowercase or uppercase, but include any underscores between words). The codes in the access column indicate if the given resource can be set at creation time (**C**), set by using **XtSetValues** (**S**), retrieved by using **XtGetValues** (**G**), or is not applicable (**N/A**).

XmScrolledWindow Resource Set		
Name Class	**Default** Type	**Access**
XmNclipWindow XmCClipWindow	NULL Widget	G
XmNhorizontalScrollBar XmCHorizontalScrollBar	NULL Widget	CSG
XmNscrollBarDisplayPolicy XmCScrollBarDisplayPolicy	XmSTATIC unsigned char	CG
XmNscrollBarPlacement XmCScrollBarPlacement	XmBOTTOM_RIGHT unsigned char	CSG
XmNscrolledWindowMarginHeight XmCScrolledWindowMarginHeight	0 Dimension	CSG
XmNscrolledWindowMarginWidth XmCScrolledWindowMarginWidth	0 Dimension	CSG
XmNscrollingPolicy XmCScrollingPolicy	XmAPPLICATION_DEFINED unsigned char	CG
XmNspacing XmCSpacing	4 Dimension	CSG
XmNverticalScrollBar XmCVerticalScrollBar	NULL Widget	CSG
XmNvisualPolicy XmCVisualPolicy	XmVARIABLE unsigned char	CG
XmNworkWindow XmCWorkWindow	NULL Widget	CSG

XmNclipWindow

Specifies the widget ID of the clipping area. This is automatically created by ScrolledWindow when the **XmNvisualPolicy** resource is set to **XmCONSTANT** and can only be read by the application. Any attempt to set this resource to a new value causes a warning message to be printed by the scrolled window. If the **XmNvisualPolicy** resource is set to **XmVARIABLE**, this resource is set to NULL, and no clipping window is created.

XmNhorizontalScrollBar

Specifies the widget ID of the horizontal ScrollBar.

XmNscrollBarDisplayPolicy

Controls the automatic placement of the ScrollBars. If it is set to **XmAS_NEEDED** and if **XmNscrollingPolicy** is set to **XmAUTOMATIC**, ScrollBars are displayed only if the workspace exceeds the clip area in one or both dimensions. A resource value of **XmSTATIC** causes the ScrolledWindow to display the ScrollBars whenever they are managed, regardless of the relationship between the clip window and the work area. This resource must be **XmSTATIC** when **XmNscrollingPolicy** is **XmAPPLICATION_DEFINED**.

XmNscrollBarPlacement

Specifies the positioning of the ScrollBars in relation to the work window. The following are the values:

- **XmTOP_LEFT** — The horizontal ScrollBar is placed above the work window; the vertical ScrollBar to the left.

- **XmBOTTOM_LEFT** — The horizontal ScrollBar is placed below the work window; the vertical ScrollBar to the left.

- **XmTOP_RIGHT** — The horizontal ScrollBar is placed above the work window; the vertical ScrollBar to the right.

- **XmBOTTOM_RIGHT** — The horizontal ScrollBar is placed below the work window; the vertical ScrollBar to the right.

XmNscrolledWindowMarginHeight

Specifies the margin height on the top and bottom of the ScrolledWindow.

XmNscrolledWindowMarginWidth

Specifies the margin width on the right and left sides of the ScrolledWindow.

XmNscrollingPolicy
Performs automatic scrolling of the work area with no application interaction. If the value of this resource is **XmAUTOMATIC**, ScrolledWindow automatically creates the ScrollBars; attaches callbacks to the ScrollBars; sets the visual policy to **XmCONSTANT**; and automatically moves the work area through the clip window in response to any user interaction with the ScrollBars. An application can also add its own callbacks to the ScrollBars. This allows the application to be notified of a scroll event without having to perform any layout procedures.

NOTE: Since the ScrolledWindow adds callbacks to the ScrollBars, an application should not perform an **XtRemoveAllCallbacks** on any of the ScrollBar widgets.

When **XmNscrollingPolicy** is set to **XmAPPLICATION_DEFINED**, the application is responsible for all aspects of scrolling. The ScrollBars must be created by the application, and it is responsible for performing any visual changes in the work area in response to user input.

This resource must be set to the desired policy at the time the ScrolledWindow is created. It cannot be changed through **SetValues**.

XmNspacing
Specifies the distance that separates the ScrollBars from the work window.

XmNverticalScrollBar
Specifies the widget ID of the vertical ScrollBar.

XmNvisualPolicy
>   Grows the ScrolledWindow to match the size of the work area,
>   or it can be used as a static viewport onto a larger data space.
>   If the visual policy is **XmVARIABLE**, the ScrolledWindow
>   forces the ScrollBar display policy to **XmSTATIC** and allow
>   the work area to grow or shrink at any time and adjusts its
>   layout to accommodate the new size. When the policy is
>   **XmCONSTANT**, the work area is allowed to grow or shrink
>   as requested, but a clipping window forces the size of the
>   visible portion to remain constant. The only time the viewing
>   area can grow is in response to a resize from the
>   ScrolledWindow's parent.
>
>   **NOTE**: This resource must be set to the desired policy at the
>   time the ScrolledWindow is created. It cannot be changed
>   through **SetValues**.

XmNworkWindow
>   Specifies the widget ID of the viewing area.

Inherited Resources

ScrolledWindow inherits behavior and resources from the following
superclasses. For a complete description of each resource, refer to the man
page for that superclass.

XmManager Resource Set		
Name	**Default**	**Access**
Class	**Type**	
XmNbottomShadowColor	dynamic	CSG
XmCForeground	Pixel	
XmNbottomShadowPixmap	XmUNSPECIFIED_PIXMAP	CSG
XmCBottomShadowPixmap	Pixmap	
XmNforeground	dynamic	CSG
XmCForeground	Pixel	
XmNhelpCallback	NULL	C
XmCCallback	XtCallbackList	
XmNhighlightColor	Black	CSG
XmCForeground	Pixel	
XmNhighlightPixmap	dynamic	CSG
XmCHighlightPixmap	Pixmap	
XmNshadowThickness	0	CSG
XmCShadowThickness	short	
XmNtopShadowColor	dynamic	CSG
XmCBackground	Pixel	
XmNtopShadowPixmap	XmUNSPECIFIED_PIXMAP	CSG
XmCTopShadowPixmap	Pixmap	
XmNuserData	NULL	CSG
XmCUserData	caddr_t	

Composite Resource Set		
Name	**Default**	**Access**
Class	**Type**	
XmNinsertPosition	NULL	CSG
XmCInsertPosition	XmRFunction	

Core Resource Set		
Name	**Default**	**Access**
Class	**Type**	
XmNaccelerators	NULL	CSG
XmCAccelerators	XtTranslations	
XmNancestorSensitive	True	G
XmCSensitive	Boolean	
XmNbackground	dynamic	CSG
XmCBackground	Pixel	
XmNbackgroundPixmap	XmUNSPECIFIED_PIXMAP	CSG
XmCPixmap	Pixmap	
XmNborderColor	Black	CSG
XmCBorderColor	Pixel	
XmNborderPixmap	XmUNSPECIFIED_PIXMAP	CSG
XmCPixmap	Pixmap	
XmNborderWidth	0	CSG
XmCBorderWidth	Dimension	
XmNcolormap	XtCopyFromParent	CG
XmCColormap	Colormap	
XmNdepth	XtCopyFromParent	CG
XmCDepth	int	
XmNdestroyCallback	NULL	C
XmCCallback	XtCallbackList	
XmNheight	0	CSG
XmCHeight	Dimension	
XmNmappedWhenManaged	True	CSG
XmCMappedWhenManaged	Boolean	
XmNscreen	XtCopyScreen	CG
XmCScreen	Pointer	
XmNsensitive	True	CSG
XmCSensitive	Boolean	

Name	Default	Access
Class	Type	
XmNtranslations	NULL	CSG
XmCTranslations	XtTranslations	
XmNwidth	0	CSG
XmCWidth	Dimension	
XmNx	0	CSG
XmCPosition	Position	
XmNy	0	CSG
XmCPosition	Position	

Callback Information

ScrolledWindow defines no new callback structures. The application must use the ScrollBar callbacks to be notified of user input.

Behavior

ScrolledWindow makes extensive use of the **XtQueryGeometry** functionality to facilitate geometry communication between application levels. In the **XmAPPLICATION_DEFINED** scrolling policy, the WorkWindow's query procedure is called by the ScrolledWindow whenever the ScrolledWindow is going to change its size. The widget calculates the largest possible workspace area and passes this size to the WorkWindow widget's query procedure. The query procedure can then examine this new size and determine if any changes, such as managing or unmanaging a ScrollBar are necessary. The query procedure performs whatever actions that it needs and then returns to the ScrolledWindow. The ScrolledWindow then examines the ScrollBars to see which (if any) are managed, allocates a portion of the visible space for them, and resizes the WorkWindow to fit in the rest of the space.

When the scrolling policy is **XmCONSTANT**, the ScrolledWindow can be queried to return the optimal size for a given dimension. The optimal size is defined to be the size that would just enclose the WorkWindow. By using this mechanism, an application can size the ScrolledWindow so that it needs to display a ScrollBar for only one dimension. When the ScrolledWindow's query procedure is called via **XtQueryGeometry**, the request is examined to see if the width or height has been specified. If so, the routine uses the given dimension as the basis for its calculations. It determines the minimum value for the other dimension that just encloses the WorkWindow, fills in the appropriate elements in the reply structure, and returns to the calling program. Occasionally, using the specified width or height and the other minimum dimension would result in neither ScrollBar appearing. When this happens, the query procedure sets both the width and height fields, indicating that in this situation the ideal size would cause a change in both dimensions. If the calling application sets both the width and height fields, the ScrolledWindow determines the minimum size for both dimensions and returns those values in the reply structure.

Keyboard Traversal

For information on keyboard traversal, see the man page for **XmManager(3X)** and its sections on behavior and default translations.

Related Information

Composite(3X),   Constraint(3X),   Core(3X), **XmCreateScrolledWindow(3X),**   **XmManager(3X),**   and **XmScrolledWindowSetAreas(3X).**

XmScrolledWindowSetAreas

Purpose

A ScrolledWindow function that adds or changes a window work region and a horizontal or vertical ScrollBar widget to the ScrolledWindow widget.

AES Support Level

Full-use

Synopsis

#include <Xm/ScrolledW.h>

void   XmScrolledWindowSetAreas   (*widget,   horizontal_scrollbar,* *vertical_scrollbar, work_region*)
        Widget   *widget*;
        Widget   *horizontal_scrollbar*;
        Widget   *vertical_scrollbar*;
        Widget   *work_region*;

Description

XmScrolledWindowSetAreas adds or changes a window work region and a horizontal or vertical ScrollBar widget to the ScrolledWindow widget for the application. Each widget is optional and may be passed as NULL.

widget   Specifies the ScrolledWindow widget ID.

horizontal_scrollbar

Specifies the ScrollBar widget ID for the horizontal ScrollBar to be associated with the ScrolledWindow widget. Set this ID only after creating an instance of the ScrolledWindow widget. The resource name associated with this argument is **XmNhorizontalScrollBar**.

vertical_scrollbar   Specifies the ScrollBar widget ID for the vertical ScrollBar to be associated with the ScrolledWindow widget. Set this ID only after creating an instance of the ScrolledWindow widget. The resource name associated with this argument is **XmNverticalScrollBar**.

work_region   Specifies the widget ID for the work window to be associated with the ScrolledWindow widget. Set this ID only after creating an instance of the ScrolledWindow widget. The attribute name associated with this argument is **XmNworkWindow**.

For a complete definition of ScrolledWindow and its associated resources, see **XmScrolledWindow(3X)**.

Related Information

XmScrolledWindow(3X).

XmSelectionBox

Purpose

The SelectionBox widget class

AES Support Level

Full-use

Synopsis

#include <Xm/SelectioB.h>

Description

SelectionBox is a general dialog widget that allows the user to select one item from a list. A SelectionBox includes the following:

- A scrolling list of alternatives
- An editable text field for the selected alternative
- Labels for the list and text field
- Three buttons

The default button labels are **OK, Cancel**, and **Help**. An **Apply** button is created unmanaged and may be explicitly managed as needed. One additional **WorkArea** child may be added to the SelectionBox after creation.

The user can select an item in two ways: by scrolling through the list and selecting the desired item or by entering the item name directly into the text edit area. Selecting an item from the list causes that item name to appear in the selection text edit area.

The user may select a new item as many times as desired. The item is not actually selected until the user presses the **OK** PushButton.

Classes

SelectionBox inherits behavior and resources from **Core**, **Composite**, **Constraint**, **XmManager**, and **XmBulletinBoard** Classes.

The class pointer is **xmSelectionBoxWidgetClass**.

The class name is **XmSelectionBox**.

New Resources

The following table defines a set of widget resources used by the programmer to specify data. The programmer can also set the resource values for the inherited classes to set attributes for this widget. To reference a resource by name or by class in a .Xdefaults file, remove the **XmN** or **XmC** prefix and use the remaining letters. To specify one of the defined values for a resource in a .Xdefaults file, remove the **Xm** prefix and use the remaining letters (in either lowercase or uppercase, but include any underscores between words). The codes in the access column indicate if the given resource can be set at creation time (**C**), set by using **XtSetValues** (**S**), retrieved by using **XtGetValues** (**G**), or is not applicable (**N/A**).

XmSelectionBox Resource Set		
Name Class	**Default** Type	**Access**
XmNapplyCallback XmCCallback	NULL XtCallbackList	C
XmNapplyLabelString XmCApplyLabelString	"Apply" XmString	CSG
XmNcancelCallback XmCCallback	NULL XtCallbackList	CSG
XmNcancelLabelString XmCXmString	"Cancel" XmString	CSG
XmNdialogType XmCDialogType	dynamic unsigned char	CG
XmNhelpLabelString XmCXmString	"Help" XmString	CSG
XmNlistItemCount XmCItemCount	0 int	CSG
XmNlistItems XmCItems	NULL XmStringList	CSG
XmNlistLabelString XmCXmString	NULL XmString	CSG
XmNlistVisibleItemCount XmCVisibleItemCount	8 int	CSG
XmNminimizeButtons XmCMinimizeButtons	False Boolean	CSG
XmNmustMatch XmCMustMatch	False Boolean	CSG
XmNnoMatchCallback XmCCallback	NULL XtCallbackList	C
XmNokCallback XmCCallback	NULL XtCallbackList	C

Name	Default	Access
Class	Type	
XmNokLabelString	"OK"	CSG
XmCXmString	XmString	
XmNselectionLabelString	"Selection"	CSG
XmCXmString	XmString	
XmNtextAccelerators	see below	C
XmCTextAccelerators	XtTranslations	
XmNtextColumns	20	CSG
XmCTextColumns	int	
XmNtextString	NULL	CSG
XmCTextString	XmString	

XmNapplyCallback

Specifies the list of callbacks called when the user clicks on the **Apply** button. The callback reason is **XmCR_APPLY**.

XmNapplyLabelString

Specifies the string label for the **Apply** button.

XmNcancelCallback

Specifies the list of callbacks called when the user clicks on the **Cancel** button. The callback reason is **XmCR_CANCEL**.

XmNcancelLabelString

Specifies the string label for the **Cancel** button.

XmNdialogType

Determines the set of SelectionBox children widgets that are created and managed at initialization. The following are possible values:

- **XmDIALOG_PROMPT** — the list and list label are not created, and the **Apply** button is unmanaged

- **XmDIALOG_SELECTION** — all standard children are created and managed except the **Apply** button

- **XmDIALOG_WORK_AREA** — all standard children are created and managed

If the parent of the SelectionBox is a DialogShell, the default is **XmDIALOG_SELECTION**; otherwise, the default is **XmDIALOG_WORK_AREA**. **XmCreatePromptDialog** and **XmCreateSelectionDialog** set and append this resource to the creation *arglist* supplied by the application. This resource cannot be modified after creation.

XmNhelpLabelString

Specifies the string label for the **Help** button.

XmNlistItems

Specifies the items in the SelectionBox list.

XmNlistItemCount

Specifies the number of items in the SelectionBox list.

XmNlistLabelString

Specifies the string label to appear above the SelectionBox list containing the selection items.

XmNlistVisibleItemCount

Specifies the number of items displayed in the SelectionBox list.

XmNminimizeButtons

Sets the buttons to the width of the widest button and height of the tallest button if False. If True, button width and height are not modified.

XmNmustMatch

Specifies whether the selection widget should check if the user's selection in the text edit field has an exact match in the SelectionBox list. If the selection does not have an exact match, and **XmNmustMatch** is True, the **XmNnoMatchCallback** is activated. If the selection does have an exact match, then either **XmNapplyCallback** or **XmNokCallback** is activated.

XmNnoMatchCallback

Specifies the list of callbacks called when the user makes a selection from the text edit field that does not have an exact match with any of the items in the list box. The callback reason is **XmCR_NO_MATCH**. Callbacks in this list are called only if XmNmustMatch is true.

XmNokCallback

Specifies the list of callbacks called when the user clicks the **OK** button. The callback reason is **XmCR_OK**.

XmNokLabelString

Specifies the string label for the **OK** button.

XmNselectionLabelString

Specifies the string label for the selection text edit field.

XmNtextAccelerators

Specifies translations added to the Text widget child of the SelectionBox. The default includes bindings for the up and down keys for auto selection of list items; it also includes the normal accelerator translations defined by BulletinBoard for dialog components.

XmNtextColumns

Specifies the number of columns in the Text widget.

XmNtextString

Specifies the text in the text edit selection field.

Inherited Resources

SelectionBox inherits behavior and resources from the following superclasses. For a complete description of each resource, refer to the man page for that superclass.

XmBulletinBoard Resource Set		
Name	**Default**	**Access**
Class	**Type**	
XmNallowOverlap	True	CSG
XmCAllowOverlap	Boolean	
XmNautoUnmanage	True	CSG
XmCAutoUnmanage	Boolean	
XmNbuttonFontList	NULL	CSG
XmCButtonFontList	XmFontList	
XmNcancelButton	Cancel button	SG
XmCWidget	Widget	
XmNdefaultButton	OK button	SG
XmCWidget	Widget	
XmNdefaultPosition	True	CSG
XmCDefaultPosition	Boolean	
XmNdialogStyle	dynamic	CSG
XmCDialogStyle	unsigned char	
XmNdialogTitle	NULL	CSG
XmCXmString	XmString	
XmNfocusCallback	NULL	C
XmCCallback	XtCallbackList	
XmNlabelFontList	NULL	CSG
XmCLabelFontList	XmFontList	
XmNmapCallback	NULL	C
XmCCallback	XtCallbackList	
XmNmarginHeight	10	CSG
XmCMarginHeight	short	
XmNmarginWidth	10	CSG
XmCMarginWidth	short	
XmNnoResize	False	CSG
XmCNoResize	Boolean	

Name	Default	Access
Class	Type	
XmNresizePolicy	XmRESIZE_ANY	CSG
XmCResizePolicy	unsigned char	
XmNshadowType	XmSHADOW_OUT	CSG
XmCShadowType	unsigned char	
XmNtextFontList	NULL	CSG
XmCTextFontList	XmFontList	
XmNtextTranslations	NULL	C
XmCTranslations	XtTranslations	
XmNunmapCallback	NULL	C
XmCCallback	XtCallbackList	

XmManager Resource Set		

Name
    Class
	Default
	    Type
		Access

XmNbottomShadowColor
    XmCForeground
	dynamic
	    Pixel
		CSG

XmNbottomShadowPixmap
    XmCBottomShadowPixmap
	XmUNSPECIFIED_PIXMAP
	    Pixmap
		CSG

XmNforeground
    XmCForeground
	dynamic
	    Pixel
		CSG

XmNhelpCallback
    XmCCallback
	NULL
	    XtCallbackList
		C

XmNhighlightColor
    XmCForeground
	Black
	    Pixel
		CSG

XmNhighlightPixmap
    XmCHighlightPixmap
	dynamic
	    Pixmap
		CSG

XmNshadowThickness
    XmCShadowThickness
	dynamic
	    short
		CSG

XmNtopShadowColor
    XmCBackground
	dynamic
	    Pixel
		CSG

XmNtopShadowPixmap
    XmCTopShadowPixmap
	XmUNSPECIFIED_PIXMAP
	    Pixmap
		CSG

XmNuserData
    XmCUserData
	NULL
	    caddr_t
		CSG

Composite Resource Set		

Name
    Class
	Default
	    Type
		Access

XmNinsertPosition
    XmCInsertPosition
	NULL
	    XmRFunction
		CSG

Core Resource Set		
Name	**Default**	**Access**
Class	**Type**	
XmNaccelerators	NULL	CSG
XmCAccelerators	XtTranslations	
XmNancestorSensitive	True	G
XmCSensitive	Boolean	
XmNbackground	dynamic	CSG
XmCBackground	Pixel	
XmNbackgroundPixmap	XmUNSPECIFIED_PIXMAP	CSG
XmCPixmap	Pixmap	
XmNborderColor	Black	CSG
XmCBorderColor	Pixel	
XmNborderPixmap	XmUNSPECIFIED_PIXMAP	CSG
XmCPixmap	Pixmap	
XmNborderWidth	0	CSG
XmCBorderWidth	Dimension	
XmNcolormap	XtCopyFromParent	CG
XmCColormap	Colormap	
XmNdepth	XtCopyFromParent	CG
XmCDepth	int	
XmNdestroyCallback	NULL	C
XmCCallback	XtCallbackList	
XmNheight	0	CSG
XmCHeight	Dimension	
XmNmappedWhenManaged	True	CSG
XmCMappedWhenManaged	Boolean	
XmNscreen	XtCopyScreen	CG
XmCScreen	Pointer	
XmNsensitive	True	CSG
XmCSensitive	Boolean	

Name	Default	Access
Class	Type	
XmNtranslations	NULL	CSG
XmCTranslations	XtTranslations	
XmNwidth	0	CSG
XmCWidth	Dimension	
XmNx	0	CSG
XmCPosition	Position	
XmNy	0	CSG
XmCPosition	Position	

Callback Information

The following structure is returned with each callback:

```
typedef struct
{
    int          reason;
    XEvent       * event;
    XmString     value;
    int          length;
} XmSelectionBoxCallbackStruct;
```

reason   Indicates why the callback was invoked

event   Points to the **XEvent** that triggered the callback

value   Indicates the **XmString** value selected by the user from the SelectionBox list or entered into the SelectionBox text field

length   Indicates the size in bytes of the **XmString** value

Behavior

The following is a summary of the behavior of SelectionBox.

<OK Button Activated>:
> When the **OK** button is activated, the callback **XmNokCallback** is called. The reason is **XmCR_OK**. When an invalid selection is made and it does not match any items in the list, the callback for **XmNnoMatchCallback** is called if **XmNmustMatch** is also True. The callback reason is **XmCR_NO_MATCH**.

<Apply Button Activated>:
> When the **Apply** button is activated, the callback **XmNapplyCallback** is called. The callback reason is **XmCR_APPLY**. When an invalid selection is made and it does not match any items in the list, the callback for **XmNnoMatchCallback** is called, if **XmNmustMatch** is also True. The callback reason is **XmCR_NO_MATCH**.

<Cancel Button Activated>:
> When the **Cancel** button is activated, the callback **XmNcancelCallback** is called. The callback reason is **XmCR_CANCEL**.

<Help Button Activated> or **<Key>F1**:
> When the Help button or **Function key 1** is pressed, the callbacks for **XmNhelpCallback** are called.

<Default Button Activated> or **<Key>Return**:
> When the default button or return key is pressed, the corresponding callback is called (**XmNokCallback**, **XmNapplyCallback**, **XmNcancelCallback**, or **XmNhelpCallback**).

<Key>Up or **<Key>Down**:
> When the up or down key is pressed within the Text subwidget of the SelectionBox, the text value is replaced with the previous or next item in the List subwidget.

<FocusIn>: When a **FocusIn** event is generated on the widget window, the callbacks for **XmNfocusCallback** are called.

<MapWindow>:

When a SelectionBox that is the child of a DialogShell is mapped, the callbacks for **XmNmapCallback** are invoked. When a SelectionBox that is not the child of a DialogShell is mapped, the callbacks are not invoked.

<UnmapWindow>:

When a SelectionBox that is the child of a DialogShell is unmapped, the callbacks for **XmNunmapCallback** are invoked. When a SelectionBox that is not the child of a DialogShell is unmapped, the callbacks are not invoked.

Default Translations

The following are the default translations defined for SelectionBox widgets:

<EnterWindow>:	**Enter()**
<FocusIn>:	**FocusIn()**
<Btn1Down>:	**Arm()**
<Btn1Up>:	**Activate()**
<Key>F1:	**Help()**
<Key>Return:	**Return()**
<Key>KP_Enter:	**Return()**

Default Accelerators

The following are the default accelerator translations added to the descendants of a SelectionBox:

#override	
<Key>F1:	**Help()**
<Key>Return:	**Return()**
<Key>KP_Enter:	**Return()**

Default Text Accelerators

The following are the default accelerators added to the Text child of the SelectionBox:

#override
<Key>Up: **UpOrDown(0)**
<Key>Down: **UpOrDown(1)**
<Key>F1:   **Help()**
<Key>Return: **Return()**
<Key>KP_Enter: **Return()**

Keyboard Traversal

For information on keyboard traversal, see the man page for **XmManager(3X)** and its sections on behavior and default translations.

Related Information

Composite(3X), Constraint(3X), Core(3X), XmBulletinBoard(3X), XmCreateSelectionBox(3X), XmCreateSelectionDialog(3X), XmCreatePromptDialog(3X), XmManager(3X), and **XmSelectionBoxGetChild(3X).**

XmSelectionBoxGetChild

Purpose

A SelectionBox function that is used to access a component.

AES Support Level

Full-use

Synopsis

#include <Xm/SelectioB.h>

Widget XmSelectionBoxGetChild (*widget, child*)

Widget *widget*;
unsigned char*child*;

Description

XmSelectionBoxGetChild is used to access a component within a SelectionBox. The parameters given to the function are the SelectionBox widget and a value indicating which child to access.

widget   Specifies the SelectionBox widget ID.

child   Specifies a component within the SelectionBox. The following are legal values for this parameter:

- **XmDIALOG_APPLY_BUTTON**
- **XmDIALOG_CANCEL_BUTTON**
- **XmDIALOG_DEFAULT_BUTTON**
- **XmDIALOG_HELP_BUTTON**
- **XmDIALOG_LIST**
- **XmDIALOG_LIST_LABEL**
- **XmDIALOG_OK_BUTTON**
- **XmDIALOG_SELECTION_LABEL**
- **XmDIALOG_SEPARATOR**
- **XmDIALOG_TEXT**
- **XmDIALOG_WORK_AREA**

For a complete definition of SelectionBox and its associated resources, see **XmSelectionBox(3X)**.

Return Value

Returns the widget ID of the specified SelectionBox child.

Related Information

XmSelectionBox(3X).

XmSeparator

Purpose

The Separator widget class

AES Support Level

Full-use

Synopsis

#include <Xm/Separator.h>

Description

Separator is a primitive widget that separates items in a display. Several different line drawing styles are provided, as well as horizontal or vertical orientation.

The Separator line drawing is automatically centered within the height of the widget for a horizontal orientation and centered within the width of the widget for a vertical orientation. An **XtSetValues** with a new **XmNseparatorType** resizes the widget to its minimal height (for horizontal orientation) or its minimal width (for vertical orientation) unless height or width is explicitly set in the **XtSetValues** call.

Separator does not draw shadows. The Primitive resource **XmNshadowThickness** is used for the Separator's thickness when **XmNshadowType** is **XmSHADOW_ETCHED_IN** or **XmSHADOW_ETCHED_OUT**.

Separator does not highlight and allows no traversing. The primitive resource **XmNtraversalOn** is forced to False.

The **XmNseparatorType** of **XmNO_LINE** provides an escape to the application programmer who needs a different style of drawing. A pixmap the height of the widget can be created and used as the background pixmap by building an argument list using the **XmNbackgroundPixmap** argument type as defined by **Core**. Whenever the widget is redrawn, its background is displayed containing the desired separator drawing.

Classes

Separator inherits behavior and resources from **Core** and **XmPrimitive** Classes.

The class pointer is **xmSeparatorWidgetClass**.

The class name is **XmSeparator**.

New Resources

The following table defines a set of widget resources used by the programmer to specify data. The programmer can also set the resource values for the inherited classes to set attributes for this widget. To reference a resource by name or by class in a .Xdefaults file, remove the **XmN** or **XmC** prefix and use the remaining letters. To specify one of the defined values for a resource in a .Xdefaults file, remove the **Xm** prefix and use the remaining letters (in either lowercase or uppercase, but include any underscores between words). The codes in the access column indicate if the given resource can be set at creation time (**C**), set by using **XtSetValues** (**S**), retrieved by using **XtGetValues** (**G**), or is not applicable (**N/A**).

XmSeparator Resource Set		
Name **Class**	**Default** **Type**	**Access**
XmNmargin XmCMargin	0 short	CSG
XmNorientation XmCOrientation	XmHORIZONTAL unsigned char	CSG
XmNseparatorType XmCSeparatorType	XmSHADOW_ETCHED_IN unsigned char	CSG

XmNmargin

For horizontal orientation, specifies the space on the left and right sides between the border of the Separator and the line drawn. For vertical orientation, specifies the space on the top and bottom between the border of the Separator and the line drawn.

XmNorientation

Displays Separator vertically or horizontally. This resource can have values of **XmVERTICAL** and **XmHORIZONTAL**.

XmNseparatorType

Specifies the type of line drawing to be done in the Separator widget.

- **XmSINGLE_LINE** — single line.

- **XmDOUBLE_LINE** — double line.

- **XmSINGLE_DASHED_LINE** — single-dashed line.

- **XmDOUBLE_DASHED_LINE** — double-dashed line.

- **XmNO_LINE** — no line.

- **XmSHADOW_ETCHED_IN** — double line giving the effect of a line etched into the window. The thickness of the double line is equal to the value of **XmNshadowThickness**. For horizontal orientation, the top line is drawn in **XmNtopShadowColor** and the bottom line is drawn in **XmNbottomShadowColor**. For vertical orientation, the left line is drawn in **XmNtopShadowColor** and the right line is drawn in **XmNbottomShadowColor**.

- **XmSHADOW_ETCHED_OUT** — double line giving the effect of an etched line coming out from the window. The thickness of the double line is equal to the value of **XmNshadowThickness**. For horizontal orientation, the top line is drawn in **XmNbottomShadowColor** and the bottom line is drawn in **XmNtopShadowColor**. For vertical orientation, the left line is drawn in **XmNbottomShadowColor** and the right line is drawn in **XmNtopShadowColor**.

Inherited Resources

Separator inherits behavior and resources from the following superclasses. For a complete description of each resource, refer to the man page for that superclass.

XmPrimitive Resource Set		
Name	**Default**	**Access**
Class	Type	
XmNbottomShadowColor	dynamic	CSG
XmCForeground	Pixel	
XmNbottomShadowPixmap	XmUNSPECIFIED_PIXMAP	CSG
XmCBottomShadowPixmap	Pixmap	
XmNforeground	dynamic	CSG
XmCForeground	Pixel	
XmNhelpCallback	NULL	C
XmCCallback	XtCallbackList	
XmNhighlightColor	Black	CSG
XmCForeground	Pixel	
XmNhighlightOnEnter	False	CSG
XmCHighlightOnEnter	Boolean	
XmNhighlightPixmap	dynamic	CSG
XmCHighlightPixmap	Pixmap	
XmNhighlightThickness	0	CSG
XmCHighlightThickness	short	
XmNshadowThickness	2	CSG
XmCShadowThickness	short	
XmNtopShadowColor	dynamic	CSG
XmCBackground	Pixel	
XmNtopShadowPixmap	XmUNSPECIFIED_PIXMAP	CSG
XmCTopShadowPixmap	Pixmap	
XmNtraversalOn	False	CSG
XmCTraversalOn	Boolean	
XmNuserData	NULL	CSG
XmCUserData	caddr_t	

Core Resource Set		
Name	**Default**	**Access**
Class	**Type**	
XmNaccelerators	NULL	CSG
XmCAccelerators	XtTranslations	
XmNancestorSensitive	True	G
XmCSensitive	Boolean	
XmNbackground	dynamic	CSG
XmCBackground	Pixel	
XmNbackgroundPixmap	XmUNSPECIFIED_PIXMAP	CSG
XmCPixmap	Pixmap	
XmNborderColor	Black	CSG
XmCBorderColor	Pixel	
XmNborderPixmap	XmUNSPECIFIED_PIXMAP	CSG
XmCPixmap	Pixmap	
XmNborderWidth	0	CSG
XmCBorderWidth	Dimension	
XmNcolormap	XtCopyFromParent	CG
XmCColormap	Colormap	
XmNdepth	XtCopyFromParent	CG
XmCDepth	int	
XmNdestroyCallback	NULL	C
XmCCallback	XtCallbackList	
XmNheight	0	CSG
XmCHeight	Dimension	
XmNmappedWhenManaged	True	CSG
XmCMappedWhenManaged	Boolean	
XmNscreen	XtCopyScreen	CG
XmCScreen	Pointer	
XmNsensitive	True	CSG
XmCSensitive	Boolean	

Name	Default	Access
Class	Type	
XmNtranslations	NULL	CSG
XmCTranslations	XtTranslations	
XmNwidth	0	CSG
XmCWidth	Dimension	
XmNx	0	CSG
XmCPosition	Position	
XmNy	0	CSG
XmCPosition	Position	

Keyboard Traversal

For information on keyboard traversal, see the man page for **XmPrimitive(3X)** and its sections on behavior and default translations.

Related Information

Core(3X), **XmCreateSeparator(3X)**, and **XmPrimitive(3X)**.

XmSeparatorGadget

Purpose

The SeparatorGadget widget class

AES Support Level

Full-use

Synopsis

#include <Xm/SeparatoG.h>

Description

SeparatorGadget separates items in a display. Several line drawing styles are provided, as well as horizontal or vertical orientation.

Lines drawn within the SeparatorGadget are automatically centered within the height of the gadget for a horizontal orientation and centered within the width of the gadget for a vertical orientation. An **XtSetValues** with a new **XmNseparatorType** resizes the widget to its minimal height (for horizontal orientation) or its minimal width (for vertical orientation) unless height or width is explicitly set in the **XtSetValues** call.

SeparatorGadget does not draw shadows. The Gadget resource **XmNshadowThickness** is used for the SeparatorGadget's thickness when **XmNshadowType** is **XmSHADOW_ETCHED_IN** or **XmSHADOW_ETCHED_OUT**.

SeparatorGadget does not highlight and allows no traversing. The Gadget resource **XmNtraversalOn** is forced to False.

Classes

SeparatorGadget inherits behavior and resources from **Object**, **RectObj**, and **XmGadget** Classes.

The class pointer is **xmSeparatorGadgetClass**.

The class name is **XmSeparatorGadget**.

New Resources

The following table defines a set of widget resources used by the programmer to specify data. The programmer can also set the resource values for the inherited classes to set attributes for this widget. To reference a resource by name or by class in a .Xdefaults file, remove the **XmN** or **XmC** prefix and use the remaining letters. To specify one of the defined values for a resource in a .Xdefaults file, remove the **Xm** prefix and use the remaining letters (in either lowercase or uppercase, but include any underscores between words). The codes in the access column indicate if the given resource can be set at creation time (**C**), set by using **XtSetValues** (**S**), retrieved by using **XtGetValues** (**G**), or is not applicable (**N/A**).

XmSeparatorGadget Resource Set		
Name Class	**Default** Type	**Access**
XmNmargin XmCMargin	0 short	CSG
nXmNorientation XmCOrientation	XmHORIZONTAL unsigned char	CSG
XmNseparatorType XmCSeparatorType	XmSHADOW_ETCHED_IN unsigned char	CSG

XmNmargin

> For horizontal orientation, specifies the space on the left and right sides between the border of SeparatorGadget and the line drawn. For vertical orientation, specifies the space on the top and bottom between the border of SeparatorGadget and the line drawn.

XmNorientation

> Specifies whether SeparatorGadget is displayed vertically or horizontally. This resource can have values of **XmVERTICAL** and **XmHORIZONTAL**.

XmNseparatorType

> Specifies the type of line drawing to be done in the Separator widget.

- **XmSINGLE_LINE** — single line.

- **XmDOUBLE_LINE** — double line.

- **XmSINGLE_DASHED_LINE** — single-dashed line.

- **XmDOUBLE_DASHED_LINE** — double-dashed line.

- **XmNO_LINE** — no line.

- **XmSHADOW_ETCHED_IN** — double line giving the effect of a line etched into the window. The thickness of the double line is equal to the value of **XmNshadowThickness**. For horizontal orientation, the top line is drawn in **XmNtopShadowColor** and the bottom line is drawn in **XmNbottomShadowColor**. For vertical orientation, the left line is drawn in **XmNtopShadowColor** and the right line is drawn in **XmNbottomShadowColor**.

- **XmSHADOW_ETCHED_OUT** — double line giving the effect of an etched line coming out from the window. The thickness of the double line is equal to the value of **XmNshadowThickness**. For horizontal orientation, the top line is drawn in **XmNbottomShadowColor** and the bottom line is drawn in **XmNtopShadowColor**. For vertical orientation, the left line is drawn in **XmNbottomShadowColor** and the right line is drawn in **XmNtopShadowColor**.

Inherited Resources

SeparatorGadget inherits behavior and resources from the following superclasses. For a complete description of each resource, refer to the man page for that superclass.

XmGadget Resource Set		
Name	**Default**	**Access**
Class	**Type**	
XmNhelpCallback	NULL	C
XmCCallback	XtCallbackList	
XmNhighlightOnEnter	False	CSG
XmCHighlightOnEnter	Boolean	
XmNhighlightThickness	0	CSG
XmCHighlightThickness	short	
XmNshadowThickness	2	CSG
XmCShadowThickness	short	
XmNtraversalOn	False	CSG
XmCTraversalOn	Boolean	
XmNuserData	NULL	CSG
XmCUserData	caddr_t	

RectObj Resource Set		
Name **Class**	**Default** **Type**	**Access**
XmNancestorSensitive XmCSensitive	XtCopyFromParent Boolean	CSG
XmNborderWidth XmCBorderWidth	1 Dimension	CSG
XmNheight XmCHeight	0 Dimension	CSG
XmNsensitive XmCSensitive	True Boolean	CSG
XmNwidth XmCWidth	0 Dimension	CSG
XmNx XmCPosition	0 Position	CSG
XmNy XmCPosition	0 Position	CSG

Object Resource Set		
Name **Class**	**Default** **Type**	**Access**
XmNdestroyCallback XmCCallback	NULL XtCallbackList	C

Keyboard Traversal

For information on keyboard traversal, see the man page for **XmGadget(3X)**
and its sections on behavior and default translations.

Related Information

Object(3X), **RectObject(3X)**, **XmCreateSeparatorGadget(3X)**, and **XmGadget(3X)**.

XmSetMenuCursor

Purpose

A RowColumn function that modifies the menu cursor for a client.

AES Support Level

Full-use

Synopsis

void XmSetMenuCursor (*display, cursorId*)
    Display   * *display*;
    Cursor   *cursorId*;

Description

XmSetMenuCursor programmatically modifies the menu cursor for a
client; after the cursor has been created by the client, this function registers
the cursor with the menu system. After calling this function, the specified
cursor is displayed whenever this client displays a Motif menu on the
indicated display. The client can then specify different cursors on different
displays.

display   Specifies the display to which the cursor is to be associated

cursorId Specifies the **X** cursor ID

For a complete definition of the menu cursor resource, see
XmRowColumn(3X).

Related Information

XmRowColumn(3X).

XmText

Purpose

The Text widget class

AES Support Level

Full-use

Synopsis

#include <Xm/Text.h>

Description

Text provides a single-line and multiline text editor for customizing both user and programmatic interfaces. It can be used for single-line string entry, forms entry with verification procedures, and full-window editing. It provides an application with a consistent editing system for textual data. The screen's textual data adjusts to the application writer's needs.

Text provides separate callback lists to verify movement of the insert cursor, modification of the text, and changes in input focus. Each of these callbacks provides the verification function with the widget instance, the event that caused the callback, and a data structure specific to the verification type. From this information the function can verify if the application considers this to be a legitimate state change and can signal the widget whether to continue with the action.

The user interface tailors a new set of translations. The default translations provide key bindings for insert cursor movement, deletion, insertion, and selection of text.

Text allows the user to select regions of text. Selection is based on the Interclient Communication Conventions (lCCC) selection model. Text supports primary selection.

Primitive's resource **XmNtraversalOn** is always True in Text.

Classes

Text inherits behavior and resources from **Core** and **Primitive** classes.

The class pointer is **xmTextWidgetClass**.

The class name is **XmText**.

New Resources

The following table defines a set of widget resources used by the programmer to specify data. The programmer can also set the resource values for the inherited classes to set attributes for this widget. To reference a resource by name or by class in a .Xdefaults file, remove the **XmN** or **XmC** prefix and use the remaining letters. To specify one of the defined values for a resource in a .Xdefaults file, remove the **Xm** prefix and use the remaining letters (in either lowercase or uppercase, but include any underscores between words). The codes in the access column indicate if the given resource can be set at creation time (**C**), set by using **XtSetValues** (**S**), retrieved by using **XtGetValues** (**G**), or is not applicable (**N/A**).

XmText Resource Set		

Name
    Class
	Default
	    Type
		Access

XmNactivateCallback
    XmCCallback
	NULL
	    XtCallbackList
		C

XmNautoShowCursorPosition
    XmCAutoShowCursorPosition
	True
	    Boolean
		CSG

XmNcursorPosition
    XmCCursorPosition
	0
	    XmTextPosition
		CSG

XmNeditable
    XmCEditable
	True
	    Boolean
		CSG

XmNeditMode
    XmCEditMode
	XmSINGLE_LINE_EDIT
	    int
		CSG

XmNfocusCallback
    XmCCallback
	NULL
	    XtCallbackList
		C

XmNlosingFocusCallback
    XmCCallback
	NULL
	    XtCallbackList
		C

XmNmarginHeight
    XmCMarginHeight
	3
	    short
		CSG

XmNmarginWidth
    XmCMarginWidth
	3
	    short
		CSG

XmNmaxLength
    XmCMaxLength
	MAXINT
	    int
		CSG

XmNmodifyVerifyCallback
    XmCCallback
	NULL
	    XtCallbackList
		C

XmNmotionVerifyCallback
    XmCCallback
	NULL
	    XtCallbackList
		C

XmNtopPosition
    XmCTextPosition
	0
	    XmTextPosition
		CSG

XmNvalue
    XmCValue
	""
	    String
		CSG

Name	Default	Access
Class	Type	
XmNvalueChangedCallback	NULL	C
XmCCallback	XtCallbackList	

XmNactivateCallback

Specifies the list of callbacks that is called when the user invokes an event that calls the **Activate**() function. The structure returned by this callback is **XmAnyCallbackStruct**. The reason sent by the callback is **XmCR_ACTIVATE**.

XmNautoShowCursorPosition

Ensures that the visible text contains the insert cursor when set to True. If the insert cursor changes, the contents of Text may scroll in order to bring the insertion point into the window.

XmNcursorPosition

Indicates the position in the text where the current insert cursor is to be located. Position is determined by the number of characters from the beginning of the text.

XmNeditable

Indicates that the user can edit the text string when set to True. Prohibits the user from editing the text when set to False.

XmNeditMode

Specifies the set of keyboard bindings used in Text. The default keyboard bindings (**XmSINGLE_LINE_EDIT**) provides the set of key bindings to be used in editing single-line text. The multiline bindings (**XmMULTI_LINE_EDIT**) provides the set of key bindings to be used in editing multiline text.

XmNfocusCallback

Specifies the list of callbacks that is called before Text has accepted input focus. The structure returned by this callback is **XmAnyCallbackStruct**. The reason sent by the callback is **XmCR_FOCUS**.

XmNlosingFocusCallback

Specifies the list of callbacks called before Text loses input focus. The structure returned by this callback is **XmTextVerifyCallbackStruct**. The reason sent by the callback is **XmCR_LOSING_FOCUS**.

XmNmarginHeight

Specifies the distance between the top edge of the widget window and the text, and between the bottom edge of the widget window and the text. This resource is forced to True when the Text widget is placed in a ScrolledWindow with **XmNscrollingPolicy** set to **XmAUTOMATIC**.

XmNmarginWidth

Specifies the distance between the left edge of the widget window and the text, and between the right edge of the widget window and the text. This resource is forced to True when the Text widget is placed in a ScrolledWindow with **XmNscrollingPolicy** set to **XmAUTOMATIC**.

XmNmaxLength

Specifies the maximum length of the text string that can be entered into text from the keyboard. Strings that are entered using the **XmNvalue** resource or the **XmTextSetString** function ignore this resource.

XmNmodifyVerifyCallback

Specifies the list of callbacks that is called before text is deleted from or inserted into Text. The structure returned by this callback is **XmTextVerifyCallbackStruct**. The reason sent by the callback is **XmCR_MODIFYING_TEXT_VALUE**.

XmNmotionVerifyCallback

Specifies the list of callbacks that is called before the insert cursor is moved to a new position. The structure returned by this callback is **XmTextVerifyCallbackStruct**. The reason sent by the callback is **XmCR_MOVING_INSERT_CURSOR**.

XmNtopPosition

> Displays the position of text at the top of the window. Position is determined by the number of characters from the beginning of the text.

XmNvalue   Displays the string value. **XtGetValues** returns the value of the internal buffer and **XtSetValues** copies the string values into the internal buffer.

XmNvalueChangedCallback

> Specifies the list of callbacks called after text is deleted from or inserted into Text. The structure returned by this callback is **XmAnyCallbackStruct**. The reason sent by the callback is **XmCR_VALUE_CHANGED**.

XmText Input Resource Set		
Name Class	Default Type	Access
XmNpendingDelete XmCPendingDelete	True Boolean	CSG
XmNselectionArray XmCSelectionArray	sarray Pointer	CSG
XmNselectThreshold XmCSelectThreshold	5 int	CSG

XmNpendingDelete

> Indicates that pending delete mode is on when the Boolean value is True. Pending deletion is defined as deletion of the selected text when an insertion is made.

XmNselectionArray

Defines the actions for multiple mouse clicks. Each mouse
click performed within a half of a second of the previous
mouse click increments the index into this array and perform
the defined action for that index. The possible actions are:

- **XmSELECT_POSITIONS** — resets the insert cursor
  position

- **XmSELECT_WORD** — selects a word

- **XmSELECT_LINE** — selects a line of text

- **XmSELECT_ALL** — selects all of the text

XmNselectThreshold

Specifies the number of pixels of motion that is required to
select the next character when selection is performed using the
click-drag mode of selection.

XmText Output Resource Set		

Name
    Class
	Default
	    Type
		Access

XmNblinkRate
    XmCBlinkRate
	500
	    int
		CSG

XmNcolumns
    XmCColumns
	20
	    short
		CSG

XmNcursorPositionVisible
    XmCCursorPositionVisible
	True
	    Boolean
		CSG

XmNfontList
    XmCFontList
	fixed
	    XmFontList
		CSG

XmNresizeHeight
    XmCResizeHeight
	False
	    Boolean
		CSG

XmNresizeWidth
    XmCResizeWidth
	False
	    Boolean
		CSG

XmNrows
    XmCRows
	1
	    short
		CSG

XmNwordWrap
    XmCWordWrap
	False
	    Boolean
		CSG

XmNblinkRate

Specifies the blink rate of the text cursor in milliseconds. The time indicated in the blink rate relates to the time the cursor is visible and the time the cursor is invisible (that is, the time it takes to blink the insertion cursor on and off is twice the blink rate). The cursor does not blink when the blink rate is set to zero.

XmNcolumns

Specifies the initial width of the text window measured in character spaces.

XmNfontList

Specifies the font list to be used for Text.

XmNinsertionPointVisible

Indicates that the insert cursor position is marked by a blinking text cursor when the Boolean value is True.

XmNresizeHeight

Indicates that Text attempts to resize its height to accommodate all the text contained in the widget when the Boolean is True. If the Boolean value is set to True, the text is always displayed starting from the first position in the source, even if instructed otherwise. This attribute is ignored when the applications using a ScrolledText widget and when **XmNscrollVertical** is True.

XmNresizeWidth

Indicates that Text attempts to resize its width to accommodate all the text contained in the widget when the Boolean value is True. This attribute is ignored if **XmNwordWrap** is True.

XmNrows Specifies the initial height of the text window measured in character heights. This attribute is ignored if the text widget resource **XmNeditMode** is **XmSINGLE_LINE_EDIT**.

XmNwordWrap

Indicates that lines are to be broken at word breaks (that is, the text does not go off the right edge of the window) when the Boolean value is True. Words are defined as a sequence of characters separated by white space. White space is defined as a space, tab, or newline. This attribute is ignored if the text widget resource **XmNeditMode** is **XmSINGLE_LINE_EDIT**.

The following resources are used only when text is created in a ScrolledWindow. See the man page for **XmCreateScrolledText**.

XmText ScrolledText Resource Set		
Name	**Default**	**Access**
Class	**Type**	
XmNscrollHorizontal	True	CG
XmCScroll	Boolean	
XmNscrollLeftSide	False	CG
XmCScrollSide	Boolean	
XmNscrollTopSide	False	CG
XmCScrollSide	Boolean	
XmNscrollVertical	True	CG
XmCScroll	Boolean	

XmNscrollHorizontal

Adds a ScrollBar that allows the user to scroll horizontally through text when the Boolean value is True. This attribute is ignored if the Text resource **XmNeditMode** is **XmSINGLE_LINE_EDIT**. This resource is forced to False when the Text widget is placed in a ScrolledWindow with **XmNscrollingPolicy** set to **XmAUTOMATIC**.

XmNscrollLeftSide

Indicates that the vertical ScrollBar should be placed on the left side of the scrolled text window when the Boolean value is True. This attribute is ignored if **XmNscrollVertical** is False or the Text resource **XmNeditMode** is **XmSINGLE_LINE_EDIT**.

XmNscrollTopSide

Indicates that the horizontal ScrollBar should be placed on the top side of the scrolled text window when the Boolean value is True.

XmNscrollVertical

Adds a ScrollBar that allows the user to scroll vertically through text when the Boolean value is True. This resource is forced to False when the Text widget is placed in a ScrolledWindow with **XmNscrollingPolicy** set to **XmAUTOMATIC**.

Inherited Resources

Text inherits behavior and resources from the following superclasses. For a complete description of each resource, refer to the man page for that superclass.

XmPrimitive Resource Set		
Name	**Default**	**Access**
Class	**Type**	
XmNbottomShadowColor	dynamic	CSG
XmCForeground	Pixel	
XmNbottomShadowPixmap	XmUNSPECIFIED_PIXMAP	CSG
XmCBottomShadowPixmap	Pixmap	
XmNforeground	dynamic	CSG
XmCForeground	Pixel	
XmNhelpCallback	NULL	CSG
XmCCallback	XtCallbackList	
XmNhighlightColor	Black	CSG
XmCForeground	Pixel	
XmNhighlightOnEnter	False	CSG
XmCHighlightOnEnter	Boolean	
XmNhighlightPixmap	dynamic	CSG
XmCHighlightPixmap	Pixmap	
XmNhighlightThickness	0	CSG
XmCHighlightThickness	short	
XmNshadowThickness	2	CSG
XmCShadowThickness	short	
XmNtopShadowColor	dynamic	CSG
XmCBackground	Pixel	
XmNtopShadowPixmap	XmUNSPECIFIED_PIXMAP	CSG
XmCTopShadowPixmap	Pixmap	
XmNtraversalOn	True	N/A
XmCTraversalOn	Boolean	
XmNuserData	NULL	CSG
XmCUserData	caddr_t	

Core Resource Set		
Name	**Default**	**Access**
Class	**Type**	
XmNaccelerators	NULL	CSG
XmCAccelerators	XtTranslations	
XmNancestorSensitive	True	G
XmCSensitive	Boolean	
XmNbackground	dynamic	CSG
XmCBackground	Pixel	
XmNbackgroundPixmap	XmUNSPECIFIED_PIXMAP	CSG
XmCPixmap	Pixmap	
XmNborderColor	Black	CSG
XmCBorderColor	Pixel	
XmNborderPixmap	XmUNSPECIFIED_PIXMAP	CSG
XmCPixmap	Pixmap	
XmNborderWidth	0	CSG
XmCBorderWidth	Dimension	
XmNcolormap	XtCopyFromParent	CG
XmCColormap	Colormap	
XmNdepth	XtCopyFromParent	CG
XmCDepth	int	
XmNdestroyCallback	NULL	C
XmCCallback	XtCallbackList	
XmNheight	0	CSG
XmCHeight	Dimension	
XmNmappedWhenManaged	True	CSG
XmCMappedWhenManaged	Boolean	
XmNscreen	XtCopyScreen	CG
XmCScreen	Pointer	
XmNsensitive	True	CSG
XmCSensitive	Boolean	

Name	Default	Access
Class	Type	
XmNtranslations	NULL	CSG
XmCTranslations	XtTranslations	
XmNwidth	0	CSG
XmCWidth	Dimension	
XmNx	0	CSG
XmCPosition	Position	
XmNy	0	CSG
XmCPosition	Position	

Callback Information

The following structure is returned with each callback.

typedef struct
{
    int   *reason*;
    XEvent   ** event*;
} XmAnyCallbackStruct;

reason   Indicates why the callback was invoked

event   Points to the **XEvent** that triggered the callback

The Text widget defines a new callback structure for use with verification callbacks. Note that not all fields are relevant for every callback reason. The application must first look at the reason field and use only the structure members that are valid for the particular reason. The following structure is returned with **XmNlosingFocusCallbacks**, **XmNmodifyVerifyCallbacks**, and **XmNmotionVerifyCallbacks**.

```
        typedef struct
        {
            int              reason;
            XEvent           * event;
            Boolean          doit;
            XmTextPosition currInsert, newInsert;
            XmTextPosition startPos, endPos;
            XmTextBlock    text;
        } XmTextVerifyCallbackStruct, *XmTextVerifyPtr;
```

reason   Indicates why the callback was invoked.

event   Points to the **XEvent** that triggered the callback.

doit   Indicates whether the action that invoked the callback is performed. Setting *doit* to False negates the action.

currInsert

Indicates the current position of the insert cursor.

newInsert

Indicates the position at which the user attempts to position the insert cursor.

startPos   Indicates the starting position of the text to modify. If the callback is not a modify verification callback, this value is the same as *currInsert*.

endPos   Indicates the ending position of the text to modify. If no text is replaced or deleted, then the value is the same as *startPos*. If the callback is not a modify verification callback, this value is the same as *currInsert*.

text   Points to a structure of type **XmTextBlockRec**. This structure holds the textual information to be inserted.

> **typedef struct**
> {
>   **char**   * *ptr*;
>   **int**   *length*;
>   **XmTextFormat** *format*;
> } **XmTextBlockRec, *XmTextBlock**;

ptr   Points to the text to be inserted

length Specifies the length of the text to be inserted

format Specifies the format of the text (for example, **FMT8BIT**)

The following table describes the reasons why the individual verification callback structure fields are valid:

Reason	Valid Fields
XmCR_LOSING_FOCUS	*reason, event, doit, currInsert, newInsert, startPos, endPos*
XmCR_MODIFYING_TEXT_VALUE	*reason, event, doit, currInsert, newInsert, startPos, endPos, text*
XmCR_MOVING_TEXT_CURSOR	*reason, event, doit, currInsert, newInsert*

Behavior

The behavior for the Text widget is determined by the **XmNeditMode** resource. Depending on how this resource is set, some of the key bindings perform different actions. The possible values for **XmNeditMode** are **XmSINGLE_LINE_EDIT** and **XmMULTI_LINE_EDIT**. The following describes the key bindings for these edit modes.

Default Behavior (Single-line Text Edit)

<Btn1Down>:

This key binding performs the action defined in the selection array depending on the number of multiple mouse clicks. The default selection array ordering is one click to move the insertion cursor position, two clicks to select a word, and three clicks to select a line of text.

It also begins text selection. Primary selected text that was previously selected becomes unselected.

Button1 <PtrMoved>:

Text is selected in the direction of the pointer cursor movement. While the pointer cursor is moved along the text, the text is selected from the point the mouse button 1 was pressed to the present position of the pointer cursor. Moving the pointer cursor back over previously selected text while mouse button 1 is pressed deselects the text. Primary selected text is shown visibly by inverted text.

<Btn1Up>: The selected text becomes the primary selection (that is, the selection is committed).

Shift <Btn1Down>:

The end points of the selection move to the point where the pointer cursor is located when the shifted mouse button 1 is pressed. If the pointer cursor is located at a position where text is already selected, the text following this position becomes unselected.

<Btn2Up>: The text is copied from the primary selection to the insertion point located at the insert cursor. This is shown by underlined text.

CTRL <Btn2Up>:
The text is copied and cut from the primary selection and is pasted to the insertion point located at the insert cursor.

<Key> Right:
The insert cursor moves one character to the right.

Shift <Key> Right:
The text character to the right of the insert cursor is selected and inverted (that is, primary selection). If text to the right of the insert cursor is already selected, this text becomes unselected one character at a time.

CTRL <Key> Right:
The insert cursor moves to the end of the line.

<Key> Left: The insert cursor moves one character to the left.

Shift <Key> Left:
The text character to the left of the insert cursor is selected and inverted. If already text to the left of the insert cursor is already selected, this text becomes unselected one character at a time.

CTRL <Key> Left:
The insert cursor moves to the beginning of the line.

<Key> Backspace:
The character of text immediately preceding the insert cursor is deleted.

<Key> Delete:
The character of text immediately following the insert cursor is deleted.

Any <Key>: This key binding inserts the character, associated with the key pressed, into the text of the Text widget.

<Key> Return:
Calls the callbacks for **XmNactivateCallback**.

Multiline Text Edit

Button1 <PtrMoved>:

Text is selected in the direction of the pointer cursor movement. While the pointer cursor is moved along the text, the text is selected from the point that mouse button 1 was pressed to the present position of the pointer cursor. Moving the cursor over several lines selects text to the end of each line the pointer cursor moves over and up to its position on the current line. Moving the pointer cursor back over previously selected text while mouse button 1 is pressed deselects the text.

<Key> Up: The insert cursor moves to the line directly above the line where the insert cursor is currently residing.

<Key> Down:

The insert cursor moves to the line directly below line where the insert cursor is currently residing.

<Key> Return:

Inserts a newline at the point where the insert cursor is positioned.

Default Translations

Default translations for Text are:

```
Shift<Key>Tab:         prev-tab-group()
<Key>Tab:              next-tab-group()
<Key>Up:               traverse-prev()
<Key>Down:             traverse-next()
<Key>Home:             traverse-home()
Ctrl<Key>Right:        backward-word()
Shift<Key>Right:       key-select(right)
<Key>Right:            forward-character()
Ctrl<Key>Left:         forward-word()
Shift<Key>Left:        key-select(left)
<Key>Left:             backward-character()
Shift<Key>BackSpace:delete-previous-word()
<Key>BackSpace:        delete-previous-character()
<Key>Return:           activate()
<Key>:                 self-insert()
Shift<Btn1Down>:       extend-start()
<Btn1Down>:            grab-focus()
Button1<PtrMoved>:extend-adjust()
<Btn1Up>:              extend-end()
Ctrl<Btn3Up>:          move-to()
<Btn3Up>:              copy-to()
<LeaveWindow>:         leave()
<FocusIn>:             focusIn()
<FocusOut>:            focusOut()
<Unmap>:               unmap()
Shift<Key>Delete:      delete-next-word()
<Key>Delete:           delete-next-character()
```

The following default translations override the above default translations when using Multiline Text Edit:

<Key>Tab:	**self-insert()**
<Key>Up:	**previous-line()**
<Key>Down:	**next-line()**
<Key>Home:	**beginning-of-file()**
<Key>Return:	**newline()**

When changing from Multiline Text Edit to Single-line Text Edit, the following default translations override the Multiline Text Edit default translations.

<Key>Tab:	**next-tab-group()**
<Key>Up:	**traverse-prev()**
<Key>Down:	**traverse-next()**
<Key>Home:	**traverse-home()**
<Key>Return:	**activate()**

Keyboard Traversal

Multiline Text Edit differs from standard traversal in the following manner:

Up or Down Arrow — moves the insert cursor between lines

Tab — inserts a tab

Home — moves the insert cursor to the first position (top) of the file

Return — adds a new line

Both Single-line and Multiline Text Edit differs from standard traversal in the following manner:

Right or Left Arrows — moves the insert cursor to the right or to the left

For more information on keyboard traversal, see the man page for **XmPrimitive(3X)** and its sections on behavior and default translations.

Related Information

Core(3X), XmCreateScrolledText(3X), XmCreateText(3X), XmPrimitive(3X), XmTextClearSelection(3X), XmTextGetEditable(3X), XmTextGetMaxLength(3X), XmTextGetSelection(3X), XmTextGetString(3X), XmTextRe<place(3X), XmTextSetEditable(3X), XmTextSetMaxLength(3X), XmTextSetSelection(3X), and XmTextSetString(3X).

XmTextClearSelection

Purpose

A Text function that clears the primary selection

AES Support Level

Full-use

Synopsis

#include <Xm/Text.h>

void XmTextClearSelection (*widget, time*)
    Widget   *widget*;
    Time   *time*;

Description

XmTextClearSelection clears the primary selection in the Text widget; it has no effect on the text that was previously selected.

widget   Specifies the Text widget ID.

time   Specifies the time at which the selection value is desired. This should be the time of the event which triggered this request.

For a complete definition of Text and its associated resources, see
XmText(3X).

Related Information

XmText(3X).

XmTextGetEditable

Purpose

A Text function that accesses the edit permission state.

AES Support Level

Full-use

Synopsis

#include <Xm/Text.h>

Boolean XmTextGetEditable (*widget*)
  Widget   *widget*;

Description

XmTextGetEditable accesses the edit permission state of the Text widget.

widget   Specifies the Text widget ID

For a complete definition of Text and its associated resources, see
XmText(3X).

Return Value

Returns a Boolean value that indicates the state of the **XmNeditable** resource.

Related Information

XmText(3X).

0.

XmTextGetMaxLength

Purpose

A Text function that accesses the value of the current maximum allowable length of a text string entered from the keyboard.

AES Support Level

Full-use

Synopsis

#include <Xm/Text.h>

int XmTextGetMaxLength (*widget*)
    Widget   *widget*;

Description

XmTextGetMaxLength accesses the value of the current maximum allowable length of the text string in the Text widget entered from the keyboard. The maximum allowable length prevents the user from entering a text string larger than this limit.

widget   Specifies the Text widget ID

For a complete definition of Text and its associated resources, see **XmText(3X)**.

Return Value

Returns the integer value that indicates the string's maximum allowable length that can be entered from the keyboard.

Related Information

XmText(3X).

XmTextGetSelection

Purpose

A Text function that retrieves the value of the primary selection.

AES Support Level

Full-use

Synopsis

#include <Xm/Text.h>

char * XmTextGetSelection (*widget*)
  Widget   *widget*;

Description

XmTextGetSelection retrieves the value of the primary selection. It returns a NULL pointer if no text is selected in the widget. The application is responsible for freeing the storage associated with the string by calling **XtFree**.

widget   Specifies the Text widget ID

For a complete definition of Text and its associated resources, see **XmText(3X)**.

Return Value

Returns a character pointer to the string that is associated with the primary selection.

Related Information

XmText(3X).

XmTextGetString

Purpose

A Text function that accesses the string value

AES Support Level

Full-use

Synopsis

#include <Xm/Text.h>

char * XmTextGetString (*widget*)
    Widget   *widget*;

Description

XmTextGetString accesses the string value of the Text widget. The application is responsible for freeing the storage associated with the string by calling **XtFree**.

widget   Specifies the Text widget ID

For a complete definition of Text and its associated resources, see **XmText(3X)**.

Return Value

Returns a character pointer to the string value of the text widget.

Related Information

XmText(3X).

XmTextReplace

Purpose

A Text function that replaces part of a text string

AES Support Level

Full-use

Synopsis

#include <Xm/Text.h>

void XmTextReplace (*widget, from_pos, to_pos, value*)
    Widget   *widget*;
    XmTextPosition*from_pos*;
    XmTextPosition*to_pos*;
    char   * *value*;

Description

XmTextReplace replaces part of the text string in the Text widget. The character positions begin at zero and are numbered sequentially from the beginning of the text.

An example text replacement would be to replace the second and third characters in the text string. To accomplish this, the parameter *from_pos* must be 1 and *to_pos* must be 3. To insert a string after the fourth character, both parameters, *from_pos* and *to_pos*, must be 4.

widget   Specifies the Text widget ID

from_pos Specifies the start position of the text to be replaced

to_pos   Specifies the end position of the text to be replaced

value   Specifies the character string value to be added to the text widget

For a complete definition of Text and its associated resources, see **XmText(3X)**.

Related Information

XmText(3X).

XmTextSetEditable

Purpose

A Text function that sets the edit permission

AES Support Level

Full-use

Synopsis

```
#include <Xm/Text.h>

void XmTextSetEditable (widget, editable)
    Widget    widget;
    Boolean   editable;
```

Description

XmTextSetEditable sets the edit permission state of the Text widget. When set to True, the text string can be edited.

widget Specifies the Text widget ID

editable Specifies a Boolean value that when True allows text string edits

For a complete definition of Text and its associated resources, see **XmText(3X)**.

Related Information

XmText(3X).

XmTextSetMaxLength

Purpose

A Text function that sets the value of the current maximum allowable length of a text string entered from the keyboard.

AES Support Level

Full-use

Synopsis

#include <Xm/Text.h>

void **XmTextSetMaxLength** (*widget, max_length*)
    Widget   *widget*;
    int   *max_length*;

Description

XmTextSetMaxLength sets the value of the current maximum allowable length of the text string in the Text widget. The maximum allowable length prevents the user from entering a text string from the keyboard that is larger than this limit. Strings that are entered using the **XmNvalue** resource or the **XmTextSetString** function ignore this resource.

widget   Specifies the Text widget ID

max_length
          Specifies the maximum allowable length of the text string

For a complete definition of Text and its associated resources, see **XmText(3X)**.

Related Information

XmText(3X) and **XmTextSetString(3X)**.

XmTextSetSelection

Purpose

A Text function that sets the primary selection of the text.

AES Support Level

Full-use

Synopsis

```
#include <Xm/Text.h>

void XmTextSetSelection (widget, first, last, time)
     Widget          widget;
     XmTextPositionfirst;
     XmTextPositionlast;
     Time            time;
```

Description

XmTextSetSelection sets the primary selection of the text in the widget.

widget	Specifies the Text widget ID
first	Marks the first character position
last	Marks the last position of the text to be selected
time	Specifies the time at which the selection value is desired. This should be the same as the time of the event that triggered this request.

For a complete definition of Text and its associated resources, see **XmText(3X)**.

Related Information

XmText(3X).

XmTextSetString

Purpose

A Text function that sets the string value

AES Support Level

Full-use

Synopsis

#include <Xm/Text.h>

void XmTextSetString (*widget, value*)
    Widget   *widget*;
    char   * *value*;

Description

XmTextSetString sets the string value of the Text widget.

widget   Specifies the Text widget ID

value   Specifies the character pointer to the string value and places the string into the text edit window

For a complete definition of Text and its associated resources, see **XmText(3X)**.

Related Information

XmText(3X).

XmToggleButton

Purpose

The ToggleButton widget class

AES Support Level

Full-use

Synopsis

#include <Xm/ToggleB.h>

Description

ToggleButton sets nontransitory state data within an application. Usually this widget consists of an indicator (square or diamond) with either text or a pixmap to its right. However, it can also consist of just text or a pixmap without the indicator.

The toggle graphics display a **1-of-many** or **N-of-many** selection state. When a toggle indicator is displayed, a square indicator shows an **N-of-many** selection state and a diamond indicator shows a **1-of-many** selection state.

ToggleButton implies a selected or unselected state. In the case of a label and an indicator, an empty indicator (square or diamond shaped) indicates that ToggleButton is unselected, and a filled indicator shows that it is selected. In the case of a pixmap toggle, different pixmaps are used to display the selected/unselected states.

Normally, mouse button 1 is used to arm and activate the button. However, if the ToggleButton resides within a menu, then the mouse button used is determined by the RowColumn resources **XmNrowColumnType** and **XmNwhichButton**.

To accommodate the toggle indicator when created, Label's resource **XmNmarginLeft** may be increased.

Classes

ToggleButton inherits behavior and resources from **Core**, **XmPrimitive**, and **XmLabel** Classes.

The class pointer is **xmToggleButtonWidgetClass**.

The class name is **XmToggleButton**.

New Resources

The following table defines a set of widget resources used by the programmer to specify data. The programmer can also set the resource values for the inherited classes to set attributes for this widget. To reference a resource by name or by class in a .Xdefaults file, remove the **XmN** or **XmC** prefix and use the remaining letters. To specify one of the defined values for a resource in a .Xdefaults file, remove the **Xm** prefix and use the remaining letters (in either lowercase or uppercase, but include any underscores between words). The codes in the access column indicate if the given resource can be set at creation time (**C**), set by using **XtSetValues** (**S**), retrieved by using **XtGetValues** (**G**), or is not applicable (**N/A**).

XmToggleButton Resource Set		
Name Class	**Default** Type	**Access**
XmNarmCallback XmCArmCallback	NULL XtCallbackList	C
XmNdisarmCallback XmCDisarmCallback	NULL XtCallbackList	C
XmNfillOnSelect XmCFillOnSelect	True Boolean	CSG
XmNindicatorOn XmCIndicatorOn	True Boolean	CSG
XmNindicatorType XmCIndicatorType	XmN_OF_MANY unsigned char	CSG
XmNselectColor XmCSelectColor	dynamic Pixel	CSG
XmNselectInsensitivePixmap XmCSelectInsensitivePixmap	XmUNSPECIFIED_PIXMAP Pixmap	CSG
XmNselectPixmap XmCSelectPixmap	XmUNSPECIFIED_PIXMAP Pixmap	CSG
XmNset XmCSet	False Boolean	CSG
XmNspacing XmCSpacing	4 short	CSG
XmNvalueChangedCallback XmCValueChangedCallback	NULL XtCallbackList	C
XmNvisibleWhenOff XmCVisibleWhenOff	True Boolean	CSG

XmNarmCallback

Specifies the list of callbacks called when the ToggleButton is armed. To arm this widget, press the active mouse button while the pointer is inside the ToggleButton. For this callback, the reason is **XmCR_ARM**.

XmNdisarmCallback

Specifies the list of callbacks called when ToggleButton is disarmed. To disarm this widget, press and release the active mouse button while the pointer is inside the ToggleButton. This widget is also disarmed when the user moves out of the widget and releases the mouse button when the pointer is outside the widget. For this callback, the reason is **XmCR_DISARM**.

XmNfillOnSelect

Fills the indicator with the color specified in **XmNselectColor** and switches the top and bottom shadow colors when set to True. Otherwise, it switches only the top and bottom shadow colors.

XmNindicatorOn

Specifies that a toggle indicator is drawn to the left of the toggle text or pixmap when set to True. When set to False, no space is allocated for the indicator, and it is not displayed. If **XmNindicatorOn** is True, the indicator shadows are switched when the button is selected or unselected, but, any shadows around the entire widget are not switched. However, if **XmNindicatorOn** is False, any shadows around the entire widget are switched when the toggle is selected or unselected.

XmNindicatorType

Specifies if the indicator is a **1-of** or **N-of** indicator. For the **1-of** indicator, the value is **XmONE_OF_MANY**. For the **N-of** indicator, the value is **XmN_OF_MANY**. The N-of-many indicator is square. The **1-of-many** indicator is diamond shaped. This resource specifies only the visuals and does not enforce the behavior. When the ToggleButton is in a RadioBox, the parent forces this resource to **XmONE_OF_MANY**.

XmNselectColor

Allows the application to specify what color fills the center of the square or diamond-shaped indicator when it is set. If this color is the same as either the top or the bottom shadow color of the indicator, a one-pixel-wide margin is left between the shadows and the fill; otherwise, it is filled completely. This resource's default for a color display is a color between the background and the bottom shadow color. For a monochrome display, the default is set to the foreground color.

XmNselectInsensitivePixmap

Specifies a pixmap used as the button face when the ToggleButton is selected and the button is insensitive if the Label resource **XmNlabelType** is set to **XmPIXMAP**. If the ToggleButton is unselected and the button is insensitive, the pixmap in **XmNlabelInsensitivePixmap** is used as the button face.

XmNselectPixmap

Specifies the pixmap to be used as the button face if **XmNlabelType** is **XmPIXMAP** and the ToggleButton is selected. When the ToggleButton is unselected, the pixmap specified in Label's **XmNlabelPixmap** is used.

XmNset Displays the button in its selected state if set to True. This shows some conditions as active when a set of buttons first appears.

XmNspacing

Specifies the amount of spacing between the toggle indicator and the toggle label (text or pixmap).

XmNvalueChangedCallback

Specifies the list of callbacks called when the ToggleButton value is changed. To change the value, press and release the active mouse button while the pointer is inside the ToggleButton. This action also causes this widget to be disarmed. For this callback, the reason is **XmCR_VALUE_CHANGED**.

XmNvisibleWhenOff

Indicates that the toggle indicator is visible in the unselected state when the Boolean value is True. When the ToggleButton is in a menu, the RowColumn parent forces this resource to False. When the ToggleButton is in a RadioBox, the parent forces this resource to True.

Inherited Resources

ToggleButton inherits behavior and resources from the following superclasses. For a complete description of each resource, refer to the man page for that superclass.

XmLabel Resource Set		
Name	**Default**	**Access**
Class	**Type**	
XmNaccelerator	NULL	CSG
XmCAccelerator	String	
XmNacceleratorText	NULL	CSG
XmCAcceleratorText	XmString	
XmNalignment	XmALIGNMENT_CENTER	CSG
XmCAlignment	unsigned char	
XmNfontList	"Fixed"	CSG
XmCFontList	XmFontList	
XmNlabelInsensitivePixmap	XmUNSPECIFIED_PIXMAP	CSG
XmCLabelInsensitivePixmap	Pixmap	
XmNlabelPixmap	XmUNSPECIFIED_PIXMAP	CSG
XmCPixmap	Pixmap	
XmNlabelString	NULL	CSG
XmCXmString	XmString	
XmNlabelType	XmSTRING	CSG
XmCLabelType	unsigned char	
XmNmarginBottom	0	CSG
XmCMarginBottom	short	
XmNmarginHeight	2	CSG
XmCMarginHeight	short	
XmNmarginLeft	dynamic	CSG
XmCMarginLeft	short	
XmNmarginRight	0	CSG
XmCMarginRight	short	
XmNmarginTop	0	CSG
XmCMarginTop	short	
XmNmarginWidth	2	CSG
XmCMarginWidth	short	

Name	Default	Access
Class	Type	
XmNmnemonic	'\0'	CSG
XmCMnemonic	char	
XmNrecomputeSize	True	CSG
XmCRecomputeSize	Boolean	

XmPrimitive Resource Set		

Name
    Class
	Default
	    Type
		Access

XmNbottomShadowColor
    XmCForeground
	dynamic
	    Pixel
		CSG

XmNbottomShadowPixmap
    XmCBottomShadowPixmap
	XmUNSPECIFIED_PIXMAP
	    Pixmap
		CSG

XmNforeground
    XmCForeground
	dynamic
	    Pixel
		CSG

XmNhelpCallback
    XmCCallback
	NULL
	    XtCallbackList
		C

XmNhighlightColor
    XmCForeground
	Black
	    Pixel
		CSG

XmNhighlightOnEnter
    XmCHighlightOnEnter
	False
	    Boolean
		CSG

XmNhighlightPixmap
    XmCHighlightPixmap
	dynamic
	    Pixmap
		CSG

XmNhighlightThickness
    XmCHighlightThickness
	0
	    short
		CSG

XmNshadowThickness
    XmCShadowThickness
	0
	    short
		CSG

XmNtopShadowColor
    XmCBackground
	dynamic
	    Pixel
		CSG

XmNtopShadowPixmap
    XmCTopShadowPixmap
	XmUNSPECIFIED_PIXMAP
	    Pixmap
		CSG

XmNtraversalOn
    XmCTraversalOn
	False
	    Boolean
		CSG

XmNuserData
    XmCUserData
	NULL
	    caddr_t
		CSG

Core Resource Set		
Name	**Default**	**Access**
Class	**Type**	
XmNaccelerators	NULL	CSG
XmCAccelerators	XtTranslations	
XmNancestorSensitive	True	G
XmCSensitive	Boolean	
XmNbackground	dynamic	CSG
XmCBackground	Pixel	
XmNbackgroundPixmap	XmUNSPECIFIED_PIXMAP	CSG
XmCPixmap	Pixmap	
XmNborderColor	Black	CSG
XmCBorderColor	Pixel	
XmNborderPixmap	XmUNSPECIFIED_PIXMAP	CSG
XmCPixmap	Pixmap	
XmNborderWidth	0	CSG
XmCBorderWidth	Dimension	
XmNcolormap	XtCopyFromParent	CG
XmCColormap	Colormap	
XmNdepth	XtCopyFromParent	CG
XmCDepth	int	
XmNdestroyCallback	NULL	C
XmCCallback	XtCallbackList	
XmNheight	0	CSG
XmCHeight	Dimension	
XmNmappedWhenManaged	True	CSG
XmCMappedWhenManaged	Boolean	
XmNscreen	XtCopyScreen	CG
XmCScreen	Pointer	
XmNsensitive	True	CSG
XmCSensitive	Boolean	

Name Class	Default Type	Access
XmNtranslations XmCTranslations	NULL XtTranslations	CSG
XmNwidth XmCWidth	0 Dimension	CSG
XmNx XmCPosition	0 Position	CSG
XmNy XmCPosition	0 Position	CSG

Callback Information

The following structure is returned with each callback:

```
typedef struct
{
    int         reason;
    XEvent      * event;
    Boolean     set;
} XmToggleButtonCallbackStruct;
```

reason Indicates why the callback was invoked

event Points to the **XEvent** that triggered the callback

set Reflects the ToggleButton's current state when the callback occurred, either True (selected) or False (unselected)

Behavior

ToggleButton is associated with the default behavior unless it is part of a
menu system. In a menu system, the RowColumn parent determines which
mouse button is used.

Default Behavior

<Btn1Down>:

> **(if unset):** This action arms the ToggleButton widget. The
> indicator shadow is drawn so that the button looks pressed, and
> the indicator fills with the color specified in **XmNselectColor**.
> The callbacks for **XmNarmCallback** are also called.

> **(if set):** This action arms the ToggleButton widget. The
> indicator shadow is drawn so that the button looks raised, and
> the indicator fills with the background color. The callbacks
> for **XmNarmCallback** are also called.

<Btn1Up>:

> **(In Button):**

> **(if unset):** This action selects the ToggleButton widget.
> Visually, it appears the same as when it is armed. The
> callbacks for **XmvalueChangedCallback** are called, followed
> by callbacks for **XmdisarmCallback**.

> **(if set):** This action unselects the ToggleButton widget.
> Visually, it appears the same as when it is armed. The
> callbacks for **XmvalueChangedCallback** are called, followed
> by callbacks for **XmdisarmCallback**.

> **(Outside Of Button):**

> If the button release occurs outside the ToggleButton, the
> callbacks for **XmNdisarmCallback** are called.

<Leave Window>:

> If the button is pressed and the cursor leaves the widget, it
> visually reverts to its previous unpressed state.

\<Enter Window\>:

> If the button is pressed and the cursor leaves and re-enters the widget, it visually appears the same as when the button was first armed.

Default PopupMenu System

\<Btn3Down\>:

> This action disables keyboard traversal for the menu and returns the user to drag mode, which is the mode in which the menu is manipulated by using the mouse. This action also causes the ToggleButton to be armed. A shadow is drawn around the ToggleButton. The callbacks for **XmNarmCallback** are also called.

\<Btn3Up\>: (**if unset**): This action selects the ToggleButton widget. The indicator shadow is drawn so that it looks depressed, and the indicator fills with the color specified in **XmNselectColor**. The menu is then unposted and the callbacks for **XmvalueChangedCallback** are called, followed by callbacks for **XmdisarmCallback**.

> (**if set**): This action unselects the ToggleButton widget. The indicator shadow is drawn so that it looks raised, and the indicator fills with the background color. The menu is then unposted and the callbacks for **XmvalueChangedCallback** are called, followed by callbacks for **XmdisarmCallback**.

\<Leave Window\>:

> Pressing button 3 and moving the cursor out of the widget's window erases the shadow around the ToggleButton. This event is ignored if keyboard traversal is enabled in the menu.

\<Enter Window\>:

> Pressing button 3 and moving the cursor into the widget's window draws a shadow around the ToggleButton. This event is ignored if keyboard traversal is enabled in the menu.

<Key>Return:

> If keyboard traversal is enabled in the menu, this event sets or unsets the ToggleButton.
>
> **(if unset)**: Sets the ToggleButton. The indicator shadow is drawn so that looks pressed, and the indicator fills with the color specified in **XmNselectColor**.
>
> **(if set)**: Unsets the ToggleButton. The indicator shadow is drawn so that it looks raised, and the indicator fills with the background color.
>
> For both set and unset cases, the menu is then unposted and the callbacks for **XmvalueChangedCallback** are called, followed by callbacks for **XmdisarmCallback**.

Default Pulldown Menu System and OptionMenu System

<Btn1Down>:

> This action disables keyboard traversal for the menu and returns the user to drag mode (the mode in which the menu is manipulated using the mouse). This action also arms the ToggleButton. A shadow is drawn around the ToggleButton. The callbacks for **XmNarmCallback** are also called.

<Btn1Up>: **(if unset)**: This action selects the ToggleButton. The indicator shadow is drawn so that it looks depressed, and the indicator fills with the color specified in **XmNselectColor**. The menu then unposts, and the callbacks for **XmvalueChangedCallback** are called, followed by callbacks for **XmdisarmCallback**.

> **(if set)**: This action unselects the ToggleButton. The indicator shadow is drawn so that it looks raised, and the indicator fills with the background color. The menu then unposts, and the callbacks for **XmvalueChangedCallback** are called, followed by callbacks for **XmdisarmCallback**.

<Leave Window>:

> Pressing button 1 and moving the cursor out of the widget's window erases the shadow around the ToggleButton. This event is ignored if keyboard traversal is enabled in the menu.

<Enter Window>:
> Pressing button 1 and moving the cursor into the widget's window draws a shadow around the ToggleButton. This event is ignored if keyboard traversal is enabled in the menu.

<Key>Return:
> This event sets or unsets the ToggleButton if keyboard traversal is enabled in the menu.
>
> **(if unset)**: Sets the ToggleButton. The indicator shadow is drawn so that it looks pressed, and the indicator fills with the color specified in **XmNselectColor**.
>
> **(if set)**: Unsets the ToggleButton. The indicator shadow is drawn so that it looks raised, and the indicator fills with the background color.
>
> For both set and unset cases, the menu then unposts, and the callbacks for **XmvalueChangedCallback** are called, followed by callbacks for **XmdisarmCallback**.

Default Translations

When not in a menu system, the following are the default translations:

<Btn1Down>:	**Arm()**
<Btn1Up>:	**Select()**
	Disarm()
<Key>Return:	**ArmAndActivate()**
<Key>space:	**ArmAndActivate()**
<EnterWindow>:	**Enter()**
<LeaveWindow>:	**Leave()**

When in a menu system, the following are the default translations:

<BtnDown>:	**BtnDown()**
<BtnUp>:	**BtnUp()**
<EnterWindow>:	**Enter()**
<LeaveWindow>:	**Leave()**
<Key>Return:	**KeySelect()**
<Key>Escape:	**MenuShellPopdownDone()**

Keyboard Traversal

When in a menu system, the following translations are added to ToggleButton.

<Unmap>:	**Unmap()**
<FocusOut>:	**FocusOut()**
<FocusIn>:	**FocusIn()**
<Key>space:	**Noop()**
<Key>Left:	**MenuTraverseLeft()**
<Key>Right:	**MenuTraverseRight()**
<Key>Up:	**MenuTraverseUp()**
<Key>Down:	**MenuTraverseDown()**
<Key>Home:	**Noop()**

For information on keyboard traversal when not in a menu, see the man page for **XmPrimitive(3X)** and its sections on behavior and default translations.

Related Information

Core(3X), XmCreateToggleButton(3X), XmLabel(3X),
XmPrimitive(3X), XmRowColumn(3X), XmToggleButtonGetState(3X),
and XmToggleButtonSetState(3X).

XmToggleButtonGadget

Purpose

The ToggleButtonGadget widget class

AES Support Level

Full-use

Synopsis

#include <Xm/ToggleBG.h>

Description

ToggleButtonGadget sets nontransitory state data within an application. Usually this gadget consists of an indicator (square or diamond-shaped) with either text or a pixmap to its right. However, it can also consist of just text or a pixmap without the indicator.

The toggle graphics display a **1-of-many** or **N-of-many** selection state. When a toggle indicator is displayed, a square indicator shows an **N-of-many** selection state and a diamond-shaped indicator shows a **1-of-many** selection state.

ToggleButtonGadget implies a selected or unselected state. In the case of a label and an indicator, an empty indicator (square or diamond-shaped) indicates that ToggleButtonGadget is unselected, and a filled indicator shows that it is selected. In the case of a pixmap toggle, different pixmaps are used to display the selected/unselected states.

Normally, mouse button 1 is used to arm and activate the button. However, if the ToggleButtonGadget resides within a menu, then the mouse button used is determined by the RowColumn resources **XmNrowColumnType** and **XmNwhichButton**.

To accommodate the toggle indicator when created, Label's resource **XmNmarginLeft** may be increased.

Classes

ToggleButtonGadget inherits behavior and resources from **Object**, **RectObj**, **XmGadget** and **XmLabelGadget** classes.

The class pointer is **xmToggleButtonGadgetClass**.

The class name is **XmToggleButtonGadget**.

New Resources

The following table defines a set of widget resources used by the programmer to specify data. The programmer can also set the resource values for the inherited classes to set attributes for this widget. To reference a resource by name or by class in a .Xdefaults file, remove the **XmN** or **XmC** prefix and use the remaining letters. To specify one of the defined values for a resource in a .Xdefaults file, remove the **Xm** prefix and use the remaining letters (in either lowercase or uppercase, but include any underscores between words). The codes in the access column indicate if the given resource can be set at creation time (**C**), set by using **XtSetValues** (**S**), retrieved by using **XtGetValues** (**G**), or is not applicable (**N/A**).

XmToggleButtonGadget Resource Set		
Name Class	Default Type	Access
XmNarmCallback XmCArmCallback	NULL XtCallbackList	C
XmNdisarmCallback XmCDisarmCallback	NULL XtCallbackList	C
XmNfillOnSelect XmCFillOnSelect	True Boolean	CSG
XmNindicatorOn XmCIndicatorOn	True Boolean	CSG
XmNindicatorType XmCIndicatorType	XmN_OF_MANY unsigned char	CSG
XmNselectColor XmCSelectColor	dynamic Pixel	CSG
XmNselectInsensitivePixmap XmCSelectInsensitivePixmap	XmUNSPECIFIED_PIXMAP Pixmap	CSG
XmNselectPixmap XmCSelectPixmap	XmUNSPECIFIED_PIXMAP Pixmap	CSG
XmNset XmCSet	False Boolean	CSG
XmNspacing XmCSpacing	4 short	CSG
XmNvalueChangedCallback XmCValueChangedCallback	NULL XtCallbackList	C
XmNvisibleWhenOff XmCVisibleWhenOff	True Boolean	CSG

XmNarmCallback

Specifies a list of callbacks that is called when the ToggleButtonGadget is armed. To arm this gadget, press the active mouse button while the pointer is inside the ToggleButtonGadget. For this callback, the reason is **XmCR_ARM**.

XmNdisarmCallback

Specifies a list of callbacks called when ToggleButtonGadget is disarmed. To disarm this gadget, press and release the active mouse button while the pointer is inside the ToggleButtonGadget. The gadget is also disarmed when the user moves out of the gadget and releases the mouse button when the pointer is outside the gadget. For this callback, the reason is **XmCR_DISARM**.

XmNfillOnSelect

Fills the indicator with the color specified in **XmNselectColor** and switches the top and bottom shadow colors when set to True. Otherwise, it only switches the top and bottom shadow colors.

XmNindicatorOn

Specifies that a toggle indicator is drawn to the left of the toggle text or pixmap when set to True. When set to False, no space is allocated for the indicator, and it is not displayed. If **XmNindicatorOn** is True, the indicator shadows are switched when the button is selected or unselected, but any shadows around the entire gadget are not switched. However, if **XmNindicatorOn** is False, any shadows around the entire gadget are switched when the toggle is selected or unselected.

XmNindicatorType

Specifies if the indicator is a **1-of** an **N-of** indicator. For the **1-of** indicator, the value is **XmONE_OF_MANY**. For the **N-of** indicator, the value is **XmN_OF_MANY**. The **N-of-many** indicator is square. The **1-of-many** indicator is diamond-shaped. This resource specifies only the visuals and does not enforce the behavior. When the ToggleButtonGadget is in a RadioBox, the parent forces this resource to **XmONE_OF_MANY**.

XmNselectColor

> Allows the application to specify what color fills the center of the square or diamond-shaped indicator when it is set. If this color is the same as either the top or the bottom shadow color of the indicator, a one-pixel-wide margin is left between the shadows and the fill; otherwise, it is filled completely. This resource's default for a color display is a color between the background and the bottom shadow color. For a monochrome display, the default is set to the foreground color.

XmNselectInsensitivePixmap

> Specifies a pixmap used as the button face when the ToggleButtonGadget is selected and the button is insensitive if the LabelGadget resource **XmNlabelType** is **XmPIXMAP**. If the ToggleButtonGadget is unselected and the button is insensitive, the pixmap in **XmNlabelInsensitivePixmap** is used as the button face.

XmNselectPixmap

> Specifies the pixmap to be used as the button face if **XmNlabelType** is **XmPIXMAP** and the ToggleButtonGadget is selected. When the ToggleButtonGadget is unselected, the pixmap specified in Label's **XmNlabelPixmap** is used.

XmNset

> Displays the button in its selected state if set to True. This shows some conditions as active when a set of buttons first appears.

XmNspacing

> Specifies the amount of spacing between the toggle indicator and the toggle label (text or pixmap).

XmNvalueChangedCallback

> Specifies a list of callbacks that is called when the ToggleButtonGadget value is changed. To change the value, press and release the active mouse button while the pointer is inside the ToggleButtonGadget. This action also causes the gadget to be disarmed. For this callback, the reason is **XmCR_VALUE_CHANGED**.

XmNvisibleWhenOff
> Indicates that the toggle indicator is visible in the unselected state when the Boolean value is True. When the ToggleButtonGadget is in a menu, the RowColumn parent forces this resource to False. When the ToggleButtonGadget is in a RadioBox, the parent forces this resource to True.

Inherited Resources

ToggleButtonGadget inherits behavior and resources from the following superclasses. For a complete description of each resource, refer to the man page for that superclass.

XmLabelGadget Resource Set		
Name	**Default**	**Access**
Class	**Type**	
XmNaccelerator	NULL	CSG
XmCAccelerator	String	
XmNacceleratorText	NULL	CSG
XmCAcceleratorText	XmString	
XmNalignment	XmALIGNMENT_CENTER	CSG
XmCAlignment	unsigned char	
XmNfontList	"Fixed"	CSG
XmCFontList	XmFontList	
XmNlabelInsensitivePixmap	XmUNSPECIFIED_PIXMAP	CSG
XmCLabelInsensitivePixmap	Pixmap	
XmNlabelPixmap	XmUNSPECIFIED_PIXMAP	CSG
XmCPixmap	Pixmap	
XmNlabelString	NULL	CSG
XmCXmString	XmString	
XmNlabelType	XmSTRING	CSG
XmCLabelType	unsigned char	
XmNmarginBottom	0	CSG
XmCMarginBottom	short	
XmNmarginHeight	2	CSG
XmCMarginHeight	short	
XmNmarginLeft	dynamic	CSG
XmCMarginLeft	short	
XmNmarginRight	0	CSG
XmCMarginRight	short	
XmNmarginTop	0	CSG
XmCMarginTop	short	
XmNmarginWidth	2	CSG
XmCMarginWidth	short	

Name	Default	Access
Class	**Type**	
XmNmnemonic	'\0'	CSG
XmCMnemonic	char	
XmNrecomputeSize	True	CSG
XmCRecomputeSize	Boolean	

XmGadget Resource Set		
Name	**Default**	**Access**
Class	**Type**	
XmNhelpCallback	NULL	C
XmCCallback	XtCallbackList	
XmNhighlightOnEnter	False	CSG
XmCHighlightOnEnter	Boolean	
XmNhighlightThickness	0	CSG
XmCHighlightThickness	short	
XmNshadowThickness	0	CSG
XmCShadowThickness	short	
XmNtraversalOn	False	CSG
XmCTraversalOn	Boolean	
XmNuserData	NULL	CSG
XmCUserData	caddr_t	

RectObj Resource Set		
Name **Class**	**Default** **Type**	**Access**
XmNancestorSensitive XmCSensitive	XtCopyFromParent Boolean	CSG
XmNborderWidth XmCBorderWidth	0 Dimension	CSG
XmNheight XmCHeight	0 Dimension	CSG
XmNsensitive XmCSensitive	True Boolean	CSG
XmNwidth XmCWidth	0 Dimension	CSG
XmNx XmCPosition	0 Position	CSG
XmNy XmCPosition	0 Position	CSG

Callback Information

The following structure is returned with each callback:

typedef struct
{
    int   *reason*;
    XEvent   * *event*;
11 Boolean   *set*;
} XmToggleButtonCallbackStruct;

reason   Indicates why the callback was invoked

event   Points to the **XEvent** that triggered the callback

set   Reflects the ToggleButtonGadget's current state when the callback occurred, either True (selected) or False (unselected)

Behavior

ToggleButtonGadget is associated with the default behavior unless it is part of a menu system. In a menu system, the RowColumn parent determines which mouse button is used.

Default Behavior

<Btn1Down>:

> **(if unset)**: This action arms the ToggleButtonGadget. The indicator shadow is drawn so that the button looks pressed, and the indicator fills with the color specified in **XmNselectColor**. The callbacks for **XmNarmCallback** are also called.

> **(if set)**: This action arms the ToggleButtonGadget. The indicator shadow is drawn so that the button looks raised, and the indicator fills with the background color. The callbacks for **XmNarmCallback** are also called.

<Btn1Up>:

> **(In Button)**:

> **(if unset)**: This action selects the ToggleButtonGadget. Visually, it appears the same as when it is armed. The callbacks for **XmvalueChangedCallback** are called, followed by callbacks for **XmdisarmCallback**.

> **(if set)**: This action unselects the ToggleButtonGadget. Visually, it appears the same as when it is armed. The callbacks for **XmvalueChangedCallback** are called, followed by callbacks for **XmdisarmCallback**.

> **(Outside Of Button)**:

> If the button release occurs outside the ToggleButtonGadget, the callbacks for **XmNdisarmCallback** are called.

<Leave Window>:

> If the button is pressed and the cursor leaves the gadget, it visually reverts to its previous unpressed state.

<Enter Window>:

>   If the button is pressed and the cursor leaves and re-enters the gadget, it visually appears the same as when the button was first armed.

Default PopupMenu System

<Btn3Down>:

>   This action disables keyboard traversal for the menu and returns the user to drag mode, which is the mode in which the menu is manipulated by using the mouse. This action also causes the ToggleButtonGadget to be armed. A shadow is drawn around the ToggleButtonGadget. The callbacks for **XmNarmCallback** are also called.

<Btn3Up>:   (**if unset**): This action selects the ToggleButtonGadget. The indicator shadow is drawn so that it looks pressed, and the indicator fills with the color specified in **XmNselectColor**. The menu is then unposted and the callbacks for **XmvalueChangedCallback** are called, followed by callbacks for **XmdisarmCallback**.

>   (**if set**): This action unselects the ToggleButtonGadget. The indicator shadow is drawn so that it looks raised, and the indicator fills with the background color. The menu is then unposted and the callbacks for **XmvalueChangedCallback** are called, followed by callbacks for **XmdisarmCallback**.

<Leave Window>:

>   Pressing button 2 and moving the cursor out of the widget's window erases the shadow around the ToggleButtonGadget. This event is ignored if keyboard traversal is enabled in the menu.

<Enter Window>:

>   Pressing button 2 and moving the cursor into the widget's window draws a shadow around the ToggleButtonGadget. This event is ignored if keyboard traversal is enabled in the menu.

<Key>Return:

> If keyboard traversal is enabled in the menu, this event sets or unsets the ToggleButtonGadget.
>
> **(if unset)**: Sets the ToggleButtonGadget. The indicator shadow is drawn so that it looks pressed, and the indicator fills with the color specified in **XmNselectColor**.
>
> **(if set)**: Unsets the ToggleButtonGadget. The indicator shadow is drawn so that it looks raised, and the indicator fills with the background color.
>
> For both set and unset cases, the menu is then unposted and the callbacks for **XmvalueChangedCallback** are called, followed by callbacks for **XmdisarmCallback**.

Default PulldownMenu System and OptionMenu System

<Btn1Down>:

> This action disables keyboard traversal for the menu and returns the user to drag mode (the mode in which the menu is manipulated using the mouse). This action also arms the ToggleButtonGadget. A shadow is drawn around the ToggleButtonGadget. The callbacks for **XmNarmCallback** are also called.

<Btn1Up>: **(if unset)**: This action selects the ToggleButtonGadget. The indicator shadow is drawn so that it looks pressed, and the indicator fills with the color specified in **XmNselectColor**. The menu then unposts, and the callbacks for **XmvalueChangedCallback** are called, followed by callbacks for **XmdisarmCallback**.

> **(if set)**: This action unselects the ToggleButtonGadget. The indicator shadow is drawn so that it looks raised, and the indicator fills with the background color. The menu then unposts, and the callbacks for **XmvalueChangedCallback** are called, followed by callbacks for **XmdisarmCallback**.

<Leave Window>:

Pressing button 1 and moving the cursor out of the widget's window erases the shadow around the ToggleButtonGadget. This event is ignored if keyboard traversal is enabled in the menu.

<Enter Window>:

Pressing button 1 and moving the cursor into the widget's window draws a shadow around the ToggleButtonGadget. This event is ignored if keyboard traversal is enabled in the menu.

<Key>Return:

This event sets or unsets the ToggleButtonGadget if keyboard traversal is enabled in the menu.

(**if unset**): Sets the ToggleButtonGadget. The indicator shadow is drawn so that it looks depressed, and the indicator fills with the color specified in **XmNselectColor**.

(**if set**): Unsets the ToggleButtonGadget. The indicator shadow is drawn so that it looks raised, and the indicator fills with the background color.

For both set and unset cases, the menu then unposts, and the callbacks for **XmvalueChangedCallback** are called, followed by callbacks for **XmdisarmCallback**.

Keyboard Traversal

For information on keyboard traversal when not in a menu system, see the man page for **XmGadget(3X)** and its sections on behavior and default translations. When the ToggleButtonGadget is in a menu system, the keyboard traversal translations are defined by the RowColumn parent.

Related Information

Object(3X), RectObj(3X), XmCreateToggleButtonGadget(3X),
XmGadget(3X), XmLabelGadget(3X), XmRowColumn(3X),
XmToggleButtonGadgetGetState(3X), and
XmToggleButtonGadgetSetState(3X).

XmToggleButtonGadgetGetState

Purpose

A ToggleButtonGadget function that obtains the state of a ToggleButtonGadget.

AES Support Level

Full-use

Synopsis

#include <Xm/ToggleBG.h>

Boolean XmToggleButtonGadgetGetState (*widget*)
    Widget   *widget*;

Description

XmToggleButtonGadgetGetState obtains the state of a ToggleButtonGadget.

widget   Specifies the ToggleButtonGadget ID

For a complete definition of ToggleButtonGadget and its associated resources, see **XmToggleButtonGadget(3X)**.

Return Value

Returns True if the button is selected and False if the button is unselected.

Related Information

XmToggleButtonGadget(3X).

XmToggleButtonGadgetSetState

Purpose

A ToggleButtonGadget function that sets or changes the current state.

AES Support Level

Full-use

Synopsis

#include <Xm/ToggleBG.h>

void XmToggleButtonGadgetSetState (*widget, state, notify*)
    Widget   *widget*;
    Boolean   *state*;
    Boolean   *notify*;

Description

XmToggleButtonGadgetSetState sets or changes the ToggleButtonGadget's current state.

widget   Specifies the ToggleButtonGadget widget ID.

state   Specifies a Boolean value that indicates whether the ToggleButtonGadget state is selected or unselected. If True, the button state is selected; if False, the button state is unselected.

notify   Indicates whether **XmNvalueChangedCallback** is called; it can be either True or False.

For a complete definition of ToggleButtonGadget and its associated resources, see **XmToggleButtonGadget(3X)**.

Related Information

XmToggleButtonGadget(3X).

XmToggleButtonGetState

Purpose

A ToggleButton function that obtains the state of a ToggleButton.

AES Support Level

Full-use

Synopsis

#include <Xm/ToggleB.h>

Boolean XmToggleButtonGetState (*widget*)
    Widget   *widget*;

Description

XmToggleButtonGetState obtains the state of a ToggleButton.

widget   Specifies the ToggleButton widget ID

For a complete definition of ToggleButton and its associated resources, see
XmToggleButton(3X).

Return Value

Returns True if the button is selected and False if the button is unselected.

Related Information

XmToggleButton(3X).

XmToggleButtonSetState

Purpose

A ToggleButton function that sets or changes the current state.

AES Support Level

Full-use

Synopsis

#include <Xm/ToggleB.h>

void XmToggleButtonSetState (*widget, state, notify*)
    Widget   *widget*;
    Boolean   *state*;
    Boolean   *notify*;

Description

XmToggleButtonSetState sets or changes the ToggleButton's current state.

widget   Specifies the ToggleButton widget ID.

state   Specifies a Boolean value that indicates whether the ToggleButton state is selected or unselected. If True, the button state is selected; if False, the button state is unselected.

notify   Indicates whether **XmNvalueChangedCallback** is called; it can be either True or False.

For a complete definition of ToggleButton and its associated resources, see **XmToggleButton(3X)**.

Related Information

XmToggleButton(3X).

XmUninstallImage

Purpose

A pixmap caching function that removes an image from the image cache.

AES Support Level

Full-use

Synopsis

#include <Xm/Xm.h>

Boolean XmUninstallImage (*image*)
  XImage   * *image*;

Description

XmUninstallImage removes an image from the image cache.

image Points to the image structure given to the **XmInstallImage()** routine

Return Value

Returns True when successful; returns False if the *image* is NULL, or if it cannot be found to be uninstalled.

Related Information

XmInstallImage(3X), **XmGetPixmap(3X)**, and **XmDestroyPixmap(3X)**.

XmUpdateDisplay

Purpose

A function that processes all pending exposure events immediately.

AES Support Level

Full-use

Synopsis

```
void XmUpdateDisplay (widget)
     Widget      widget;
```

Description

XmUpdateDisplay provides the application with a mechanism for forcing all pending exposure events to be removed from the input queue and processed immediately.

When a user selects a button within a MenuPane, the MenuPanes are unposted and then any activation callbacks registered by the application are invoked. If one of the callbacks performs a time-consuming action, the portion of the application window that was covered by the MenuPanes is not redrawn; normal exposure processing does not occur until all of the callbacks have been invoked. If the application writer suspects that a callback will take a long time, then the callback may choose to invoke **XmUpdateDisplay** before starting its time-consuming operation.

This function is also useful any time a transient window, such as a dialog box, is unposted; callbacks are invoked before normal exposure processing can occur.

widget   Specifies any widget or gadget.

Index

E

F

FileSelectionBox functions
    XmFileSelectionBoxGetChild,
    2-390
    XmFileSelectionDoSearch, 2-392

focus policy
    click to type, 2-19
    explicit, 2-5, 2-19
    pointer, 2-19
    real estate, 2-5, 2-19

I

icon box, 2-4

icons, 2-4

input focus, 2-5, 2-19

L

List functions
    XmListAddItem, 2-473
    XmListAddItemUnselected, 2-475
    XmListDeleteItem, 2-477
    XmListDeletePos, 2-479
    XmListDeselectAllItems, 2-481
    XmListDeselectItem, 2-483
    XmListDeselectPos, 2-485
    XmListItemExists, 2-487
    XmListSelectItem, 2-489

XmListSelectPos, 2-491
XmListSetBottomItem, 2-493
XmListSetBottomPos, 2-495
XmListSetHorizPos, 2-497
XmListSetItem, 2-499
XmListSetPos, 2-501

M

MainWindow functions
    XmMainWindowSep1, 2-511
    XmMainWindowSep2, 2-513
    XmMainWindowSetAreas, 2-515

manual page
    format, xi

maximize, 2-3

menu, 2-3

MessageBox functions
    XmMessageBoxGetChild, 2-548

minimize, 2-2

mwm, 2-1

O

Object, 2-68

OverrideShell, 2-70

P

R

S

T

OPEN SOFTWARE FOUNDATION

INFORMATION REQUEST FORM

Please send me the following:

    ( ) OSF Membership Information

    ( ) OSF/Motif™ License Materials

    ( ) OSF/Motif™ Training Information

Contact Name   _____

Company Name   _____

Street Address   _____

Mail Stop   _____

City   _____ State _____ Zip _____

Phone   _____ FAX _____

Electronic Mail   _____

MAIL TO:

Open Software Foundation
11 Cambridge Center
Cambridge, MA 02142

Attn: OSF/Motif™

For more information about OSF/Motif™, call 617-621-8755.